Praise for *Fierce Patriot*

"Robert O'Connell's *Fierce Patriot* is a sharply drawn and propulsive march through the tortured psyche of the man known to his army as 'Uncle Billy'—a man on a lifelong march of his own, not to Atlanta or the sea but to his own independence."

—*The Wall Street Journal*

"Robert L. O'Connell's new biography is so welcome and valuable. 'Biography' is actually something of a misnomer in this case: O'Connell … has written a study that has little relation to the 800-page lives that come and go with such frequency and seem designed for coffee tables rather than actual reading.… In their place is an engaging series of chapters (occasionally not in chronological sequence) that explain what a fascinating and complex life Sherman led and, most strikingly, make the persuasive argument that his fingerprints can be found on America even today."

—*National Review*

"O'Connell's biography is unconventional and multifaceted, organized thematically rather than chronologically. By untangling Sherman the strategist from Sherman the leader and Sherman the husband, *Fierce Patriot* gives a more three-dimensional picture of his fiery but magnetic personality.… [It] is the best kind of biography, filled with insights beyond a mere recitation of events."

—*USA Today*

"[O'Connell's] narrative of the March to the Sea is perhaps the best I have read about that ever-controversial subject."

—*The Washington Post*

"An insightful biography of a complex man."   —*The Economist*

"O'Connell, the author of several works of military history, has some striking and, in some cases, unique insights into Sherman's life and personality."
—*Chicago Tribune*

"O'Connell writes vividly and clearly.... A deep understanding of military history often flashes through that lively writing."
—*Bookforum*

"*Fierce Patriot* is a bold, revisionist portrait of how this iconic and enigmatic figure exerted an outsize impact on the American landscape—and the American character.... In this rich and layered portrait, Robert L. O'Connell captures the man in full for the first time. . . . A masterful character study whose myriad insights are leavened with its author's trademark wit, *Fierce Patriot* will stand as the essential book on Sherman for decades to come."
—*Bookreporter*

"O'Connell displays warmth and occasional humor as he considers Sherman's more memorable traits."
—*BookPage*

"O'Connell [shows Sherman's] humanity with impressive clarity."
—*Kirkus Reviews*

"William Tecumseh Sherman is one of the great characters in American history—protean, highly effective, cunning, outrageous, and in every way memorable. He has found just the right biographer in Robert L. O'Connell. *Fierce Patriot* is a surprising, clever, wise, and powerful book."
—Evan Thomas, author of *Ike's Bluff: President Eisenhower's Secret Battle to Save the World*

"For those who think they know a lot about William Tecumseh Sherman, this book will be a revelation. Those who are meeting him for the first time will be equally mesmerized."
—Thomas Fleming, author of *A Disease of the Public Mind: A New Understanding of Why We Fought the Civil War*

"To his family and friends he was Cump; to his soldiers he was Uncle Billy; to generations of Southern whites he was the devil incarnate. But to biographer Robert L. O'Connell, William T. Sherman was the quintessential nineteenth-century American: full of energy, constantly on the move, pragmatic, adaptable, determined to overcome all obstacles, a nationalist and patriot who teamed with Grant and Lincoln to win the Civil War and launch America as a world power. This readable biography offers new insights on Sherman as a husband and father as well as a master strategist and leader."

—JAMES M. MCPHERSON, Pulitzer Prize–winning author of *Battle Cry of Freedom: The Civil War*

"A fascinating dissection of the multifaceted lives of William Tecumseh Sherman—military genius, brilliant organizer, inspired observer, and occasionally wayward husband. Sherman, O'Connell reminds us, was as brilliantly unpredictable on the battlefield as he was off it."

—VICTOR DAVIS HANSON, The Hoover Institution, author of *The Soul of Battle* and *Ripples of Battle*

"William Tecumseh Sherman has to be our premier grand strategist, who set unexpectedly bold boundaries, not just for war but for peace, and kept to them. In *Fierce Patriot*, Robert L. O'Connell has fashioned a remarkable, and remarkably original, portrait of one of the people who truly defined America."

—ROBERT COWLEY, founding editor of *MHQ: The Quarterly Journal of Military History*

"William Tecumseh Sherman was the most fiery, complicated, and inconsistent of America's great generals. In Robert L. O'Connell's aptly titled *Fierce Patriot,* he brings this conflicted American hero vividly to life. For both the Civil War buff and the general reader, *Fierce Patriot* offers new and arresting insights into this remarkable figure and his impact on the world in which he lived."

—CHARLES BRACELEN FLOOD, author of *Grant and Sherman: The Friendship That Won the Civil War*

Fierce Patriot

Fierce Patriot

THE TANGLED LIVES OF
WILLIAM TECUMSEH SHERMAN

Robert L. O'Connell

RANDOM HOUSE
NEW YORK

2015 Random House Trade Paperback Edition

Copyright © 2014 by Robert L. O'Connell
Map copyright © 2014 by Hal Jespersen

Published in the United States by Random House Trade Paperbacks,
an imprint of Random House, a division of Random House LLC,
a Penguin Random House Company, New York.

RANDOM HOUSE and the HOUSE colophon are registered
trademarks of Random House LLC.

Originally published in hardcover in the United States by
Random House, an imprint and division of Random House LLC, in 2014.

Library of Congress Cataloging-in-Publication Data
O'Connell, Robert L.
Fierce patriot: the tangled lives of William Tecumseh Sherman/ Robert L. O'Connell
pages cm
Includes index.
ISBN 978-0-8129-8212-1
eBook ISBN 978-0-6796-0469-3
Sherman, William T. (William Tecumseh), 1820–1891. 2. United States—History—
Civil War, 1861–1865—Biography.   3. Generals—United States—Biography.
4. United States. Army—Biography.   I. Title
E467.1A55O25 2014   973.7092—dc23   2013028999
[B]

Printed in the United States of America on acid-free paper

www.atrandom.com

4   6   8   9   7   5   3

Book design by Christopher M. Zucker

To Benjie O'Connell, wife of a lifetime

Contents

Introduction

＝＝＝

NAME RECOGNITION would not be the problem. William Tecumseh Sherman—about as memorable a moniker as exists in American military history. "He and Grant won the Civil War." "Named a tank after him." Broad segments of the American public, albeit mostly male, can probably conjure up at least this much.

But from here on, the general reputation of the general takes a dive, caricatured by a T-shirt sold at the 1996 Olympics featuring Sherman's image emblazoned on a penumbra of flames along with the motto "Atlanta's Original Torchbearer." This is mostly just darkly funny now, since it's broadly understood that the satanic Sherman was an invention of the postwar South, specifically those intent on turning the Confederacy into a "Lost Cause"—a noble endeavor rather than an unmitigated disaster. Sherman as intruder and dark destroyer made a perfect foil for the South's marble man, Robert E. Lee, the great defender. But if the myth of the Lost Cause was ripped to shreds in the civil rights era, it still hasn't done Sherman's reputation much good.

That's because he still stands indicted as one of the originators of what is termed "modern war"—wholesale assaults on civilian populations as an integral part of military strategy. Thinking along these lines, we can easily draw a direct path from Sherman's March through Georgia and the Carolinas to the superlethal industrial wars of the twentieth century, then on to holding entire populations hostage to nearly instant nuclear destruction. Not exactly a sunny consequence to drape over a legacy. Yet it too is about as flimsy and transparent as the Lost Cause. Sherman was not clairvoyant; he had only the foggiest notion of where military technology was heading. He was enveloped in his own time, intent upon accomplishing specific strategic objectives. He did what worked, and the idea of his being at the root of the future of war would have struck him as laughable. But there he remains, perhaps conceded a measure of absolution on these grounds, but still a resident of history's darker side.

Actually, that's part of the attraction. Initially, at least—until it becomes apparent that this was hardly Sherman's image among contemporaries. Still, any attempt to capture or even approximate the actual Sherman is fraught with pitfalls. For one thing, the very nature of his personality makes it easy to lapse into caricature.

There is an undeniably daffy aspect to Sherman. Calling him a motormouth understates the case: he was a veritable volcano of verbiage, as borne out by a mountain of letters, memoranda, and other official papers, not to mention the uniformly gabby impression he left among contemporaries. If there were a contest for who spoke the most words in a lifetime, Sherman would have been a finalist—he lived a long time and slept very little; otherwise he was talking. He said exactly what was on his mind at that instant, until his quicksilver brain turned to an entirely different matter, then to a third, and perhaps to a fourth, then back to the first—unceasing—spewing orders, analysis, advice, and anecdotes in a random pattern that often left listeners stunned and amazed. One prominent Civil War historian, Gary Gallagher, described Sherman as lacking cognitive filters. It all came out. And this is a real problem in trying to resurrect the man's nature.

One approach that seems to help is to draw a distinction between the Sherman of vast opinion and the walk-around, quotidian Sherman. The former said and wrote a great deal that could be used against him; the latter was an almost compulsively gregarious individual who normally treated other people, even adversaries, courteously and reasonably. He could even be a good listener. He almost never lost his temper. The worse the situation, the more clearheaded Sherman became. To contemporaries he was a jumble of sagacity, rectitude, shoot-from-the-hip sincerity, prepotency, and grumpiness—all rolled into a unique being known and beloved by Americans simply as "Uncle Billy"—the nickname originally bestowed upon him by his men during the Civil War. Other military heroes were similarly revered—Jackson, Grant, Eisenhower—but partially as politicians. Uncle Billy was always just a soldier, our only true celebrity general.

But he was also one with a sardonic, at times even self-mocking, sense of humor. Consider Sherman answering the door in the middle of the night for an important dispatch with a cheery, "I have seen the devil. Have you?" Or imagine him in the middle of a battle coming upon a soldier cowering behind a tree and loudly proclaiming his intention to desert—prompting Sherman to shower the tree with rocks, convincing the reluctant warrior he was under even heavier fire. Crazy Billy—that too was part of the image.

We have no analogue today. If you wanted to point to an individual in recent memory who most resembles Sherman, one choice might be Katharine Hepburn—a supermasculine version, but with the same prickly combination of irrepressible self-righteousness, good sense, and charisma.

If nothing else, this comparison calls attention to an aspect not much noted: Sherman was, to an extraordinary degree, theatrical. This quality is useful militarily, especially when convincing others to risk their lives. But Sherman took it well beyond that. The theater was his favorite form of recreation, and players (often female players) would one day occupy a large portion of his social life.

More to the point, Sherman was instinctively theatrical in much that he did. His famously disheveled Civil War uniforms—tailored by Brooks Brothers, incidentally—were absolutely on the mark for the democratic volunteers manning the Army of the West. Later in his career, there is little of that. Photographs capture a sartorially appropriate, even dapper, Sherman acting out his role as commanding general of the United States Army. His life was undeniably dramatic, but you also have the feeling he framed it as such, the central character in his personal production. All the controversies, his endless battles with the press, his famous feuds—it seems apparent he would have had it no other way.

Yet we will never actually see him in character. For we are separated by an electronic divide that precludes hearing the voice and cadence of this most talkative of men. Similarly, the few images we have freeze a figure who was almost never at rest and reduce his famously spiky red hair and grizzled beard to a kind of black-and-white mediocrity. So Uncle Billy must remain largely a creature of our imagination. We are left to deal with what has been preserved—his words; the Sherman of vast opinion.

Words are a problem along a number of dimensions. Sheer volume, for instance. Studying Sherman means becoming conversant with the Civil War, one of the most heavily documented conflicts in history.

The process began shortly after the last shots were fired, when Sherman's sometime friend and full-time rival Henry Halleck sponsored a huge gathering and collation of operational evidence, resulting in the monumental *War of the Rebellion: Official Records of the Union and Confederate Armies* (*OR*), a true blockbuster at 128 volumes. Since then it's been followed by an avalanche of memoirs, regimental histories, diaries, collections of letters, and reminiscences from all manner of perspectives and localities, not to mention the secondary literature that has formed around it at the rate of hundreds of volumes a year.

Not surprisingly, William Tecumseh Sherman proved a significant contributor to this process. At this stage of his career, he and his machine-gun mouth were increasingly surrounded by staff aides armed with notepads, all struggling to capture his stream of words and convert them into orders, official correspondence, and memos of all sorts, much of it destined for the pages of the *OR*. Meanwhile,

Sherman forged ahead with his own pen in hand, corresponding in a nearly indecipherable script with wife, family, and a huge circle of friends and acquaintances.

Studying Sherman in detail can be compared to a really bad day at the beach. At first you are merely intrigued, getting your feet wet with a biography or two. Next, you are hit with the equivalent of a rogue wave and sucked in over your head, caught in a riptide drawing you inexorably into a sea of Sherman. The far shore is nowhere apparent, the beach is barely visible. So you plod on until finally you come to understand you will never get through all of Sherman, that you are drowning in Sherman.

But there is a lifesaver. Sherman was a general, and almost by definition generals are judged by their deeds, not their words. He did a great deal, but it's all been well documented and amounts to a finite body of evidence, something to cling to. Gradually, you realize that an accurate Sherman could potentially be made to float on such a basis. It's not walking on water, but it does promise a realistic strategy that parallels the split between the Sherman of vast opinion and the walk-around Sherman. Focus on what he did, not what he said.

Still, there will always be the temptation to do the opposite. The words are all there—Sherman's words—to build and document several extremely unflattering portraits.

Sherman as war criminal? Certainly not impossible. He not only bulldozed the Plains Indians aside, but wrote repeatedly of exterminating them (not to mention the buffalo). During the Civil War, his view of collective responsibility clearly exceeded what are now the standards of international law—he banished several hundred civilians from Memphis and Atlanta and burned some hamlets that harbored guerrilla sharpshooters along the Mississippi. He even threatened to hang a respected journalist.

But he never came close to doing so. Nor did his operations against the Indians actually approach genocide. Sherman was a hard and determined man, but not a cruel one. He got the big things right. His March through Georgia and the Carolinas was accompanied by none of the rape and slaughter that all too often have been an integral part of such foraging-based campaigns. The peace he offered

Joseph E. Johnston and the last of the Confederate armies was so generous, it was summarily rejected in Washington. Sherman waged war to win, never simply to destroy.

A more credible case can certainly be built against Sherman as racist—again with Sherman's own words serving as the chief witness for the prosecution. Morally, he was never much troubled by slavery, and he adopted emancipation reluctantly and only as a means of punishing the planter class he believed had spearheaded secession. On paper, he plainly thought blacks were inferior to whites, and plenty of disparaging comments to that effect can be found in his writings, along with a liberal use of the word *nigger*. He wanted nothing, or as little as possible, to do with black freedmen as troops and sent off a stream of blistering memos to that effect. It all builds toward an airtight, open-and-shut case—except for the testimony of the sole witness for the defense: the record of what Sherman actually did.

The fact remains that Sherman and his army catalyzed the liberation of countless slaves—and did so in the most spectacular fashion. The March across Georgia became a road show for emancipation, putting to rest the notion that slaves were somehow satisfied with their condition. You could say it broke the back of slavery and brought to fruition the Emancipation Proclamation. Granted, Sherman was not exactly overjoyed. As a military man seeking to move as quickly as possible, he viewed the freedmen who attached themselves to his army like so many barnacles on a racing hull. But he also knew from experience that they were his best source of intelligence on the Confederates.

It is in these interrogations, some of which have been preserved, that another aspect of Sherman becomes apparent: He invariably treated these people respectfully and without condescension. Secretary of War Edwin M. Stanton discovered the same thing when he raced to Savannah, worried that Sherman might jeopardize the positive racial atmosphere the March had created. He quizzed a number of black leaders about this, and to a man, they maintained that Sherman had treated them simply as fellow human beings.

It has been argued that it was in their best interest to say this, so it's worth mentioning an incident where nothing was at stake. Years later, at a Yale University commencement, Sherman became bored and, Sherman-like, walked out—only to be found afterward on a park bench, happily sharing cigars with a black man with whom he had struck up a conversation. Mere anecdotes, perhaps, but also telling and consistent ones contradicting the portrait of a virulent racist.

Sherman craved crowds and ceremonies; both were basic to his personality and life pattern, beginning with West Point. Invite him and he'd be there—troop reunions, conventions, expositions, professional gatherings, testimonials, parties, and weddings (especially weddings: he literally expired as the result of attending one too many), not to mention as many theatrical performances as he could manage. Basically, he enjoyed being anywhere he could mix and mingle. Of course, he was perfectly capable of blowing a fuse should the crowds press too close or the handshakes become painful. "Out of my way, damn you!" he might bellow. Folks took little offense and kept showing up—and so did Uncle Billy; he needed them.

Without doubt, Sherman was a product of the upper crust; but his sheer gregariousness seems to have overwhelmed class consciousness. In person, he appeared perfectly comfortable with the egalitarian enthusiasm that defined mid-nineteenth-century America. Yet you would never know it from his correspondence: brimming with antidemocratic diatribes, dark forebodings over social and labor unrest, and an apparent willingness to use decisive force to suppress them. Sherman as authoritarian, Sherman as capitalist enforcer. Yet again, the words exist to build such a case.

But yet again, the real Sherman undermines it through his abhorrence of politics and marked disinclination to get personally involved with strikebreaking, knowing full well that many of "his boys"—veterans of the Army of the West—were part of the labor movement.

This could go on—a male chauvinist Sherman is a possibility, as is a postmodernist critique of virtually his entire mind-set. But both are likely blind alleys to a better understanding of the man.

The fruitlessness of this sort of analysis results from trying to apply contemporary standards to a nineteenth-century person, something historians deplore but can never fully avoid. Each generation looks to the past with a perspective colored (and influenced) by contemporary problems and interests, so it's inherently difficult to predict where Sherman's reputation will head. One day he may stand accused or be praised from angles not now apparent. Good Sherman, Bad Sherman, it's a flip of the coin. Yet some kind of Sherman, a continuing historical presence, seems likely. For underlying all is the man's importance.

Beneath those four individuals without whom America would be a very different place—Washington, Jefferson, Lincoln, and FDR—resides a second tier of epic overachievers with substantial roles in furthering the national extravaganza. Sherman's place here is secure, his significance in transcontinental consolidation being no small matter. America was built just once, so his achievements in this regard are almost guaranteed to remain unique. As long as we live here, Sherman will be remembered.

Not unexpectedly, he has already sired a string of biographies. All deserve some credit simply for having attempted to capture such a lollapalooza of a life. Yet many share a staccato, even frantic, quality as they jump from topic to topic, racing to keep up with one frenetic life story. A corporate cry can almost be heard: "So much Sherman, so little time!" Granted, this hectic approach mirrors the man's scattered nature, but it's also distracting.

The more I studied the secondary literature and recalled my exhausting swim through the primary documents, the more I became convinced that any attempt to confine Sherman to a single chronological track was bound to create confusion. Instead, it seemed to me that three separate story lines, each deserving independent development, emerged out of the man's life.

I. If Jefferson was the architect of continental expansion, Sherman would become the general contractor. It took decades after the end of his formal military education for him to become a master strategist, but Sherman was on the job site almost from the beginning of his career.

In Florida for the last two years of the Second Seminole War,

Sherman accomplished little beyond learning of the effectiveness and cruelty of guerrilla combat. Still, when he left in 1842 with today's equivalent of the campaign badge, the territory was just three years away from statehood.

His time in California, beginning in 1847, was similarly frustrating—troops deserting en masse for the gold fields, and the settlers, not the army, taking over the place. Meanwhile, his fellow officer Henry Halleck completely outperformed and outclassed him. This too was a learning experience, a bitter one, but at least when he left, California's American destiny was settled.

The Civil War arrived with Sherman at last ready to ply his trade effectively as a key member of a national reconstruction project. Secession took Sherman by surprise, and he reacted as if the South were trying to make off with the family room. Even more than Lincoln and Grant, Sherman waged war with a ferocity aimed at driving the Confederate states back into the larger Union structure, getting the house divided back together.

This accomplished, Sherman devoted much of his remaining career to further shoring up the framework, masterminding the construction of the transcontinental railroad and literally binding East and West together with bands of steel.

By the time he retired from the U.S. Army in 1884, Sherman had become virtually a human embodiment of Manifest Destiny. Florida, California, reclaiming the Confederacy, winning the West: He had been just about everywhere. This is a story well worth following from beginning to end.

II. The coevolution of the Army of the West and Sherman as its commander was a process with the profoundest import for all future U.S. ground forces. Under his auspices, the legions that marched through Georgia and the Carolinas had mastered one of the rarest and most valued of military skills: the ability to adapt.

This was a force that morphed a crowd of farm boys into an army capable of conducting effective conventional field operations, siege warfare, amphibious assault, and anti-insurgency. It learned to move and maneuver with astonishing rapidity and then to apply devastating firepower on the flanks. Much, if not all, seems to have been picked up by trial and error, regiment by regiment, and then passed along by what we would call an information network, a force born of self-organization.

Sherman, who had begun the war with nearly total contempt for these volunteers, sensed something like this was taking place and had the good sense to let it proceed, even to foster it. He too was experimental and creatively disobedient, but he was still able to operate effectively in a fairly rigid hierarchy—something Americans do particularly well.

This seems to have been the key element passed forward, the military equivalent of genetic instructions for adaptability, ones that would enable later U.S. ground forces to perform so many missions, so far from home, all the time adjusting on the fly, change coming from above and below. The Army of the West prophesied the future of the American military, augured its fighting edge. It was far from the first American army, but it was the first one that was together long enough and subjected to sufficiently varied challenges to fully enlist the innovative potential of its members. As such, it was not just the prototype, but the archetype of the American forces that followed. Like the story of Sherman the strategist, the tale of how Uncle Billy and his boys invented a new kind of army remains compelling enough to deserve a complete and uninterrupted telling.

III. Not only did Sherman live a personal life worthy of Dickens or James, but in his public guise as Uncle Billy, he created a model of how to grab and hold on to fame in America, one that still works today.

Ordinarily, it's not a good career move to marry your sister, even if it's your foster sister; but for Sherman it was brilliant, leaving him with political connections as powerful as any other general in American history, and also with the redoubtable Ellen Ewing. Every bit as intelligent and determined as Sherman and religious to the point of loopyness, Ellen stood up to him during thirty-eight years of marriage—the South only managed four. To further complicate matters, a tug-of-war developed between Sherman and his foster father, the rich and politically powerful Thomas Ewing, as Cump (the family nickname for Sherman) sought to drag his foster sister/

bride along the many godforsaken stops in his army career, while the foster father/father-in-law struggled manfully to keep her in his mansion in Lancaster. Ever the Ohio American princess, Ellen preferred home. Yet she was and remained Sherman's key confidante, his ultimate ally, at one desperate point in her husband's career interceding personally and successfully with Lincoln on his behalf. Ellen and Cump: It was a lifelong saga; they were mated like geese.

Nonetheless, Sherman also proved to be something of a wild goose. He loved women, was surrounded by them throughout his life, and even through a shroud of Victorian propriety it's apparent he was frequently interested in more than just a chat. How frequently is debatable, but letters exist that show he carried on at least two long-term affairs—the one with the plucky and alluring sculptor Vinnie Ream is worthy of a novel by itself.

This was exceedingly dangerous, and had it become public, it would have ended his celebrity masterpiece, the persona of Uncle Billy. But it didn't, and Uncle Billy, tended tenaciously by his crusty creator, soldiered on to the grave. Sherman virtually pioneered the abusive/symbiotic relationship with the press that has kept famous people famous in America ever since. With or without guns, he was always armed with a pithy quote, courting controversy and staying in the public eye, all the while selling newspapers. And it worked for all parties to the day he died. Uncle Billy remains a remarkable life story, a personal odyssey clearly worth our undivided attention.

So Sherman boils down to a sort of three-ring circus; each is interesting, but it's too distracting to watch all simultaneously. A sequential offering, on the other hand, has the potential to do justice to all three successive stories of Sherman—the strategic man, the general, the human being. The order may be debatable, but in this case it's based on the historical importance of each Sherman, beginning with the first. Ideally, one will blend with and build on the next, and by the end there will remain but one Sherman, a better-understood one. This is a lot to ask, and with another character, even an interesting and important one, the dangers of repetition might outweigh the advantages. But in this case, we can more or less rest assured there will always be enough Sherman to go around.

Part I

THE MILITARY STRATEGIST

Chapter I

TYRO

I

ON JUNE 12, 1836, a Hudson River steamer nosed into the dock at West Point and deposited, among others, sixteen-year-old William Tecumseh Sherman. As he stared up at the bluffs upon which sat the United States Military Academy, it's a safe bet that young Sherman had only a glimmer of what he was getting into. He knew the place was strict and "the army was its natural consequence," but what that implied would have escaped him—that he was beginning a process that would induct him into a warrior elite, forging bonds that would last a lifetime.

Admission was not assured. Because appointment to West Point was open to young men from all classes in a nation of wildly variable primary education, an entrance exam, testing for literacy and arithmetic skills, was administered upon arrival.[1] For Sherman, this amounted to a formality. His foster father, the powerful Whig politician Thomas Ewing, had not only engineered his appointment, but also ensured his charge was academically prepared. Although the family base in Lancaster, Ohio, remained less than a generation removed from the frontier, the boy had been rigorously schooled and apparently knew enough to bone up on French and math, exactly the subjects that would be stressed plebe year.[2] Not surprisingly, he aced the test and academically, at least, never looked back.

Ever gregarious, he fit in easily with his fellow cadets. In particular, he forged what would prove to be lifelong bonds with his two roommates, Stewart Van Vliet and George Thomas. Thomas, who would gain fame in the Civil War as the "Rock of Chickamauga," became a vital and continuing presence in Sherman's career. Even as a veritable pebble, Thomas was already formidable, at one point threatening to throw an upperclassman out the window if he didn't cease his attempts to haze them.[3] Sherman himself was less physical, but he must have appreciated his roommate's bravado and marked him as someone who would not back down in a tough situation. Still, such outbursts were best kept hushed and infrequent at West Point.

Cadets were subjected to a relentless system of regulation, observation, and meticulous evaluation. Their long days were consumed with a monotonous string of planned activities, most of them arduous and all, it seems, subject to some kind of sanction. The system was the masterpiece of Sylvanus Thayer, whose short but indelible tenure as superintendent set the academy irrevocably on the course of "appraisal by numbers," based on the assumption that cadets could be usefully ranked according to a precise order of merit (or demerit, really).

The keystone was the academic program, administered by faculty set in place by Thayer and led by the brilliant but peevish professor Dennis Hart Mahan.[4] It has been said that Thayer effectively turned West Point into an engineering school, but this can be seen as serendipitous, the result of a math-heavy curriculum, which not coincidentally proved useful in rating and weeding out cadets.[5] Sherman and his fellows were graded daily in all subjects, the results of which were tabulated with exam scores and fed into a complicated formula that included dress and disciplinary infractions. This produced an annual and ultimately final class rank used to assign graduates to the various service branches—the Corps of Engineers receiving those

Cadet Sherman's drawing of Theseus slaying the Centaur, an early indication of a nearly photographic memory. *West Point Museum Collection, United States Military Academy*

standing at the front of the long gray line, followed by artillery, cavalry, and then infantry.

Because at West Point everything counted and everything was counted, the system was also applied to a series of upper-class courses, including topography, geography, chemistry, physics, rhetoric, political philosophy, and drawing—a two-year requirement presumed useful in creating maps.[6] Sherman proved particularly adept at capturing images—his teacher Robert W. Weir was an accomplished painter of the Hudson River school—but rather than any real artistic talent, this probably reflected an eidetic or photographic memory, especially for terrain, which proved to be one of

Sherman's core military talents.[7] At any rate, he prospered academically, maintaining himself near the top of his class of around forty-five survivors of the seventy or so who entered with him—though his disdain for spit and polish lowered his final standing enough to preclude entry into the elite engineers.

Meanwhile, he may have noticed that with the exception of Mahan's capstone Science of War course in his final year, there was little that was specifically military about the academic diet fed to those supposedly preparing for careers as professional soldiers. Even Mahan went heavy on the military engineering and light on strategy, relying on the writings of French general Antoine-Henri Jomini to implant an almost exclusively Napoleonic view of warfare in his young charges (who, if the past was any indication, would probably spend most of their time fighting Indians).[8]

This sort of disconnect raises questions as to West Point's actual mission. Sherman arrived at the crest of the age of Jackson, a high tide of egalitarian and democratic enthusiasm. Old Hickory was undeniably a general, but military elites and the kinds of schools that bred them were viewed with suspicion.[9] West Point's survival depended upon accommodation, and by offering a free college education that stressed engineering-friendly subjects to boys of all classes, the academy undoubtedly provided a service to a developing nation much in need of infrastructure.

It was understood that many cadets would not pursue careers as officers much beyond graduation but would turn instead to civilian pursuits. "I tell you Coz," wrote Cadet Ulysses S. Grant, "if a man graduates from here he is set fer life, come what may."[10] Still, the Civil War would offer Grant a much better fit for the skill set he picked up at West Point than his prewar clerkship at his father's store. So too with Sherman, Henry Halleck, and George McClellan, key luminaries of the great struggle, who would briefly leave the service, only to return to what proved to be their true calling. Today's notion that West Point was essentially dedicated to producing "engineers who could also function as soldiers rather than the reverse"[11] would have seemed odd indeed to these men. Just about everything cadets experienced at West Point was militarily derived or motivated.

A case in point is drill, the training that teaches soldiers to move together. Plebe Sherman was thrilled at first sight of the old cadets "stepping as one man—all forming a line"; suddenly, he wrote his foster brother Hugh, he understood what West Point was all about.[12] He would have plenty of opportunity to confirm the observation. Cadets marched and drilled daily, sometimes with a rigor and intensity that caused a number to faint.

This was no casual pursuit. Ever since Maurice of Nassau, Prince of Orange, had pioneered these routines in the Netherlands at the end of the sixteenth century, they had formed the basis of firefighting tactics. The explanation lay with the weapon everybody used, the single-shot, muzzle-loading, smoothbore musket, which also had not changed fundamentally over this time. Because bullets bounced up their barrels, the accurate range of these guns did not exceed around eighty yards, enabling combat formations to blast away at each other out in the open in relative proximity. Thus the key lay not in aiming, but in loading and firing as fast as possible, using a complicated series of motions first analyzed and regularized by Maurice and then drilled relentlessly into subsequent generations of infantrymen so they might be performed reliably and automatically in the chaos and terror of battle.

Maximum firepower also demanded that soldiers do their shooting in long thin lines only several ranks thick. Firing lines, however, were not only brittle, but incapable of rapid and precise maneuver. This required short, thick columns, which moved much faster but were also more vulnerable since the men were bunched together. Safety, or at least relative safety, lay in the rapid and orderly transition from column to line and the reverse, which in turn demanded the disciplined movement of smaller combat units—in the case of the Corps of Cadets, four companies, subdivided into platoons and sections. Whether on the parade ground of West Point or on an actual battlefield, choreographing all these elements so they didn't collide or otherwise fall apart required almost endless practice, men marching at exactly the same pace with exactly the same stride almost ad infinitum, turning into metronomes, at least until they stopped and became loading machines.

Cadet Sherman soon grew bored with the ponderous evolutions of infantry tactics, but otherwise he said very little about them.[13] No wonder. They were by intent mind-numbing. Frederick the Great probably had the last word on the subject: "I come from drill. I drill. I will drill—that is all the news I can give you."[14] Yet there was a great deal more to be learned on the parade ground than Sherman probably realized, subtle lessons but pervasive ones.

Courage had changed since the gun proliferated. Earlier, heroism had consisted of close fighting, hand to hand, and battle, especially in the Western military tradition, was understood to be a matter of intimate confrontation. But a hail of supersonic projectiles had eventually rendered this standard pretty much suicidal. As a compromise, fighting formations backed off, and bravery became largely a matter of standing fast and ignoring the bullets.

Among officers, this meant keeping a cool head and focusing on directing the fighting. Within the ranks, it consisted of a routinized determination to faithfully execute a series of movements drummed in by endless practice. To harness this kind of human energy, to use it effectively, leaders needed to grasp its repetitive power. So it made sense to give cadets the same experience. And as they drilled, Sherman and his cohort would have found themselves growing together, enlisting what historian William McNeill believes to be the primal penchant for dance—shared patterns of movement performed in unison, stirring a deep sense of corporate identity.[15] Individual cadets bonded into a whole, exactly the message the academy wanted to impart.

Still, the entire enterprise was by its nature dehumanizing and fostered the notion that soldiers (to officers of the day, this generally meant long-term enlistees, or regulars) were basically expendable, things to be dressed up, marched around, and shot. In part, this was a function of the necessities of organized warfare itself, but it also reflected the aristocratic origins of firefighting as it had evolved in Europe. "The army," in the words of the eighteenth-century courtier Claude Louis, Comte de Saint-Germain, "must inevitably consist of the scum of the people....We must therefore rely on military discipline to purify and mold the mass of corruption and turn it into something useful."[16] While Sherman and his classmates might not have put it so bluntly, the comment basically characterized the outlook they took away from the parade ground.

This is important, because one day they would come to command men who thought themselves as good as any other, who believed officers ought to be elected, and who, when they got new guns that made fighting in the open a great deal more dangerous, tended to take matters into their own hands. Some, like Sherman, reacted appropriately, others less so. But it is in this clash of outlooks that much of the combat history of the American Civil War is to be found.

Those arguing that West Point was more civilian than military could always point to the professorial confab who controlled the core curriculum, only one of whom had ever seen combat or even been on active duty for more than a few years.[17] Beyond the lecture hall, a number were prominently published in their fields, none more so than Mahan, whose knowledge of Jomini was widely equated with strategic wisdom. Plainly these were academics, not soldiers.

Yet they were also not alone on the faculty. The Thayer system dictated that each senior faculty member be supported by section instructors, young officers who saw the cadets daily and on a more personal basis, in the barracks as well as the classroom. They were brought in on rotation from all over the regular army and were consistently among the best and brightest.[18] Of the Civil War generation, George McClellan, William Hardee, Robert Anderson, John Schofield, Oliver O. Howard, Simon Bolivar Buckner, Fitz-John Porter, and William Rosecrans all served as "schoolmasters" at West Point. This was important duty.

Yet as with drill, its most lasting impact was probably more subtle and psychological than formal and academic. In effect, these young lieutenants and captains were the cadets' umbilical cord to the real world of the U.S. Army. They ran the summer encampment where cadets were taught the practical aspects of service—how to set up a camp, post a picket, run a skirmish line, fire an artillery piece, even wield a sword and ride a horse if they didn't know already. More important, they learned by example—the way these young officers looked and acted would have been the way cadets wanted to look and act.

These were role models and future commanders, and the cadets would have hung on their words in ways that eluded the senior faculty. These men could describe what it was like to command a lonely outpost, recount the splendors of a largely unoccupied continent, and, of course, tell war stories. Since a soldier on the frontier could expect combat every five years, there would have been plenty to tell. This is where West Point's supposed gap in Indian removal instruction would have been filled: these men were the academy's voice of practical wisdom on the nature of irregular warfare. Sherman and his classmates would adapt quickly to their first assignment, the Second Seminole War, in part because they had been told what to expect. Quietly, though.

Cadets also learned from one another, mostly from the inevitable process of sizing up and sorting out status. A pack of high-spirited late adolescents, living in close quarters, constrained on every side by a tyrannical behavioral model, brought out a lot of interesting behavior. Sherman himself cruised through most of it unperturbed, making friends but no apparent enemies. Already something of a newspaper junkie, he had a subscription to the *National Gazette*, which he loaned out freely.[19] He was respected but low-key, choosing to abstain from involvement with the Point's most obvious pecking order.

Cadet rank ("captains" and "lieutenants" from the first class, "sergeants" from the second, and "corporals" from the third) was West Point's official standard of prestige. These positions were reserved for the spotless cadets, individuals of high academic standing who were also unsullied by demerits. But the academy's version of success and subsequent military success did not necessarily coincide. Using the example of Henry Halleck and George McClellan, you might even say that an obsessive following of the rules actually in-hibited fighting initiative and opportunism. Of course, no cadet was more spotless than Robert E. Lee, accumulating no demerits in four years, and on the battlefield nothing slowed him down.

Still, academy rank meant nothing to the real army, so a cadet might reasonably conclude that it was all a bit of a farce. Sherman later wrote that he remained a private the "whole four years," having been "found not to excel" in "neatness in dress" and "strict confor-mity to the rules," taking care to add that he averaged around 150 demerits a year—50 below expulsion level.[20] In another time, this would be called "gaming the system." At least he was in good com-pany: Ulysses S. Grant and "Stonewall" Jackson also graduated as "high privates."

Yet if you asked them or any of their classmates, even long after graduation, who were the "captains" during their time at West Point, they likely would have remembered. In the small world of the United States Military Academy, such things mattered a great deal, conferring almost celebrity status on chosen cadets. "Private" Sher-man, for instance, probably knew that "Captain" Henry Halleck, one class ahead of him, had already ingratiated himself sufficiently with Dennis Hart Mahan to assume a kind of strategic protégé sta-tus, even becoming part of the faculty while still an undergraduate.[21] But such precocity was not the norm. Halleck was clearly an over-achiever, an outlier who himself recognized he had made few friends in the process.[22] More to the point, his lonely (if spotless) path was just one of several a cadet might navigate to win the respect of his peers.

"Sam" Grant seemed invisible. Just over five feet tall and prover-bially silent, he occupied the opposite side of the order of merit, graduating in the lower half of his class. Sherman, his future friend and collaborator, three years his senior, could barely conjure an image of Grant as a cadet, nor could many others. Still, he was not without a reputation, something he could stand, or at least ride, on. Grant was hands down the best horseman at West Point, holding the record for jumping that stood for twenty-five years.[23] This was the nineteenth century, and all officers rode horses; it was part of their professional behavioral package. Those who did it well were admired. It mattered.

Notoriety of a still more unorthodox sort was also a cadet possibility. War is cruel and nefarious; fooling one's opponent, taking lethal advantage, is encouraged. In the context of West Point, the motto "Rules are made to be broken" seems to apply. Elite military training establishments frequently set up conditions that encourage initiates to play fast and loose with the rules and then punish those maladroit enough to be caught. Not exactly a war game, but definitely a parable about war and its consequences.

Traditionally, this often played out in terms of food. Sparta, perhaps the West's most thoroughly militarized society, incentivized trainees to steal from subject Helots by starving them and then savagely beating those found with the purloined consumables. West Point managed a parallel set of circumstances—keeping the cadets hungry on a miserable cuisine of boiled food and mealtime harassment, then forbidding, on penalty of dismissal, forays to nearby Benny Havens tavern, the home of roast turkey, shellfish, and beer. Perhaps prophetically Sherman proved a regular forager, once smuggling a half bushel of Benny's oysters into the barracks and preparing an "extraordinary supper" for himself and his friends.[24] There was also the possibility of an inside job. Henry Heth, who graduated at the bottom of his class in 1847, managed, through stealth, speed, and a few conspirators, to filch an entire holiday meal from the officers' mess.[25]

This was the stuff of cadet legend, but still not nearly so spectacular as what was undoubtedly the master prank of the time: John Schofield's day off. The future Medal of Honor winner, lieutenant general, and West Point superintendent lined up for morning roll call and then, instead of marching to class, he raced to the wharf and caught a steamer for New York City, purchased a return ticket to verify reaching his destination, and rode the boat back up the Hudson, arriving just in time to make the evening lineup before his name was called.[26] Logistics under pressure—who could argue this wasn't a military skill?

All of this—the joint participation in pranks; living and eating together; marching and drilling; sharing the rigors and the boredom over the course of four years—amalgamated cadets in a way few experiences could. West Point forged its graduates into a band of brothers, or at least cousins, their futures linked by cords of loyalty, obligation, and trust. No professional group in nineteenth-century America was as closely bonded and networked, exactly what worried some cabal-wary citizens. It shouldn't have. This was no monolith. Abolition and secession were destined to cleave the long gray line and send its members to opposite sides of the battlefield. But even here, and especially after, fellowship persisted.

While at West Point, Sherman was surrounded by young men who would one day lead the fighting of the American Civil War. Braxton Bragg, Jubal Early, Joseph Hooker, John Pemberton, and John Sedgwick were all in their last year when Sherman was a plebe. Besides Halleck, other cadets ahead of him included P. G. T. Beauregard, Irvin McDowell, William Hardee, and Edward Ord. George Thomas was a classmate, while coming up behind were Grant, Don Carlos Buell, Daniel Hill, James Longstreet, Nathaniel Lyon, John Pope, John Reynolds, William Rosecrans, and Earl Van Dorn. All took their place in the army's officer corps, which itself numbered fewer than eight hundred members in the early 1840s—a cadre within a cadre, bound by their formative days as cadets.[27]

Sherman may have gagged on the absurdity of many of the rules, but the West Point experience penetrated to the depths of his soul. From the moment he departed in June 1840 to his retirement in 1884, Sherman's identity would be defined by his affiliation with the school and its graduates. In California during the 1850s, when several West Pointers suffered heavy financial losses investing through him, Sherman—at a point when he could least afford it—felt honor-bound to return their money in full.[28] And professionally, at least, he never really trusted any officer who had not gone to the academy. To Sherman, West Point was the vital cornerstone of any respectable military career.

The academy served him well. He emerged appropriately schooled in things military and ready to take his place as an officer in the U.S. Army. The curriculum, despite its emphasis on rote memorization, had sharpened his intellectual skills. Sherman may have neglected the rules, but never the books. Even the dearth of strategic studies and Mahan's focus on the works of Jomini rather than the more astute analysis of the Prussian war theorist Carl von Clausewitz did not hinder him. Unlike Halleck the eager beaver, Sherman had barely begun to think about strategy. Besides, he and his classmates would eventually face a future of egalitarian volunteers, rifled muskets, telegraphs, and railroads, all of which would change war in ways unanticipated by either author. It was better to let time and actual experience gradually build Sherman's strategic portfolio.

Still, he was about to embark on an absurdly difficult career path. Military strategy is among the most complex, esoteric, and unlikely of all human pursuits. This is important to consider since one of the enduring questions raised by Sherman's life is why it took someone so plainly capable so long to become successful. Certainly timing and a string of bad breaks and decisions played a role. As did a proclivity for depression. But it's worth proposing that the sheer difficulty of what he was about to undertake—grope for, really—was at the root of his problems, especially since his famous bouts with depression prior to the Civil War all seemed based on career frustrations. So let's examine what he was attempting to become.

2

A military strategist, simply defined, is a person who plans, conducts, and (hopefully) wins wars. Yet this masks the nearly preposterous notion that a single individual can enlist and synchronize the lethal aggression of his own militarized multitudes—forever thirsty and hungry and at times frantic—in a way that will inflict defeat not just on the enemy's forces, but on his will to be anything but abject.

Paradoxically, this sort of warlike wizardry entails both a great deal more and somewhat less than might be expected. This is symptomatic. Military strategy is, almost by definition, deceptive. It can be compared with very few human activities. Certainly there are other kinds of strategists—heads of state and diplomats, corporate leaders and investment bankers, all manner of institutional planners—but ultimately, win or lose, very few (if any) go to the hospital or the morgue. War is about killing and dying; this changes the psychological dimension entirely and also the basis for comparison. In drawing any kind of plausible analogy, the possibility of dying must be a factor.

Let me propose an admittedly unconventional but useful analogy—big-wave surfing. Not nearly so many die as in war, but it does happen—crushed and drowned beneath a mountain of water or occasionally between the teeth of a white shark. But the real parallel is in the difficulty. As hard as it looks, surfing is actually a lot harder than it looks.

First and most basic, the opportunities are limited. Mostly there are no good waves, and in the few places where they occasionally roll in, the truly great days, even in the career of a master waterman, are infrequent and therefore easily missed. So too with wars. Globally, armed conflict has been a common occurrence throughout recorded history; but the probability of combat at any one location is low, and the chances of a single individual being in a position to direct it are even lower. Sherman basically missed the whole Mexican War. Clausewitz, Western military strategy's most brilliant expositor and a professional officer of merit, never reached sufficient rank to test his theories. About the best that can be done is to try to place oneself in a position to get lucky. Nothing is certain, but shrewd, well-informed planning, a determined use of every possible advantage, and a continuous awareness and acceptance of an ever-shifting environment can raise the odds.

A big-wave surfer could certainly relate. If ever there was a full-immersion activity, it's this, and the environment is literally liquid, changing from flat to mountainous in a matter of seconds. Not only is the surfer tiny compared with the huge walls of water to be faced, but he or she is slow, capable of paddling a board at not much more than four miles an hour when breaking waves move at around twenty-five. Plainly, strategy is crucial, finding the spot where the most waves will come at a point when they can be picked up and ridden—and this in turn demands plenty of firsthand knowledge of tides, currents, wind conditions, and even terrain of the seafloor and the shifting sands that change it constantly.[29]

But there will always be competition for such spots, the "lineup," as it's called, peopled by those with the skill and reputation to claim a spot (others are rather brutally excluded). It's all a matter of safety; the dangers are too great, especially of crashing into each other. So surfers have learned to cooperate, take turns, share the waves. This too is the way of war. Competition for position is relentless, but it must be tempered by the necessity for loyalty and cooperation in the face of danger and death. Big waves and battle leave little room for piggishness.

Streaking down the face of a monster breaker, attached to your board by nothing more than a coat of wax, agile feet, and an awesome sense of balance, and then leaning in at precisely the right instant at precisely the right angle that will send you rocketing out from under just before the whole thunderous mass comes crashing down—or being buried in the attempt—that is the essence, the whole point, of everything else.

The parallel with military strategists shouldn't be missed. War is not a matter of armchairs. Real strategists are warriors and must be willing and able to fight battles, to "see the elephant," as Civil War soldiers were fond of saying.[30] Few came to understand this better than Sherman, and this in part is why he spoke with such authority about war. Yet he fought with a larger purpose, not just as a vision, but carefully calculated. And this is what separated him from most other warriors and all surfers.

Here the analogy breaks down, and the challenge of wave riding pales in comparison with that of military strategy. To see the difference, consider a hypothetical Sherman plunging down the same giant wave—only instead of merely riding it, he reaches out, manipulates it, and gradually bends it in a direction cunningly designed to smash the maximum number of the enemy's sand castles lined up on the beach. Considering the degree of difficulty involved, this roughly approximates the military strategist's task.

Still, difficulty should not be confused with ultimate agency. The expression "plans, conducts, and wins wars" is not all encompassing; it says nothing about who starts the conflicts or who decides what to do with the results. For the most part, that is not the role of the military strategist. Although it is possible to point to examples of transcendent rulers who were also great strategists—typically sharing the epithet "Great" (Alexander, Frederick, Peter, and so on)—they amount to no more than a handful. Far more often, the job description designates the strategist as an instrument of higher authority. This is worth considering for a moment, since the outlook implied here was very much Sherman's.

History is not exactly packed with periods when strategy became a self-conscious profession—mostly environments of multiple competing states of roughly equal power, such that military planning and skill were critical attributes much prized. Eighteenth-century Europe certainly qualifies as a strategist incubation zone, but there are other examples earlier and much farther afield—the squabbling statelets of Italy around the time of the gun's proliferation, the network of Hellenistic successor states occupying the shards of Alexander the Great's broken empire, and in China during the Warring States period immediately preceding imperial unification.

The last is particularly suggestive, since it produced a rich literature of strategic thinking, consolidated during the Sung dynasty and preserved as *The Seven Military Classics*.[31] Without exception, the tracts of Sun Tzu and his six less famous colleagues explain in detail and with considerable sophistication how to wage war, but they never ask why war is being waged. Ultimate questions are simply not considered; theirs is the mind-set of an employee—influential, but not ultimately in charge. Thus, Sun Tzu did not hesitate to behead the King of Wu's two favorite concubines when they giggled during a military experiment, but never would he have dared to tell the king what the Mandate of Heaven might demand of him.

If we judge by their actions and what writings are available, this was emblematic of strategists throughout history. More to the point,

it exactly characterized William Tecumseh Sherman's range of aspirations and accomplishments. As substantial as they were, the impetus was always provided by others, and the ultimate goal of Sherman's
career—national consolidation of the central band of the North
American continent—was the same Manifest Destiny shared and
supported by millions of his fellow citizens. If you can say one thing
about Sherman with certainty, it's that he never wanted to be ultimately in charge. It was hard enough to become a military strategist,
and once he found his groove, he stuck to it. The first step involved
Indian removal.

3

Largely forgotten today, the Second Seminole War—what
amounted to Native America's last stand east of the Mississippi—
began in 1835 with the massacre of all but 3 of Major Francis Dade's
110-man command in the vicinity of Fort Brooke, Florida. It would
sputter on until 1842, ultimately costing the lives of almost 1,500
troops—nearly a quarter of the regular army—and damaging the
reputations of Generals Zachary Taylor and Winfield Scott, who
left frustrated and exhausted.[32]

The same basic story line had been going on for two hundred
years. In this case, the United States wanted the Seminoles out,
pushed far west with their supposed Creek "brothers." The Native
Americans, claiming no such allegiance, wanted to stay put. To
compound matters, local southerners alleged that the Indians were
harboring runaway slaves.[33] There were no grounds for reconciliation; it would be a fight to the ugly finish. Operationally, the war
boiled down to a sporadic series of raids and counter-raids, carried
out brutally in the heat and saw grass and swamps of central
Florida—green hell epitomized.

Second Lieutenant William Tecumseh Sherman arrived late in
the war, months after graduating from West Point, and got off lightly.
After delivering a company of recruits to the base at St. Augustine in

October 1840, he headed for his duty station at Fort Pierce, the Atlantic anchor point of his regiment's line of posts strung south as far
as Key Biscayne and west across the peninsula to Tampa Bay. He
went by ship but had to be steered in a whaleboat through the
treacherous surf at the Indian River Outlet by a veteran helmsman,
known locally as the Pilot Ashlock.[34]

The fort was across a broad lagoon perched on sand bluffs, three
rows of log-and-palmetto-thatched barracks joined by stockades to
form a defensible perimeter, with a parade ground to the rear. Officers had separate quarters, six or seven stilt houses, which they had
festooned with varicolored feathers, animal skins, and shark teeth. It
was not an unattractive environment, especially considering the inland alternative. White sand, clear, luminous aqua water, even the
burning sun tamed by the breeze coming off the Atlantic—war in
the tropics could be beautiful.

Sherman was reporting toward the end of the traditional summer
lull in the fighting.[35] Unlike West Point, here there was plenty of free
time. Ashlock—"the best fisherman I ever saw"—taught the new
lieutenant to spear sharks and net green turtles and filled him with
tales of Indian fighting. The base commander and its surgeon also
provided war stories over whiskey punch. They plainly liked young
Sherman: he was bright, animated, and, thanks to his foster father's
political connections, aware of what was going on in Washington.
Familiar faces from West Point were filtering in. Both Edward Ord
and George Thomas were not far down the coast in Fort Lauderdale, and Stewart Van Vliet soon joined Sherman at Fort Pierce. He
gave every sign of enjoying himself.

But this was a war zone, not a Florida vacation, and it quickly
became evident. As the weather cooled, expeditions inland resumed—a hit-and-miss process of locating Seminole bands scattered through the wetlands. Sherman went in repeatedly but found
nothing.

He did see the violent results, though. In January, one party, using
a captured black man as guide, set upon a group of natives with
muskets blazing and then returned with thirty-four survivors, in-

cluding several badly wounded young women whose stoicism astonished Sherman.[36] Around the same time, one of Stewart Van Vliet's patrols stumbled into nearly fifty natives and slaughtered them. One of the sergeants, Broderick, managed to kill three, while Van Vliet, an excellent shot, cut down a warrior at full run through the trees.[37] Broderick brought back one of the scalps and staged a monumental drunk to celebrate. He didn't last long, shot by the enraged husband of a flirtatious base cook.[38] Ashlock was next. After testifying at the Broderick murder trial in St. Augustine, the pilot brought his new bride and her sister through particularly heavy surf and back to Fort Pierce. He then returned to the steamer to pick up a load of ten soldiers, only to capsize and drown with all but one, leaving Sherman on the beach to console the young wife. The next day, he and Ord found a couple of the corpses washed up and "torn all to pieces by the sharks."[39] If combat eluded Sherman in Florida, death did not.

Sherman was aware that military operations were slowly grinding down the Seminoles. But he wanted the pace quickened, and this prompted his first spate of concerted strategic thinking. He pored over available maps to get a better idea of local topography, declaring it "essential to a true military execution."[40] He wrote his foster brother Phil that he wanted "a war of extermination—the most certain and economical method."[41] More men were needed. But further militarizing the white settlers would not help, he concluded, dismissing the local militia as "a pack of rascals" unable to defend themselves, much less conduct offensive operations.[42] Instead, Sherman wanted Florida filled with regulars (long-term enlisted troops) until active resistance ceased—the gradually escalating sledgehammer strategy that conventional soldiers so often propose to deal with guerrillas.[43] What he got was something more sophisticated.

In May 1841, Colonel William Worth took over in Florida. A man with an instinctive feel for irregular warfare, Worth proposed sealing off the south of the peninsula and then conducting unrelenting operations against the remaining Seminoles. First, Worth streamlined rather than enlarged the force—cutting nearly a thousand civilian supernumeraries and then paring down combat teams, which had been slowed and bloated through fear of ambush, to leaner and more numerous units of twenty. Most important, Worth was ready to use them continuously.

Militarily, the Seminoles were determined and resourceful fighters, but they were betrayed by the vulnerability of their support base. It had been the same story since the European colonists first encountered them. Native Americans could not wage war continuously. As advanced hunter-gatherers and slash-and-burn agriculturalists, they needed time and solitude to exploit these slender staffs of survival. Later irregulars—the white Southern guerrillas who would confront Sherman in the Mississippi Valley during the Civil War, as well as the many insurgent groups of the twentieth century—would have vastly better access to food and were therefore harder to deal with. But the Indians were cursed by their lifestyle, falling prey to winter operations in the North and the West and here in Florida to Worth's determination to send his forces into the depths of the interior in all the summer's heat.

Sherman doubted if half the soldiers at Fort Pierce were ready for the rigors of such an agenda, especially with yellow fever about. He needn't have worried. Seventy of the healthiest men were chosen to fan out inland, while he was left at the fort with the "sick, halt, and blind," as he sardonically put it.[44]

Results were not long in coming. Marines and sailors supported the soldiers, moving relentlessly through the Everglades, hunting down the isolated bands of Seminoles in the midst of their growing season. From Fort Lauderdale, Sherman's former roommate George Thomas helped lead an expedition that captured more than fifty Indians. Sherman's own superior, Major Thomas Childs, conducted a twenty-five-day search for Sam Jones, one of the last at-large chiefs, and the young lieutenant was soon bragging that his regiment "had caught more Indians and destroyed more property ... than the rest of the army."[45] Sherman even lent a hand, finding the local chief Wild Cat in a hammock and escorting him peacefully to Fort Pierce, where Childs later had him arrested. Plainly, resistance was being drained like water out of a wetland.

Another incident occurred while Sherman was back at the fort, one that tells us a good deal about his professional outlook and that of his superiors. The post surgeon had wanted ten days' leave, and Sherman agreed to fill in. At sick call the next morning, the young substitute was presented with a groaning enlisted man. Rather than send him to bed, Sherman decided he was faking and ordered a sergeant to run him around the fort. The soldier dropped dead.[46] In the modern U.S. military, this would spell the end of a career; but absolutely nothing came of it—no letter of reprimand, no sign of disapproval. Sherman was young and inexperienced, but he was also practicing what he had learned at West Point: soldiers were essentially pawns, dispensable items. One day this would change, and Sherman would play a key role in that process. But for the foreseeable future, he would subscribe to the elitist code of firefighting, just like his superiors.

They clearly thought he was doing a fine job, and in November 1841, he was promoted to first lieutenant, a jump that usually took five to eight years rather than his seventeen months of service. Some see the fingerprints of Sherman's foster father, Thomas Ewing, who was now (if briefly) new president John Tyler's secretary of the treasury. But one of Winfield Scott's former aides, Erasmus D. Keyes, testified to Sherman's impressiveness: "thin and spare, but healthy, loquacious, active, and communicative to an extraordinary degree."[47] The promotion meant leaving Fort Pierce and doing nothing more exciting than commanding a detachment of twenty men guarding the road between Picolata and St. Augustine. But that didn't matter much, since within two months Worth would write Scott, now commanding general of the army, that hostilities should cease since there were too few Seminoles left in Florida to make it worth chasing them.

The war was over, and Sherman had done well. Within three years, Florida would become the twenty-seventh state, so it is possible to say the interlude marked his first experience with national expansion. He would later grouse that Florida was gaining population slowly and didn't seem to be worth much, but he never suggested relinquishing it.[48] And although his role there may have been minuscule, it was a solid beginning for a young military career. Still, if he was off to a fast start, so was he destined to slow down.

4

After a brief sojourn in Mobile, Alabama, William Tecumseh Sherman found himself bogged down for the next four years at Fort Moultrie on Sullivan's Island in South Carolina, across the harbor from Charleston. His regiment, the Third Artillery, had been brought north and then concentrated there on more or less permanent garrison duty. At least it reunited him with classmates Van Vliet and Thomas, along with Braxton Bragg, who had been three years ahead at West Point. All got a huge helping of boredom.

Life consisted of rising for reveille, drill at sunrise, breakfast at seven, parade at eight, changing of the guard at eight thirty to nine, and then...nothing. Militarily, the day was over. Enforced leisure prevailed.[49]

A certain amount of time was filled with shoptalk. Sherman later remembered long bull sessions in his room among officers on "Tactics & History—discussing the relative merits of the old Flint lock and modern innovation of the percussion cap," adding that one captain "contended that there could be no better weapon than the old revolutionary firelock...and in spite of regulations clung to his old Steuben's Tactics."[50] Reactionary or progressive, this sort of discussion, spaced over days and weeks, was bound to get old.

Sherman took to amusing himself. He read continuously. He wrote home, particularly to his younger foster sister, Ellen—a relationship soon destined to escalate dramatically. He even acquired paint and easel, characteristically turning to landscape and with an intensity that "made it painful to lay down the brush."[51] This may have been just a measure of his own idleness, since he never painted with any seriousness again.

Nevertheless, it did bring him closer to his former West Point instructor and now immediate superior, Robert Anderson. He and his wife were avid collectors and were happy to spend hours with Sherman, showing him their many paintings and engravings. In the process, a friendship blossomed, one that would have significant consequences for both of them. Sherman recalled standing on the battlements with Anderson and watching cotton ships from the North dump their rock ballast on a designated spot within the harbor, where the army engineers were building a new, far more defensible fort. It would be called Sumter, and it would make Robert Anderson famous.

In the interim, however, the city of Charleston continued to extend a hand of welcome to the officers stationed at Moultrie. Armed mostly with their full-dress uniforms, they in turn staged frequent invasions across the harbor, gaining easy entrée to the best parties and drawing rooms. Sherman already had an eye for the ladies and regularly joined in the fun to be had among Charleston's famously winsome belles.

Yet the experience wore thin. The officers and their epaulets were obviously a decorative motif, there to flatter the aristocratic conceits of the local planter class. Partying became a chore, and then a bore. He wrote home: "Smirks, smiles, pride and vanity, hypocrisy and flippance reign triumphant."[52] So did states' rights and nullification, a local brand of politics Sherman, already the staunch nationalist, found contemptible, and one he believed was keeping South Carolina isolated from the American mainstream.[53] He also thought they were bluffing, which they weren't.[54]

He had no quarrel with their economic system, though. Seeing slavery in action in probably its most brutal North American manifestation, the rice plantations of the steamy coastal lowlands, left Sherman unfazed. He accepted the argument that nobody else could do this work in such heat and that it required compulsion. The slaves he saw, at least the ones in Charleston, were "all well dressed and behaved, never impudent," and he thought they felt "very lightly indeed the chains of bondage."[55]

Still, he remained skeptical of the entire social order. In his eyes, it was a structure forged from necessity and pretension and as such hardly preferable to what he had grown up with or had seen subsequently. This pretty much characterized Sherman's thinking up to the Civil War. Slavery was a natural part of the social framework, as was free labor; each could and should coexist for the sake of national unity. A strategic blindfold, you might say.

As time ground on at Moultrie, Sherman increasingly found reasons to get away—and a career as an officer in the U.S. Army offered numerous opportunities to wander the land. Several soldiers deserted, and Sherman jumped at the chance of pursuit. Inspection details and court-martials brought trips to neighboring states.[56] But most significant, three years of continuous service entitled him to a long furlough in the summer of 1843, one that turned into a momentous journey of discovery.

First, back in Lancaster, Sherman discovered he had fallen in love with his foster sister, Ellen, and she with him. But there were many obstacles, even if you overlooked the most obvious: Ellen was by upbringing and inclination hyper-Catholic, and she wanted the instinctively agnostic Sherman to convert. She also wanted him to quit the army. The Ewings were all about the law and public service, making money, and running the family salt mine. Those were the acceptable career options. Finally, she made it clear that Lancaster was home. So clear that you can almost imagine her asking: "Why, oh why, oh why, oh—why would I ever leave Ohio?"

Altogether, this was a pretty strict set of betrothal conditions, but Ellen laid them down softly and Sherman took them up with the same spirit. At least they gave everybody, including the very possessive prospective foster father/father-in law, Thomas Ewing, time to mull things over and get used to the new relationship. Marriage, meanwhile, remained on the horizon.

Plainly in the mood for love, Sherman found a new object of fascination on the way back to Moultrie—not a woman this time, but a river, the mighty Mississippi. Traditionally, strategists focused on such arteries for their ease of transport and also because they generally defined the corridors of power and ultimately the military center of gravity. On the deck of his riverboat, Lieutenant Sherman instinctively knew he was someplace important, furiously scribbling notes on everything he saw: the sights and sounds of water traffic, the lay of the land along the banks, and the towns and cities—New Orleans, Memphis, Vicksburg, and especially St. Louis.

Geography, or at least Sherman's version of geography, prophesied a wonderful future for any place positioned at the confluence of the Missouri and the Mississippi, and to make his point, he moved there six times in his life.[57] But it was this initial trip down the river that seems to have crystallized the image that "in a few Short years the Inhabitants of the Mississippi & tributaries will command this continent."[58] For as historian Charles Royster notes, this liquid network symbolized for him "the unity and complementary harmony" his countrymen must seek.[59] It was "the spinal column of America," as Sherman later put it, and as such was never again far from his mind, a mind that was learning to place great emphasis on movement and central position.[60]

Back at Moultrie, the strategic apprentice didn't so much think geography as devour it. In February 1844, he was detailed to Georgia under the army's inspector general, to investigate some claims by former volunteer troops. As the hearings moved from Marietta to Bellefonte, Alabama, then back to Augusta, Sherman roved the countryside on horseback, exploring points of interest and making what he termed a "topographical sketch of the ground."[61]

It amounted to a great deal more, a kind of nineteenth-century prototype of Google Earth's effort to image everything terrestrial. He was a visual vacuum cleaner, sucking in terrain, placing it in the context of the larger mapping effort, and then storing it in a manner that gave him precise photographic access decades later when he and his army were marching through.

Sherman was a prodigy of geography. During the Civil War, no matter how befuddling the swamp or forest or mountain range, if Sherman had been there, he remembered it exactly. And since he had seen so much of the South, he became a kind of human geolocation system. It was an awesome military talent, but at the time he was developing it, it was nearly invisible to those around him. It may not have even struck Sherman as that unusual; it was simply something he did and assumed others shared.

Besides, there were soon more pressing matters to consider. With the annexation of Texas at the end of 1845, the slide toward war with Mexico was nearly complete. The imminent possibility of adventure, combat, and quick promotion electrified the languid atmosphere of Moultrie. Sherman immediately applied to escort a detachment of recruits to Corpus Christi, and when this was pigeonholed, he wrote the adjutant general in mid-January 1846, asking to be transferred to any regiment being readied for "Western service."[62] Nothing happened. Bragg and Thomas had already been sent to Texas, and Sherman waited, increasingly fretful. Then his regimental commander was ordered to pick two lieutenants for duty elsewhere—one with the dashing horse artillery plainly destined for war and the other as a recruiting officer in Pittsburgh. The selections were made, and Sherman found himself headed for Pennsylvania, not Mexico—a wallflower of war, the cruelest fate for an ambitious young soldier. Missing combat was becoming a habit. The immediate future did not look promising.

Chapter II

THE GOLDEN STATE

I

MAROONED AT THE St. Charles Hotel in Pittsburgh, Sherman alternately processed a line of motley recruits—including a group of maimed veterans who wanted to reenlist—and read newspapers. The headlines only stoked his frustration: Zachary Taylor's forces had moved south toward the Rio Grande and had routed the Mexicans at Palo Alto and Resaca de la Palma; the horse artillery had performed brilliantly. "That I should be on recruiting service, when my comrades are actually fighting is intolerable," he fumed.[1]

Then a letter from his West Point and Florida friend Ed Ord promised a way out—Ord's unit, the Third Artillery, had just received orders for California—an outlier, but still part of the Mexican War—and he urged Sherman to apply.[2] He jumped at the chance, taking all the recruits gathered in Pittsburgh and herding them to an assembly point in Cincinnati, where he dumped them on the colonel in charge, only to be dressed down, "cursed," and sent back.[3] Fortunately, orders for California awaited him along with news that the unit was in New York and ready to sail. He raced east and arrived with two weeks to spare, using the interim to gather maps and documents on California. He would have plenty of time to study them.

For the next six months Sherman would be confined to the USS *Lexington,* an armed supply sloop measuring 127 feet long by 38 feet at the beam—space he shared with around 160 others, including soldiers, sailors, and officers. Because the cargo hold carried artillery too heavy to cart across the Isthmus of Panama, they were headed south the long way, around Cape Horn to Alta California, a huge and treacherous journey for any sailing ship.

The army officers aboard were all West Pointers and therefore used to close quarters and enforced boredom. They tolerated the journey and one another well, gathering in the wardroom daily for meals and chatter and cards. Sherman bunked with Ed Ord and got to know his brother, a civilian physician. But the man who plainly caught his interest was Henry Halleck, former spotless cadet and protégé of Mahan's.

Halleck's career had thrived since he'd left the Point, at least in an academic sort of way—he'd lectured at Boston's prestigious Lowell Institute and published a well-received book on strategy.[4] But he too had missed out on Mexico and was left with the choice of California or working on harbor fortifications. He'd chosen the former and was apparently determined to make the best of it.

Sherman was beginning to think seriously about the nature of warfare, and it's a safe bet that he engaged Halleck—caught him in his usual fusillade of questions and observations. Both were very bright and liked to talk shop. Each was doubtless caught up in the importance of the mission or, as Sherman wrote Ellen the day before they had all left, "to precede the flow of population thither and become one of the pillars of the land."[5] The fighting may have begun elsewhere, but the thought of taking over a substantial chunk of the Pacific coast had to be energizing to the two young strategists in the making, a catalyst to an apparently budding friendship.

When the *Lexington* reached Rio, Sherman went ashore with the Ord brothers for sightseeing and to ogle the girls; but more interesting to him was his hike with Halleck up Corcovado to examine the design of the city's aqueduct—just the sort of geeky adventure he might expect from his sober shipmate. Back aboard, he came to marvel at Halleck's sheer persistence in translating Jomini's biography of Napoleon. "When others were struggling to kill time," he recalled later, "he was using it in hard study. When the sea was high... he stood on a stool, his book and candle on the upper berth and a bed strap round his middle... to support him in the wild tossing of the ship."[6]

As they proceeded south, the weather and the waves grew worse. Sherman and the other officers resorted to albatross "fishing"—baiting a line with pork and then reeling in the voracious birds—which unnerved the crew, who didn't have to read Coleridge to know this was tempting fate. The passage around the Horn took twenty-six ice-storm- and gale-filled days, the most frightening any of the tars could remember, and they blamed it all on the West Pointers.

The worst had passed with the weather, but not necessarily with the tidings. When they reached Valparaiso, Chile, the frigate *Independence* was there, along with word that the war in California was over: the U.S. Navy had already captured all the ports.[7] The only thing left for the army contingent would be fortification of some of the key strategic points like Monterey or the Golden Gate. "No fighting," Sherman wrote in disgust. "That's too bad after coming so far."

2

The *Lexington* finally glided into Monterey on January 26, 1847, after 198 days at sea. Fog clung close to the coast. "Slowly the land came out of the water, the high mountains about Santa Cruz, the low beach....Then the line of whitewashed houses of adobe," Sherman remembered.[8] It didn't look like much.

Lieutenant Wise from the *Independence*, which had also sailed north, came aboard to pilot them to the anchorage. Insurrection, he told them, had broken out. The fleet under Commodore Robert Stockton was far south, around San Diego. General Stephen Kearny had marched in with an expeditionary force of dragoons from Santa Fe but had been roughly handled by the Mexicans at San Pascual. There was fighting in Los Angeles, and guerrillas were everywhere. The army units aboard the *Lexington* took him literally, going ashore in full battle array.[9] They needn't have bothered. Monterey was as quiet as a tomb.

California—all 165,000 square miles of it—was barely inhabited, and most of those people would have had only the foggiest idea that an American takeover was in progress. Over half the population, which did not number more than twenty-five thousand, were Indians. The great bulk of the whites were self-styled Hispanic Californios and traditionally oblivious to whoever claimed to rule them. That left about a thousand recently arrived Americans, a handful of whom took matters into their own hands in 1846 and established the Bear Flag Republic in Sonoma. Virtually nobody elsewhere in Alta California even knew the republic existed before it was superseded by the arrival of the U.S. Navy.[10]

Mexican resistances collapsed, and from this point Americans were clearly in charge. But the question remained: "Which Americans?" General Kearny, Commodore Stockton, and a third player, John C. Fremont, a lieutenant colonel who had fallen in with local Americans to form the California Battalion, all claimed they had orders granting them supremacy. Kearny, his tiny force clearly outnumbered, retreated to San Diego to bide his time. Stockton was due for replacement. And Fremont, as always, remained a wild card. "Who the devil is Governor of California?" Sherman and his fellows wondered in Monterey.[11]

It was a moot point, really. Everybody was on the same side and, in the case of the general and the commodore, all were military professionals. They would work it out. Kearny came north to Monterey and allied himself with Stockton's substitute, William Shubrick, which left Fremont the odd man out. Shortly after, Colonel Richard B. Mason arrived, carrying orders from Winfield Scott that explicitly gave Kearny command.[12] Fremont (Sherman met him briefly

The Monterey Customs House, where Sherman first demonstrated his talent for moving money, in this case disbursing his unit's expeditionary funds. *Library of Congress*

and wasn't impressed) backed down. The army was officially in charge. But what exactly were they supposed to do?

Exert themselves, take control, make sure this place ended up American. That was the obvious answer, but this was a tiny force, and the points of leverage in the vastness of California were hardly apparent. Halleck was already referring to Monterey sarcastically as "the great capital of California," and since he "had neither men nor mean for constructing fortifications," he was "left almost without occupation."[13] Bored and professionally disoriented, Halleck was thrown back on his own resources. In the midst of war, he was in the middle of nowhere. If this tour was to prove anything but a disaster, he would have to figure out a way to invent his own version of success. That in essence was the army's problem as well as his.

Sherman, at least initially, appeared more adaptable. As unit quartermaster, he had gone ashore with $28,000 and set himself up in the customs house, disbursing the money to obtain what the troops needed. It kept him busy, doing something that had tangible results. It was also an ideal way to make local contacts, and the ever-outgoing Sherman plainly made them, even moving in with a family of high repute. The husband, he wrote, "passes most of his time on his rancho about forty miles off so that I am a species of guardian to the family," which of course included the young mother, Doña Augustias.[14]

Since late adolescence, Sherman had been intensely aware of women, particularly attractive women. This is a consistent theme in his correspondence, even to Ellen, to whom he could not resist relating the prevalence of whores in Valparaiso.[15] He was in his mid-twenties, a young man with a healthy sex drive thrust into intimate circumstances with a "kind and intelligent" and apparently available young woman. Los Californios had their own ways of adjusting to the Yankee invaders, and this apparently was one of them.[16] How this looked to his brother officers goes unrecorded.

Sherman's days and nights also left lots of time for his favorite outdoor activity, terrain mapping on horseback, heading out in wider and wider circles through the beautiful countryside up and down the spectacular coast and inland toward the Salinas valley. "And here I must mention that the country is lovely in the extreme," he wrote Ellen, "the hills are bare but covered with high grass and wild oats, the slopes and valleys near towns are wooded with pine and live oak."[17] Soon official business would send him all over northern California, but by then he would wander the land in an increasingly darker mood.

News began filtering in of great American victories far to the south. While Zachary Taylor waged a grinding and inconclusive campaign below the Rio Grande, Winfield Scott had staged an audacious assault aimed at taking Mexico out of the war. After landing at Veracruz, he followed the 1519 route of Spanish conquistador Hernán Cortés, his troops foraging for food. Then, when blocked at Cerro Gordo Pass by the Mexican general Santa Anna, Scott flanked and routed him, moving on to Puebla and ultimately the capital, where the issue was settled at the culminating Battle of Chapultepec.[18] This was strategy deluxe, everything aimed at decapitation. "These brilliant scenes nearly kill us," Sherman wrote home, "who are so far off, and deprived of such precious pieces of military glory."[19] It was apparent now that the real war, the one in Mexico, would produce a host of heroes and promotions, while the California gambit of Sherman and Halleck was looking like a charade.

The two were not getting along. The dispute began in June, when Sherman pressed Halleck over the progress of fortifications on the Presidio, and he in turn took umbrage over the implied lack of professional deference—he was, after all, an elite engineer. "One word led to another till some rather bitter and perhaps improper remarks were made."[20] It was the beginning of a long quarrel, one based on something much deeper: competition. These were two intensely bright and ambitious men, stuck in a bad situation. As each struggled to make the best of it, relative success (Halleck's) and frustration (Sherman's) would only poison the brew.

Colonel Richard Mason, who had replaced Kearny, was determined to at least organize things in the Tenth Military District, as California was now officially titled. With equivalent grandiosity of terminology, in August 1847 he named Halleck district secretary of state, with authority to deal with public law issues, and Sherman as adjutant in charge of implementing military orders. They were his two right-hand men, and almost immediately their paths diverged sharply.

Unexpectedly, Halleck managed to gather a little glory. The U.S. Navy was heading toward Baja California in October, and Commodore Shubrick asked him to join the expedition as his chief of staff. The resulting campaign down the long coast and over to Mazatlán— basically a series of landings and skirmishes—found Halleck repeatedly in the middle of the action, and when he returned to Monterey eight months later, he was promoted to captain, albeit on a brevet (or temporary) basis.[21] Given the scant prospects for heroics in California, this certainly constituted making the most of limited opportunities.

Doubtless Sherman didn't bother congratulating him, since the two were no longer speaking. Rather than combat, he had found depression. "I am so completely banished that I feel I am losing all hope ... I feel ten years older than I did when I sailed," he confessed to Ellen.[22]

Sherman's role as the long arm of the U.S. Army was proving to be that of a straight man in a farce. In Sonoma, a local administrator, or alcalde, elected under the previous regime was refusing to step down. Colonel Mason sent Sherman to evict him. With what might be considered an excess of enthusiasm, he arrived with a detachment of sailors, burst in at dinner with pistols in hand, then kidnapped what turned out to be quite an old man, bringing him back to Monterey "half-dead with sea sickness and fear," only to be released and never heard from again.[23] Sherman may have told himself he had saved the citizens of Sonoma from "a dangerous state of effervescence" and chalked this up as a victory for law and order, but he must have known it amounted to considerably less. Meanwhile, when he was not out on such goose chases, the workload in Monterey was crushing him beneath a pile of Mason's unenforceable orders. "There is nothing new here. No strange events, no hair breath escapes, no battles, no stirring parties, no nothing."[24]

Then, without warning, everything changed. One day in the spring of 1848, Mason called Sherman into his office and directed him to some shiny chunks on the table. "What is it?" Sherman bit it to check for luster, then pounded the largest piece flat with the head of an ax. There was no question: it was gold. And a great deal more than he had ever seen.

It had been sent by Johann Sutter, the discovery of his workmen building a sawmill along the American fork of the Sacramento River. Sherman's mind raced, but it was obvious what they had to do. "I convinced Col. Mason that it was our duty to go up and see with our own eyes that we might report the truth to our Government."[25]

The resulting mission—Sherman, Mason, and four soldiers—proceeded to Sutter's Fort (where he threw them an Independence Day bash) and then up the American fork, where an amazed Sherman estimated four thousand men were already working various sites, producing around $50,000 worth of gold per day.

As soon as the party returned to Monterey, the lieutenant prepared "with great care" the letter Mason would forward to Washington officially confirming the find. He also suggested sending proof in the form of an oyster can full of nuggets.[26] The timing was uncanny.

The gold, all twenty pounds of it, arrived in December the day after President James Polk's last annual message informed Congress of the "extraordinary" finds in California. It set off the great Gold Rush of '49 and marked William Tecumseh Sherman's first brush with destiny.[27] Like the sorcerer's apprentice, though, he would find the results overpowering.

Gold, economics' version of the universal solvent, immediately began dissolving the U.S. military presence in California. Soldiers deserted in droves and sailors jumped ship, all headed for the river of gold where any laborer could earn more in a day than the military paid in a month. Sherman seethed with frustration. Each morning's roll call seemed to show more troops missing. One regular even took off with his favorite double-barreled shotgun.[28]

Finally, one evening the orderly sergeants reported to the assembled officers that a total of twenty-eight men had apparently headed for the hills. Sherman took the lead in rounding them up, knowing that when they hit the flat Salinas valley at daybreak, they would be easy to spot. His plan worked, and he proudly recorded having captured all but one, thereby preventing the desertion of the entire Second Infantry.[29] But the leakage continued, and Sherman's efforts to stop it were largely ineffective. He and his brother officers were in command of an evaporating force.

Compounding their humiliation, gold impoverished them. As nuggets proliferated, the price of goods skyrocketed, and officers' pay soon became inadequate for even the barest necessities. Sherman remembered how his new commander, General Persifor Smith, "had to scratch to get one good meal a day for his family!"[30] and eventually had to send them back east. Smith at least was a realist: he encouraged his subordinates "to go into any business that would enable us to make money." That suggestion soon found Sherman back in gold country, surveying for Sutter and trading plots of land in Sacramento, an endeavor that netted him the amazing sum of $6,000 in two months.[31]

The money may have turned his head. When he returned to San Francisco, a place he hated, he told Smith he wanted to resign his commission and was persuaded to stay only with the promise of an eventual trip east to deliver dispatches. He was plainly miserable during this period,[32] and the absence of military power in California prompted fantasies of societal collapse: "All the women of the lower country may be ravished & killed, horses stolen & houses burnt & you couldn't get a dozen men to leave the Gold district to go to their aid."[33]

Sherman and his brethren were feeling overwhelmed—and indeed they were, deluged by an inexorable tide of their fellow citizens. One hundred thousand avaricious souls had headed west initially, and around eighty thousand actually reached California in 1849, more than quadrupling the population, which was now overwhelmingly American. They, not the army, were taking the place over for Uncle Sam, conquerors armed with picks and shovels instead of swords and muskets. By census year 1850, California's population exceeded Delaware's and Florida's, and it was clamoring for statehood. That was the future.

Given his instinct to establish and maintain military control, Sherman proceeded to fight the wave rather than use it. Halleck, on the other hand, was prepared to go with the flow. Since returning from Baja California, he had been collecting Spanish and Mexican archives, studying maps and property titles, and becoming an expert on the disposition of public lands.[34] Consequently, when his commander issued a proclamation calling for a convention aimed at formulating a state constitution, Halleck was a logical choice to assign as a delegate. He quickly took a leading role in the proceedings and skillfully helped produce a document that broadly paralleled the U.S. Constitution but, significantly, prohibited slavery. Within a month of adjournment in October 1849, it was ratified by popular vote and sent to Washington, where California—albeit controversially—soon became the thirty-first state as part of the Compromise of 1850. The United States of America was inexorably planted on the Pacific, and Halleck was enshrined as a Founding Father—west coast version. It's hard to argue that he hadn't made the most of things.

Sherman attended the convention as General Smith's observer, but the continuing feud with Halleck and his instinctive hatred of politics precluded any influential role. His time in California was winding down, and he spent much of it on horseback, moving about on official business and "fetching up occasionally at Dona Augustias."[35] Finally, news came that the dispatches to army headquarters were ready, and his promised return east had materialized. On January 1, 1850, he departed, taking two of the doña's adolescent sons, Antonio and Porfirio, for delivery to the Jesuits at Georgetown College.

He left in a sour mood. And with some reason. He had been bested in an obvious rivalry with another talented and ambitious officer. Strategy is all about adapting to changing circumstances, making the most of the unexpected. Henry Halleck, who was more intellectually mature, had done this better than Sherman. He was more self-disciplined. He knew how and what to prepare. And he was more strategic in his opportunism. Sherman had displayed considerable energy and initiative, but sometimes they had been aimed in a questionable or even wrong direction. With time the balance would shift—Halleck revealing faults and Sherman talents not yet apparent; but for now there was little doubt who was ahead.

Still, from a career perspective both men probably regretted coming to California and felt stigmatized by having missed the great battles fought in the heart of Mexico. The army would be composed of combat initiates and non-initiates, heroes and the unheroic, and through no fault of their own, Sherman and Halleck were now relegated to the latter category. Very likely it was an important factor in their later decisions to leave the service, albeit temporarily.

Looking beyond immediate career prospects, though, it becomes evident that such pessimism was unwarranted. In war, it's results that matter. California was now a state, and each man had played a significant role in the process: Sherman by inadvertently setting off the Gold Rush that made the place American; Halleck for taking care of the formalities. To a strategist, battles are simply a means to an end. If there are other means to that end, so be it. Only winning matters—a lesson both noncombatants had yet to appreciate.

Thomas Ewing, Sherman's formidable foster
father, sponsor, and sometimes rival.

3

Good fortune awaited William Tecumseh Sherman back on the
east coast, but with his head still under a cloud, he had trouble recognizing it. First, when he delivered the dispatches from California
to the Office of the General of the Army in New York, he was ordered to dine with the great man himself the next day. Winfield
Scott, whose campaign against Mexico City the Duke of Wellington
had labeled the most brilliant in modern warfare,[36] was a lover of
good food, fine literature, elevated conversation, and fancy
uniforms—Old Fuss and Feathers in person. The dinner left Sherman dazzled but also misled.

Scott wanted the Whig presidential nomination in 1852 and was
aware of the lieutenant's connection to Thomas Ewing, now secretary of the interior, so a good reception was likely. Still, the old general didn't suffer foolish junior officers lightly, and what Sherman
had to say plainly interested him, especially on the politics of the

Pacific coast. He launched a zinger of his own, telling Sherman that "our country is on the eve of a terrible civil war"—a pronouncement bound to have shaken the intensely nationalistic lieutenant.

He then shifted to anecdotes of the Mexican War and what some of Sherman's former comrades had accomplished. The stories sent Sherman into an emotional nosedive. "I had not heard a hostile shot. Of course, I thought . . . that my career as a soldier was at an end," he recalled later.[37] Quite the contrary: the savvy old general found the lieutenant "an officer of intelligence" able to "give many explanations of interest" and sent him to Washington to talk to the secretary of war.[38] This was not the first time Sherman would make a good first impression on a major player without even realizing it.

An even better reception awaited him in Washington. Secretary of War George Crawford from Georgia wasn't interested in California "except as it related to slavery."[39] But that didn't matter much. Zachary Taylor—a worse general but a better politician than Scott—had leveraged his Mexican War credentials to vault himself into the White House, and now, when he heard the young lieutenant was in town (perhaps from Thomas Ewing), he extended an invitation. The president received Sherman "with great kindness, told me that Colonel Mason had mentioned my name with praise, and that he would be pleased to do me any act of favor."[40] For a lieutenant without a combat record, this amounted to career exoneration; even Sherman must have perked up.

Things only got better. After depositing Antonio and Porfirio at Georgetown, thoughts of Doña Augustias vanished. For within minutes of his arrival at Blair House, where the Ewing family was living, Sherman and Ellen decided the time had come to marry. None of the issues separating them had really been resolved, but she was now twenty-six and he thirty, and both seemed to realize it was now or never. The emotional complexity of their relationship is a story in itself (and will be dealt with separately), but the implications of the union for Sherman's future success were immediate and profound. He was about to become a full member of a political phalanx—one that would foster and guard his career for the foreseeable future.

The sad and unusual circumstances of Sherman's upbringing had

unexpectedly produced family solidarity, an interlocking directorate of two families. Sherman's father, Charles, an Ohio State Supreme Court justice, had died unexpectedly when William was nine,
leaving his wife, Mary, with eleven children and no money. Fortunately, there was a network of friends and colleagues around the
state willing to provide foster homes. Six of the middle children
went out. In Lancaster, Charles Sherman's best friend, Thomas
Ewing, stepped in fast, looking for intelligence. "Take Cump, the
red-haired one," suggested Sherman's eldest sister, Elizabeth. "He's
the smartest."[41] He did, and she was right.

Sherman fit remarkably well into the thriving Ewing family and
bonded deeply with his foster brothers: Phil, Hugh, Thomas Jr., and
Charley—all of them bright, energetic, and on their way to successful careers. Now, by marrying Ellen, he would link himself irrevocably to them and what would soon become one of the two most
politically influential families in the Midwest (the other being the
Blairs of Missouri). The Ewings, of course, got Sherman, destined to
reveal himself as a military genius, and to complete the package,
they got his full brother John, soon to become the equal of any of
them—even the father—politically.

After a short bout of adolescent rebellion,[42] John Sherman zeroed
in on success like a guided missile. At seventeen, he was reading law;
at thirty-two, he took his seat in the U.S. Congress; at thirty-eight,
he was elected senator from Ohio, fully launched on a trajectory that
would render him a fixture in national politics for nearly half a century and land him the offices of both secretary of the treasury and
secretary of state. Nicknamed "the Ohio Icicle," he was as cool and
calculating as his older brother was volatile and mercurial. But he
was also utterly dedicated to Sherman and would provide wise
counsel and support in what soon would become a very difficult period. Fire and ice, they had their differences. Sherman hated politicians, so he could hardly approve of John's career choice or of his
brother's growing reputation as an enemy of slavery. For his part,
John would find Sherman's various vendettas, especially with the
press, embarrassing. Yet they were and would remain locked together, utterly loyal, rock solid; and Sherman in turn would tie John

John Sherman, the other refugee from the broken Sherman clan, who eventually soared to stratospheric success, but in politics, not the military. *Library of Congress*

to the Ewings, to generate a sort of Ohio steamroller—Team Ewing/ Sherman. All for one, one for all: it would work for everybody, but especially for William Tecumseh Sherman.

Ellen herself would become an integral part of the alliance, reaching out and forging an increasingly strong relationship with John and participating in various Ewing/Sherman advancement and rescue missions. For all her eccentricities, Ellen was both highly intelligent and educated to the exacting standards of her doting father. If anyone could stand up to Sherman—look him square in the eye and tell him exactly what she thought—it was she. He may have known Ellen since she was a child, but on the night of their wedding, May 1, 1850, Sherman still had a lot to learn.

The ceremony held at Blair House was a great success—three hundred guests attended, including the president, his cabinet, Daniel Webster, and Henry Clay—an absolute A-list D.C. gala. Ellen got so excited on the receiving line that she broke protocol and kissed the president.[43] And the happy groom, surrounded by family and those at the pinnacle of power, caught perhaps a glimpse of himself as Fortune's red-haired boy. But the image, at least for now, was a mirage.

Nine days after he and Ellen returned to Washington from their honeymoon, Zachary Taylor died of acute gastroenteritis, apparently contracted at a Fourth of July groundbreaking for the Washington Monument. Sherman's career prospects dimmed accordingly. To compound matters, "hardly was General Taylor decently buried in the Congressional Cemetery" than the new president, Millard Fillmore, named "A.H.H. Stuart to succeed Mr. Ewing."[44] Ewing was immediately appointed by the governor of Ohio to fill the state's vacant senate seat, but the change meant the family would move back to Lancaster—Ellen's dream and increasingly Sherman's nightmare.

From the beginning, the marriage had its difficulties—the same difficulties. Sherman refused to convert to Catholicism, Ellen refused to convert to cosmopolitanism—sticking to home and Daddy whenever possible—and the Ewings still wanted Sherman to resign his commission. Given the latest developments, he may have been softening on that front.

Thomas Ewing did learn from Winfield Scott that Sherman was about to be promoted to captain. When Sherman reported to Jefferson Barracks in St. Louis, his new posting, Ellen didn't go with him; she was pregnant, and at the Ewings' insistence she stayed home. He plainly missed her, but the job and the place had its attractions. Brevet Colonel Braxton Bragg, his old West Point friend and now a war hero, was company commander. Sherman's duties left plenty of time for wandering on horseback, adding most of Missouri and eastern Kansas to his personal terrain database.

His strategic instincts also told him St. Louis had a brilliant future, so he took the opportunity to make all the contacts he could and to worry Ellen in the process. "Alone, I shall be forced for mere occupation's sake to go and seek company at the hotels, at Theatres and concerts."[45] That he did, diving into the city's social life and making a series of wealthy and influential acquaintances he would continue to draw on and cultivate even decades later.

He also got Ellen back, along with the new baby, Minnie, but it took a year, and he had to go to Lancaster and fetch them over the Ewings' objections. They moved into the Planter's Hotel, St. Louis's finest, but Ellen found it confining, so he bought a house on the outskirts of town. She liked it, especially the big guest room. "Come all you can and stay as long as you can" she wrote the Ewings.[46] Instead, West Point friend Stewart Van Vliet moved in with his wife. Minnie was a happy baby, and with three live-in servants it must have seemed a bit like a perpetual double date. Ellen seemed content and soon found herself pregnant again.

Yet Sherman was plainly uneasy. Braxton Bragg's war stories only reminded him of his own unheroic professional status and the likelihood that his next promotion would be decades in coming.[47] He started suffering from asthma attacks, particularly when Ellen was away.

And the pull of Thomas Ewing was hard to avoid. By virtue of a huge legal settlement he won for a local landholder, Ewing and his family found themselves in possession of a great deal of St. Louis property, and Sherman, being there, had to manage it. Then Ellen herself was drawn back to Lancaster, spending the summer of 1852 with her parents. Ewing soon wrote asking that the stay be extended the length of her confinement, and Sherman, cognizant of the tight constraints imposed by the interlocking family directorate, blamed Lancaster. "I have good reason to be jealous of a place that virtually robs me of my family."[48] So did death. That September, his natural mother, Mary, who had been living with John in Mansfield, Ohio, quietly passed away, which only deepened his gloom.[49]

After two years, St. Louis itself was beginning to bore him. His military and property management duties compounded his paperwork to the point that even memories of California and "wild gold seekers is enough to strip quiet life here of all interest & charm."[50]

Relief was on the way, though, and once again it involved a move. Down the great river in New Orleans, the commissary general believed his contracting office was involved in shady dealings and personally ordered Sherman to investigate. He picked the right man.

Sherman arrived in October, set up an office in Lafayette Square, and then cleaned house: cutting previous relationships with the local mercantile establishment; wandering the levee for the best deals; and checking quality to the point of fishing through barrels of salt pork. He rented a warehouse and hired a guard so he could purchase nonperishables at the best price and then store them.[51] Most of all, he followed the money. "If Sherman does not find the error of three cents, necessary to balance his accounts, he will resign his commission and commit suicide," suggested one officer, perhaps hopefully.[52]

Because he was one of the city's largest customers, and because he was Sherman, he soon found himself immersed in a steady round of dinners, balls, and theater parties, as always making friends and contacts. Emotionally, things seemed to be looking up. Back in Lancaster, Ellen gave birth in November to another healthy baby girl, Lizzie, and then departed with the two children, a nursemaid, and one of Sherman's natural sisters to join him in late December, after a concerted campaign to sell her on the city.

Ellen once in place had no trouble buying. New Orleans was an expensive place to live. And if Sherman had stopped the hemorrhaging of U.S. government funds, he soon found his household finances leaking badly. His army pay was inadequate to the task, and he told his brother John that if he stayed put, he would have to begin liquidating the real estate he had acquired in St. Louis.[53] To Ellen, who had no intention of curbing her spendthrift ways, the alternative was as simple as a letter of resignation and a switch to the civilian sector. Sherman resisted for the moment, but the logic of the situation demanded that he do something. He had always been ambitious, yet now it was personal. He was coming to realize that truly winning Ellen involved outshining her father, becoming a bigger man than him. This was not currently in the offing, but it left him open to career options.

In fact, he had already heard from Henry Turner, an army friend he had met in Monterey and later seen a good deal of in St. Louis.[54]

Now a civilian, Turner was tightly linked with that city's power structure, and this was frankly a recruiting letter: "The duties of a subaltern in time of peace are wholly incompatible with your intellect or energy." He went on to tell Sherman of his own "California venture," a branch bank of the St. Louis firm of Lucas, Turner & Co., to be opened in San Francisco. He then popped the question: "Would a fair consideration [partnership] induce you to embark in the same business with myself?" Turner knew his man well, arguing that Sherman's quartermaster and commissary tours, along with the management of the Ewing properties, had provided him with skills readily transferable to the financial sector. Sherman trusted and respected Turner and would have known James Lucas to be the richest man in St. Louis.[55] This was a serious offer by serious people, made all the more manifest when both Turner and Lucas came down to New Orleans to complete the negotiations.

Sherman not only drove a hard bargain, but characteristically hedged his bets, which the partners were only too happy to cover. Rather than have him resign his commission immediately, Turner used his army connections in Washington to smooth the way for a six-month leave of absence, during which time Sherman would travel to San Francisco and manage the bank on a trial basis at the rate of $5,000 per year (around $150,000 in 2012 dollars) plus one-eighth of the profits. It was a sweet deal by any measure. He shipped his family back up the river to Ohio and left New Orleans on March 6, 1853, telling John somewhat skeptically: "I will not throw away my present position without a strong probability of decided advantage."[56] Nevertheless, he was on his way out of the army.

He left without bitterness. His assignments in St. Louis and New Orleans witnessed a clear maturation of his administrative skills and general competence; he departed widely respected by important figures both within the army and without. Also, it is significant that this time frame marked the height of commerce along the Mississippi River and just before railroads began to redirect traffic in alternative directions.[57] It was this Mississippi, full of paddle wheelers, that Sherman remembered when he later helped formulate a Union strategy focused on getting it back.

4

Sherman's timing was terrible. Though it was not fully apparent when he arrived in San Francisco, the boomtown's first great growth spurt had already crested. As the wave of gold from nearby fields ebbed, the city's inflated property values sank, the banks became overextended, and a run on deposits followed—one that ruined a number of prominent firms. Through prudence and good management, Sherman survived the run, but the general erosion of confidence and declining business conditions doomed his banking career in California. He would fight a losing battle to keep the San Francisco branch of Lucas, Turner & Co. afloat.

Meanwhile, the family drama with Ellen and her father continued to bedevil him. She hated San Francisco but insisted on living large, which Sherman's status as a banker also demanded. So he regularly, if grudgingly, burned through his large salary and borrowed heavily to build a suitable dwelling on tony Rincon Hill. Literally and figuratively, it was founded on shaky ground. Through it all, Sherman handled his business affairs carefully and honorably— especially when it came to fellow West Pointers—but he plainly needed more stability in his life.

If he wanted an example of charting a sound course through uncertain times, he had only to look across the neighborhood to the impressive residence of Henry Halleck—a galling role model indeed. Now also a civilian, Halleck had capitalized on his knowledge of Spanish and his Monterey research into colonial deeds to zero in on a particularly sweet economic niche—he became a title lawyer. Soon enough, his fortuitously named firm, Halleck, Peachy & Billings was charging up to $1,500 a case at a time when a carpenter made $5 to $7 a day. "I shall decline all offers for paltry fees, & let the petty foggers take the cases."[58] Why not? The firm was the wealthiest on the west coast, the gold standard of the Golden State. Yet again, Halleck had figured out what was most important—who owns the land—and capitalized on it: as neat a strategic solution as even his mentor, Dennis Mahan, might have demanded.

Henry Halleck, alternately Sherman's collaborator and competitor, and, ultimately, betrayer.
Library of Congress

Halleck's personal life also had stabilized. Paunchy, bug-eyed,
and thinking himself a confirmed bachelor, he had unexpectedly
married, at age forty-one, a woman twenty years his junior, the
granddaughter of Alexander Hamilton and also the sister of his West
Point roommate Schuyler Hamilton. Doubtless Sherman knew all
this, since Hamilton was also employed as the chief clerk in his bank.
Sherman had told him of the bad feelings shared between him and
Halleck. Hamilton decided to play peacemaker, relaying Halleck's
words: "Your friend Sherman deserves a good deal of credit for the
manner in which he conducted his banking affairs during the past
crisis."[59] Obviously he was ready for reconciliation; he could afford
to be. But Sherman only turned a cold shoulder, and the freeze between the two continued for his entire stay in California.

The low point of Sherman's San Francisco period was marked by
his becoming embroiled in the city's penchant for vigilante politics.

The spring of 1856 found Sherman a public figure of sorts: acting as chairman of a committee boosting a national wagon route from Missouri to California, speaking at the dedication of a twenty-two-mile railroad heading east, and accepting a commission as major general of the California militia.[60] In the last instance, his timing couldn't have been worse, since it put him on a collision course with the very hand that fed him: the city's business community.

Like most things here, politics in San Francisco were extreme, and extremely corrupt—speculation, extortion, rigged bids, and stuffed ballot boxes were key instruments of municipal government. Public reaction was spasmodic, what historian Lee Kennett terms "a kind of spontaneous combustion of extra-legality," manifested in the so-called committees of vigilance.[61] This first took place in 1851, when such a committee temporarily displaced city government, hanged a few purported malefactors, and then withdrew. The business community prided itself on the episode—their version of cleaning up city hall—and they were ready to do it again should the occasion arise.

It did, just as Sherman took command of the militia. A member of the board of supervisors, James Casey, had openly gunned down a political opponent and then turned himself over to the sheriff, a trusted associate, thereby galvanizing the elite to go vigilante. A throng of armed men surrounded the jail holding Casey, protected by a nervous and greatly outnumbered posse, virtually a cinematic archetype. Sherman, in his military capacity, inspected the jail, promptly declared it indefensible, and left, only to watch helplessly with the governor and mayor from the roof of the International Hotel as Casey and another suspect were removed by a crowd of twenty-five hundred men several days later, their fate a quick and public hanging.

Sherman wasn't sorry to see Casey go, but he was determined to support Governor John Neely Johnson's efforts to checkmate the vigilantes. On June 1, he and the governor met with General John Wool and Commodore David Farragut, the senior U.S. military representatives, in nearby Benicia, asking for muskets and a ship to land

The public hanging of Casey and Cora symbolized Sherman's inability to thwart San Francisco's vigilantes and the beginning of his endless feud with the press. *Library of Congress*

them in San Francisco. Farragut promised only a naval demonstration (which he delivered), but they thought they had a deal with Wool to supply the guns.[62]

On this basis, two days later Johnson declared a state of insurrection in San Francisco and ordered Sherman to call out the militia. At this point, things didn't simply unravel, they dissolved. Sherman suffered the indignity of learning from a bank customer that General Wool had no intention of delivering the proffered weapons.[63] Meanwhile, the governor's proclamation had produced precious little in the way of volunteers, "the fizzle-call of General (?) Sherman," one local paper called it.[64] In less than a week, Sherman resigned his commission as general without arms or an army; but retaining his sardonic sense of humor, he recommended Halleck as his replacement.[65]

Along with pretty much everybody else in authority, Sherman found himself in the crosshairs of the press, publicly lampooned as "a Mighty Man of War taken from the desk of a counting house."[66] For the first time in his life, he felt the sting of journalistic ridicule, and it revealed a very thin skin. "I conceived a terrible mistrust of the press in California," he wrote long after.[67] While Sherman was actually handled much less roughly than others, he remembered that the papers "poured out their abuse of me."[68] He would continue to read newspapers compulsively, but now it was with an anger seething and growing until seeing his name in print became virtually synonymous with seeing red.

It has been suggested—and Sherman's own words can be used to support the view—that his retreat in the face of the vigilantes was politically transformative and imprinted a kind of nightmarish fear of grassroots democracy gone wild and one that was at the root of his fury over secession.[69] The impact was apparent, but not the whole story. Sherman was far too gregarious and egalitarian in the way he treated people to become a pure authoritarian. He liked much that democracy had created and feared just its logical conclusion, which he believed he had seen in California and again in the Confederacy.

More significant, perhaps, for his fate as a strategist was a trait he first exhibited here in the face of overwhelming odds: He knew when to quit and cut his losses. This is a much-overlooked military capacity: in the heat of the moment to retain sufficient objectivity to recognize the prospect of sure defeat and then to summon the self-control to reverse course and withdraw. For some—Grant, for instance—this proved impossible. But Sherman's military career was studded with such moments, epiphanies of defeat, and they were emblematic of his eventual success. He came to realize that in war there would be good days and bad days, but the ultimate objective must always remain paramount.

The remainder of Sherman's stay in California also turned out to be about cutting his losses. Boomtown's bubble had burst, the easy river of gold was long gone, and the economy was only scraping along. Lucas decided to shut down his bank's San Francisco branch, and Sherman handled the closing in an orderly and responsible fashion. A new branch was being opened in New York, and Lucas would put Sherman in charge.

Sherman departed in a dark state, with many regrets. Halleck persisted; he did not. The dream of big money in the Golden State had hardly panned out. And then there had been the vigilantes. In his mind, at least, the whole interlude had been a litany of failure;

but in spite of everything, he liked California and wanted to stay. He had held his own in a tough environment and continued to impress capable and powerful people. His skills as a banker were sufficient for Turner and Lucas to send him on to the real financial big leagues. Meanwhile, his strategic skill set was gradually, silently, growing, his capacious mind filling with useful knowledge and experience. He would need it all. He was headed for even worse times.

Chapter III

INTO THE GLOOM

I

IN THE SUMMER OF 1857, William Tecumseh Sherman entered probably the worst period of his life. Before it was over, he would come to feel washed up and old beyond his years, a true failure. His unusual family circumstances only exacerbated his perceived inadequacy; self-respect along with possession of mate and offspring came to turn on somehow outdoing the family heavyweight, Thomas Ewing. This was not a delusion: Sherman was caught up in a unique web of family ties that were both his making and his undoing. But Sherman allowed it to color everything. Career frustrations came to be equated with personal frustration in a peculiarly intimate way that ultimately sent him into an emotional tailspin.

But it also seems that the world saw Sherman differently. The impression he left was that of a competent man of affairs, someone who could be trusted in tough times and, increasingly, looked to for leadership. Opportunities continued to come his way. No one seemed to doubt his abilities, energy, or intelligence. Nothing he did during this time detracted from his growing reputation. Even in the gloomy recesses of the inner Sherman, it's possible to see progress. He was becoming less impulsive, more calculating. His knowledge base and skill set were continuously growing. His various career deviations served to sharpen his adaptability. The strategic man was being unveiled; but the veil itself remained a problem. For it allowed him to ignore the central problem of the age.

Sherman arrived in New York and moved in with several West Pointers, one of whom, James McPherson, proved to be particularly good company—the beginning of a long friendship and a key alliance during the Civil War. There was a lot to talk about. Barely a month after opening the New York branch of Lucas & Co. at No. 12 Wall Street, a financial meltdown occurred. Because he had little as yet out in loans, Sherman at first observed the deepening panic with amused comparisons to the San Francisco collapse. But this was entirely different, arguably the first worldwide financial crisis. That reality hit Sherman on the morning of October 7, when his cousin woke him with the news that James H. Lucas & Co. of St. Louis had suspended payments.[1] Almost as soon as they began, his days as a New York banker were over.

It had never been a good fit, and now Sherman began referring to himself as the "Jonah of Banking." "Banking & Gambling are synonymous terms," he told his brother John, a sentiment that was both revealing and true.[2] It is an enduring verity of capitalism that the big money is made at the margins, the product of big risk. But this translates poorly to warfare, where the coin of the realm is human lives, not dollars and cents. The difference in battle between defeat and disaster is huge: in the former, the loser typically suffers a few percent more casualties than the winner; in the latter, annihilation and loss of an entire force structure are real and horrific possibilities. With this in mind, commanders instinctively hedge their bets and cut their losses. This was always Sherman's outlook as a banker; it saved him during the San Francisco run, but as a long-term strategy it would have left him as little more than a capitalistic also-ran. He was a military man with a military mind, and this would become increasingly obvious as he struggled to find himself.

Sherman dutifully returned to St. Louis with the assets he had been able to scrape together from No. 12 Wall Street and spent until the middle of December helping Lucas gather the pieces of his panic-scattered empire. Otherwise, about the only notable thing that happened was an encounter with former cadet Sam Grant, now running his father-in-law's farm on the outskirts of St. Louis and plainly sinking. Sherman could relate; he "concluded that West Point and the regular army were not good schools for farmers [and] bankers."[3]

In fact, Sherman was no longer a banker, but a repo man. He continued to work for Lucas, but his job entailed returning to San Francisco and salvaging what he could from their delinquent debts and deflated real estate. He arrived at the end of January 1858 and spent the next five months dunning deadbeats. The spectacle of hyperenergetic Sherman chasing them down went largely unrecorded, but the results indicate he remained a relentless and effective bill collector. Meanwhile, word came of improvements in the St. Louis bank, allowing Sherman to head back east "justly entitled," Turner wrote him, "to an honorable discharge from further care & trouble so far as Mr. Lucas' affairs are concerned."[4]

This may have come as a relief, but it was only a partial one. Sherman's days as a banker in San Francisco also left him saddled with what he would have described as a debt of honor. Several West Pointers, including Braxton Bragg, Don Carlos Buell, William Hardee, and George Thomas, had entrusted him with around $130,000, money he'd kept in a separate trust account and used largely to purchase San Francisco municipal bonds, which had subsequently defaulted.[5]

Sherman considered this a personal obligation and set about liquidating his own assets to cover their losses.[6] How much this ended up costing him is unclear, in part because his finances were so tied up with those of the Ewings, but it probably amounted to at least $20,000, an enormous sum at the time. Sherman's natural father had taken on a similarly huge debt, and combined with his early death, it had nearly ruined the family. Plainly, the son would not take on such a burden lightly. But he did and in so doing demonstrated where his true loyalties lay. This was in essence a tithe to the long gray line, painful but done without hesitation, honorific union dues that he did not even bother mentioning in his own memoirs. Yet it certainly pointed the way toward his future.

2

August 1858 found Sherman back in Lancaster, reunited with his family and in close consultation with Thomas Ewing. His preferred future from this quarter (undoubtedly with Ellen's input) was deemed to be a life in Ohio managing the family salt mine—a persistent and recurring career nightmare. From California, Sherman had already made it clear to Ewing how he felt about home base. "In the army I know my place, and out here am one of the pioneers and big chiefs. At Lancaster I can only be Cump Sherman."[7] There was an option, however. Ewing had substantial landholdings around Leavenworth, Kansas, and not coincidentally, sons Hugh and Tom Jr. also had established a law practice there; Sherman could join them and manage the property. Serendipitously—at least from a Ewing perspective—Ellen and the children would remain home until her husband could establish himself. It was better than the salt mine.

Almost as soon as he arrived in Leavenworth, he set out across the prairie for Fort Riley 140 miles west, to see his West Point roommate Stewart Van Vliet, who was serving as quartermaster. "He asked me how I stood, and I told him at once the whole fact that I was adrift seeking employment."[8] Van Vliet fixed that quick, offering him a contract to oversee the maintenance of the road back to Leavenworth.[9]

It was exactly what Sherman needed. It brought some money into Hugh and Tom's firm, but mostly it was a tonic for his spirits. He set up shop out on the range, reconnoitering the road, spotting the bad stretches, and letting contracts for repair—all the while, no doubt, adding the terrain to his personal mapping project. He met up with a column of cavalry returning from summer scouting on the plains and spent the night with them trading stories. His time at Fort Riley was equally pleasant; he was "perfectly at home with sound of bugle and drum." More to the point, he missed it. "It makes me regret my being out of the service thus to meet my old comrades, in the open field, just where I most like to be."[10] This marked the first time since Monterey that Sherman had spent time with troops in the field, and it apparently brought back a flood of happy memories and equivalent regrets over the life he had given up.

During this same time frame, he wrote a long report for his brother John on the prospects of a transcontinental railroad, one in which he accurately projected the most feasible route, its unifying effect on the nation, and the inevitability of federal involvement.[11] When his brother had it published in a Washington newspaper—a public unveiling of the Sherman plan for national expansion—it received rave reviews.

Even more suggestive was a letter he wrote in May to John, who was planning an official visit to Europe. The subject was the ongoing Franco-Austrian War, and Sherman demonstrated a sophisticated understanding of its dynamics and the strategic motivation of the participants. Plainly, he had been keeping up—no doubt through his obsessive reading of newspapers—with foreign and military affairs; beneath all his personal travails, the mind of the strategist continued to mature. The letter also revealed his preferences: "I wish I were there to watch the operations and changes; but alas! I am in Kansas scratching for a living."[12]

He must have known this was temporary. Lucas still had confidence in him, and other offers from friends in St. Louis came his way. But his lonely stretch on the prairie clarified at least one thing: Sherman wanted his military life back and began calling in chits to get it. In early June, he wrote Don Carlos Buell, one of the officers whose San Francisco investments Sherman had rescued and who was now well-placed in the Department of War, asking him about a rumored vacancy in the Office of the Paymaster. Buell wrote back almost immediately, but with the bad news that it probably would be filled by the secretary for political reasons. He did have an alternative, though. The state of Louisiana was setting up what they called a military seminary, and its board of supervisors was looking for a superintendent.[13]

Sherman wasted little time in applying to the governor of Louisiana, using Braxton Bragg, another of the investment returnees, as a reference. The head of the board of supervisors, General Graham, recognized Sherman through a network of army connections stretching back to Monterey and was so impressed with Buell's recommendation that he engineered the appointment, despite some grousing over him "being the son-in-law of that blackhearted Abolitionist Tom Ewing."[14]

Back in Lancaster, Sherman weighed his options. He still coveted the paymaster position, but his campaign failed. A job offer in Utah came in, then the possibility of managing an American bank in London. Thomas Ewing put in a pitch for the salt mine and favored the bank as a fallback. But Ellen was about to give birth to "Number 5," Elly, and Sherman considered the seminary "more certain & reliable."[15] The pay was good, $3,500 a year, and even though Ellen and the children would remain in Ohio, they might come south later. Finally, after what he considered due diligence, Sherman signed the letter of appointment. But there was one question he never asked: Why was it that Louisiana wanted a military academy?

3

Sherman had been doing his best to overlook the issue of slavery for a long time, virtually his entire professional career. It was more than simply accepting the institution as a given, part of the natural order of things. Sherman's alternate reality encompassed suppressing the ever-growing political controversy surrounding slavery, not only in his own mind, but in the minds of those closest to him.

Some have suggested his "moderate" position on slavery was inherited from the old-line Whig Thomas Ewing; but the family was also shot through with abolitionists. Ellen, guided by her faith, had no sympathy for slavery. Tom Jr. was steeped in Free Soil politics and was now chief justice of the Kansas State Supreme Court. His natural brother John was a rising star in the Republican Party and in 1856 had served on the three-man congressional committee investigating the slavery-induced violence in Kansas—nearly becoming the first member of the family shot at over the issue. Yet with all three, Sherman sought to paper it over, advising Tom and John repeatedly to avoid abolitionist politics and even chuckling that Ellen might have to purchase some slaves if she moved to Louisiana.[16] His descriptions of his own stay in Kansas—now "Bleeding Kansas" to many—were devoid of references to the violence of the nearby Border War. He had blinded himself to a crisis that had been building all his life.

Nothing in history is inevitable, but sometimes probabilities combine to make events look as if they were. Historian James McPherson points to a central dynamic leading up to the Civil War that is compelling in this regard. While the morality of slavery alone might have eventually led to a showdown, it was America's sprawling growth that made the issue explosive. All parties were committed to expansion, but the South was addicted.

Economically, slave-based cotton production was a great success, providing at this point three-quarters of the world's supply and profits to match. But unlike the North's increasingly industrialized version of prosperity, it couldn't be intensified. Expanding production required expanding the area under cultivation, and since the system was hard on the land, this meant continuous acquisition of new territory. In the southern version of Manifest Destiny (which would eventually look toward Latin America), the key was extending the "peculiar institution," and this would provoke a sequence of bitter political crises as Americans relentlessly moved west and it was decided which new states would become slave or free.

With each confrontation, even when resolved, anger grew, especially in the South, which came to see its whole social structure under assault. The equivalent rise of true abolitionists, particularly ones like John Brown with guns, provided a further element of demonization. From here it was just a short step to secession and then war.[17]

Winfield Scott had seen it coming and had told Sherman. Ulysses Grant, exiled to his father's store in Galena, Illinois, saw it, too, telling a friend exactly how it would happen.[18] Sherman remained steadfastly blind. He likened the Southern states to a "fox who lost his tail and wanted all others to cut theirs off.... I would indulge them in their delusion," he told John, "with the complacency of a strong man."[19] This from someone destined to become one of history's greatest strategists. It requires further explanation.

Anyone can be wrong, of course. But students of history and politics have long puzzled over how otherwise competent leaders can, in moments of extreme crisis and high anxiety, warp the facts of a situation to produce an interpretation basically at odds with reality. Recent explanations have tended to cluster around two poles: that it is largely an emotional response or that it is a reflection of how the mind works. In the first, the stress is placed on the human need to perpetuate conceptions of self and situation that are conducive to emotional well-being.[20] Typically this plays out in denial, procrastination, and incrementalism as the individual struggles to maintain equilibrium and feel better.

Alternately, this sort of behavior can be seen simply as the result of the way the brain processes and prioritizes incoming information—a cognitive structure that filters reality in a manner consistent with preexisting stereotypes necessary to make sense of the world. The phrase *failure to connect the dots* reflects exactly this exclusionary or filtering function along with the brain's systematic bias toward cognitive consistency.[21]

Whatever their ultimate roles, these two paradigms don't seem mutually exclusive, and in Sherman's case signs of both can be readily inferred. His personal ambition compounded by his relationship with his tightly wired family must have infused him with plenty of emotional incentive to seize this opportunity to establish a military academy—his own little West Point—and ignore the implications in light of the looming crisis with the South. He was nearing forty, and this might be his last chance of success on his own terms rather than Thomas Ewing's. Emotionally, the stakes could hardly be higher, and obliviousness promised relief.

It might also be said that Sherman had an extraordinarily rigid and exclusive cognitive framework. His education, professional experience, and internalized vision of a transcontinental America unified and governed under the Constitution left little room for alternative developments. Meanwhile, the whole thing was veiled in a way that let in light only from certain angles, ones that illuminated the structure and preserved cognitive consistency; the rest was filtered out.

This degree of misperception, whatever its causes, does not seem to cast Sherman in a positive light in terms of his prospects as a military strategist. If nothing else, a strategist must stare reality square in the face. But that's never as simple as it seems. Meanwhile, until a war is won, victory remains an intellectual construct in the mind of the strategist, one that must be firm enough to withstand the vicissitudes and bizarre mischance of war. Everything here has to be made rugged, including frames of reference. Better too strong than too weak. Sherman's own had to become more adaptive to changing circumstances, but mainly he had to lose the veil. That would be traumatic.

4

Sherman got on well with his Louisiana hosts from the beginning, and progress toward opening the seminary was immediate and impressive. He had done his homework, consulting with his West Point superintendent and writing the head of the Virginia Military Institute, along with George McClellan, for advice. He found a powerful local ally in the head of the board of supervisors, General Graham, and the two worked effectively together for the length of his stay.

As head of the Louisiana State Seminary of Learning and Military Academy, Sherman never asked his hosts why they thought they needed a military academy.
Louisiana State University Libraries Special Collections

Graham's plantation was close to the school's site in rural Alexandria, providing frequent contact and a conduit to sources of patronage and funding.

Sherman was his usual whirlwind of energy and effectiveness. The academic building—"a gorgeous palace, altogether too good for its purposes"[22]—was nearly complete after three years of work: seventy-two large rooms, all of them devoid of furniture, books, faculty, or students. Yet within two months of his arrival, everything had been assembled and the Louisiana State Seminary of Learning and Military Academy opened on schedule, January 2, 1860.

Sherman completely dominated the place; his vision and personality were electric and compelling. His talent for leadership and charisma were now plainly evident as both students and faculty fell into step and turned the seminary into exactly what he intended.

Some initially wanted the school to stress liberal arts, but Sherman understood that Graham, Governor Thomas Moore, and influential local West Pointers like P. G. T. Beauregard and Braxton Bragg (now a rich Louisiana sugar planter) wanted a military academy, and this was, after all, why he had been brought in. He simply let it be known that only military discipline could effectively control young men and then turned the place into a mini–West Point.[23]

Predictably, there was some push-back from the cadets, some real rebelliousness (not unexpected given the times), but he effortlessly reestablished order and soon had them eating out of his hand, gathered in his room at night to hear stories of California Gold Rush days.[24] Maybe you can find the origins of Uncle Billy right here, a surrogate family, just as the Army of the West would one day become a much bigger one. He was enjoying himself and thoroughly in control.

This went for the faculty, too. Given the rapidity of their assembly, they were a surprisingly distinguished group. Most had teaching experience, but not in a military context and not with Sherman. When one member delivered a lecture that left the cadets mystified, Sherman was heard to mutter: "Every damned shot went over their heads"—a prelude to prompt remediation. "He soon clipped the wings of our grandiloquently soaring eagle, and made him a plain barnyard fowl—a practical, useful instructor."[25] Yet he did it in a manner that did not alienate; he was dominant without becoming domineering.

He became particularly close to linguist David French Boyd, really the only true friend he ever made outside the army and family. Both were unattached, and they apparently spent long evenings in deep conversation. Boyd seems to have served as a sounding board and confessor, but the friendship was mutual, deep, and lifelong. Boyd would one day resurrect the seminary and transform it into Louisiana State University, but he always considered Sherman the founder.

He made an equivalently good impression on Baton Rouge and the corridors of power. But first he had to overcome more than just some initial skepticism. Back in Washington, John, having enjoyed a quick rise to power in Congress, had just stumbled badly in endorsing abolitionist Hinton Helper's book *The Impending Crisis of the South,* a move that so enraged Southern congressmen that ultimately it cost him elevation to Speaker of the House. In Louisiana, William

Sherman was John Sherman's brother until otherwise proven inno-
cent.

He was up to the task. As usual, John had his back, providing a
letter packed with phrases like "thoughtless, foolish, and unfortunate act" and "the ultra sentiments in the book are as obnoxious to
me as they can be to any one," to be shared with Graham and the
others.[26] Mollified but unconvinced, the governor held a banquet for
Sherman in Baton Rouge and made sure the topic of slavery was
broached. Sherman mouthed the right phrases—"the people of
Louisiana were hardly responsible for slavery, as they had inherited
it." He suggested reform, not separating families, and repeal of anti-
literacy laws on the grounds that "property" would be worth more if
it could read. "By God, he is right," uttered one guest, slamming his
fist on the table.[27] This was a man who could be trusted with the
future of Louisiana's youth…whatever that might be.

It was apparent the school was working well but needed more
resources. Sherman had additional leverage, a renewal of the London banking offer at the princely sum of $15,000 for two years. Gra-
ham and the board didn't want him to leave and responded
immediately, tripling the school's budget, raising Sherman's salary
to $5,000 a year, and agreeing to build him a house suitable for Ellen
and the children.[28] It was certainly a vote of confidence, but Sherman hesitated and pondered leaving.

He must have realized the banking offer was more than just an
offer; it had Thomas Ewing's fingerprints all over it. On the face of
it, he wanted Sherman to get out while he had an attractive option,
but there was a deeper undercurrent of disapproval, one reflected by
the whole family. The South was careening toward secession, and
Sherman was running a military academy in Louisiana. From their
perspective, it was not a matter of making excuses for Tom Jr.'s and
John's politics, it was a matter of making excuses for Cump. The Ewings had a reputation to protect, and this was not appropriate.

Sherman's response was to go through the motions, making obei-
sance to the family agenda, but not really. In March 1860, he went
north and met with the bankers in Cincinnati; made impossible demands that were rejected; and then promptly returned to the school

to finish the term, which stretched into the summer. The authorities were delighted at his return and raised his salary another $500; the house for Ellen was under construction, and he planned for her arrival. He went north again to obtain books and supplies, including two hundred cadet muskets personally requisitioned from the Ordnance Office.[29] Meanwhile, the world around him continued to break apart.

The approaching presidential election must have looked like a train wreck. The Democratic Party had split into Northern and Southern factions, each with its own candidate, giving Republican Abraham Lincoln an apparent edge. His election meant secession for many in the South; that was apparent. To try to head off the crisis, Thomas Ewing and remnants of the old-line Whigs cobbled together a Constitutional Union Party with their own candidate, John Bell. No sooner had Sherman picked up on Bell and the idea of a four-year truce to work out the problem of slavery than he discovered that Ewing himself had defected to Lincoln. The Republican victory in November sent shock waves throughout the South, and in mid-December word reached Alexandria that South Carolina had seceded, with other states ready to follow.

David Boyd was with Sherman when they read the news, recalling he "burst out crying like a child, and pacing his room in that nervous way of his, he turned to me & exclaimed: 'Boyd, you people of the South don't know what you are doing! You think you can tear to pieces this great union without war! But I tell you there will be blood-shed—and plenty of it.'" Sherman's agony was real. Secession cut him to the depths of his nationalistic soul: what he had been avoiding all his life had come to pass.[30] It made no sense. "The North can make a steam-engine, locomotive or railway car; hardly a yard of cloth or shoes can you make. You are rushing into war with one of the most powerful, ingeniously mechanical and determined people on earth....You are bound to fail. Only in your spirit and determination are you prepared for war."[31] Clairvoyant words, proof of the strategist resident all along beneath the veil of self-deception. His illusions in tatters, Sherman would have to deal with the consequences.

David French Boyd, Sherman's friend at the seminary and later
head of Louisiana State University, recalled vividly Sherman's
agony at the news of secession. *Louisiana State University Libraries
Special Collections*

Governor Moore ordered the forts along the Mississippi and
Lake Pontchartrain seized along with the U.S. arsenal at Baton
Rouge, while a secession convention was called for early January.
Two thousand of the purloined muskets were shipped to the school
for storage, an act that particularly galled Sherman, who recognized
their packing crates with "'U.S.' Simply scratched off."[32] Being made
technically responsible for stolen Federal property was something
Sherman never forgave. He continued to mention the seizure of U.S.
arsenals as among the most grievous of Southern outrages. His resignation was inevitable and followed shortly, though still with some
regret.[33]

They were sorry to see him go, too. Letters of praise came from
the governor, Graham, and Bragg, and all agreed he had done an
excellent job for them. None, though, tried to convince him to stay
and join their cause; it was obvious where he stood. "Secession was
treason, was war," he told everybody who would listen. It might as

well have been a tattoo. He had a pleasant final meeting with the governor and the board of supervisors and laughingly promised to hang Moore the next time he saw him. He wasn't necessarily kidding.[34]

Sherman left Louisiana a bitter and angry man. He was not unmindful of the kindness and hospitality of his hosts, but it's hard to imagine him not also feeling used. His outrage at the seizure of U.S. property, along with the cadet muskets he had personally requisitioned, suggested an underlying realization of how bad it looked to have been training officers for what now promised to be an army of rebellion.

But mainly his gathering fury was directed at secession itself. It mangled and debased the most profound pillar in his frame of reference, the Union, and he truly took that personally. Historian Charles Royster argues that Sherman based his identity and sense of coherence on the security of the nation: "The alternative was madness."[35] And anarchy. He spun out scenarios by which secession might atomize the political structure down to the county level: "It will be Mexico, only worse."[36] Sherman craved order, and secession implied the opposite, bringing back memories of the vigilantes in California, who had also taken things into their own hands.[37] Ultimately, his personal integrity demanded that the process be reversed and the Union restored. But for the moment, he was out of a job and depressed, and he returned to Lancaster in a state that left the family shaking their heads.

5

It was a complete reversal. Ellen, Thomas Ewing, Tom Jr., Hugh, and John all wanted him back in the army immediately, while Sherman hedged. Militarily, the situation was in flux, neither peace nor war. He needed time to get oriented. Besides, he was in a sour mood, wondering openly whether the North would actually fight.

There were two letters waiting for him when he arrived. The first was from Henry Turner, offering the opportunity to run the Fifth

Street Railroad Company in St. Louis at a decent salary of $2,500 a year—a welcome alternative to the ever-available Ewing salt mine and yet another chance to return to the city of his geostrategic dreams.

The second was less substantial but more intriguing. John had recently been appointed senator (replacing Salmon Chase, who was now in the cabinet), and he wanted his brother to come to Washington to discuss the evolving crisis. It was an open invitation to show himself off, and Sherman dutifully headed east.

John's connections went straight to the top, and in early March 1861, for the second time in his life, Sherman found himself conferring with the chief executive. "Mr. President, this is my brother, Colonel Sherman, who is just up from Louisiana, he may give you some information you want." "Ah!" responded Abraham Lincoln. "How are they getting along down there?" Sherman had no doubts: "They think they are getting along swimmingly—they are preparing for war." "Oh, well!" Lincoln shrugged. "I guess we'll manage to keep house." End of conversation. Sherman for once was at a loss for words, and they soon left.

Outside, he remembered, "I broke out on John, damning the politicians generally, saying, 'You have got things in a hell of a fig, and you get them out as you best can,' adding that the country was sleeping on a volcano that might burst forth at any minute, but that I was going to St. Louis to take care of my family."[38] This was the thanks the long-suffering John got for setting up a meeting with the president. Sherman could be temperamental, to say the least. Yet neither his brother nor anyone else in the family seems to have have doubted his abilities or their own duty to see he got back in the military in some suitable position. Neither, quite possibly, did Honest Abe.

It has been said that Lincoln, caught up in the turmoil of his administration's earliest days, had dismissed Sherman as simply a job-seeking relative of a pol.[39] But it's hard to imagine the tall, twitchy redhead not making an impression on someone as shrewd as Lincoln, even at his busiest. Later, once the war had begun and the South proved surprisingly prepared for combat, he might well have remembered Sherman's words. From the day of that first meeting forward, Lincoln never seemed anything but favorably disposed toward Sherman. He would stick by this odd (some said crazy) commander when others were more than ready to cast him aside. And in the end, it would pay big dividends. For the redhead was destined to save Lincoln's political career.

For the moment, however, Sherman retreated to St. Louis—joined at last by a reluctant Ellen (pregnant yet again), the five children, and two servants—to run his urban railroad. But there was a slim chance of him staying. Sherman was at base a professional military officer, and his skill set naturally included angling for the right posting. He plainly intended to get back in the military, but he also realized that officers of his training and capabilities were now at a premium. "The time will come...when professional knowledge will be appreciated, when men that can be trusted will be wanted, and I will bide my time," he told John.[40] Some of what the family took for stalling was really calculation, but it was also complicated by his own depressed and irritable state and the situation on the ground.

If he was looking for peace and quiet, St. Louis was the wrong place. The city was being torn apart by North/South politics. On one side, the secessionist governor Claiborne Jackson, both Lucas and Turner, and much of the population were obvious Southern sympathizers; on the other were large numbers of recent German immigrants, the Unconditional Union Party, and the U.S. Army in the person of the very determined captain Nathaniel Lyon, commander of the troops guarding the Federal arsenal. Sherman felt caught in the middle. "On the question of secession...I am an ultra. I believe in coercion....On the slavery question, as much forbearance should be made as possible."[41]

It didn't help that the Unconditionals were led by Frank Blair, a forthright abolitionist, son of one of Lincoln's advisers, and brother to the postmaster general, Montgomery Blair. Sherman seems to have taken an instant dislike to Blair, considering him an amateur in over his head in a violent game and his family "a selfish and unscrupulous set."[42] Actually, Blair had plenty of military talent—ironically, he would prove to be one of Sherman's best corps commanders—and the clan was plainly not averse to cooperation.

Back in Washington, John had convinced Montgomery Blair to offer Sherman the chief clerkship of the War Department—a position projected to transform into assistant secretary of war. His brother rejected the offer, a move that caused several in the cabinet to question his loyalty.[43] They need not have worried on that score: it was the job he spurned. Earlier he would have accepted such an administrative post, but as war neared, his instincts shifted. Sherman was a soldier, not a military bureaucrat, and this position would have decoupled him from directing troops.

Undaunted, Frank Blair personally offered to make Sherman a brigadier general of the recently organized volunteer Home Guard gathered in St. Louis.[44] He rejected that, too, as well as a similar possibility of commanding the Ohio militia as a major general. Both were telling but puzzling moves if he really wanted to fight.

Meanwhile, the pressure was being ratcheted up by outside events, particularly the defense and fall of Fort Sumter during the first part of April 1861—the clash that ignited the Civil War. This was the same Fort Sumter that Sherman and his friend Robert Anderson watched being built in Charleston harbor, the same Anderson who was now responsible for its heroic defense. Here was yet another case of a close acquaintance involved when Sherman was not; the need to do something could only have grown accordingly. As it turned out, the pull of local events clarified where he stood and what direction he would take.

In the immediate aftermath of Sumter, the governor tried to stage a putsch to bring Missouri into the Confederate camp—taking control of the St. Louis police, mobilizing pro-Southern militia, and setting up Camp Jackson on the outskirts of the city.

Frank Blair and Captain Nathaniel Lyon matched him move for move, secretly transferring the U.S. arsenal's twenty-one thousand muskets across the Mississippi to safety in Illinois, mustering the Home Guard into Federal service, and then incorporating them with the regulars. Sherman was impressed with what Lyon, a West Pointer, was doing and visited the arsenal repeatedly. How could he stay away? This was St. Louis, his geographic center of gravity, key to the Mississippi River.

But it was Lyon who was determined to seize the initiative. Disguised as Frank Blair's mother-in-law, he scouted Camp Jackson and the next day, May 10, surrounded the place with four Home Guard regiments and two companies of regulars. Seven hundred pro-Southern militia surrendered without a shot being fired.[45]

Sherman had heard of the surrender and was headed in that direction, accompanied by his son Willy, when he encountered Frank Blair's volunteers with their prisoners on their way back. They had been stalled by an angry mob, and Sherman moved ahead to the regular soldiers, chatting with their commander until the column resumed its progress. Moments later, a pro-Confederate drunk shot one of the volunteers' officers and they opened fire, killing twenty-eight civilians before they could be stopped.

For the first time in his life, William Tecumseh Sherman found himself under sustained fire, "the balls cutting the leaves above our heads."[46] He reacted coolly, grabbing Willy and racing for a gully, where he threw himself on top and waited for the firing to stop. These moments of danger only reinforced what Sherman had been saying all along, that volunteers and militia could not be trusted for difficult duty. The regulars had held their fire; the Home Guard had panicked. This was key to his reticence, why he avoided becoming a general in the militia. As far as he was concerned, volunteers were incapable of waging the kind of war he believed necessary, invasion of the South.[47] Fortunately, relief came within days, when Sherman learned he was being appointed colonel of the Thirteenth U.S. Infantry Regiment, a defunct unit now being reconstituted. He accepted immediately, presuming he now had something to work with.

Sherman was and would remain a regular army kind of guy, but as he stood on the precipice of war, he was an incomplete military package, a good ways from the warrior wizard he would one day become. His chief problem continued to be his contingent relationship with reality, a complex and ambiguous problem for any military strategist. If the perceptual filters that had allowed him to ignore the coming of secession were in abeyance, there remained those that would exaggerate danger—a potentially paralyzing affliction in warfare, and nearly Sherman's undoing before he finally learned to effectively balance limited information with an ever-changing reality.

He was also filled with doubts about himself and his abilities, most also exaggerated. Sherman's career to date had not been wildly successful, but he had also run into an extraordinary amount of bad luck. Throughout, he had effectively handled increasing levels of responsibility and consistently impressed important people. Nonetheless, his letters during this period, particularly to Ellen, are filled with self-castigation and trepidation. He feared neither battle nor death, only failure in his first and only true calling.[48] So as he left St. Louis and headed toward Washington and the supreme challenge, he was not a happy warrior.

Chapter IV

THE BLACK HOLE

I

IT BEGAN auspiciously enough, filled with familiar faces. He arrived in Washington on June 11 to find his command of the Thirteenth U.S. Infantry confirmed, though it remained a paper unit. He then found his way to the Office of the General of the Army, still Winfield Scott, to discover Schuyler Hamilton, his former chief bank clerk in San Francisco, operating as Old Fuss and Feathers's personal aide. When Sherman suggested returning west to begin recruiting his unit, he was informed that a subordinate could do that. Hamilton apparently wanted to keep him close at hand, and he was not alone. The old general remembered Sherman well and wanted to talk things over at dinner.

A visit with Winfield Scott at this point, someone said, "was like paying a call on a sick bear." Now seventy-five, bloated to more than three hundred pounds, and tormented by gout, he had raised irascibility to the level of an art form. But the intellect, particularly the strategic intellect, remained keen as ever, and a good conversation still held its magic. That would have been Sherman's entrée, and it seems plausible the two had some sort of meeting of the minds. Certainly neither would have been at a loss for words.

Scott's strategic vision for ending the rebellion was informed by moderation; these Confederates were fellow Americans, after all, and a war of conquest could only bring "fifteen devastated provinces!" and much unnecessary bloodshed.[1] Since exported cotton was the South's lifeblood and it had no navy, inflicting defeat remained essentially a matter of envelopment—closing down its ports, cutting off the basic source of income, and then waiting until poverty and sanity took hold. The problem was the waiting, and the North, particularly its press, was impatient, labeling it derisively "the Anaconda Plan."[2] Why not march on Richmond, as Scott himself had marched on Mexico City?

But there was more: the part B that Sherman and Scott might have been discussing. As Scott envisioned, an invading spearhead would use the Mississippi as a highway to thrust through the Confederacy and cut it in half, followed by a larger occupying force to secure the victories and create a lasting presence that would utterly demoralize the South.[3]

Both men would have agreed that only regular troops could act as the initial spearhead, and this seems to have had something to do with Scott's decision to keep the regular army together, rather than disperse its units among the volunteer force to act as drill instructors and tactical leaders.[4] Like the eventual blockade, the invading force would take time and preparation—expanding and training the regular units and gradually bringing volunteers to the standards necessary for garrison troops. But the overall plan was entirely representative of military professional opinion and, given Sherman's personal enthusiasm for the Mississippi River, particularly convincing. This was not how things worked out in terms of force structure, but it did accurately forecast Union strategy through Vicksburg, an approach Sherman personified.

Scott briefly made Sherman an inspector general, and in this capacity he soon encountered George Thomas in charge of a brigade near Washington. Thomas had never left the army, served with distinction during the Mexican War, been wounded by a Comanche arrow out west, and now, even though a Virginian, remained the same loyal and resolute presence Sherman had known since his first days at West Point. They were soon bent over a map spread out on the floor, picking out points of strategic importance, Vicksburg and Chattanooga in particular[5]—places that would one day make them famous.

But for the immediate future, Sherman's peregrinations reporting on the military status of units and facilities around Washington apparently convinced him that Scott's determination to avoid any precipitous forward movement was unsustainable. The signs were everywhere that the fat old general was being circumvented and ignored, like an aging alpha ape about to be overthrown. "On to Richmond!" was the cry of the day, whether directly overland from Washington or up the Kanawha River, as proposed by jack-of-all-schemers George McClellan.

Sherman stopped by the headquarters of General Irvin McDowell, whom he knew from West Point and California, and found the beginnings of an army of invasion, which he was promptly asked to join. He had missed too many chances for combat in the past, and despite his skepticism of an invasion scheme based largely on volunteer units, Sherman probably made up his mind very quickly to go. At any rate, when he received his orders assigning him on June 30 to McDowell's force as commander of the Third Brigade of the First Division, there were no complaints.[6]

Those would come later. He had gone to war banking on commanding regulars; now he had volunteers—thirty-four hundred of them, three regiments of Irish New Yorkers and one from Wisconsin. Neither knew what to make of the other. Sherman arrived in a straw hat and a threadbare uniform several sizes too small and began drilling them incessantly and yelling at them until he was hoarse. They did the best they could, then started to insist on going home as their absurdly short ninety-day terms of service neared. To Sherman, this signaled they were plainly still civilians. He began referring to them as "Raw Material," complaining that Napoleon had three years to prepare his brigades, whereas "here it is expected in nine days."[7]

There was a general belief at this stage, both North and South, that one big victory would end the conflict.[8] Therefore, when the Confederates built up a force of twenty thousand around the railhead at Manassas Junction, the pressure to attack it became overwhelming. Lincoln thought it was worth a try and directed McDowell to form a plan. He produced an excellent one for veteran troops and seasoned officers, an overland flanking assault with forces numbering around thirty thousand. Still, he was worried about the status of his troops and begged for a postponement and more training. But the president ordered him to proceed with the offensive: "You are green, it is true, but they are green, also; you are all green alike."[9]

That may have been the case generally, but the Southern leadership was hardly green. Overseeing the buildup at Manassas was the dapper captor of Fort Sumter, P. G. T. Beauregard, whom Sherman knew from his days in Louisiana and elsewhere in the army to be highly competent. He was a good deal more, a truly creative tactician who would serve the entire length of the Civil War, making the best of virtually every increasingly miserable command he would be given. For now, though, his problem was simple: He knew McDowell was coming, and he needed more soldiers.

That was the province of Joseph E. Johnston, commanding eleven thousand Confederate troops in the adjacent Shenandoah Valley. A fastidious, pinched little man, Johnston had been known in the antebellum army as a superb strategist. He would do little in the subsequent four years to contradict this notion. He proverbially fought within his means, always conserving his men—something that could be said of few Confederate generals—but in doing so, he earned a reputation for caution that hurt him with superiors. Still, when the opportunity arose he was capable of decisive action, and this was just such an occasion. Blocking his way to Beauregard was a force of fifteen thousand Federals under Robert Patterson, an ancient veteran of the War of 1812 who sought to maneuver rather than pin down the Confederates. Almost effortlessly, Johnston slipped by him, marched from Winchester to the nearest railhead, and got on the train for Manassas—his last units arriving just as the fighting climaxed. The numbers would be essentially even.

Sherman would see a great deal more of both Beauregard and Johnston—it was primarily on these two swords that he honed his strategic skills—but for now his problems were more mundane. From his perspective, the march down to Manassas and Bull Run Creek was a kind of slow-motion nightmare. Burdened by fifty pounds of equipment, the men tired quickly in the heat and then simply sat down to rest or wandered off in search of water and food. As the columns lurched forward and then accordioned to a stop, turning a one-day march into three, Sherman fumed at the presumptuousness of it all. Given the later depredations of his armies, some have found a certain irony in Sherman's early outrage over free-for-all foraging. But at the root of his objections was the implied disobedience this entailed—these troops did what they wanted, not what he wanted; they were hardly the automata he had expected since his days at West Point.

When battle did come at Manassas on July 21, in what would be called the First Battle of Bull Run, his men fought surprisingly well, though in their own way. McDowell's flank attack nearly succeeded, since Beauregard had placed most of his brigades on the opposite side to protect the railroad. Through the morning, the Yankees gradually pushed the outnumbered Confederate left up a promontory called Henry House Hill. At this point, Confederate general Thomas J. Jackson, hitherto an eccentric professor at Virginia Military Institute, became "Stonewall" Jackson, holding back the Union surge long enough for Beauregard and Johnston to arrive with fresh reinforcements, reinforcements given to an unnerving yelping, the signature rebel yell that would be heard in hundreds of future charges.[10]

Sherman and his brigade were in the thick of the action. Twice grazed with bullets and having had a horse shot out from under him, he remained cool and aggressive, though shocked at the carnage of actual battle.[11] Through most of the day, his men had fought with a stubbornness he hadn't expected. But the failed afternoon assault on Henry House Hill and the hail of Confederate small-arms fire it provoked appeared to have broken their spirit. Sherman probably didn't help matters by attacking in piecemeal fashion, one regiment at a time.[12]

At any rate, as if prompted by some universal signal, the men on the blue side decided they'd had enough, retreating at first slowly and then with increasing haste and finally panic. Units on all sides were falling apart, but notably Sherman retained enough control to form a hollow square, the traditional defense when Confederate cavalry threatened his infantry.[13] But then this too broke apart and everything dissolved into chaos. McDowell's army became a crowd intent only on getting out of Virginia and across the Potomac to safety.

Sherman's brigade suffered more casualties (609, including the brother of the secretary of war, Colonel James Cameron, who was killed) and is considered to have fought as well as or better than any equivalent Union unit that day.[14] But Sherman left Bull Run mortified. His first battle and he had been chased off the field. The fact that he had performed courageously, kept his head throughout, and was still alive was plainly secondary to his sense of defeat and utter disgust with his volunteer soldiers.

Bull Run bore paradoxical results. Tactically, it was one of the most decisive defeats inflicted during the entire Civil War; but strategically, its impact is harder to pin down. Jefferson Davis, the ever-querulous Confederate president, arrived on the scene at the moment of victory and immediately urged hot pursuit: "On to Washington! The Union plan reversed." But Beauregard and Johnston knew their army was as shot as the Yankees' and could not pursue and capitalize on the win. It was the right decision, but it permanently undermined the position of both in the eyes of the unforgiving Davis. At least the cost when compared with later battles was light—around two thousand Confederate casualties compared with the Union's sixteen hundred, with another twelve hundred captured.[15] Nevertheless, Bull Run had a profound impact in another regard: It convinced both sides that the fighting would continue, that the war would persist. Figuratively, both sides stalked back to their corners and readied themselves for further rounds.

Back in Washington, Sherman had managed to reassemble his brigade from "the Shameless flight of the armed mob we led into Virginia,"[16] but he remained angry and worried. There were rumors that he had abandoned the brigade (he confided to John, now an influential voice in the Senate, that he had briefly lost track of them during the retreat),[17] a potentially damning offense. Along with a number of other officers involved in the Bull Run debacle, he half expected to be cashiered.

Plainly, he was not popular with the brigade. At one point, he evicted soldiers from a barn on a rainy night so he could shelter some horses, and on another occasion he thwarted a nascent mutiny by threatening the recalcitrants with artillery manned by his sole company of regulars.[18] This was not simply insubordination. Future terms of enlistment would be extended to three years, but these soldiers had signed up for ninety days and they wanted to go home. To Sherman, they were "a pack of New York loafers and thieves,"[19] and this constituted desertion.

The issue came to a head on July 26, when an officer in one of the regiments announced, "Colonel, I am going to New York today. What can I do for you?" A small crowd of enlisted gathered, and Sherman, ever theatrical, conspicuously stuck his hand in his coat and replied: "Captain, if you attempt to leave without orders, it will be mutiny, and I will shoot you like a dog!" The officer slunk away and the crowd evaporated, but that was not the end of it.

Later on that same day, Abraham Lincoln and his secretary of state, William Seward, were on their way to encourage this most battered of Union brigades when they encountered Sherman and invited him to join them in the carriage. As usual, the redhead was full of advice: "Please discourage all cheering, noise, or any confusion....What we needed were cool, thoughtful, hard-fighting soldiers—no more hur-rahing, no more humbug." Lincoln took it in good humor, and when they arrived at the first of the regiments he delivered a rousing address, but he cautioned the men: "Don't cheer boys. I confess I rather like it myself, but Colonel Sherman here says it is not military." Hitherto, likely on the basis of their earlier meeting, Lincoln had appeared to be something of a lightweight in Sherman's estimation. But his presence and what he said to the men prompted a dramatic reassessment, especially after what happened next.

As the party reached the adjacent regiment, the captain he had browbeat earlier stepped forward: "Mr. President, I have cause of grievance. This morning I went to speak to Colonel Sherman, and he threatened to shoot me." Lincoln stared at him for a moment, then glanced at Sherman, and finally leaned close to the officer and said in a stage whisper: "Well, if I were you, and he threatened to shoot, I would not trust him, for I believe he would do it."[20] Laughter erupted on all sides, and the homesick captain was again squelched in Sherman's recounting. There is another, less flattering version of the visit, one in which angry enlisted men recount the barn incident to the president; yet his assessment of Sherman is similar: "Well boys, I have a great deal of respect for Colonel Sherman, and if he turned you out of the barn I have no doubt it was for some good purpose."[21]

Clearly by this time Sherman was no longer just the brother of an important Republican politician in Lincoln's mind. William Tecumseh Sherman had made a distinct impression. The rapid-fire delivery, the apparently vast military knowledge, the sheer energy of the man, must have caught the attention of a president who would struggle throughout the war to prod his generals into action. If there was one thing Sherman did not have, it was the "slows." The previous comments indicate Lincoln already saw Sherman as someone who would do what he said he would do, that he was decisive. And it soon became apparent the president was ready to act on these assumptions.

"'Tis said I am to be a Brigadier General," he wrote Ellen in early August, adding characteristically, "If so, I know it not yet."[22] But it was true; the president had selected him first on the list of new brigadiers—in front of Ambrose Burnside, George Thomas, and Ulysses S. Grant, among others. And there was more.

Shortly afterward, Sherman received a note from his friend Robert Anderson, inviting him to a meeting at the Willard Hotel. After

Sumter the closest thing the Union had to a war hero, Anderson had just been appointed commander of the Department of the Cumberland—encompassing Kentucky and Tennessee, which had seceded but contained many Federal adherents. At the meeting they were joined by Tennessee senator Andrew Johnson (temporarily out of a job), along with a number of other key border state politicians. But the focus was clearly on Sherman. Anderson told him he had three brigadier slots; he had already chosen George Thomas and Burnside, but he wanted Sherman as his deputy. Friends, West Pointers, the situation seemed ideal.

He and Anderson held several subsequent meetings with the president to talk strategy and discuss the mission. They apparently went well enough, but a number of revealing things happened. Lincoln was concerned about Thomas, a Virginian who might "play false"—others had. The two soldiers jumped to their friend's defense: if Thomas was anything, he was steadfast beyond the pull of state or family.

Sherman, on the other hand, was harder to figure out. For no apparent reason, he wanted Lincoln's assurance that he would serve only as deputy and not have to assume command. What each knew about Anderson's health is hard to gauge, so the context in which this arose remains ambiguous. Still, at the least it struck Lincoln as odd. Chuckling, he indicated that his chief problem was too many generals who wanted to be at the head of affairs; but he was probably also wondering why this one didn't.[23]

Arguably, Lincoln was encountering a key aspect of Sherman's personality—his comfort zone was that of the second, the sidekick. A good deal has been written about the general's chronic bouts of depression, and he was heading into what may have been his worst. Yet with few exceptions, no matter how bad he was feeling about himself, Sherman's energy and intelligence allowed him to perform his duties creditably.

On the other hand, this passion for being not quite in charge would seem to have had a much greater impact on his career. Sherman was a classic wingman, seeking positions that promised de facto autonomy but still allowed him to request permission and elicit praise from a trusted and admired associate. It doesn't take a psychologist to suspect this mirrored his relationship with Thomas Ewing and his own ambiguity about emerging from his foster father/father-in-law's substantial shadow. Similarly, his banking career had been characterized by near independence, but always under the auspices of Lucas, the moneyman in St. Louis. During the war, the pattern would be repeated, briefly with Halleck and then, most importantly, with Grant—indeed, it would persist until Sherman's own success and fame at last overwhelmed it. For a military strategist, it was an odd outlook (they may be agents of the state, but they characteristically want to run things), but Sherman made it work brilliantly, doing his best nestled beneath a strong wing. But as things turned out, success also turned on finding the right wing, and in this case it was not Robert Anderson's.

2

"I hope to have God on my side; but I must have Kentucky," Lincoln reputedly said.[24] This was certainly his sentiment when he sent Anderson and Sherman west. With the Ohio River marking its northern border with Ohio, Indiana, and Illinois, Kentucky's defection to the South would have meant a much more defensible Confederacy in the West, along with a jumping-off point for invasion. "I think to lose Kentucky," Lincoln wrote in 1861, "is nearly the same as to lose the whole game."[25]

Politically, the place seemed poised on a knife edge—Kentucky was a slave state, and Confederate sympathy abounded (eventually, two in five of its fighting men would wear gray). But it was also the home of Henry Clay and his nationalist legacy, along with many Unionists; so the legislature originally tried to split the difference by declaring its neutrality. Lincoln, who had been born in Kentucky, treaded with caution and considerable forbearance, looking the other way as Governor Beriah Magoffin leaned ever southward by permitting a vast trade with the Confederacy and even allowing its military recruiting agents on state soil.[26]

It proved to be an overreach. During the summer of 1861, two successive legislative elections put the political momentum in the hands of the Unionists and marked the start of neutrality's end as military events forced everybody's hand. The action took place at the critical confluence of the Ohio and Mississippi, where several Federal regiments stationed in Cairo, Illinois, under Ulysses S. Grant were faced off against an equivalent Confederate force commanded by General Leonidas Polk. When Polk seized the high bluff looming over the Mississippi at the railhead of Columbus, Kentucky, Grant responded by moving into Paducah and Smithland at the mouths of the strategically vital Tennessee and Cumberland Rivers. Both had pushed into the Bluegrass State, but Polk had moved first, making him the aggressor in the eyes of the Kentucky Legislature, which declared on September 18, "The invaders must be expelled," and placed all its volunteers under Anderson, who had just arrived in Louisville.[27] In retrospect, the tide had plainly turned in a blue direction.

This was anything but apparent to William Tecumseh Sherman. Of the three key Federal commands—McClellan in Virginia, Fremont west of the Mississippi, and Anderson's—the last was by far the smallest. So much so that before even going to Kentucky, Sherman embarked on a blitz of Indiana, Illinois, and Missouri in search of men and supplies. About all he got out of the journey were protestations of overcommitment and a distinct impression that Fremont's command was a corrupt mess. Shortages of everything: This set the tone for Sherman's arrival in Louisville.

He began with his usual burst of energy, working furiously to bring the Union cause together, train recruits, and arm and equip them, all on a shoestring (he and George Thomas both had to take out personal loans to supply their commands).[28] But Sherman's central problem was simply coming to grips with the situation in Kentucky. He arrived believing the place was pro-Confederate, and now that he looked around, he was convinced. "The young active element is all secession, the older stay at homes are for Union & Peace," he told John.[29] It is important to remember that at this point, the U.S. military was devoid of dedicated intelligence functions; there was no stream of sophisticated politico/military analysis such as is automatically supplied theater commanders today. Instead, Sherman was left to make of the situation what he would, and he was not in an optimistic state of mind; his threat filters were wide open.

He had been in Kentucky less than a month when Anderson told him that he could stand the "mental torture" of his command no more and resigned.[30] The strain of Sumter had been too much, Anderson was a spent man, and now what Sherman dreaded, what he had made Lincoln promise would not happen, was coming to pass: he was in charge; his protective wing had vanished.

The added burden only made the situation appear worse. Figuratively, at least, Sherman began seeing a Confederate under every rock. This was not an unusual affliction during the Civil War. Commanders instinctively plan against the worst case on the grounds that everything else will follow. But it can also be demoralizing and even paralyzing (McClellan is a case in point), since the threat is easy to inflate. Sherman's projections of enemy strength began to leapfrog: on October 20, he estimated Federals to be outnumbered three to one; six days later, he put the ratio at five to one; and on November 4, he telegraphed Washington warning of a Confederate "force and numbers the country never has and probably never will comprehend."[31] In reality, by December 1, 1861, Kentuckians in Union service outnumbered those on the Confederate side by more than three to one, and Southern commanders Simon Bolivar Buckner and Albert Sidney Johnston were equally pessimistic about their own numbers and operational capabilities.[32]

The problems associated with acting as your own intelligence analyst were graphically illustrated by two New York reporters who joined Sherman nightly in the Louisville telegraph office, poring over Associated Press cables until three in the morning. Fueled by whiskey and up to ten cigars a night (the janitors called them "Sherman's Old Soldiers"), the general was plainly wired—"twitching his red whiskers—his coat buttons—playing a tattoo on the table—or running his fingers through his hair....And on and on he talked, nervously and obsessively...making his odd gestures...which emphasize his language. He never hesitates at interrupting anyone, but he cannot bear to be interrupted himself."[33] Sherman did not like journalists, and presumably the feeling here was reciprocated; but this was a profile almost anyone would find alarming, especially if that anyone was from Washington.

Secretary of War Simon Cameron and Adjutant General Lorenzo Thomas were on a western inspection tour and were to be briefed by Sherman in Louisville. History does not have much good to say about Cameron—"incompetent," "vicious," and "corrupt" are representative epithets—and he was not necessarily well-disposed toward Sherman, since his own brother had died under his command at Bull Run. Still, the performance he was treated to that night transcended bias and bad character; Sherman left everybody in the room, including several reporters, aghast.

While Fremont and McClellan were receiving all the new recruits, Kentucky was starving, Sherman announced after locking the door theatrically, and now there was little hope of preventing the Confederates from capturing Louisville. Unwell and draped on a couch, Cameron blurted: "You astonish me! Our informants, the Kentucky Senators and members of Congress, claim that they have in Kentucky plenty of men, and all they want are arms and money."[34]

Nevertheless, he ordered Thomas to shuttle any of the region's unassigned troops to Kentucky, pointedly suggesting that they be used to recapture the Cumberland Gap (taken in mid-September by a small Confederate force under Felix Zollicoffer) and then move through it into east Tennessee, where Union supporters abounded.

Sherman responded by producing a map of the United States marked to show that while Fremont and McClellan had fronts of only one hundred miles to defend, his own stretched for three hundred. Yet he had only eighteen thousand men, while Fremont had sixty thousand and McClellan one hundred thousand. To securely defend Kentucky, Sherman continued, he needed at least sixty thousand; but to go on the offensive, he would require two hundred thousand. "Great God! Where are they to come from?" Cameron exclaimed. Sherman was ready for that, too: Plenty of Northerners would volunteer if only the War Department would stop discouraging them.[35] The meeting ended with the secretary ordering Thomas to make note of the conversation and Sherman convinced he had aroused Cameron to the dangers of the situation. In fact, it was a performance worthy of Daffy Duck (or, given the hair color, perhaps Woody Woodpecker)—in terms of politics and reality, a birdbrained disquisition bound to become public, since it was delivered in front of several journalists. Dramatically speaking, Sherman laid an egg.

The situation grew worse as his judgment and mental state spiraled downward. When five east Tennessee Unionists were summarily hanged for burning railroad bridges in anticipation of an invasion, Sherman blamed himself; but he still called off the planned incursion, even though George Thomas, calm and steady as ever, was within forty miles of the Tennessee border and ready to go.[36]

Meanwhile, in Washington the long knives were coming out. "Sherman is playing the fool in Ky," wrote Montgomery Blair.[37] Assistant Secretary of War Thomas Scott was even more blunt: "Sherman is gone in the head, he's luny."[38] Cameron and Lorenzo Thomas arranged for the *New York Herald* to publish their version of the Louisville meeting, one that left Sherman stunned. But worse, perhaps, Sherman had seriously undermined Lincoln's confidence by sending him directly a string of dispatches, which the president told John were "complaining and almost insubordinate."[39] When even his own brother believed Sherman "not only in error but...laboring under some strange illusions," the end could not be far off.[40]

Winfield Scott had been forced into retirement, and on November 1, George McClellan assumed overall command of the Union army. He asked Sherman for regular reports and was bombarded with such a string of gloomy assessments in response that he sent a personal observer, Colonel Thomas Key, to Louisville to have a look at the author. After several days with the general, Key concluded he was on the edge of nervous exhaustion; it was the stress of command and not real shortages that was the source of these unsettling missives. This would have finished him, had Sherman not already wanted out and urgently requested a replacement.

On November 8, Ellen in Lancaster received a summons from Sherman's aide and immediately went to Louisville, arriving after a fourteen-hour train ride. "Knowing insanity to be in the family and having seen Cump on the verge of it once in California," she wrote John, "I assure you I was tortured by fears, which have been *only in part relieved* since I got here."[41] She found he had been eating and sleeping irregularly, if at all, and junior officers described him as despondent and uncommunicative. "He thinks the whole country is gone irrevocably & ruin and desolation are at hand."[42] Fortunately, his old friend and replacement, Don Carlos Buell, arrived and on November 13 took command. In the span of less than two months, Sherman's time in Kentucky and possibly his military career were over.

3

Help would come from an unexpected quarter—a very unexpected quarter, from Sherman's perspective. Henry Halleck had left California a local hero and joined the Union war effort a made man, widely respected as a military authority with connections throughout the army establishment.[43] It took him a while to reach Washington, so most of the key commands were already taken. But it was increasingly clear where he would end up.

Fremont had made a mess of things in the Department of the West. After he proved slow to assert himself in Missouri, Nathaniel Lyon took things into his own hands and attacked the Confederates at Wilson's Creek, only to be killed in a sharp Northern defeat, with casualties proportionally higher than at Bull Run.[44] When Confederate general Sterling Price invaded, Fremont seemed to have no plan to counter him, except to issue a proclamation promising to shoot guerrillas and free the slaves of all Confederate activists. His administration was sloppy and notoriously corrupt. All of this did not sit well with Abraham Lincoln, who sent Halleck west to replace Fremont, which he did just four days before Sherman resigned his command in Kentucky.

Halleck's responsibilities were huge (basically everything west of the Mississippi) and his time was short. Results were what he was sent for, and he understood he had to produce them quickly. Accordingly, Halleck set himself up in St. Louis's Planter's House with his brother-in-law Schuyler Hamilton and threw himself into the task: annulling fraudulent contracts, imposing order, and streamlining staff procedures.[45] A superb bureaucrat, he made considerable progress, but the job seemed enormous, especially coming to grips with the military situation. He wrote McClellan that the lack of good officers made it hard to know anything for certain.[46] At this point, military experience and the ability to think things through were precious commodities in the Union army, and both knew Sherman was available. So, probably with reservations on all sides, he was sent to St. Louis.

It had to have been an awkward reunion. Sherman arrived in bad shape, nearly suicidal from the Kentucky experience, and it must have shown.[47] Halleck could afford to be magnanimous, yet with rumors of insanity swarming around Sherman like angry bees, he was plainly a man under suspicion. But the nebulous military environment demanded action, so he sent Sherman out on an initial inspection of the Union camp at Sedalia, authorizing him to assume command if General John Pope was unavailable and he thought the place threatened. Sherman saw both to be true, so he took over on November 26, causing Lieutenant Colonel Alfred Gilbert to note in his diary: "From the manner in which the Commanding general acts many think he is out of his head."[48]

He was certainly worried. Sherman saw Union forces west of St. Louis as scattered and vulnerable to Sterling Price's Confederates as well as the winter wind. Their safety and well-being demanded that they be immediately consolidated in protected localities, and he issued orders to that effect. Halleck was in no way convinced and reversed the orders, sending his medical director to evaluate Sherman's mental condition. The physician found "such nervousness that he was unfit for command," and Halleck immediately ordered him back to St. Louis, where Ellen was waiting. Halleck tried to soothe his frazzled subordinate and got him to agree to twenty days' leave. But as Sherman left for Lancaster with Ellen, Halleck wrote McClellan on December 2 that Sherman had been "completely stampeded" and was "stampeding the entire army....Perhaps a few weeks rest will restore him. I am satisfied that in his present condition it would be dangerous to give him a command here."[49] Still, throwing this particular general under the locomotive was not a simple matter, nor was Halleck entirely disposed to do so.

Team Ewing/Sherman circled like a pack of wolves around a wounded member. They threatened lawsuits against his public detractors but concentrated mainly on shoring up previous supporters. Hugh Ewing, now a brigadier general, made the rounds of army brass in Washington, talking up his foster brother and being assured of his high standing.[50] Lincoln was key. John met with him and freely admitted his brother's "serious mistakes" and "inexcusable impertinence," but he added that the newspapers had exaggerated the situation, prompted by Sherman's hostility toward reporters.

Ellen was convinced that Halleck, McClellan, and Pope were conspiring against her mate and jumped into the fray with fangs bared. On January 10, she wrote the president to that effect, and when a week passed with no reply, she took a train to Washington.[51] She was plainly not the first military wife demanding an audience with the chief executive to right an injustice real or imagined; but she was also Thomas Ewing's daughter and a member of a political clan with enormous sway in Ohio and Kansas.

Lincoln probably realized there was no avoiding them, but when the meeting took place on January 29, he was at his sympathetic best, promising nothing specific but leaving both Ellen and Thomas Ewing relieved and satisfied with his attitude. There was probably more to this than political astuteness. Lincoln had suffered from deep bouts of depression since early manhood (he called it the "hypo"), and it's likely he recognized a similar condition lurking behind Sherman's excessive pessimism.[52] He also must have known from his own experience that these bleak episodes eventually passed and so remained open to giving his fellow sufferer additional responsibility once he recovered. Mental illness of any sort carried a tremendous stigma in nineteenth-century America, but not with Lincoln when it came to a general he instinctively liked and believed in.

Back in Lancaster, the man in question was feeling better. For once, the quiet backwater of Ohio did him some good. Before long he was eating and sleeping regularly and approaching something that might be called relaxation, at least until the December 11 issue of the *Cincinnati Commercial* arrived with the headline GENERAL WILLIAM T. SHERMAN INSANE. To make it worse, his own cousin Murat Halstead had authored the accompanying article, and the details seemed to reflect not just the Louisville meeting with Cameron, but Halleck's report to McClellan about Sherman's condition.[53] Plainly, someone in the family had not gotten the message.

This was a blow easily capable of driving a depressed individual into complete withdrawal. But significantly, Sherman jumped to his own defense. He immediately wrote Thomas Ewing, apologizing for "the disgrace which has befallen me" and admitting that "'tis hard to say who are sane and who insane," but then justifying in detail his conduct in Kentucky and at Sedalia.[54] The same day, he wrote Halleck to inform him of the article and blaming it on press bias: "These newspapers have us in their power, and can destroy us as they please."[55] Halleck could hardly miss the feisty tone and was aware of the team defense being put up by the Ewing/Sherman clan. He chose to make light of the entire matter, telling Phil Ewing: "No one who was personally acquainted with him thought that anything was the matter with him except a want of rest."[56]

More significant, he wanted Sherman back. Before the year was out, Halleck designated Sherman to command Benton Barracks, a sprawling training base in St. Louis, where he could keep an eye on him and also pick his brain in the cause of winning the West.[57]

Henry Halleck brought a number of core capabilities to the job. He was a superb administrator, as reflected by the rapidly improving situation in Missouri. Untangled logistics and better organization revealed that the state was solidly in Union hands and Price and the Confederates were largely a chimera.

Yet these skills also reflected the heart of a bureaucrat; Halleck was a backbiting manipulator and a compulsive seeker of power and position. It was in this spirit that he eyed his colleague in Kentucky, Don Carlos Buell, not as a candidate for joint operations—as Lin-

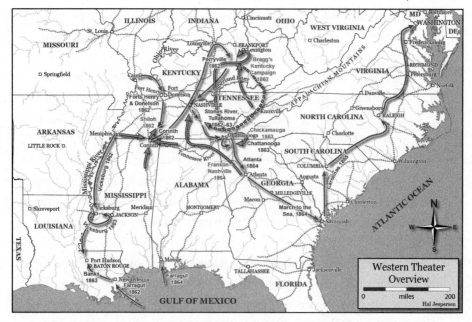

coln and his new secretary of war, Edwin Stanton, were hoping—
but as a rival and a threat to his own grand scheme.[58]

Halleck was also extremely intelligent; he had a firm grasp of
military strategy and was intent on hammering out plans to drive a
spike into the South from the west. Both Schuyler Hamilton and his
friend George Cullum had moved from Winfield Scott's staff to St.
Louis, so Halleck was well acquainted with part B of the Anaconda
Plan, the move down the Mississippi. Now they were joined by the
Mississippi-centric Sherman, who could energize any strategic conversation. Whatever had gone on in the past between the two men,
Halleck plainly felt comfortable enough to encourage a real intellectual exchange.

This spirit is captured in a scene that took place one evening
in midwinter of 1862, in Halleck's room on the second floor of
Planter's House. It found Halleck, Cullum, and Sherman gathered
around a map, discussing the projected advance. Doing his best
Dennis Hart Mahan, with pencil in hand, Halleck asked: "Where is
the rebel line?" As if in class, Cullum drew a line from Bowling
Green, Kentucky, through Forts Henry and Donelson on the paral-

lel Tennessee and Cumberland Rivers, to Columbus, Kentucky, on the Mississippi—the vast circumference that Albert Sidney Johnston, the Confederate commander in the West, had set up as his defensive perimeter. "That is their line," Halleck responded as Sherman remembered it. " 'Now where is the proper place to break it?' And either Cullum or I said, 'Naturally the center.' " When Halleck drew a perpendicular line at that point, it corresponded with the course of the Tennessee River: "That's the true line of operations."[59]

Considering what was to happen, this was certainly a prescient bit of strategic deduction. But making it happen was something else entirely. And the man who did was already thinking along the same lines.

Ulysses S. Grant, the unlikely author of the move into Paducah the previous fall, twice asked Halleck's permission to visit him in St. Louis to discuss future military operations, before being granted what amounted to an audience. Grant arrived in his usual disheveled state and announced that he wanted to move up the Tennessee and Cumberland Rivers, exactly Halleck's plan. "I had not uttered many sentences," Grant remembered, "before I was cut short as if my plan was preposterous.... I returned to Cairo very much crestfallen."[60]

Plainly, Halleck didn't like the look of Grant. He could forgive Sherman's threadbare excuses for uniforms, but this man was not only sloppy, he was known in army circles as a drunk and had been forced to resign because of it. Now there were rumors abroad that he had fallen off the wagon yet again. Worst of all—and Halleck was a good reader of men—Grant had that look about him, the same look that Lincoln noticed in Sherman when he told the aggrieved captain: "I believe he would do it." This was a man who would rather ask forgiveness than permission. To Halleck's sort, such men were dangerous.

This suspicion of pugnacity was one thing, at least, that Halleck shared with rival Don Carlos Buell (and George McClellan, for that matter). Lincoln and Stanton were having a great deal of trouble getting any of them off the mark. It had been ten months and still the

North had not scored a substantial victory; they were getting very impatient. Halleck had a keen political sense, and it forced his hand: he told Grant to go ahead. It was like letting a bulldog off a leash.

Grant's plan was an amphibious assault, employing Flag Officer Andrew Foote's new riverine gunboats to transport an infantry force of fifteen thousand to the poorly defended Fort Henry on the Tennessee River and then bombard from the front and attack from the rear. The bombardment did it. On February 6, he telegraphed Halleck: "Fort Henry is ours...I shall take and destroy Fort Donelson on the 8th."[61]

This proved to be wishful thinking. In the initial barrage, Foote's gunboats were badly shot up, and a land assault became inevitable. Fortunately for Grant, he received ten thousand reinforcements on February 14; he needed them. The fighting on the next day did not go well, and Grant was left believing two of his division commanders, John McClernand and Lew Wallace, neither of them West Pointers, had hesitated.

Things were worse for the Confederates. Demoralized, the commander called off a breakout attempt, although fifteen hundred Virginians and a battalion of cavalry under one Nathan Bedford Forrest managed to escape. As for the rest, there seemed no choice but surrender. The officer in charge, Simon Bolivar Buckner, was a friend of Grant's and had loaned him money when he was short in New York; now he asked for terms. The reply couldn't have been more blunt: "No terms except unconditional and immediate surrender can be accepted. I propose to move immediately on your works."[62] With that, it was over. Grant had bagged around thirteen thousand Confederates and opened two key river highways into the Deep South. Cannon and church bells erupted all over the North. Lincoln made Grant a major general, leaving him second in command in the West. And back in St. Louis, Henry Halleck found a rival and a loose cannon.

Sherman wouldn't see it that way. As his confidence grew, Halleck had gradually expanded his duties, particularly in the area of logistics, where Sherman excelled. This became abundantly clear after

Halleck sent him down to Paducah to support the fight at Donelson and Sherman within a day managed to move the ten thousand key reinforcements forward.[63] No one was more grateful than Grant, who moved fast and expected alacrity in others. Over the months following Donelson they got to know each other much better, and both liked what they saw. From the beginning, these two military eccentrics were on the same high-frequency wavelength.

Halleck, on the other hand, wanted a measured military pace, and Grant scared him. When he learned that the hero of the moment had gone to see Buell in Nashville, which he had recently occupied, Halleck exploded. He wrote McClellan that Grant had gone without orders, that he didn't communicate, and that his army was "demoralized."[64] There was no question where the general in chief's sympathies lay: he suggested that Halleck arrest Grant.[65]

This he didn't do, but he did temporarily remove him from field command, giving the post to C. F. Smith, Grant's friend and mentor. It didn't stick, though. Smith caught a splinter jumping into a rowboat, and the subsequent infection incapacitated and then killed him. Meanwhile, on March 10, Lincoln demanded Halleck tell him why he had replaced Grant, then softened the blow by promoting him the next day to overall command in the West. Grant was back in, but Halleck's position was also strengthened. The rising Union tide in the West also lifted Sherman. He was given a field command, a volunteer division directly under Grant. It would prove to be a momentous combination.

Sherman and Grant. Grant and Sherman. The names are linked inextricably. They should be, since it was this alliance that eventually won the Civil War in the field. At the end they were the strategists in charge, a unique team. Other generals in the war worked well together—Lee and Stonewall Jackson are obvious examples—but always in the conventional commander-subordinate mold. Sherman and Grant were different; their relationship was more complex. True, Grant remained in charge, but Sherman wanted it that way. There was a give-and-take to the way they eventually operated that is best described as collegial. They were friends. They were fellow

In Ulysses S. Grant, Sherman found at last the shelter to operate in his true role, that of a wingman.

strategists. Each had the other's back. Nobody epitomized the relationship better than Sherman himself: "He stood by me when I was crazy and I stood by him when he was drunk; now, sir, we stand by each other always."[66] For two vulnerable men, it was a unique and effective shield against attack, but it was also strong because it was based on mutual dependence.

Grant had grown up in Ohio, the son of a loudmouth tanner with negligible political influence; he had to be aware of Sherman's disproportionately greater backing. Friendship meant an opportunity to align himself with Team Ewing/Sherman, a chance to cement his own budding relationship with Abraham Lincoln and also with the increasingly powerful John Sherman.

Grant was also very bright, a natural strategist with an extraordinarily intuitive grasp of warfare. Prior to this he had done most of his strategic thinking in isolation, but now he welcomed the intellectual stimulation someone like Sherman promised. Although inarticulate in public, Grant was far from that among those who knew him well. Conversationally, he would prove a perfect foil for Sherman, the fire hose of ideas, playing the role of "the decider," paring everything down to a few key principles. Grant was certainly an innovative and opportunistic strategist in his own right, but he seemed to have understood that he needed someone like Sherman to open up the range of possibility. In war anything can happen, and Grant must have realized that required a protean strategic imagination.

For his part, Sherman seems to have decided very quickly that Grant was exactly what he was looking for, a strong wing under which to operate. Until the war's very last days, Sherman remained extremely grateful to Halleck for resuscitating his career; but after California and all that followed, a relationship of relative equality seemed far-fetched. Grant, on the other hand, was unassuming and trustworthy. And there was something else: Sherman and Grant were fighters; they recognized that in each other. Both were inherently decisive and ready to risk combat if it looked promising. Sherman, it seemed, had found his soul mate. His mood soared; he almost seemed a happy warrior.

But there was another side to Grant. Perhaps his best quality on the battlefield was an extraordinary ability to focus, but with this came an equivalent lack of concern that the agents of his will were made of flesh and blood. He was a kind and gentle man personally, yet at this level of engagement casualties were just numbers, the cost of his plan. Grant would also prove an extraordinarily demanding commander and equally unforgiving of subordinates who didn't meet his standards. His rules were simple: "Do what I want and do it now." He didn't require victory. But complaint and hesitation, especially the latter, were neither forgotten nor excused.

Fortunately for Sherman, he was inherently fast, and his relationship with Grant was more complex. But still it would boil down to a series of herculean tasks imposed on the aspiring wingman, one after another, until at last he truly had won his feathers. The first of these was just a short way off, in fact, down the Tennessee River near a little church called Shiloh.

4

The next move on the campaign was pretty obviously Corinth, Mississippi, the rail junction of the east–west link between Memphis and Charleston and the north–south Mobile and Ohio, and also just over twenty miles from the Tennessee River at a point known as Pittsburg Landing, which Sherman came upon during an initial reconnaissance.[67] It was high enough to avoid spring flooding and a good place to disembark troops. Grant checked the site himself and then endorsed a massive buildup, an invading army of volunteer divisions of the same sort he had used at Donelson. Anaconda B had morphed from a spear tip of regulars to a massive battering ram of volunteers. Sherman may have had private reservations, but his own volunteer division was among the first to come ashore at Pittsburg Landing, and he was plainly at the core of the operation.[68]

In the days that followed, five divisions moved in by boat and set up camp—Sherman's own, three others headed by Illinois politicians Stephen Hurlbut, Benjamin Prentiss, and John McClernand, and finally one under Lew Wallace that was placed five miles north. There were more on the way. Halleck ordered Buell to join the buildup with his thirty-five thousand troops—a planned force of seventy-five thousand, which Halleck then intended to come down and lead in a procession toward Corinth, most likely expecting to lay siege to the place.

The Confederates had other ideas. They meant to strike first, before Buell and Halleck could arrive. Corinth had been filling up with troops as Albert Sidney Johnston's defensive line crumpled, and now the wily P. G. T. Beauregard wanted to use them, forty-one thousand strong, to crush the Yankee force already at Pittsburg Landing. It was an audacious plan for what were mostly green troops, but Corinth was an unhealthy environment for such a large body of men and not the sort of place to be caught in a siege; so Johnston agreed.

The march proved to be a mess, akin to the Yankee saunter to Bull Run, only a lot soggier in the spring rains. A distance veterans would have covered in one day stretched into three. As they got close, Confederate soldiers kept firing their guns to make sure the powder was dry. Beauregard, having lost all hope of surprise, wanted to call off the operation. The two-day delay meant that Buell must have reinforced Grant. Yet Albert Sidney Johnston, now that his troops were finally deployed, had gained rather than lost enthusiasm. "I would fight them if they were a million," was his answer. He told his corps commanders to make their final preparations for battle: "Gentlemen, we shall attack at daylight tomorrow."[69]

The morning of April 6, 1862, found Sherman at Pittsburg Landing, his division parked out front next to Prentiss's, and Grant at his headquarters nine miles downstream, neither of them expecting an attack.

Since he had arrived, Sherman appeared to have picked up more than a little of Grant's supreme confidence. Rather than have his troops dig defensive entrenchments, which he and Grant agreed might rob volunteers of aggressiveness, he drilled them relentlessly for the coming offensive.[70] Rather than seeing a Confederate behind every tree, as he had in Kentucky, Sherman now refused to recognize them even when they were there. During the night of April 5, when a cavalry major interpreted an earlier contact as indicating the enemy was present in large numbers, Sherman called it a "mere skirmish sir."[71] He was less polite to a colonel who spoke nervously about thousands of Confederates out in the woods: "Take your damned regiment back to Ohio. Beauregard is not such a fool as to leave his base of operations and attack us in ours."[72]

Sherman was in for the surprise of his life. One of his volunteer colonels was sufficiently jumpy to order his regiment into battle formation. At first Sherman ignored it, but then he rode out with his staff around four hundred yards in front of the division's bivouac. Shots rang out, and next to him, Sherman's orderly toppled off his horse, dead. "My God, we're attacked," he screamed.[73]

In war, this is about as bad as it gets, especially if you are a general and a strategist. An enormous wave of Confederates was about to break right in front of him, and he had completely missed it. Whatever his later protestations to the contrary, it seems apparent that

Sherman was utterly surprised by a huge enemy force, now in total possession of the initiative. Figuratively speaking, he was left gaping at the void, a military black hole from which there must have seemed no escape.

But William Tecumseh Sherman was not about to be wiped out. He righted himself and took on the wave. And in doing so, he changed the course of his life. The jolt he received that morning near the church called Shiloh seems to have thrown his hitherto wildly oscillating threat filters into proper alignment. He learned definitively that in war anything can happen; that the threat profile changes constantly; and that the key to survival is the ability to adapt to it.

And adapt he did. Fortunately, his own division and Prentiss's had just enough warning to deploy into battle formation, when the rebels arrayed along a broad front crashed into them. Many of the raw Union soldiers—probably amounting to several thousand—simply ran away and cowered by the landing; but most stayed and fought, grimly giving ground and taking horrific casualties.

Sherman was everywhere: arranging units as reinforcements came up from the divisions to the rear, encouraging troops to hold the line, making sure ammunition got to the front, and inspiring everybody. He was wounded twice (slightly) and had three horses shot out from under him; yet he impressed those around him as being calmer than usual and utterly clearheaded. He was de facto in charge, giving orders to McClernand, who was senior brigadier.[74] When Grant finally arrived two hours into the carnage, he paid Sherman the compliment of leaving without issuing orders of his own.

Still, the situation remained desperate. Shiloh had devolved into the most elemental kind of battle; if the blue line broke, it would be pushed into the river. It was probably Prentiss who saved the day. His division found shelter along a sunken lane and turned it into what was remembered by Confederates as "the hornet's nest," a stubborn bastion of resistance that took the steam out of their attack and allowed Sherman to pivot behind and successively reestablish the line. Prentiss would have to surrender, but by four in the afternoon, Sherman had stabilized the line about a mile from the river directly in front of Pittsburg Landing. Nevertheless, he was down to three divisions. Buell was in the area, but his lead brigade had yet to arrive. Lew Wallace's division had gotten lost and was just straggling in. Who could know what would happen if another attack came?

It didn't. In midafternoon, Albert Sidney Johnston had ridden out to rally his exhausted rebel troops when he was hit by a ball in the leg, bled out, and died within a matter of minutes. P. G. T. Beauregard was now in charge. He considered his tired troops, massive casualties, and crumbling brigade structure and decided a night's reorganization rather than one last assault would better finish the job. He would get them in the morning.

Grant had the same idea. At around five, he informed the incredulous Sherman to plan for the next day's offensive. Sherman assumed there must be some mistake. Their army had barely escaped a rout. He wanted to talk to Grant again, this time about plans to get their troops out of this vulnerable position.

It was a terrible night, with only the cold spring rain muting the screams and groans of the thousands of wounded strewn about the battlefield. Sherman, his arm in a sling and hand throbbing from a buckshot wound, finally found Grant at about eleven standing alone beneath a tree, his hat turned down against the rain. He wanted to bring up his plan for a retreat, but something told him not to. "Well, Grant, we've had the devil's own day, haven't we?" he opened instead. "Yes," Grant replied chewing on a cigar. "Lick 'em tomorrow, though."[75]

Another defining instant was at hand. Sherman saw the real Grant for the first time and also the unforgiving nature of their alliance. There was no reclama with this man. Reservations, alternative plans, would be seen only as vacillation. With Grant, particularly in the heat of battle, there was no escape: "Do what I want and do it now." For the second time that day, Sherman rose to the occasion. The chatterbox shut himself down, bit the proverbial bullet, and got ready for the next day's attack.

So did his former associates P. G. T. Beauregard and Braxton Bragg, piecing together their order of battle and operational plans in

Sherman's own tent of the night before. They were in a confident mood and telegrammed Richmond to that effect. But they were misled by intelligence indicating that Buell was heading away from the battlefield. In fact his brigades were flowing in steadily throughout the night, adding huge numbers of fresh troops to the Union lines. Nathan Bedford Forrest's scouts watched them cross the river, but his warnings made no impression on the Southern leadership. "We'll be whipped like Hell," he concluded in disgust.[76]

The day began with Shiloh's second surprise attack, the Yankee one, as Buell's and Grant's armies surged forward all along the front, initially sweeping the befuddled Confederates before them. But by the middle of the morning, their resistance had stiffened and the fighting became as intense and stubborn as the day before. Gradually, though, the Union weight of numbers and fresher bodies began to tell in a grinding, relentless advance that finally reached the original Confederate starting point. Around two thirty, Beauregard's chief of staff thought to put the situation as sweetly as he could to his boss: "Do you not think our troops are very much in the condition of a lump of sugar thoroughly soaked with water, but yet preserving its original shape, though ready to dissolve? Would it not be judicious to get away with what we have?"[77] Beauregard, whose considerable military talents apparently included recognizing a good analogy, replied that he intended to start the withdrawal momentarily.

The exhausted Confederate army staggered back toward Corinth, slowly slogging over a spiderweb of mud-soaked roads. But by this time the boys in blue were almost as tired and incapable of much more than crashing for the night in their original campgrounds.

Grant waited until the next day before sending Sherman out with two brigades in what was obviously a halfhearted pursuit. On the way, they ran into the cavalry of Nathan Bedford Forrest, who promptly attacked and temporarily scattered them until Sherman stabilized the line. Meanwhile, the ever-aggressive Forrest got far in front of his troops and was surrounded and wounded before he escaped by using a Union foot soldier as a shield.[78] Sherman decided to forgo further pursuit, a terrible mistake. Had he been blessed with a window on his own future, he would have told his troops: "Boys, forget the rest of the Confederates, run down that man and kill him. Bring me his body; I want to see him dead." He didn't, of course, and Forrest remained a thorn in his side for the remainder of the war.

But for the moment (and really for the rest of his life), things were looking up for William Tecumseh Sherman. As he returned to the battlefield, still littered with corpses, cheers rang out in great waves as soldiers recognized him. "He rode slowly, his grizzled face beaming with animation, his tall form swaying from side to side, and his arms waving. 'Boys,' he yelled, 'you have won a great victory. The enemy has retreated to Corinth.'"[79] For the first time, he felt the adulation of victorious troops sweep over him. These volunteers had fought hard, and he was their general. The long slide (at least in his mind) that began with missing the Mexican War was over. Shiloh marked the turning point of his life. He may not have expected to survive the war,[80] but he and Grant were still alive and they had won. It must have seemed so clear at that moment.

But it was more complicated. Shiloh was a truly terrible battle. Sherman himself said the scene "would have cured anybody of war."[81] More than twenty thousand men—about equally distributed between blue and gray—were dead or wounded, casualties that dwarfed those of the Civil War's previous battles or, for that matter, any battle in prior U.S. history. This was a new order of violence, and it shocked everybody.

The press made it sound particularly bad, since they initially had access only to the skulkers in the rear. Influential journalist Whitelaw Reid's story of April 6 spoke of nearly total ruin, and others who had never been near Shiloh picked up the beat until the continent reverberated with it.[82] Fingers were also pointed at Sherman and, particularly, Grant. It seemed obvious they had been surprised. Grant had been slow getting to the battlefield in part because he had hurt his leg by falling off a horse. Now the rumors swirled again that he'd been drunk. Sherman took it all personally but was especially enraged by the attacks on Grant. As far as he was concerned, these war correspondents were cowards and spies intent on turning a victory into a defeat.

He need not have worried. Team Ewing/Sherman was busy in Washington: John defended him on the floor of the Senate, and pressure on Lincoln from John and Thomas Ewing secured a promotion for Sherman to major general of volunteers. It was deserved. Shiloh was a strategic success of major proportions, blunting the South's great effort to recover the initiative in the Mississippi Valley and opening the way to a dramatic reordering of the military balance in the West.[83]

On the same day Beauregard headed back toward Corinth, John Pope, working with Andrew Foote's gunboats, captured Island No. 10 and its fifty-two big guns, a key Confederate spike blocking the Mississippi. Before the month was out, David Farragut's fleet moving relentlessly upriver had taken New Orleans, the South's biggest city and gate to the Gulf of Mexico. Then, as the result of another riverine gunfight on June 6, Union troops occupied Memphis. Very suddenly, only Vicksburg was blocking traffic on the Mississippi and the fulfillment of Anaconda B seemed just a step away.

Henry Halleck, however, was not happy. Whatever had been gained at Shiloh strategically was overwhelmed in his mind by the harsh realities of war. And he blamed it on Grant. He had proved every bit as reckless and disorganized as Halleck had feared, and the result had been unnecessary slaughter. Leaving inexperienced troops without entrenchment was inexcusable. It was time for adult leadership. He would take the field himself and lead the assault on Corinth.[84]

Halleck knew Grant still had Lincoln's support (after Shiloh, Lincoln told an important Pennsylvania Republican who called him a drunkard and wanted him removed: "I can't spare this man; he fights"), so he outflanked him bureaucratically, making Grant his second in command and removing him from field responsibility shortly after arriving at Pittsburg Landing on April 11. Sherman remained on Halleck's good side, but he instinctively took the part of his friend.

After hearing rumors that Grant was about to leave, Sherman raced to Grant's tent to find him and his staff in the midst of packing. Seeing the partnership in jeopardy and remembering Kentucky,

Sherman was at his most convincing. He reminded Grant that after Shiloh nobody was calling him crazy. In war, everything changed fast. He needed to stay and wait for the next roll of the dice. It was excellent advice, and Grant took it. It also cemented the friendship, and Sherman knew it.[85]

Meanwhile, Henry Halleck was doing what he did best: organizing and consolidating. During the month of April, he brought together what amounted to the entire Army of the West (it would not be joined again until the Chattanooga campaign in late 1863), a juggernaut of more than one hundred thousand men and a massive statistical overmatch for the Confederates at Corinth.

Halleck wanted to take no chances, and the subsequent operation was a monument to that assumption—literally. The giant force lurched toward its objective with baby steps, each day's short march followed by hours devoted to entrenchment if it encountered so much as a Confederate outpost. It was hard work and consumed much of the month of May, but after Shiloh many of the men may not have minded digging something they could hide behind. They even gave Halleck a nickname—something they never did for Grant—"Old Brains," they called him.[86] Not, it should be noted, "Old Blood and Brains." These men weren't stupid.

Neither were Grant and Sherman, and it was becoming obvious to both that the warrior component was largely missing from this military strategist. Sherman called the advance toward Corinth "provokingly slow," and Grant characteristically questioned the whole point of taking places rather than destroying rebel troop formations.[87]

In the end, the fox, P. G. T. Beauregard, settled the matter on May 25 by making it look as if he were being reinforced while actually evacuating his army by rail, leaving Corinth for Halleck to occupy unopposed. It was a poison prize. Without adequate water supply, it had already killed more Confederates than Shiloh, and a third of the soldiers and half of the Union generals, including Sherman, became sick as a result of the campaign—subsequently known to some wags as "the Evacuation of Corinth." Still, Halleck seemed satisfied and was proud of taking the place through maneuver "and…with very little loss of life"—just as Jomini or Dennis Hart Mahan might have been.[88]

But Halleck had not gotten this far without a measure of self-awareness. As another resident of the Monterey peninsula famously advised, "A man's got to know his limitations," and Halleck, it seems, knew his. Barely a month would pass before he left the field of battle permanently.

George McClellan's short stint as general in chief was over, though he was still in the field. After briefly trying to do the job themselves, Lincoln and Secretary of War Stanton conceded they needed a military replacement. On July 2, over Stanton's objections, the president appointed Halleck "to command the whole land forces of the United States." This, Halleck intended to do as an administrator. He would let others do the fighting; he would coordinate.[89]

Lincoln may not have known what he was getting at the time and later disparaged Halleck as "little more...than a first-rate clerk," but he performed a vital function as the interface between civilian and military, and one that has been growing ever since. Operations in the Civil War were already vast, and someone had to have his fingers on the details, monitoring the ebb and flow of men and matériel and bringing them together at critical moments, all within the context of overall strategic objectives—a daunting task and one Halleck was uniquely qualified to perform. As many have in Washington, he worked himself into a frenzy, but on the whole he performed creditably. No longer a rival, he even became a vocal supporter of Grant.

Sherman remained profoundly grateful to Halleck for saving his career, but the fact remained that Old Brains was gone and he and Grant were now the key players to fulfill Anaconda B and remove the last obstacles to opening the Mississippi River. But this would prove more complicated than it seemed, and before it was over, William Tecumseh Sherman would find himself waging war in ways he never expected.

===

SWAMPED

I

TOWARD THE END of July 1862, newly minted major general William T. Sherman arrived at his next assignment, the city of Memphis, as an occupier, not a conquering hero—but also inclined to split the difference if he could. As military governor, he maintained his position since the beginning of the war: secession was illegal, which meant apostate Southerners remained citizens of the United States, to be treated as such *if* they obeyed its laws and dictates. That, of course, was a big if.

Memphis was plainly a nest of Confederate support; Sherman had only to look at the flags flying defiantly from private homes. It was also a major commercial center almost at a standstill: stores and businesses were shuttered, and only the smugglers seemed active. The population was plainly suffering; they needed work.

With a kind of sardonic ingenuity, Sherman moved along two tracks. By fiat he breathed life into the place, ordering all the stores, churches, schools, and theaters—along with the bars and brothels—

open for business, priming the pump with an army's worth of customers. He restored the mayor and city government along with the courts and police. He even allowed newspapers, though he watched them closely.[1] Ever gregarious, he attended church, social functions, and plays, a smiling if supervisory presence.[2]

Meanwhile, to leave no doubt who was in charge, he intensely drilled his six thousand troops and began to rebuild Fort Pickering, massively enlarging it along the southern bluffs of the city. To supply the labor, Sherman employed huge gangs drawn from the thousands of escaped slaves who had fled to the safety of this Union garrison town. He didn't free them, and wages consisted of food, clothing, and tobacco, not specie; but neither did he allow their former owners to use "force or undue persuasion" to recover them.[3]

Superficially, it all sort of worked. Sherman enjoyed the stiff little social evenings and found himself liking the place. And even if the guests were technically his prisoners, he was a hard man to hate face-to-face. A number even found themselves attracted, intrigued by his constant chatter and argumentation. The city streets were suddenly full of people bustling, buying, and selling. Business was plainly better, especially cotton. Northern mills and the war effort in general were clamoring for fiber. Prices were high, and Memphis had plenty to sell. But the traders wanted, and were getting, gold in return as the market took off.

It didn't take Sherman long to conclude that the gold flowing into the city was being smuggled out just as fast, eventually being used to pay for rebel arms slipped through the Northern blockade.[4] He decreed that cotton could not be paid for with gold or even treasury notes, but his order was quickly countermanded by Washington. The more he looked, the more he came to believe that Memphis was a kind of sub-rosa distribution point for the Confederate army and that trade here in salt, bacon, powder, and firearms was secretly flowing mainly in that direction.[5] Smugglers seemed to be everywhere, typically evading pickets at night, but also packing the stomachs of dead animals with contraband and even using the hearse at a funeral procession to ship the Johnnies medicine.[6] Most problematic were the women, constantly moving in and out in their broad crinoline skirts, which Yankee guards along the five trade roads were reluctant to search. Not all engaged, but many did, and a lot of boots and whiskey found their way into rebel hands strapped to the haunches of wives, sisters, and girlfriends.

Memphis was full of single women, and with good reason. Sherman knew from a captured roster that the city had already contributed sixty-two companies of men to the Confederate army.[7] Many others were operating in the countryside as guerrillas. As reports came in of ambushes and opportunistic cavalry attacks, Sherman began to realize Memphis was an isle of staged tranquillity surrounded by a sea of rebellion.

The invading Union army remained big, even after it broke up following Corinth. All of it was being supplied by rail or along newly opened river routes, logistical threads that grew ever longer and more vulnerable as the Yankees penetrated farther south. Garrisons proliferated at narrow points on rivers and at regular intervals along the rails, and these in turn provided targets for rebel cavalry and irregulars staging raids meant to distract as much as destroy.

They were fighting a different kind of war, one we call insurgency. Their aim was not to confront, but to enervate. Small units formed quickly, striking in random patterns and then melting away into the countryside. They were maddeningly hard to find, because they looked like everybody else. They were everywhere and nowhere. Relatively small, they had the potential to paralyze whole armies. And to make matters worse, they were being brilliantly led by one of Memphis's most prominent citizens.

Nathan Bedford Forrest grew up big, barely literate, and violent on a series of frontier farms, but he quickly moved to the world of commerce. He tried his hand initially at trading horses but soon moved on to human beings. Since the slave market in Memphis was the South's biggest, he transferred operations there in 1851 and within a decade was among the richest and most respected of its residents—a slaver version of the American dream.[8]

But Forrest found his true calling in the chaos of warfare—or at least his style of warfare. He was certainly a member of the Confederate armed forces; he performed exceptionally well in a number of big battles and rose eventually to the rank of lieutenant general. But his idea of military discipline and protocol was far different from that of a West Pointer—he dispatched one of his own junior officers with a knife in a fight and also threatened to kill his commanding officer, Braxton Bragg, who said of him: "The man is ignorant, and does not know anything of cooperation."[9] True, Forrest was almost uncontrollable in a conventional military sense, but this was because he was motivated differently.

Nathan Bedford Forrest was a masterful insurgent, one of the best of all time.[10] He instinctively understood that surprise and terror were his best weapons ("Do all you can to keep up the scare," he advised)[11] and that his personal magnetism and bravery, not the chain of command, would keep his kind of men fighting. In combat, he was a Homeric throwback, behaving as if bullets did not exist and closing with the most lethal of intent—killing up to thirty Union soldiers with sword and pistol, yet somehow he survived.

That killer reputation along with a notable backwoods charisma turned Forrest into the epicenter of the rebellion in the countryside, a magnet for supporters and recruits. He knew just what to tell them: "Come on, boys, if you want a heap of fun and to kill some Yankees."[12] They came, always—many deserting from other Confederate units—and he used them to great effect. Instinctively, Forrest kept them dispersed, scattered but still networked; then he brought them suddenly together against surprised adversaries, whom they further demoralized with swarming tactics—the classic guerrilla moves.[13]

More important at the operational and strategic level, they were linked into the countryside through an analogous net of sympathizers, supporters, and actives—the classic triad of modern insurgency. Operating in such an environment, the guerrillas always found places to hide and rest and gather willing locals, whose knowledge of the terrain imparted a key advantage over the invaders. They also provided something even more important.

Intelligence is critical in irregular warfare. Insurgent forces are by nature small and must seek only momentary tactical advantage. To be successful, Forrest or any of the other spear points of the rebellion (Price, Van Dorn, Morgan, Wheeler, and others) needed really good information on the size and location of blue units, and it's plain from their string of successes that they got it. Wherever the Yankees went, there were rebel eyes watching them and then broadcasting over a network of neighbors and friends, a web of connections over which news traveled fast.

Sherman—who never killed anybody (neither did Grant)—plainly had trouble coming to grips with this kind of adversary and this kind of war. He was certainly familiar with guerrilla tactics; the Seminoles had used them in Florida. But these Southerners were massively more capable of supporting themselves and far more sophisticated politically. Besides, according to Sherman's own logic, they were still Americans, and this limited his military options.

On the other hand, he was beginning to feel he was fighting an entire society. When snipers grounded a packet boat by firing concealed from the riverside town of Randolph, Sherman sent a regiment to burn the place.[14] He also began expelling Confederate sympathizers from Memphis, forcing around forty individuals to leave.[15] These were pretty mild reprisals and probably legal under contemporary interpretations of the laws of war,[16] but the fact remains that in modern times such tactics increasingly serve to enrage, not pacify. And in such a charged atmosphere, there was little chance that Union sympathizers among the farmers and planters would come forward to help close the blue information gap. This was not the way to undermine an insurgency, nor did Sherman seem to fully understand the military dangers it constituted.

From the perspective of the twenty-first century, it's easy to see that such insurgencies were and remain capable of paralyzing whole armies, turning them into targets, not instruments of coercion, emasculating them strategically. This Southern rebellion had all the ingredients for success—inspired leadership, a clever and bellicose support network, and a commitment to wait out the invader. Yet the main reason Sherman never realized the danger was that it never actually materialized. For all their tactical success, Confederate raiders never succeeded in bogging down the Northern invaders, keeping them from tightening their grip on the Mississippi and ultimately piercing the heart of the Confederacy. The insurgents underperformed. And from a contemporary understanding of irregular warfare, this is puzzling.

The answer, though, may well have been hiding right out in the open. There was another network in play, a true army of the night, populated by people who had become by necessity masters of covert activities. They were the slaves. They penetrated to every level of Confederate society; they listened and remembered; but they remained invisible. Southerners bought their own propaganda,[17] assuming their slaves were loyal and resigned to their condition. This was hardly the case, and the slaves were quick to realize that these boys in blue coats constituted their best chance in over two centuries to change things or at least escape. If and when they could, they would help the Yankees, supplying the most valuable of commodities in this kind of war: information.

It is important to understand that this went on at all levels of engagement. Runaways flocked to Union troop concentrations, where they were debriefed by officers of every rank, including Sherman himself, who learned to trust their honesty and good intentions. But such cooperation also consisted of a field hand sidling up to a group of Yankees at night and warning them of an ambush up the road; of servants pointing out a cache of arms; of an old man quietly explaining the fastest and safest way from point A to point B ... all repeated thousands of times. This was intelligence manna indeed: a parallel network, fully established and available.

The exact worth to the Yankee invaders is hard to calculate. Sherman, because he didn't fully comprehend the nature and magnitude of the threat he was facing, never seems to have considered his African American informants critical to his operations. But from a contemporary perspective, it's possible to disagree. This network was a true windfall and likely provided a significant, though subtle, military advantage. It is highly suggestive that the areas where the rebel insurgency thrived—Kansas, Missouri, western Virginia—possessed very few slaves; here, the white network went unbalanced.[18] But the Deep South, where the invaders were headed, would remain rich in informants, rich enough, apparently, to allow Sherman and Grant to pursue their central strategic aims, controlling important places and destroying Confederate armies. It is unfortunate that Sherman never fully appreciated the worth of the blacks and even came to view them as an encumbrance when they flocked to his armies. Down south, he had no better friends.

2

By December 1862, Vicksburg had become the focal point. During the previous summer, Buell's move against Chattanooga, the major Federal effort in the West, had ended just as badly as McClellan's Richmond campaign. Now Buell was gone, replaced by William Rosecrans, and it was Anaconda B's turn to try to clear the Mississippi.

John McClernand, the Illinois politician turned general, had been pressing his friend Abraham Lincoln to let him organize "a special force" aimed at Vicksburg and opening the river.[19] Without telling Grant—who also had his sights set on Vicksburg and had already advanced to Oxford with an army of forty thousand—the president gave his approval to McClernand. Not surprisingly, this did not go down well with the West Pointers—Halleck, Grant, and Sherman—and they set about organizing a countercampaign. Though it failed militarily, it featured some dazzling bureaucratic sleight of hand.

Put simply, they stole McClernand's army. As soon as Grant learned the troops he had recruited were arriving at Memphis, he sent Sherman there to take charge before McClernand arrived. The operational plan was a parallel movement: Sherman would move his forces down the Mississippi on a flotilla of transports and gunboats commanded by David Dixon Porter; and Grant would proceed overland, simultaneously preventing Vicksburg from being reinforced and acting as a pincer.[20]

The key to this larcenous endeavor was moving fast, and nobody was a better getaway man than Sherman. Within a matter of days, he put together an expedition of thirty-two thousand and had them ready to leave on December 20, with no McClernand in sight.[21] Porter's own description wonderfully captures the sheer manic energy of the man the night of departure: "Halloo, Porter, I am glad to see you; you got here sooner than I expected, but we'll get off to-night. Devilish cold isn't it? Sit down and warm up.... Here, captain tell General Blair to get his men on board at once. Tell the quartermaster to report as soon as he has six hundred thousand rations embarked. Here, Dick"—to his servant—"put me up some shirts and under-clothes in a bag.... Here, Captain tell the steamboat captains to have steam up at six O'Clock and to lay in plenty of fuel, for I'm not going to stop every few houses to cut wood. Tell the officer in charge of embarkation to allow no picking and choosing of boats; the generals in command must take what is given them— Glad to see you Porter; how's Grant?"[22] Plainly, Sherman could multitask with the best; unfortunately, this was probably the high point of the mission.

Vicksburg—situated on bluffs two hundred feet above the east bank of the Mississippi and flanked on the north by a triangle of swamps and bayous generated by the slow-flowing Yazoo—was inherently a tough target. The cannons on Porter's gunboats couldn't be elevated high enough to do any harm to the Confederate artillery on the bluffs, so an approach along the soggy ground to the north was the only tactical option for now.[23]

Despite the quick takeoff, there was no surprise. Nor was there any Grant. A raid by Van Dorn's cavalry had captured his supply base at Holly Springs, and Forrest had severed his rail link, so he called off the land assault. That left fourteen thousand dug-in Confederates free to give Sherman their full attention when he landed at Chickasaw Bayou, marched his force across the swamp, and assaulted the bluffs on December 29. In repeated attacks they were shot to pieces, losing eighteen hundred men (compared with the rebels' two hundred) before Sherman mercifully "became convinced that the part of wisdom was to withdraw."[24]

That night found Sherman aboard Porter's flagship, discouraged but far from despondent, more full of ideas than lamentations. He had changed remarkably in the nine months since Shiloh, truly grown into his role as military strategist, and this day of defeat in his first independent command reflected it, perhaps better than a victory. For it marked the debut of one of his best military qualities, prefaced by his time as a banker: He knew when he was beat and moved quickly to cut his losses. This is not to be discounted. In the heat of battle, too many commanders, thwarted in their objectives, simply begin throwing their men at hopeless objectives—a surefire recipe for slaughter in an era of rapidly improving weapons, as the Civil War was demonstrating. Sherman once marched a man to death in Florida, but those days were long gone. He never lost track of the fact that these were human lives he was playing with. Not coincidentally, it was an ideal approach to take with volunteers, who were already calling him Uncle Billy.

His attitude toward them as soldiers was also changing.[25] They had fought long and hard at Chickasaw Bluffs under the most difficult conditions. Many were inexperienced in combat and probably drilled only briefly, but they demonstrated the same self-reliance and adaptability Sherman had noticed in other volunteer units. This had been an amphibious operation, traditionally the most difficult of military tasks; yet it was carried out with relatively little confusion and considerable determination. If these volunteers could do this, then their military possibilities were practically endless. With a strategic imagination like Sherman's, this had to be stimulating.

That night, though, he and Porter conjured up more of the same, a military consolation prize for these neophyte swamp rats. Fort Hindman (also known as Arkansas Post) was low-hanging fruit. A cache of five thousand Confederates stashed fifty miles up the Arkansas River, it was an easy target for the much larger Union amphibious force. This was just the sort of operation that rebuilds confidence in defeated troops. There was really only one hang-up: McClernand had finally caught up with his purloined army, and the reunion with Sherman and Porter had been frosty.[26] Still, McClernand was enough of a soldier to realize this was a sure thing and enough of a politician to foresee the advantages of being associated with such a coup. At Porter's insistence, he allowed Sherman to retain command of the ground troops, and the operation proceeded up the Arkansas without further delay.

On January 12, 1863, following two days of hard fighting and a thorough pounding by Porter's gunboats, Fort Hindman surrendered and the blue force bagged all the Confederates. Sherman played a conspicuous role in the action, scouting enemy lines and coming under repeated artillery fire, while McClernand waved his hat along the riverbank surrounded by newsmen.[27]

That's how the West Pointers saw it, at least. Sherman seems to have taken a particular dislike to McClernand, but this was really all about who would control military operations, politicians or professionals—at least in the eyes of the professionals. They all had it in for McClernand. Grant never forgave him for hesitation at Donelson; Sherman had given him orders at Shiloh; and Halleck considered him a rank amateur. But their larger point was that professionals had to control operations of Vicksburg's importance. That was their point when McClernand complained to Lincoln and, soon after, when Halleck made it official and gave Grant overall command of the expedition against Vicksburg.[28] Indeed, that obstacle still loomed and was assuming more importance as each day passed.

Shiloh had been no aberration. The Civil War had turned into a bloodbath, with subsequent battles bringing just as bad or worse. Worse, certainly, for the Union in the East. The Peninsula Campaign had been followed by a succession of hammer blows—Second Bull Run, Antietam, and most recently the disaster at Fredericksburg. A string of Union generals—McClellan, Pope, Burnside—all of them West Pointers, had been set up and then knocked down like bowling pins. In the West just days after Chickasaw Bluffs, Yankee troops had suffered 31 percent casualties at the welcome but inconclusive victory at Stones River.[29] The Confederate strategy of survival and raising the cost of rebellion suppression seemed to be working. The Union cause desperately needed a big victory and one its adherents could see constituted real progress.

Sherman and Grant understood the stakes at hand: the fulfillment of Anaconda B would cut the Confederacy in half—the war's most tangible strategic achievement and something no one North or South could miss. The eyes of the nation were upon them. Plainly this was their moment, but the military problems presented by

Vicksburg had not gone away. In fact, they were growing worse by the day as the winter rains fell and the rivers rose.

Grant's initial concept was to dig his way around the problem, employ the forty-five thousand men they had accumulated to slice a series of canals—first a short cutoff to avoid Vicksburg's guns, then a much more ambitious attempt to cut through an oxbow to bypass the place entirely. Neither worked, flooded out despite the best efforts of Sherman's men and those of General James McPherson, his friend from New York and one of Grant's favorites.

Not to be denied, Grant sent Sherman and his waterlogged swamp rats to probe the Yazoo Delta accompanied by Porter's gunboats, with the intent of finding a way down to Vicksburg that would flank its bluffs and defenses.[30] What they found was a morass of vegetation that slowed Porter's gunboats to a crawl and left them easy targets for Confederate cavalry, had not Sherman come to the rescue. "Halloo Porter....What did you get into such an ugly scrape for? So much for you navy fellows getting out of your element; better send for the soldiers always. My boys will put you through."[31]

They did. The Steele's Bayou Expedition demonstrated just how far Sherman and his boys had come as an army. Sherman's nearly inhuman grasp of terrain revealed itself in this mass of channels and dead ends; he never got lost. And as his troops, now toughened into real soldiers, realized he knew what he was doing and where he was going, they marched and fought all the harder. But in the end, it led nowhere. Porter and Sherman backed out of Steele's Bayou and Vicksburg remained unapproachable.

Not perpetually, but for a while. It was probably inevitable that Grant and Sherman would eventually find a way around Vicksburg's defenses. But this sort of operation took time, and an impatient nation was watching. For Sherman, this proved to be a swamp of another order—an information environment where reporters lurked behind every tree and their stories traveled at the speed of light—and one where he really lost his bearings.

Sherman's anger with the press had been building since Kentucky and had hardened into true hatred after Shiloh. Now it became explosive. Press censorship in the South was certainly more effective than in the North. It was also true that journalistic coverage of the war was distorted and overdramatized. But these imbalances for Sherman had transformed reporters into spies, Jefferson Davis's secret weapon.[32] At Vicksburg, he tried to treat one as such.

The reporter was Thomas Knox of the *New York Herald,* who had violated Sherman's order banning journalists from the Chickasaw Bayou/Arkansas Post expedition and then filed an unflattering and inaccurate account of his leadership. Knox offered a retraction, but then he named Frank Blair as his source and admitted, "You are regarded the enemy of our set, and we must in self-defense write you down."[33] Sherman went volcanic, questioning Blair closely (he was not the source) and insisting on the only court-martial of a journalist in U.S. history—for Knox.[34]

The general plainly wanted him convicted as a spy and given a death sentence (whether it would have been carried out remains open to question), but he had to content himself with a verdict of expulsion from Union lines. Everyone close to Sherman—Grant, his brother, and Ellen—all thought he was way wide of reality on this one. "You cannot stand up against newspaper power alone...," she wrote just before the Knox trial. "Instead of resisting why not use it."[35]

This was good advice, and he never again attempted to exclude reporters from his operations; but Sherman's vitriolic conduct at Vicksburg also reflected the sheer frustration of the campaign and its importance to the war effort. Three months had passed since Chickasaw Bluffs. It was early April, the beginning of the wettest time of the year, and the nation was still awaiting some tangible signs of progress—Grant and Sherman seemed as bogged down as the generals in the East. Lincoln was under tremendous pressure. Stanton was getting itchy and sent his assistant secretary of war, Charles Dana, to look over the situation.[36] He liked what he saw, but the basic problem, Vicksburg, remained.

It was time for a new plan. Sherman wanted to reboot: move back to Memphis and start over.[37] Grant hated to retrace his steps and understood that any shift back from Vicksburg would be seen by the public as a retreat and admission of failure. Instead, he proposed moving forward, characteristically doubling down his bets in the face of adversity. Grant's plan called for Porter running the guns of Vicksburg, moving his army down the west bank of the Mississippi, having the flotilla ferry him across, and then maneuvering around in back of the fortress city. Significantly, this meant that once the army reached the east bank, it would operate without dedicated supply lines but would live off the countryside instead.

Sherman objected, and considering what happened later, it's worth asking why. Foraging was nothing new in warfare; armies had been doing it since war began. Sherman also knew that Winfield Scott's brilliant campaign against Mexico City had been based on cutting his supply lines and allowing his troops to gather sustenance from the campesinos. At this point in the war, Sherman had few moral and no legal reservations against troops helping themselves to Southern farm products, nor did he lack trust in his army's ability to conduct such operations. He simply considered it too risky, "one of the most hazardous and desperate moves of this or any war," he told Ellen.[38] It was a telling reaction from a man remembered for the apparent audacity of his military campaigns. Just as he operated as a banker, Sherman remained a conservative and calculating risk taker. Grant's plan was inferior to his own simply because it involved more risk. But he also knew Grant, and once he made up his mind, Sherman did everything he could to help.

On the night of April 16, while Vicksburg held a ball to celebrate the apparent withdrawal of the Yankees, Porter ran the Confederate gauntlet, losing only one of his eleven gunboats and transports. Sherman was waiting for Porter in a rowboat. "Are you all right, old fellow?...You are more at home here than you were in the ditches grounding on willow-trees....There are a lot of my boys on the point ready to help you if you want anything....Good-night! I must go and find out how the other fellows fare."[39] He visited every vessel.

Grant's plan turned on rapidity and strategic surprise. To move an army of forty thousand while keeping the Confederates guessing, he needed diversions. First he sent horse-hating cavalryman Benjamin Grierson on a spectacular raid (the subject of John Ford's film *The Horse Soldiers*) through the entire state of Mississippi, tearing up railroads and raising commotion until finally reaching Union lines at Baton Rouge after sixteen days, exhausted but virtually unscathed.

Sherman drew the short straw, a mock attempt on the bluffs yet again through Chickasaw Bayou. Grant knew the men (who couldn't be told it was a ruse) would hate the idea and was "loath to order it."[40] But of course he did, and Sherman and his swamp rats dutifully slogged into position facing the bluffs while artillery and gunboats shelled Confederate positions in apparent preparation for an attack that never came. But it did cause John Pemberton, Vicksburg's defender, to recall a force of three thousand he had sent to challenge Grant, whose plans he did not fully understand.

By the time he did, it was too late: Grant had transferred his entire army to the east bank, recalled Sherman, who marched his boys eighty-three miles south to join him, then went inland rather than approach the city directly to the north. They headed instead for Jackson, where the new Confederate commander in the West, Joseph E. Johnston, was concentrating troops. On May 14, in the middle of a downpour, Sherman's corps along with McPherson's overwhelmed six thousand rebels and sent them scampering through the city's streets. While the rest of the army headed toward a notable victory at Champion Hill two days later, Sherman's boys stuck around and provided a demonstration of things to come.

Despite its small population, Jackson had come to be a key Confederate rail and industrial center, and Sherman set about wrecking it—methodically tearing up track, smashing rolling stock, and torching foundries, arsenals, and anything else that looked useful to the war effort. His troops were also hard on symbols of the rebellion, burning (among other icons) the Confederate Hotel.[41]

This is significant, since Jackson was also the state capital, the local seat of secession. Sherman left quickly to rejoin Grant, but in early July he returned to lay siege to the place and then completely burned it—"Jackson, once the pride and boast of Mississippi is a ruined town," he wrote.[42] More than any Northern general, even Grant, Sherman waged war on political and psychological levels; his overarching and everlasting aim was to destroy the rebellion and drive its member states back into the Union. Rebel state capitals provided Sherman exactly the stage he wanted to conduct this psychodrama of domination and then forgiveness—no sooner had he conquered Jackson than he urged Grant to let him feed the battered inhabitants.[43] He did it repeatedly, and Confederate leaders wondering where he and his boys might wander had only to look to their own state capitals. He almost always paid them a visit.

Meanwhile, Grant's plan had closed the vise on Vicksburg. After Champion Hill, Confederate forces had staggered back to their fortress city, barely beating the Yankees but in doing so sealing their doom. They were surrounded; it was just a matter of time.

Nevertheless, they staged a spirited defense behind the war's most elaborate and formidable fortifications. Hoping for a breakthrough while the rebels were still demoralized, Grant ordered an immediate assault by his whole army on May 19, only to be turned back by a hail of Confederate lead. Three days later, they tried again. This time, McClernand (still in the field as a corps commander) reported a breakthrough that proved nonexistent and probably caused unnecessary casualties when Sherman and McPherson renewed their attacks. He compounded his sins by publicly congratulating his own troops and casting aspersions on the others. The West Pointers moved in like antibodies, and by mid-June, Grant had fired him, eliminating what had been, at least from the academy grad perspective, one of the campaign's two major obstacles.

The other, Vicksburg, had no brighter future. Through Halleck's skillful use of telegraph and rail, Grant was able to build his force to seventy thousand and basically wait.[44] "All day and night continues the sharp crash of the Rifle and deep sound of mortars," Sherman wrote Ellen in early June. "I think we have shot 20,000 cannon balls and many millions of musket balls into Vicksburg....The truth is, we trust to the Starvation."[45] In an attempt to break Grant's now restored supply lines, the Confederates staged a raid on the Union garrison at Milliken's Bend, but two regiments of newly enlisted freedmen and a few gunboats fought them off. Pemberton kept hoping that the five divisions Joseph Johnston had managed to assemble would challenge the siege, but the Confederate commander in the West informed Richmond on June 15: "I consider saving Vicksburg

Sherman's sketch for his children of the Union batteries at
Vicksburg. *Archives of the University of Notre Dame*

hopeless."[46] By the end of the month, Confederate troops and the
city's citizens were where Sherman trusted they would be, at the
edge of starvation. Three days later, Pemberton asked for a truce
and sat under a tree with Grant to work out the surrender of Vicksburg, to take effect on July 4, 1863.

It was the most joyous Independence Day in U.S. history. A thousand miles away at Gettysburg, the battered Army of the Potomac
had at last decisively defeated its chief tormentor, Robert E. Lee,
and on this day sent him staggering south to end his invasion of
Union territory. Combined with the news from Vicksburg, the results at Gettysburg sent a wave of relief sweeping across the North;
after more than two years of terrible war, victory seemed in sight.
George Meade, the commander at Gettysburg, was a dour individual, and this was his first major victory. Grant and Sherman were the
men of the hour.

And rightly so: Vicksburg was, in the words of historian James McPherson, "the most important northern strategic victory of the war."[47] When the news reached the Confederate garrison at Port Hudson, the last obstacle blocking the Mississippi, it too surrendered, and Abraham Lincoln could proclaim: "The Father of Waters again goes unvexed to the sea."[48] Anaconda B was fulfilled, the Confederacy was cut in two, and it was these two unlikely characters, the drunk and the crazy in popular mythology, who had accomplished it. Henceforth, they were the military strategists who mattered; it fell to them to figure out a way to win. But before they could, disaster struck and everything had to be put on hold.

3

Up to this point, the Army of the West had been brought together only once, at Corinth by Henry Halleck. Otherwise, it had essentially operated in parallel—the Grant-Sherman team and their Army of the Tennessee achieving spectacular success along the Mississippi, and its plodding brother force the Army of the Cumberland mostly underachieving in Kentucky and western Tennessee, first under Buell, now under William Rosecrans. In the summer of 1863, it mounted its second stately campaign against Chattanooga, the sole rail link between the eastern and western Confederacy.

Facing the Union advance was Sherman's old associate Braxton Bragg. After P. G. T. Beauregard's sly evacuation of Corinth, Jefferson Davis, who had little appreciation for military subtlety, replaced him with Bragg, a considerably blunter instrument. He had already fought bloody but indecisive battles, first at Perryville, then at Stones River, and had earned the reputation of being careless with his men's lives. He had also alienated virtually all of his subordinates, including Forrest, who would soon threaten to kill him. Nevertheless, he was technically competent and had a large, experienced force, which made him a dangerous foe.

It began well for blue. Rosecrans was nothing if not methodical, and his careful planning paid off at the end of June, when his four infantry and one cavalry corps swept through separate gaps in the Cumberland foothills and arrived on both flanks of the Confederates waiting in the Duck River Valley. Bragg knew when he was out-maneuvered and fell back all the way to Chattanooga.

The blue forces clearly had the initiative, and the way was now open to both Knoxville and Chattanooga. Lincoln and Stanton urged him forward, but Rosecrans persisted with his calculated and deceptive advance. It took the rest of the summer to put in place, but after that it unfolded like clockwork. At the same time, Ambrose Burnside's army of twenty-four thousand moved through four passes to bloodlessly take Knoxville. Rosecrans, after feinting north, crossed the Tennessee south of Chattanooga and put himself and sixty thousand Union troops between Bragg and the railroad to Atlanta.

Surrounded by river and mountains, Chattanooga was an easy place in which to get trapped, so on September 8, Bragg evacuated his army, now joined by the Confederate division that had abandoned Knoxville in the face of Burnside. Bragg's concept was a retreat into northern Georgia, but Jefferson Davis reminded him that Lee had turned the war around in the east in 1862 by attacking McClellan and ordered him to try the same thing against Rosecrans. Two divisions from Joseph Johnston's force in Mississippi had already joined Bragg; now Davis proposed to transfer two more by rail from the Army of Northern Virginia under James Longstreet. For a commander as aggressive as Bragg, this was all he needed for a fight.

After setting a number of traps for Rosecrans, which Bragg's subordinates failed to spring, Bragg and his army—now pumped up to sixty-five thousand with the arrival of the first of the Virginia divisions—was intent on turning the Yankees left, when they ran into George Thomas's large Union corps slightly west of Chickamauga Creek on the morning of September 19, igniting one of the most horrific battles of the entire war and certainly the most dumbfounding.

These were substantial armies full of veterans, and they settled in for a two-day kill fest, with Bragg throwing division after division at George Thomas's corps and Rosecrans feeding him reinforcements, when, as suddenly as a bolt of lightning, everything changed. Rose-crans got a report that one of his divisions was missing from the line, creating a quarter-mile gap (the force was actually concealed in the woods), and he responded by moving another over, thereby generating a real division-sized hole.

It was right in front of James Longstreet, one of the war's very best generals, who was about to demonstrate that in battle, a game of chance, it's always better to be lucky than good. Under orders to stage another of Bragg's man-killing frontal assaults, he sent his yelping Confederates racing forward instead into a Yankee-less void, cutting the entire army in two and sending Rosecrans and his troops reeling back toward Chattanooga in disarray.

Now vastly outnumbered, the remainder of the Union force was in terrible danger, with Longstreet screaming for reinforcements to finish it off. Fortunately, he didn't get them and the Yankees were able to form a new line along a ridge perpendicular to the old one before Longstreet went at them again with what he had.[49] They were fortunate also to have George Thomas.

Thus far, Sherman's old roommate had waged a solid war—steady performances, increasing responsibility, nothing spectacular, but deliberate like Rosecrans, in keeping perhaps with his prewar nickname, "Slow Trot."[50] Now, in this moment of crisis George Thomas revealed a critical difference: He was utterly obdurate. He organized the defense, beat back Longstreet's repeated assaults until dark, then disengaged in good order for a nighttime retreat to Chattanooga—all in the process of earning what may be the best military moniker in U.S. history, better even than "Stonewall." George Thomas would be known forevermore as "the Rock of Chickamauga."

Still, like an athlete after an epic performance in a losing cause, Thomas would not have been happy with the results. Union forces had been driven from the field, had suffered more than sixteen thousand casualties, and were now bottled up in Chattanooga, surrounded by Bragg. To the outside world, Washington especially, it looked like disaster, a Confederate Gettysburg, maybe worse. Stanton and Halleck raced to reinforce the battered Army of the Cumberland, sending the Army of the Potomac's Eleventh and Twelfth

Corps by rail in eleven days—the longest and fastest movement of such a large number of soldiers prior to the twentieth century,[51] but also adding twenty thousand mouths to what amounted to a besieged army. Lincoln worried that its commander, William Rosecrans, remained "confused and stunned like a duck hit on the head."[52]

It was plainly time for new management, time for the boys from Vicksburg. Halleck called Grant, who replaced Rosecrans with Thomas and then quickly headed for Chattanooga to oversee the operation.[53] But not before he in turn called Sherman, which was hard, very hard.

His friend was in the midst of the worst personal tragedy of his life. After torching Jackson for a second time, Sherman had parked his army near the Big Black River for a well-deserved rest in early August. "Handsomest camp I ever saw," he wrote his brother; so salubrious, it seemed, that he invited the whole family for an extended stay. Ellen loved the place—there was a priest to say Mass, a military band played at night, and a regiment of regulars adopted little Willy as one of its sergeants. It was a rare interlude of family intimacy.

But then Grant sent word for Sherman to go immediately to Memphis and get as much as possible of the Army of the Tennessee on the way to Chattanooga as quickly as possible. As the family boarded a riverboat to leave, nine-year-old Willy complained of diarrhea. A physician thought it was a combination of dysentery and malaria; it may have been typhoid. At any rate, he died on October 3.[54] Sherman was shattered, virtually paralyzed with grief, and he told Grant as much: "Can hardly compose myself enough for work," then added, "but must and will do so at once."[55] He knew his man, knew there was no reclama or exemption. He had only to gather the troops and get them going.

By October 11, he had the best part of four divisions on the way; but that was just the beginning. The route to Chattanooga traversed more than three hundred miles of rugged terrain, following the path of the Memphis and Charleston Railroad, every foot of it vulnerable to guerrillas. Just twenty-four miles down the line at Collierville, Sherman's train was hit by a combination of Confederate cavalry and insurgents, and he found himself in the midst of a firefight.[56]

Sketch of the tents at the camp on the Big Black River, a visit that would prove fatal to his beloved son Willy. *Archives of the University of Notre Dame*

When the Confederate commander demanded surrender, he coolly stood his ground. "General . . . you will surely be hit if you don't keep under cover," warned one soldier. "Sergeant attend to your business, sir; attend to your business, I will take care of myself, sir."[57] He did, and after several hours the rebels withdrew.

The journey resumed, but the need to protect the railroad was slowing him down and robbing him of troops to guard it. Finally, Grant told him to forget the repairs and concentrate on getting to Chattanooga. Mainly they marched, following the tracks, riding when they could. On November 8, they were still more than a hundred miles away; but five days later, it was down to thirty-six and the first columns were nearing the rail link into Chattanooga. Sherman jumped a riverboat and walked into Grant's headquarters on November 15, with the Army of the Tennessee not far behind.

Amid the other commanders, including Thomas, he got the greeting he deserved from the man who mattered: "Take the chair of honor Sherman." "Oh, no! that belongs to you, general." But Grant insisted. "I don't forget Sherman, to give proper respect to age."[58] So he took the seat, knowing full well, as did everybody else in the room, that a great deal more was involved.

The team was assembled, ready to consider the matter at hand—their own desperate condition. The next morning, the two generals and their staffs walked out on a parapet with a panoramic view. As Sherman remembered: "Lookout Mountain, with its rebel flags and batteries, stood out boldly....All along Missionary Ridge were the tents of the rebel beleaguering force; the lines of trench from Lookout up toward Chickamauga were plainly visible; and rebel sentinels, in a continuous chain, were walking their posts in plain view, not a thousand yards off. 'Why,' said I, 'General Grant, you are besieged'; and he said, 'It is too true.' "[59]

"But not for long," he might have added. Supplies were now trickling in from the west; yet men were eating the corn meant for the horses, and more troops were flowing in all the time. He also knew Bragg, following Jefferson Davis's advice, had detached the more than capable Longstreet to Knoxville to confront Ambrose Burnside, the goat of Fredericksburg, an obvious mismatch. Grant felt he had to do something quickly. It was either break out or go hungry and suffer still another Union setback in east Tennessee.[60]

But things had a different slant from a Confederate perspective. Chickamauga had savagely decimated the rebel force, which had lost more men (twenty thousand) than even the Yankees. By this time, virtually all of Bragg's subordinates had turned on him, including Longstreet, whose detachment with fifteen thousand men further weakened the gray side numerically. The Confederate noose around Chattanooga was already seriously frayed as Grant considered how to break it.

His plan was to go after both ends, a double-flank attack. To the south, "Fighting Joe" Hooker, who had been inherited along with the Eleventh and Twelfth Corps, was slated to lead an assault against Bragg's left on Lookout Mountain. On the opposite side, in the main effort, Sherman would hit the northern edge of Missionary Ridge with his own four divisions—one of which was commanded by his foster brother Hugh (Charley, the youngest Ewing son, was also attached to Cump's staff, so Team Ewing/Sherman was well represented). Meanwhile, the Army of the Cumberland under George Thomas would simply be asked to hold the middle, since Grant considered them too demoralized after Chickamauga to do much else.[61] Little worked out as expected when the attack got under way on November 29.

Hooker and his troops, hitherto the lambs of Chancellorsville, performed surprisingly well, launching their assault on Lookout Mountain through a ground fog and sweeping what turned out to be only three Confederate brigades down the reverse slope in short order. The next morning, a huge Stars and Stripes was seen by both armies flying from the highest point on the peak, Braxton Bragg having been forced to concentrate all his defenses on Missionary Ridge.

Meanwhile, Sherman was getting stuffed—flummoxed, of all things, by the terrain. He had been in the vicinity during the 1840s but may have missed Chattanooga; in any case, for the first and only time in the war, he became seriously disoriented. Sherman sent his troops up the wrong ridge, a spur separated from Missionary Ridge by a rocky ravine. When he got over his bewilderment, he launched an attack on the correct objective the next morning, with his foster brother's division out front: "I say Ewing, don't call for help until you actually need it."[62] They all needed it after running into the oversize division of Patrick Cleburne, one of the best in the Confederate army, and being pushed back repeatedly by a buzz saw of fire. Sherman liked to claim later that the attacks forced Braxton Bragg to fatally divert troops from his center, but this never happened.[63] It also didn't matter. This was not a battle determined by generals, good or bad. The soldiers decided this one.

Sensing Sherman was in trouble and wanting to prevent Bragg from sending reinforcements against him, Grant told Thomas to order the Army of the Cumberland in the center forward against the first line of Confederate trenches at the base of Missionary Ridge. A two-mile-wide frontal assault against a well-entrenched adversary with a broad field of fire: This smelled suicidal, Pickett's Charge II.

Instead, amazingly, it sent the rebels racing back toward the next line of trenches. Even more amazing, the boys in blue didn't stop but continued chasing them. "Thomas, who ordered those men up the ridge?" Grant fumed. "I don't know," he replied, "I did not."[64]

They ordered themselves. Not from an excess of enthusiasm or bloodlust, though some was involved, but from a keen situational awareness. These men were mostly veterans; they had been under fire before and understood lines of sight. In the first set of trenches, they were easy targets from above. Also, it made sense to follow the retreating rebels as closely as possible to suppress the fire of their comrades. As they moved up the ridge, the Union troops began to realize the Confederates at the top were consistently firing high or into the ground, that the dips and swells in the terrain offered sure cover. Likely few understood exactly why—Bragg's combat engineers mistakenly located the uppermost fortifications at the topographic crest, not the military one, where lines of fire could not be blocked by such features[65]—but the Yankees just kept coming, sixty regimental flags advancing relentlessly in the face of what should have been irresistible fire.

For the rebels, it proved too much. As the blue forces neared, the entire line broke in panic and raced down the opposite slope, leaving the boys of the Army of the Cumberland to occupy their trenches and scream, "Chickamauga! Chickamauga!" at their backs.[66] It was an extraordinary moment and an important one. Bragg's entire army was chased from the battlefield, not stopping to gather itself until it was thirty miles down the tracks toward Atlanta. But perhaps even more significant, it was the besmirched Army of the Cumberland that had done it, winning back its military reputation in front of the rest of the Army of the West, a truly amalgamating event. After Missionary Ridge, it would finally become possible to consider the Army of the West as a single entity, unified in spirit and under the command of one universally recognized individual. That would soon be William Tecumseh Sherman, but not yet. Grant had one more miserable job for his long-suffering wingman.

Burnside was still in Knoxville, boxed in by Longstreet and purportedly starving. For relief, Grant initially looked to Gordon

Granger, who on his own initiative had joined Thomas's last stand at Chickamauga but now proved slow to get his corps moving. That was unforgivable in Grant's eyes, and he turned immediately to Sherman, who found himself the next day on the road with his seriously beat-up army.[67] Many of their uniforms and shoes were already in tatters when they'd arrived in Chattanooga; they'd fought a battle and had been roughly handled; and now they were on an eighty-mile trek across frigid mountainous country. Yet they managed better than ten miles a day, Sherman at their head, until on December 5, nearing Knoxville, they all learned that Longstreet had retreated back to Virginia the night before. The emergency was over.

Sherman found Burnside sitting down to a turkey dinner. When the general admitted that the supply situation had never been as bad as it seemed, the redhead had the good sense to shut up, eat turkey, and take his army limping slowly back to Chattanooga and then to winter quarters, where they could finally rest, recuperate, and ready themselves for subsequent adventures with Uncle Billy.

He now fully understood what he had in them. Since Shiloh, they had performed virtually every kind of mission—amphibious assault, siege warfare, conventional combat, anti-insurgent operations, combat engineering—and were plainly capable of doing anything he wanted. "No better body of soldiers in America," he told Grant.[68]

So it was that just as Sherman was about to emerge a strategic magician, he found himself with a wand in hand, capable of morphing into anything he wanted. He would need every bit of it, for the war was far from over. Anaconda A had cut off Confederate trade; Anaconda B had cut the rebels in two; but still the Confederacy refused to admit it was dead. Now it was up to Sherman and Grant to think of a scheme to really kill it.

Chapter VI

ATLANTA

I

SHERMAN WAS NOW a made man, finally perched where he wanted and could best operate. He had been promoted to brigadier general of regulars,[1] which meant perpetual employment at that rank should he survive the war—something he wasn't necessarily expecting. Still, to a West Pointer this was a dream slot and a profound endorsement from Washington and Halleck, who had engineered it. Even better, he had finalized his relationship with Grant. His herculean labors were over and he was now truly the trusted associate of the man just designated to run the entire war effort in the East. Sherman would take over in the West, remaining the wingman, perpetually asking permission, which Grant, as good as his name, always granted.

Sherman was ruefully aware of Southern tenacity: "No amount of poverty or adversity seems to shake their faith. . . . I see no signs of let up—some few deserters—plenty tired of war, the masses determined to fight it out," he wrote Ellen in March 1864,[2] just before meeting with Grant in the first of a series of strategy sessions that culminated in Cincinnati. Sherman spoke of "constant interruptions"—Ellen was pregnant again but remained deeply depressed over Willy and the recent death of her mother, and the Grants were in the midst of their move eastward—but the two men found time to finalize what had been outlined first at Nashville and then at Louisville.[3]

It was very Grant-like, amounting to a full-court press aimed at killing Southerners until, in essence, they ran out of Southerners.[4] The intent was to engage in great battles and shatter Confederate field forces, not just Sherman and Grant, but everybody—Nathaniel Banks's Army of the Gulf would move on Mobile, Benjamin Butler's Army of the James would head up the peninsula toward Richmond, and Franz Sigel would traverse the Shenandoah Valley—all of them supposed to be looking for a fight. The days of episodic combat were over; Grant and Sherman would present the Confederacy with one apparently never-ending battle until it bled to death.[5] That was the main plan, "the Grand Plan," as Sherman called it,[6] but there was likely more.

Their actual conversations went unrecorded, but given the deeply defined personalities of each man, they are not hard to imagine: Sherman a fire hose of ideas, contingencies, and opportunities; Grant saying just a few words, encapsulating everything, and then deciding...subject probably to more argumentation from Sherman. Thesis/antithesis, yin and yang, Mutt and Jeff. Because of this dynamic, it does seem likely that much that was to come later strategically was prefaced here, predigested by the two men. Both recognized the need to attack Southern morale and its relationship to crushing the rebellion. Each had come to accept abolition as a means of undermining the slaveholding leadership class. Both understood the psychological effect of their blue-clad armies barging across the landscape, taking what they wanted, and wrecking anything that looked Confederate.

Sherman still had it in for Forrest and had come to view Meridian, Mississippi, as a key staging area for his insurgency. The response was a punishing raid in February 1864. His own combat divisions were resting and in no shape to go anywhere, so he assembled twenty-five thousand garrison troops, along with a separate cavalry contingent under William Sooy Smith; both forces were essentially inexperienced. He was plainly inviting an attack from Forrest and so informed Smith, who gave every sign of being terrified.[7] His intelligence also told him (accurately) that there were two Confederate divisions plus more cavalry waiting in Meridian under Polk.[8] Finally, he made no plans for provisioning.

The infantry component left Vicksburg on February 3 and upon crossing the Big Black cut loose from its supply lines and sent foragers fanning out laterally, combing the countryside for food and livestock. The weather was miserable and the roads awful, but the columns had plenty to eat and made good progress, first pounding Jackson yet again and then marching to Meridian by February 14, a distance of 133 miles.

Rebel harassment was present but ineffective. Sherman had divided his force into two wings and realized as they moved along parallel roads how hard it was to concentrate against one without being flanked by the other. He employed calculated misdirection, first feinting at Mobile and later drawing Polk out of Meridian so that he faced no opposition when he arrived. And he did all of this with virtually no cavalry support. Smith did not depart until the day after he was supposed to be in Meridian and was promptly run down by Forrest, who then trounced and scattered his force at Okolona.

Sherman was furious at Smith, but the mission remained unaffected. His troops settled in for five days of deindustrialization at Meridian, then marched with impunity back to Vicksburg, leaving a fifty-mile-wide swath dotted with fires and picked clean of foodstuffs to remind the locals of the visit. The army also drew escaped slaves like a magnet, picking up some five to eight thousand, something Sherman hadn't anticipated and unwisely viewed as an encumbrance.[9] Still, army-induced self-emancipation was certainly in line with the political message he wanted to send Southern civilians: that continued support of the Confederacy inevitably meant individual loss.

There was also plenty of food for thought here, and those who argue the Meridian raid provided Sherman with a template for the March to the Sea do not seem far off the mark.[10] With the exception of wanting to kill Forrest, the whole thing seems to have been undertaken in an experimental frame of mind, a validation phase for something already contemplated. "Lessons learned," as the army calls them now, filed away for the future.

For the Grand Plan, the one he and Grant finalized in Cincinnati, gave precedence to the physical over the psychological—engaging Confederate field armies and pulverizing them, killing rebels, not discouraging them. This was what they would now undertake, a blueprint that would turn Grant into a battering ram in the East and Sherman into a master of operational and strategic dance on his way to Atlanta.

2

It was tough to be a general in the Confederate army, especially if you placed a high priority on strategic maneuver and preserving your men's lives through defensive tactics. Almost by definition, Jefferson Davis didn't like you; nor did you fit the aggressive image prevalent among the most admired commanders—the Stonewall syndrome. This was the fate of James Longstreet, P. G. T. Beauregard, and in particular Joseph E. Johnston—never favored, turned to only in adversity, given rebel forces so beat up that there was no option but less enthusiasm.

Consider the bedraggled Army of Tennessee (not to be confused with the Union Army of *the* Tennessee, which was at the heart of the Army of the West) facing Sherman in the spring of 1864, much of it the same force that was last seen scampering down the reverse slope of Missionary Ridge. Armies, like prizefighters, suffer grievously from a severe defeat. Lest they collapse completely, they must be handled carefully. Bragg was no man to do this, but Johnston was. He understood them, what they could and could not do.

It was still basically a very good army, soon to be sixty-five thousand strong,[11] many of them veterans and famously ferocious fighters. But Johnston could not ask them to take the offensive, to engage in slug-fests like Chickamauga and expect positive results. He understood Sherman was coming to try to destroy his army.[12] He would make it as hard as possible, resisting behind fortifications where his men were safer and could maximize their veteran marksmanship. Like Halleck, Joseph Johnston knew his own limitations and those of his soldiers. In the subsequent campaign, he always remained within them. The boys in the butternut coats came to love him for that and did everything he asked. Against many opponents, it would have been enough.

Sherman was more than ready, at the height of his strategic powers with almost the perfect force at his disposal. He looked forward to the matchup as his moment, the culmination of his career. He was very much aware that Johnston had "the most exalted reputation with our old army as a strategist,"[13] but he took it as a challenge, not a cause for concern.

He had every reason for optimism. He had a combat-hardened force of nearly one hundred thousand commanded by trusted subordinates—George Thomas's Army of the Cumberland, now numbering sixty thousand; the Army of the Tennessee with twenty-five thousand tough troops under Grant-Sherman protégé James McPherson; and finally John Schofield, the same West Pointer who had steamed to New York and back without being missed, with his Army of the Ohio adding another fourteen thousand.[14]

Sherman also had an exceptional grasp of the terrain they would be covering. It was certainly challenging, filled with mountainous slopes, steep ravines, and dense forests. But this time Sherman had explored it extensively, working with the inspector general in the 1840s, and there it remained in his personal geo-spatial database.[15] He knew exactly where he was going every step of the way, which was critical for such a complex operation.

Near the end of March, Sherman had met with his three army commanders at Chattanooga and set about planning the campaign.[16] They all wanted and expected a decisive battle with Johnston; their force was much bigger and brimming with confidence. When that would come remained a question, but the intent was to keep advanc-

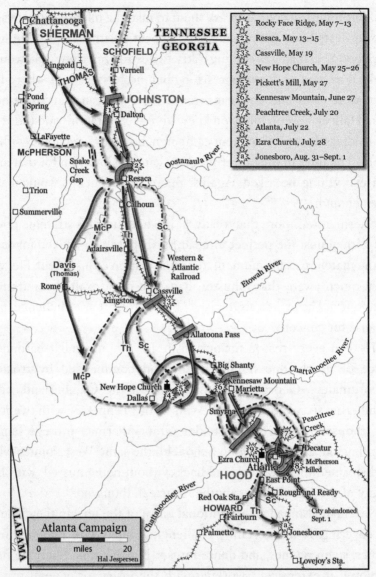

Atlanta Campaign
0 miles 20
Hal Jespersen

ing until it did and to ensure that all elements of the force operated together.[17]

This meant supply by rail, which almost dictated the general line of advance, along the tracks of the Western and Atlantic, linking Chattanooga to Atlanta.[18] There was no other way to bring this large a force into play and keep it always ready for combat. Sherman went to elaborate lengths to calculate the exact number of carloads necessary (145) and then proceeded to commandeer and cajole ("If you don't have my army supplied and keep it supplied, we'll eat your mules up sir—eat your mules up")[19] until he got what he wanted. Large-scale positional warfare made such a link necessary, but it also sent a political message—this was an invading army that could stabilize its position deep in enemy territory. Foraging was certainly useful, but it turns an army into a shark that must keep moving to survive. Sherman's intent here was different.

Johnston was waiting for him at Dalton, Georgia, with at least fifty thousand troops deeply entrenched along an eight-hundred-foot-high ridge called Rocky Face, which the Western and Atlantic pierced at Buzzard Roost. Sherman had seen a lot of fighting by this time; watched men out in the open mowed down by increasingly accurate rifle fire; noted his men's proclivity to find shelter and dig trenches whenever possible. Although he never fully articulated what he thought weapons were doing to warfare, he seems to have grasped intuitively what was happening and declined to throw his men at such objectives if there was an alternative. Intent on saving them from what he called "the terrible door of death" at Buzzard Roost,[20] he had Schofield and Thomas stage a demonstration there to fix Johnston's attention, while sending McPherson on a wide sweep to the right through Snake Creek Gap to get in behind Johnston and cut his rail link at Resaca.[21] It was a move that calls to mind the ring tactics of the boxer Muhammad Ali ("float like a butterfly, sting like a bee"), and it set the pattern for the entire campaign.

Sherman almost scored a knockout in the first round. On May 9, McPherson and the Army of the Tennessee poured through Snake Creek Gap and got within a mile of Resaca when they encountered some earthen fortifications manned by a rear guard that turned out to be fewer than four thousand strong. Had McPherson attacked promptly, Johnston would have been trapped. Yet he hesitated and dug in instead. "Well Mac, you have missed the great opportunity of your life," Sherman told him later.[22]

But all was hardly lost. Johnston was immediately forced to give up his defenses at Rocky Face and set up around Resaca. May 14 and 15 brought several more sharp actions, and once again Johnston found himself on the verge of being flanked by McPherson and retreated south toward Cassville, twenty-five miles down the tracks.

Here, it looked as if Johnston would at last strike out, as one of his corps commanders, John Bell Hood, had been urging all along. The quintessence of Southern aggressiveness, Hood had been schooled by Lee in the Army of Northern Virginia, and his body was now a monument to the costs of taking the offensive, having lost the use of an arm at Gettysburg and a leg at Chickamauga. Still, his division had led the assault that ruined Rosecrans, and he could always be counted on to attack, or so Johnston thought when he believed he had Sherman where he wanted him.

In hot pursuit, the Union commander had sent the columns of his army along several roughly parallel roads across a front of about a dozen miles. Johnston reacted by concentrating most of his forces under Hood and Polk in order to strike two of Sherman's corps seven miles separated from the rest. Rebel troops seemed anxious for a fight, but at the last minute Hood uncharacteristically worried about being flanked himself and aborted the attack.

This meant another fourteen-mile retreat from Cassville southeast to the Allatoona Pass, where slaves had already constructed defensive works overlooking the railroad along the Etowah River. It was all very demoralizing, and fingers were being pointed. The Army of Tennessee's corps commanders were once again squabbling with their chief, just as in the days of Bragg. But Johnston was still in an inherently strong position; these defenses were formidable and well located, another "terrible door of death." It was an ideal place to take a stand.

But Sherman knew that from his days exploring the pass as a lieutenant and had already resolved to go nowhere near.[23] Instead, he stopped short, gave his troops a rest, repaired the railroad, and then brought forward twenty days' worth of supplies, enough to cut loose for another grand sweep around Johnston's left.[24]

It began on May 23, the objective was Dallas, and now the whole army would move, Schofield on the left, Thomas in the middle, and McPherson as usual on the right. This time Johnston caught on and was able to shift his own force along the inside path so they reached New Hope Church near Dallas and entrenched before the Federals arrived. When they did, fierce firefights erupted on May 25 and 26, so fierce that the men remembered the place as "the Hell Hole."[25]

Afterward, both sides fell into a pattern of skirmishing and sniping, each probing for a place to attack or an angle for maneuver, in this terrain a deadly form of blindman's bluff.[26] At Pickett's Mill, Sherman tried to turn the Confederate positions and ended up taking sixteen hundred casualties.[27] But gradually he was able to work his way around, by sending McPherson and Thomas to the left and Schofield to the right. By the end of the first week in June, they were astride the Western and Atlantic near Marietta—but once again facing Johnston and the Confederates, now formidably entrenched in a line across Kennesaw Mountain.

Despite his success at moving Johnston around like a distressed chess piece, Sherman became increasingly agitated as this campaign progressed. The friction of war appeared to have caught hold of his army; everything seemed to be slowing down.[28] He was particularly impatient with Thomas's force, "which is dreadfully slow," he told Grant. "A fresh furrow in a plowed field will stop the whole column, and all will begin to entrench."[29]

Then there was track-induced entropy. The farther Sherman's army progressed, the more railroad there was to protect, and the losses in manpower weren't trivial. The men necessary to guard his rail link all the way back to Louisville were almost equal to the number of his combat troops, and the toll seemed to grow by the foot, the recent fighting having necessitated garrisons at Dalton, Kingston, Rome, Resaca, and now Allatoona Pass.[30] Considering what had happened elsewhere, his military situation was good and the rails were being repaired practically as fast as they could be broken up. But keeping them open was vital to the kind of campaign he was waging, and he was bound to worry. Sherman was an emotional man and an expressive one; if asked then to sum up the source of his unease, he might well have replied with a single appellation: "Forrest."

3

Nathan Bedford Forrest was no student of conventional warfare, but he instinctively grasped his role in the larger context of the conflict east of the Mississippi—the more hell he could raise in western Tennessee and Kentucky, the fewer bluecoats would be available against Johnston.[31] Garrison troops therefore became his primary focus and target of opportunity, his efforts intensified by the fact that the Union was now employing freedmen selectively in this role, something that infuriated Southerners.

This aspect reached a grim crescendo on April 12, 1864, when Forrest's cavalry and irregulars overwhelmed Fort Pillow along the Mississippi River and massacred the surrendered African American soldiers. There has been some debate over whether this was a deliberate act of terror, but in light of contemporary events, this seems somewhat naive. Terror is one of the key weapons in an insurgent's arsenal, and a practitioner as talented as Forrest must have recognized that the Fort Pillow attack would send a chill of dread through garrisons across the region.

Sherman knew exactly what he was doing. "Forrest's whole movement," he wrote less than a week after the massacre, "was intended to divert our attention from this concentration [against Johnston]."[32] "As soon as we move," he wrote Ellen just before pushing off, "they will attempt to cut in behind & cut our Roads . . . so we are forced to detach men."[33] In his eyes, this meant a threat to the entire campaign. So yet again, Sherman resolved to get Forrest.

He ordered the garrison commander in Memphis, Samuel Sturgis, to take a force of eight thousand and hunt down the exasperating Confederate. Sturgis found him on June 10 at Brice's Crossroads in Mississippi, where Forrest with a force half his size swarmed and routed him.

Although the lure of an easy target in Sturgis had diverted Forrest from breaking up railroads in Tennessee, that was little comfort to Sherman. "I cannot understand how he could defeat Sturgis with

8,000 men," he cabled Stanton in Washington. "Forrest is the very devil, and I think he has got some of our troops under cower." Still, Sherman was far from through with him. "I have two officers at Memphis that will fight all the time—[A. J.] Smith and [Joseph] Mower . . . I will order them to make up a force and go out and follow Forrest to the death if it costs 10,000 lives and breaks the Treasury. There will never be peace in Tennessee till Forrest is dead."[34]

A. J. Smith and Joseph Mower were among Sherman's most aggressive commanders, and their force numbered fourteen thousand when assembled. But Forrest wasn't intimidated, and as the Union column headed toward Tupelo to destroy the railroad, he promised to "be on all sides . . . attacking day and night,"[35] a classic description of swarming. By this time, Sherman was regularly receiving important tactical intelligence from a variety of African Americans he encountered, and Smith and Mower likely received similar information as they moved. In any case, the results of Forrest's swarms were lackluster, and the blue force, though stung, arrived at Tupelo intact.

At this point, events moved out of Forrest's control. His commanding general, Stephen Lee, arrived with reinforcements and decided to attack on July 14—this, despite the fact that his force was half the size of the Yankees'. It was a Confederate disaster, costing almost 1,250 killed and wounded, one of whom was Forrest, shot in the foot. It was not his kind of fight, and he may have preferred to avoid it; but the fact remained that Smith and Mower kept Forrest away from Sherman's supply lines at a critical moment. Still, Sherman's reaction to the news was rather reserved, perhaps because, as one source suggests, he wanted Forrest not just hurt, but dead.[36] Then again, he had lots of other distractions.

4

The Grand Plan had not gone well; the concept of simultaneous operations was sound, but the pieces necessary to accomplish it proved faulty. Banks never went to Mobile but instead wandered up the Red River. Here he met defeat at Sabine Crossroads and then further frustration until finally he decided to retreat, not returning to southern Louisiana until the last days in May.

Butler, another slow mover, fared no better. After steaming up the James and landing between Richmond and Petersburg, he ran into P.G.T. Beauregard, who staged a masterful defense and by the middle of May had his army completely sealed off, "as if it had been in a bottle strongly corked," Grant wrote glumly.[37]

In the Shenandoah Valley, Franz Sigel proved that he lacked any aggressive instincts at all and had to be replaced with David Hunter, who by the middle of June had been scared into West Virginia by the arrival of Jubal Early with Stonewall Jackson's old corps.

But most disappointing had been the performance of Grant himself. His nearly oxymoronic Overland Campaign had stumbled through the Wilderness, been staggered at Spotsylvania Courthouse, and then smashed disastrously into the Confederates at Cold Harbor, accumulating forty-four thousand casualties in four weeks before settling into a siege of Petersburg by the middle of June. Here he would stay for most of the next year.

All of this came at great political cost. Abraham Lincoln had welcomed the Grand Plan of simultaneous operations as reflecting his own "old suggestions so constantly made and as constantly neglected."[38] Yet the terrible spring of 1864 had shattered his hopes along with his political prospects. By the middle of June, although he had been renominated, Lincoln believed that he would lose the presidential election to George McClellan and the Democrats in November.[39] This likely would have meant some form of armistice and to Southerners their last and perhaps best hope of independence.

So it's fair to say that emancipation and the sanctity of the Union hung in the balance as William Tecumseh Sherman stared up at the Confederates entrenched on Kennesaw Mountain and considered what he would do about them. Thus far, his campaign had gained a lot of ground and cost relatively few casualties but failed to produce a decisive victory. Meanwhile, his preferred approach, flanking, was being complicated by incessant rain that had turned the roads to gumbo, and he didn't want to leave the Western and Atlantic supply link under such circumstances. In his mind, there were but two choices: Wait until the roads dried and he could accumulate surplus supplies; or attempt a frontal assault on the dug-in Confederates.

On June 5, he told Halleck he would "not run head on his fortifications," but as the month dragged on, he gradually reached the opposite conclusion. Since the enemy and even his own subordinates thought he would never attack head-on, he would "for moral effect" do exactly that. If it succeeded, he would not just put an end to the "belief that flanking alone was my game,"[40] he would cut Johnston's forces in half and rout them—exactly the kind of victory the Union and the Grand Plan so desperately needed. Or that, at least, might have been what the siren of slaughter whispered in Sherman's ear.

The attack came on June 27, aimed at the southern spurs of Kennesaw. It began badly and then degenerated. The temperature climbed to over a hundred. The rebels' fire was accurate and brutal. Eventually, a few bluecoats got within feet of the gray entrenchments, but most had been pinned down or simply shot. By the midafternoon, around three thousand Union soldiers had been killed or wounded, nearly four times Confederate casualties.[41] At this point, Sherman resorted to one of his best military traits: He recognized he was beat and cut his losses.

He had already seen a great deal, but Kennesaw seems to have had a chastening effect. "It is enough to make the whole world start at the awful amount of death and destruction ... ," he wrote Ellen; "I begin to regard the death and mangling of a couple thousand men as a small affair, a kind of morning dash."[42] After hearing from George Thomas that "one or two more such assaults will use up this army," Sherman let it be known that futile frontal attacks were over. "All the soldiers knew," one of Thomas's cavalrymen remembered: "The word was given out that night."[43] And he stuck to it. There would be more hard fighting, but nothing suicidal.

Instead, Sherman waited until the roads dried and he had enough supplies to leave the tracks. Then he sent McPherson and the Army of the Tennessee surging around the right, south toward the Chattahoochee.[44] It worked again. With the Yankees in behind him, threatening his rail connection, Johnston had no choice but to withdraw from Kennesaw on July 2.

At this point, the game changed. Instead of Johnston's army, Atlanta itself became Sherman's objective. "If I can take Atlanta without too large a sacrifice I may then allow my friends to claim for me the Rank of a General," he told John.[45] Whether he understood from the beginning that forcing Johnston progressively farther south and closer to Atlanta would inevitably shift the focus of the campaign remains unclear. But that was the effect. For outside of Richmond, there was no greater prize in the Confederacy. Over the course of the war, the city's population had doubled to twenty thousand as it added foundries, munitions plants, gun factories, and supply depots, all of which sprang up naturally at this key rail hub.[46] If the South had a workshop for war, it was Atlanta. And now Sherman was closing in.

Flanked and flanked again, Johnston fell back to the Chattahoochee, crossed the river, and took up secretly prepared positions on its banks by the end of the first week in July.[47] On the other side, one officer remembered Sherman and Thomas together with the prize now clearly in view: "Sherman stepping nervously about, his eyes sparkling and his face aglow—casting a single glance at Atlanta, another at the River... to see where he could cross... how he best could flank them. Thomas stood there like a noble Roman, calm, soldierly, dignified; no trace of excitement."[48]

On July 9, Sherman wrong-footed the rebels, having McPherson feint in his usual direction, while sending Schofield quietly several miles upriver from Johnston's right for a surprise crossing in the face of nothing more than cavalry pickets.[49] For the umpteenth time, it seemed, Johnston found himself outmaneuvered and was forced to withdraw, this time to trenches in back of Peachtree Creek, just four miles from center city.

Meanwhile, Jefferson Davis had lost all patience with Johnston and sent his new military adviser, none other than Braxton Bragg, on what amounted to a predigested fact-finding mission. When he arrived he spoke mainly to John Bell Hood, who wanted Johnston's job. "We should attack,"[50] he told Bragg, advice that would have surprised no one who knew him and was bound to be well received by the Confederate president. Hood was his kind of general, and although even Robert E. Lee warned against him ("all lion, none of the fox"), Jefferson Davis had pretty much decided on him as Johnston's replacement, when on July 16 the latter made it a certainty by hinting he would withdraw his maneuver forces and turn over the city's defense to the Georgia militia.[51] That did it. The next day, the thirty-three-year-old Hood became Atlanta's chief defender. He, at least, would not give up without a fight.

For Sherman, who knew all about him, Hood was the Confederate from Central Casting, "just what we wanted," a commander "bold even to rashness" and guaranteed to "fight in open ground, on anything like equal terms."[52] He was a military caricature, calling to mind Monty Python's Black Knight, missing all his limbs and spurting blood but still fulminating aggression. Frequently dosed with the opiate laudanum for his almost constant pain,[53] Hood had sacrificed his body on the altar of war and expected the same of his men. He had no regard for their lives, and they knew it. Something like a shudder of despair must have coursed through the Army of Tennessee when he took command.

Two days later, on July 20, to no one's surprise, he attacked. Sherman had sent his three armies sweeping toward Atlanta's final rail link to the upper South, and Hood thought he could catch Thomas, who was separated from the others, as he was crossing Peachtree Creek. But he was several hours too late and found himself instead in a stubborn firefight that cost him three thousand men and yielded no appreciable result.[54]

Hood was just getting started. After withdrawing into the city's defensive ring, that night he sent one of his corps out again on an all-night march to attack what he thought would be McPherson's exposed flank. It proved less exposed than expected, and once the Yankees got over their surprise, they fought ferociously, counterattacking at the end of the day and inflicting another five thousand casualties—eight thousand in two days, more than Johnston had lost in ten weeks.[55]

The rebels did exact a significant price: McPherson himself. After meeting with Sherman, he blundered into a gaggle of Confederates and in attempting to escape was shot out of the saddle. They brought the body back, and Sherman had it laid out on a door. Pacing back and forth, tears streaming down his cheeks, he took turns giving orders as reports came in and bemoaning the fate of this thirty-four-year-old golden boy. It brings to mind Achilles mourning the corpse of Patroclus: the warrior confronted at last with the ultimate cost of his deadly game. One officer remembered him saying after the battle: "I had expected him to finish the war. Grant and I are likely to be killed, or set aside . . . and McPherson would have come into chief command at the right time to end the war. He had no enemies."[56] Just bad luck. Instead it was these two unlikely characters who were Destiny's children.

Sherman replaced him with West Pointer Oliver O. Howard, an Army of the Potomac transplant, rather than the able politician turned general John Logan, who had been with the Army of the Tennessee since Donelson and had filled in admirably when McPherson fell. Logan never forgot the slight, and as House Military Affairs chairman after the war, he sought to shrink military budgets and tweak West Pointers, particularly Sherman, whenever he could. So much for the clairvoyance of the strategist.

Of course, you didn't need much with Hood. When Sherman sent Howard sweeping around in the direction of Atlanta's last rail link, Hood reflexively sent a corps to attack them at Ezra Church crossroads on July 28. Sherman learned of the assault and was elated: "Just what I wanted, tell Howard to invite them to attack, it will save us trouble, save us trouble, they'll only beat their own brains out, beat their own brains out."[57] That's what they did: making six separate charges and taking another five thousand casualties, only to give up the attack and entrench themselves.[58]

In eight days, John Bell Hood managed to carve the heart out of his army. Many of his most aggressive fighters lay dead or wounded, and the rest were exhausted from almost constant fighting and marching. He had little choice now but to settle into the fortifications that ringed Atlanta and try to recuperate.

Meanwhile, Sherman took advantage of the pause to soften up the city with siege artillery and further disrupt communications by sending cavalry well south to tear up the railroad. This they did, but only temporarily, as the Confederates were able to make repairs.

There was also another objective. At least twenty thousand Union prisoners, the majority captives from the Army of the West, were known to be penned up under horrible conditions at Andersonville about 140 miles south. Sherman reluctantly agreed to let George Stoneman take his division of horse soldiers in an attempt to rescue them. He was plainly torn. His soldiers were furious over the treatment of their captured compatriots, and he shared those sentiments; but he also knew that these men, having suffered such privation, would be useless as troops and very likely an encumbrance.[59] So when on July 30 Stoneman and seven hundred men were surrounded and captured by Joseph Wheeler's cavalry (then promptly delivered to Andersonville), Sherman made no further attempt in this direction, nor did he ever make a concerted effort to rescue prisoners of war. Military strategy is a harsh mistress, in part because the priorities of war must be pursued without regard to human sentiments. So while it's safe to say that Sherman at this point truly loved his soldiers, other things were more important. Like Atlanta.

To the ever-hopeful Southern press, it looked as if the city was holding out, even interpreting Hood's self-defeating assaults as wins.[60] The *Atlanta Intelligencer,* which tellingly was being printed in Macon, went so far as to suggest: "Sherman will suffer the greatest defeat any Yankee General has suffered during the war.... The Yankee forces will disappear before Atlanta before the end of August."[61]

Actually that is what happened, but not because of any Union defeat. After Stoneman's capture, Sherman had decided that truly cutting the railroad and sealing Atlanta's fate required moving the main army across it well below the city.[62] He made his move on August 26 after nearly a month of preparation, removing six out of seven infantry corps from the trenches and heading south.

Hood thought the city saved, until he realized the Yankees were now tearing up huge stretches of track unmolested. He sent out two corps to stop them, and on August 31, heavily outnumbered, they assaulted well-entrenched Union forces at Jonesboro, twenty miles south, only to be thrown back with heavy and disproportionate losses. The next day, Sherman staged a counterattack with his Fourteenth Corps under the coincidentally named and even more ill-tempered Jefferson C. Davis. The fighting proved brutal, at times hand to hand: "Our boys scaled their re-doubts . . . and then a slaughter commenced the likes of which I never witnessed before and pray I may never see again."[63] Those rebels not killed trying to surrender were captured or ran, forcing the remainder of their army from the field.

Atlanta's lifeline was officially severed. That night, Hood burned or blew up the military supplies he couldn't carry and then evacuated the city to join the rest of his weary field army. On September 2, blue-clad forces replaced them, and Sherman wired Halleck: "Atlanta is ours, & fairly won."[64]

That was putting it mildly. This was the best news for the Union in over a year, since the twin victories of Gettysburg and Vicksburg. Once again, a wave of joy and relief swept over the North and cannon salutes boomed from its cities. Combined with David Farragut's victory at Mobile Bay, which stopped the last blockade-running port east of Texas in early August, the capture of Atlanta and its war industries dealt a devastating strategic body blow to Southern hopes of somehow emerging victorious.

Of still greater importance, it had the inverse effect on the career prospects of Abraham Lincoln, who had been facing what amounted to the Grim Reaper in November. Instead, the path to victory in the presidential election of 1864 was now not only open, but wide open.[65] He would win and the South would lose, courtesy of the crazy redhead who, along with Grant, had been the president's personal reclamation project. Few long shots ever paid off bigger for a betting man.

The Atlanta campaign initiated a period that, without too much exaggeration, might be labeled High Sherman. The master of his trade in nearly the perfect circumstances, he now began a string of truly important accomplishments. Halleck told him after Atlanta's fall that he did not "hesitate to say your campaign has been the most brilliant of the war."[66] Even the hated press swung decisively in his favor, calling him the greatest general since Napoleon.[67] He was certainly the most creative. Saving Lincoln would have been enough for most men, but William Tecumseh Sherman, in his sweet spot at last, was just getting started.

Chapter VII

THE MARCH

I

JOHN BELL HOOD still had dreams of glory—those of a chess player who sees one move ahead. Now that Sherman was in Atlanta, he would reverse the play, cut the Yankees' rail links, and starve them. Jefferson Davis was encouraged after he paid a visit and Hood blamed Atlanta's loss on irresolute corps commanders, particularly William Hardee, who was removed and sent east to Charleston.[1] In the future, Hood's troops would be on the offensive, circling north and devastating Union logistics. Forrest was back in business; together they would chop up the railroad like a big snake and then engage and defeat the Yankees in detail. Despite having heard Army of Tennessee boys crying out, "Give us General Johnston,"[2] Jefferson Davis picked up the beat, telling cheering crowds in Georgia and South Carolina: "I see no chance for Sherman....The fate that befell the army of the French Empire in its retreat from Moscow will be re-enacted."[3]

Grant wanted to know who would furnish the snow,[4] but Hood did get a rise out of Sherman as he implemented his plan in September and October and supplies suffered accordingly. Not about to be engaged in detail and hoping that Hood might still be lured into a crushing battle, Sherman left one corps to guard Atlanta and set out after him with the rest of his army. It was difficult and frustrating skirmishing northward over the same hills and valleys he had recently traversed in the opposite direction, and Hood, because he had abandoned so much equipment and munitions in Atlanta, was now light and hard to catch. Sherman finally chased him back into Alabama and reconnected the rail link, but at this point he was through playing Hood's game.

In fact, Sherman was thinking in much larger terms. Beyond Hood, beyond his own command in the West, he was thinking about winning it all, or at least how to win it all. Anaconda B had worked, but the South fought on. The Grand Plan had inflicted terrible punishment, and Atlanta's capture had closed off the last plausible avenue to victory, but still the South fought on. Would they ever quit? What would it take to inflict defeat?

In an era of nuclear weapons, when a first strike would almost by definition render any society incapable of waging further war, it's easy to forget how hard it is to cause enough damage and casualties and general havoc to physically subdue a society that is truly stirred up. Even near the middle of the twentieth century, the German population took extraordinary punishment and never really lost its will to endure.

Obviously Sherman had a great deal less available in terms of destructive capability, no bombers, no tanks. But he had something better: he had come to understand that defeat was ultimately a state of mind and that he was in a position to utterly demoralize the Confederacy by making it look helpless. He could stamp across it and pummel and destroy every symbol and implement of that hated secessionist entity he could find. He had fought this war from the beginning with the unalloyed purpose of driving the seceding states back into the Union, and just how far he would go to achieve that end would be revealed in subsequent months. But not revealed would be the rape, mass murder, and population displacement that became so much a part of war in the twentieth century. These were his fellow citizens; he would never do such things to them. What he had in mind was more akin to a super-realistic horror show, one that didn't leave a dry seat in the house, scored and directed by Crazy Billy Sherman, the modern Attila.

The plotline was nothing new. He and Grant had likely already spoken in detail about the implications of cutting loose, and the Meridian raid had provided proof of concept for marching across the Confederate heartland. On September 20, he previewed his ideas to one of Grant's key staff members, Horace Porter, then followed up that same day with a letter to Grant proposing a line of march to Milledgeville and then Savannah.[5]

What was new, and distinctively Sherman, was the degree to which the March was designed to produce a psychological reaction among Southerners and how that, in turn, could be used to undermine their war effort. "I can make this march, and make Georgia howl!" he cabled Grant on October 9.[6] "This may not be war, but rather statesmanship," he continued. "If the North can march an army right through the South, it is proof positive that the North can prevail in this contest.... Even without a battle, the result operating upon the minds of sensible men would produce fruits more than compensating for the expense, trouble, and risk."[7] Sherman was proposing a trek across the mind of the South as much as a march across its territory.

Grant had one key reservation. He remained wedded to the concept of smashing Confederate armies and wanted Hood and his bedraggled force dealt with first before they could move into Tennessee.[8] But Sherman had that covered. "Why will it not do to leave Tennessee to the forces which Thomas has...?" he asked Grant.[9] If there is such a thing as a strategic sense of humor, this came close. Hood was to Sherman little more than an annoyance now and also an utterly predictable one. If he moved into Tennessee, Sherman would send him the Rock of Chickamauga along with more than fifty thousand men, knowing he would smash his army to pieces against them. This wasn't just prescient; it was a sure thing.

Grant remained skeptical, mostly because of Thomas's proverbially stately operational pace, but he thought enough of the plan to stand up for it in Washington. Lincoln was worried and told Grant so on October 12: "A misstep by General Sherman might be fatal to his army."[10] Grant was back to him through Halleck the next day: "On mature reflection I believe Sherman's proposition is the best that can be adopted."[11] That did it. If both of his wonder boys were in lockstep over this, Lincoln was not about to object, though he likely didn't understand how completely Sherman planned to cut loose.

The March was uniquely Sherman's, not only conceptually, but in terms of staging and execution. He was already considered a magician of military planning—of turning ideas into the concerted activity of thousands of people in an astonishingly short time—but the March was his masterpiece. There was a huge amount to consider, and in the space of a month and a half of preparation, he caught almost everything.

Reasoning that Hood would be held up in Alabama waiting for supplies long enough to assemble a blocking force in Tennessee, Sherman had Thomas in Nashville with selected troops on September 28, and Schofield's corps was moving into position by October 20. But while they proved to be capable troops and certainly accomplished their mission, they were plainly not the first team.

Sherman reserved those for the March—the Army of the Tennessee and the Fourteenth and Twentieth Corps—the true veterans, the hard core of his force structure. And just to make sure they were ready for the road, Sherman had his medical inspectors go through regiment by regiment, man by man, culling out any considered to be remotely unfit and sending them to Thomas.[12] Those who remained, around sixty-two thousand, were incredibly fit, and the weeding-out process had left them feeling like members of a truly elite force.[13] Nothing but the best, that's what Sherman was convinced he needed. To be truly effective, his soldiers had to leave exactly the impression he desired, virtually an army full of Shermans.

This had political implications. Sherman had adopted abolition as a means of undermining the secessionist ruling class and therefore the Confederacy. But other than that, he was halfhearted on the

issue, to put it mildly. This was especially true with regard to recruiting freedmen into the Union ranks. His reaction was dilatory to
the point of insubordination, inviting a tactful admonition from
Lincoln himself in July 1864, reminding Sherman that this was now
the law and he had no choice but to follow it.[14] "I have the highest
veneration for the law, and will respect it always," he assured the
president. But he retained his own agenda for the military integra-
tion of African Americans. "I prefer some negroes as pioneers, teamsters, cooks and servants; others gradually to experiment in the art
of the soldier, beginning with duties of local garrisons."[15] Notably,
their inclusion in maneuver units was not even considered. At the
end of October, he wrote Secretary of War Edwin Stanton that he
remained in favor of keeping black soldiers "for some time to come
in a subordinate state, for our prejudices, yours as well as mine, are
not schooled for absolute equality."[16] This was the wrong message
and the wrong man to confide in.

Sherman missed something very important. He was about to set
off on an operation of immense scale and complexity, keyed on
speed and purposeful movement, and not everybody had his own
unerring sense of direction. As one of his many duties, Orlando Poe,
his chief engineer, was charged with supplying maps—ones that
were expected to chart the way for four separate columns advancing
in parallel across long stretches without many landmarks.[17] Given
the reality of nineteenth-century roads, especially in the rural
South, such tactical maps were seldom more than generally accurate. Frequently, marked roads either didn't exist or were in no condition to allow the passage of large bodies of men. Getting lost was
always a possibility.

Yet Union forces would also encounter a network of guides,
friendly blacks who would provide not only reliable directions, but
information on Confederate and guerrilla ambushes, along with
showing foragers where food and valuables were hidden. The tactical and operational value of all this is difficult to specify, but it is
likely to have been substantial, akin to a military lubricant coating
Sherman's army and helping it slide more freely through the friction of war. Although he treated the blacks he encountered well and

appreciated the intelligence they provided, Sherman never considered the cumulative effect these contacts were having, the fact that it was going on at all levels of his army. As far as he was concerned, overall success was due to his own cleverness and the streamlined force structure he had put together back in Atlanta.

Sherman's casual, ad hoc approach to intelligence was also reflected in an army that wasn't much good at keeping secrets—an attitude with dire implications for the March. On November 9, one week before operations would commence, the *Indianapolis Herald* published a brief account that accurately reflected Sherman's plans, a story that *The New York Times* picked up and published the next day. Grant moved quickly to have all copies confiscated before they reached the South; but Stanton was furious, blaming Sherman's own officers for the leak, since the *Herald*'s source had apparently come from loose lips in Chattanooga.[18] The net effect on Sherman, however, was to deepen his hatred of the press.

Otherwise, though, he didn't miss much. Although his plan to provision through foraging was not only prefaced by Grant's success at Vicksburg and his own during the Meridian raid, Sherman hedged his bets to the maximum extent possible. He obtained from the Department of the Interior an annotated map with the population, livestock, and agricultural produce of Georgia in 1860 superimposed over the counties he intended to traverse, a sort of Michelin guide for fleecing the countryside.[19] On top of that, he had his chief commissary officer, Amos Beckwith, gather and issue 1.2 million rations to the troops along with a herd of three thousand beef cattle— enough for at least twenty days on the march.

Virtually everything else was devoted to mobility. While troops were ordered to carry all their equipment, wagons and ambulances were cut only from fifty to forty per thousand, ensuring spare rolling stock.[20] Sherman's ultimate route demanded getting over nine creeks or rivers, and Confederates could be expected to wreck crossings and guard fords as a chief means of slowing him down; so he provided his army with two regiments' worth of mobile pontoon bridges. Artillery was cut to a minimum, just over one gun per thousand men, a tip-off that he wouldn't be laying siege to anything.

Sherman had even managed—really for the first time in the war—to put together a credible cavalry force under Judson Kilpatrick, a sort of serviceable villain in his commander's eyes: "I know that Kilpatrick is a hell of a damned fool, but I want just that sort of man to command my cavalry on this expedition."[21]

Yet ultimately this army moved on the feet of his infantry—almost 90 percent of the whole[22]—hardened now to a level of fitness those of us living a sedentary life can barely imagine. Still, for the March Sherman stripped them down like a racing mechanic. There would be no tents, not even for officers. Each man carried a blanket, a pot, an extra shirt and pair of socks, a canteen, a haversack for food, a gun, and forty rounds of ammunition. Personal effects consisted of writing paper and maybe a pack of cards.[23] That was it. These were true road warriors, utterly confident, ready to go anywhere at a clip of fifteen to twenty miles a day, and certain that Sherman knew exactly where he was going and what he was doing.

Before he left, though, there was the matter of Atlanta. Originally, he had planned to turn the place into an arsenal, "a pure Gibraltar," and he set about expelling the civilian population.[24] When both Hood and the mayor of Atlanta protested vociferously, Sherman answered both. While he basically toyed with Hood ("If we must be Enemies let us be men, and fight it out...not deal in such hypocritical appeals to God"),[25] his answer to the mayor's charge of cruelty was more serious and revealing: "War is cruelty and you cannot refine it....But you cannot have peace and a division of our country....When peace does come, you may call on me for any thing. Then will I share with you the last cracker."[26] But in the meantime, since he was leaving, Atlanta would burn.

It wasn't exactly Scarlett O'Hara's holocaust; but Sherman's boys, with Poe at the helm, worked over Atlanta with the hands of seasoned veterans, under the boss's orders to destroy "all depots, carhouses, shops, factories, foundries, & etc...fire will do most of the work."[27] They had plenty of time, and they went over the place in detail. At one point, after torching a machine shop, a cache of hidden Confederate shells exploded and continued exploding all night, scattering sparks everywhere. One source notes that at least four

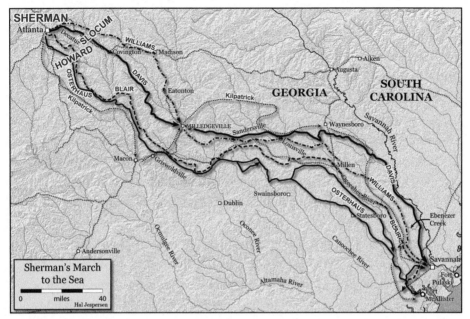

Sherman's March to the Sea

hundred structures were left standing when the Yankees departed, not pausing to consider that this was not a lot for a city that had recently been home to twenty thousand people.[28]

Sherman, like many of his soldiers, remembered pausing to look back as the March to the Sea began on November 16, 1864, and he caught the scene remarkably: "Behind us lay Atlanta, smoldering and in ruins, the black smoke rising high in the air, and hanging like a pall over the ruined city. Away off in the distance . . . was the rear of Howard's column, the gun-barrels glistening in the sun . . . and right before us the Fourteenth Corps marching steadily and rapidly, with a cheery look and a swinging pace. . . . Some band, by accident, struck up the anthem of 'John Brown's soul goes marching on'; the men caught up the strain, and never before or since have I heard the chorus of 'Glory, glory, hallelujah!' done with more spirit. . . . The day was extremely beautiful, clear sunlight, with bracing air, and an unusual feeling of exhilaration seemed to pervade all minds . . . and many a group called out to me as I worked my way past them, 'Uncle Billy, I guess Grant is waiting for us at Richmond!' "[29] Actually, a lot of people would be waiting for them, some scared to death.

2

Following the lessons of the Meridian raid, Sherman marched out of Atlanta in two wings—the right, or southern, arm under Oliver Howard; and the left, to the north, commanded by Henry Slocum. These in turn were divided into two columns apiece, to produce a total of four. Sherman's scheme called for keeping the wings in as tight a formation as possible; but armies take up space, and this one's contact patch was at least twenty miles wide and around ten miles long when wagon trains and artillery were included.[30] This sounds like a lot, but considered in light of the entire countryside, it really isn't. Meanwhile, information continued to travel either electronically at the speed of light or at the rate of a train or a fast horse. Sherman had purposely cut his link to the telegraph, which meant that those trying to ascertain his whereabouts were reduced to the latter two. In effect, it was as if he had turned strategic magician: he waved a wand and, as his audience watched in rapt attention, vanished both himself and the core of his army.

For those in Washington and the North, this was worrisome; in the South, it was a nightmare. P. G. T. Beauregard, whom Jefferson Davis had designated to somehow concoct an overall Confederate strategy in the West, agonized over where Sherman might be heading and how to choreograph a response. Based on past performance, Augusta or Macon, both munitions and manufacturing centers, were the logical choices. Of the two, Macon, swelled with refugee workers from Atlanta, seemed the best bet, and Beauregard sent Richard Taylor there with all the troops he could spare to stage a defense.

This was exactly what Sherman wanted him to conclude; he even sent Kilpatrick's cavalry and Howard's wing feinting in that direction.[31] Like Johnston, Beauregard was a good general but a conventional thinker, and therefore he did not guess that Sherman had changed the game yet again. Now his objectives were psychological. What he wanted to do was besmirch the image of the Confederacy. And for this sort of thing, there was no better destination than state capitals. Taking up where he'd left off in Jackson, Mississippi, his

March was destined to be a tour of them—in his mind the viper's nests of the rebellion, the very localities from which secession had sprung.

They headed first toward Milledgeville, Georgia's seat of government. On the way, his army became a living embodiment of his famous Field Order No. 120, stalking along at "about fifteen miles a day," foraging "liberally on the country," and, should guerrillas or citizens interfere, "enforce[ing] a devastation more or less relentless"[32]—a big human land shark, in other words.

While the great majority of soldiers remained in the columns, marching along with their units, it was the foragers (or "bummers," as they were soon being called) who largely earned the March its reputation, put their distinctive mark on it with a torrent of crazy stolen costumes, antic behavior, and darkly funny anecdotes. If you were a boy in blue, you might have thought of them as a kind of traveling entertainment and catering service, coming in every night after a hard day's march laden with food and stories that would keep you laughing for half the night.

"Fun" is not a word usually associated with a military campaign, but compared with what they were used to, this walk through Georgia was shaping up as a frolic for Sherman's army—no sign of battle, plenty to eat, and interesting things to do besides marching. Many got to indulge their skills at creative destruction on almost a daily basis—tearing up railroad tracks, smashing cotton gins and anything that looked military-industrial, and setting fire to the dwellings of prominent Confederate functionaries when they could find them.

Of course, one man's "fun" could be and frequently was another's disaster. For Southerners who actually experienced a visit from Sherman's foragers, it was a terrifying and humiliating occurrence. The fact that Joseph Wheeler's Confederate cavalry were helping themselves to agricultural resources in virtually the same manner did not mitigate the fact that these were Yankees, whose sneering demeanor was epitomized by the words of one bummer: "We're Bill Sherman's raiders—you'd better git."[33]

Many white Southerners did, fleeing at the last moment. But those who stayed—while they may have been personally insulted, vexed as their soon-to-be-ex-slaves led the bluecoats to the consumables, or horrified as they watched their houses go up in flames because concealed arms or symbols of particular Confederate enthusiasm had been found—were never lined up and shot or mass raped. It's easy to forget that the military past is filled with such atrocities; that as this is written, we are separated by less than seventy years from the worst episodes of this kind in human history; or that this was exactly what went on in supposedly postmodern Europe in places such as Srebrenica as recently as 1995. Many of these Yankees had been campaigning since 1861; they had seen lots of friends die and had scores to settle. But never this way. Instead, they displayed remarkable (admittedly, relative) self-control in their depredations—frightening Southerners, making them feel unprotected by their supposed government, transmitting exactly the message Sherman wanted to send. It's a rare army that can do such a thing, for it demands not merely military discipline, but self-discipline.

Nor was there any stopping them, as was made tragically clear six days into the March in the thrifty little town of Griswoldville, the home of a pistol factory. The Union cavalry had already trashed the installation, so a brigade of infantry from the Fifteenth Corps on the right wing was resting when someone looked up to discover three brigades of Georgia militia from nearby Macon, plus artillery lined up across a broad field, ready to charge.

Almost without orders, these veterans from the Midwest moved into line, found cover where they could, and opened fire when the Confederates got within 250 yards. The rebels who survived remembered the Yankee fire as being continuous. This was because several regiments were now equipped with Spencer seven-shot repeating rifles, and the results were murderous. Before it was over, they inflicted nearly ten times the number of casualties they had suffered, many of them "old grey-haired and weakly-looking men and little boys not over 15 years old."[34] The South really was a hollow shell; this army could go anywhere it wanted.

Not surprisingly, Sherman arrived in Milledgeville with the left wing unscathed. As they neared, an aide turned to him: "First act of drama well played General!" "Yes sir," he replied. "The first act is well played."[35] He spent a night in the governor's mansion, sleeping on the floor. The boys were in a good mood; some officers took over the capital building, held a mock assembly, and rescinded Georgia's ordinance of secession. But then, improbably in the midst of a Thanksgiving Day feast, several escaped prisoners from Andersonville wandered in. Emaciated and in rags, they wept at the sight of so much food and the American flag.

This was not soon forgotten; the party mood was over. Before they left town, the boys ransacked the state's offices and library, leaving Confederate records scattered like dandruff. Meanwhile, Kilpatrick reported that several of his men had been summarily executed after they had surrendered, and the corpses of bummers were being discovered with their throats slit or hanging from trees.[36] Grimly, Sherman told his cavalry commander to inform Wheeler that if substantial evidence was obtained of rebel soldiers committing these excesses, retaliation in kind would be authorized.[37] From this point, the March would get harder—both in physical difficulty and in application.

Sherman's road show resumed on November 24. This time he headed toward Millen, which left open the possibility of a bolt to Augusta. William Hardee, given the unenviable task of organizing a regional defense after his exile from Hood's army, was nearly certain that Sherman would bypass Augusta for Savannah. But the importance of the former city's arsenal caused him to hesitate, sending Wheeler's cavalry to help out with the defense.[38] So the Yankees made it to Millen unopposed, tearing up track as they went, at which point Sherman pivoted southeast and removed all doubt: they were headed to Savannah.

The objective was in a sense reflective of the man. As adventurous and risky as the March may have seemed, William Tecumseh Sherman remained all about cutting risk. His army was in excellent shape and could have continued its land shark path in virtually any direction. But Sherman chose an objective where it could rest and reestablish communications and supply lines, in this case courtesy of the U.S. Navy—a contingency he had already arranged and was banking on when he arrived. In the meantime, his intent having been re-vealed, the March became a race: the faster he could get to Savan-nah, the less time the rebels had to organize its defenses and block his access to the sea.

Earlier, Sherman had assumed a low-key approach to command by letting Howard and Slocum manage their wings independently. Now they would operate in close concert, squeezed together in as tight and fast-moving a formation as possible.[39] The countryside changed from rich farms to scarcely inhabited longleaf pine forests, a dead zone for foragers and further incentive to move swiftly.

Crossing rivers quickly was imperative, since they were natural points of defense—particularly the Ogeechee—where small bodies of Confederates might stop his army in its tracks. But the skill and speed of his pontoon-bridging regiments proved to be all he could have hoped. "The facility in crossing this country of many rivers and insufficient roads was one of the hardest blows inflicted on the Con-federates," Sherman maintained.[40]

Also of note in this regard were pioneer units increasingly made up of freedmen, who attached themselves to the March and subse-quently proved extremely useful lugging bridge components, cor-duroying roads, and blazing trails. This was no time to get lost, and Sherman by now habitually met with local blacks, relying on them almost exclusively for information on the local roads. "'Don't want white man,' says Sherman," one of his aides recorded.[41] In fact, through both their brawn and brains, African Americans were help-ing to push Sherman's army through territory one participant la-beled "swamp, swampy, swampier"—fighting the friction of war at a key point when slowing down might mean disaster. This is why what happened at Ebenezer Creek on December 9 just twenty miles from Savannah remains tragically ironic, even to this day.

The commander of the Fourteenth Corps, the coincidentally named Jefferson C. Davis, was another of Sherman's serviceable vil-lains. Competent and aggressive, he was also a blunt instrument and a notably bad-tempered one. In 1862, he had shot and killed his commanding officer during an argument but had avoided trial be-cause of the Union's desperate need for good field commanders.

And as he approached Ebenezer Creek, he was plainly not in a good mood: his corps was behind Sherman's schedule, picking its way through the swamp and intermittent roadways.[42] The throng of African Americans who had attached themselves seemed to be making matters worse, slowing everything down. In Davis's eyes, they should have stayed on their plantations. Now he saw a way to get rid of them.

Once the Fifty-eighth Indiana had thrown a bridge across the hundred-foot ribbon of water, the engineers were ordered to take up the pontoons and let none of the blacks cross. The details of what happened next are open to some dispute, but the overall effect was apparent. Wheeler's cavalry had been following, yapping at the heels of the columns, and when the crowd of freedmen realized they were caught between the rebels and the river, a number threw themselves in and drowned. Some may have been shot or beaten by the Confederates, hundreds were sent back to their former owners.

Davis likely assumed he had come away clean, having stripped down his columns so they could make better time. But he was mistaken. The military aide to Brigadier General Absalom Baird, Major James Connolly, was enraged by the "inhuman, barbarous proceeding" and determined to bring it to light. Ten days later, he had finished the draft of a letter he would send to the Senate Military Affairs Committee, the substance of which would be published in the *New York Tribune*. What happened at Ebenezer Creek would not be forgotten.[43]

Had he heard about it at the time, racing against the clock and nervous, Sherman probably would have approved, though he certainly didn't order it, nor would he have done it himself. But as he approached the coast, the situation was nearing a crisis. The army was getting hungry, and there were no signs of available food. Had they arrived too late to grab Savannah without a struggle?

Initially, the situation didn't look good. There were only five narrow corridors of approach, and Hardee had already ordered his men to flood the salt marshes and rice fields, construct an inner parapet, and train most of the city's artillery inland.[44] To make matters worse, the way down the Ogeechee to the sea was blocked by Fort McAllister, an apparently formidable structure that had already survived eight separate Union naval bombardments.[45]

Sherman had no trouble sorting his priorities. He ordered an assault on the fort as soon as William Hazen's division could be deployed on December 13. He watched from the other side of the river, on a rice mill's roof, pacing and worrying that Hazen would not manage to attack before sundown. Then, in the midst of these jitters, he looked up and saw a puff of smoke out in the sound, one that in minutes turned into a vessel flying the flag of the U.S. Navy. Sherman signaled: CAN YOU ASSIST WITH THE HEAVY GUNS? The reply was equally direct: BEING ONLY A TUG BOAT NO HEAVY GUNS ABOARD. This was followed a few minutes later by: IS FORT MCALLISTER TAKEN? Sherman now had no doubt: NOT YET BUT IT WILL BE IN A MINUTE.[46]

Actually, it took fifteen. As if on cue, Hazen's troops burst out of the woods and charged over a minefield (the pressure-sensitive buried "torpedoes" so incensed Sherman that he had Confederate prisoners dig them up), punched through an abatis full of spikes, and swarmed over the entrenchments for a brief bout of hand-to-hand fighting before overwhelming the defenders at a cost of eleven dead and eighty wounded.[47] Given the implications, it was a small price to pay, and Sherman knew it. "I've got Savannah!" he whooped, messaging Slocum: "Take a good big drink, a long breath and then yell like the devil."[48] When the rest of the army realized what had happened, a great roar of approval and relief rolled through their camps. "Hello, Yanks," some rebel pickets called across the lines. "What's all that yelling about?" "Fort McAllister's taken—the cracker line is open—that's what's the matter—how are you, Johnny!"[49]

Not good. Once Sherman had firmly linked up with Admiral John Dahlgren's flotilla, he knew he had access to large-caliber siege guns that could fire into the heart of Savannah. A bloody infantry assault would not be necessary; he could simply pummel the defenders into submission. P. G. T. Beauregard, in town for an inspection, could see that and angrily prodded Hardee to hasten work on the pontoon bridge across the Savannah River that would constitute the only escape route to South Carolina for his troops.

Curiously, Sherman seemed in no hurry. When an enterprising

subordinate outlined a plan to push two brigades into the Palmetto State to cut off this line of retreat, he greeted it with moody silence.[50] On the night of December 20, he was not even with the army—having left to arrange for delivery of the siege guns—when Hardee's own batteries erupted, lobbing shells over the heavy fog. Union troops sensed something was happening. "I think our officers knew they were going and did not try to stop them," one recalled, "for we could hear them all night moving about."[51] By two a.m., there was only silence: the rebels were gone. Although he expressed some concern to his ever-demanding father-in-law that he had not caught the garrison, many in the army concluded that Sherman had left the way open—that their Uncle Billy was looking out for his boys and was no longer about battles anyway.[52]

Sherman claimed in his official report that the March to the Sea inflicted $100 million of damage on Georgia's infrastructure. He actually had no idea; this was a symbolic figure chosen to reflect what had been a campaign of focused targeting and instructive damage. So too the peaceful occupation of Savannah. It sent a message of inevitability, and he announced it with a dramatist's flair in a cable to Abraham Lincoln on December 22: "I beg to present you as a Christmas gift the city of Savannah, with one hundred and fifty heavy guns and plenty of ammunition, also about twenty-five thousand bales of cotton, W. T. Sherman, Major-General."[53]

3

As it unfolded, Sherman's whole strategic scheme—the March to the Sea and sending the Rock to deal with Hood—caused official Washington increasing worry. Lincoln was particularly concerned about Sherman's whereabouts. In effect, the commander of the West and sixty-two thousand friends and colleagues had disappeared for more than a month. When John approached him for news of his brother, the president was downcast: "Oh, no, we have heard nothing from him. We know what hole he went in, but we don't know what hole he will come out of."[54] Newspapers took to counting the days

since Sherman cut the telegraph and dove into the Georgia countryside. At one point, Lincoln became so preoccupied that he had to
apologize to a guest he ignored in a receiving line, explaining: "I was
thinking of a man down south."[55] Around the same time, a colonel in
charge of delivering the missing army's mail asked the president if
he had any personal message. Taking the man's hand and near tears,
Lincoln replied: "Say to General Sherman for me, whenever and
wherever you meet him, God bless him, and God bless his army!"[56]

Adding to the pressure was the campaign in Tennessee. As might
be expected given the participants, Thomas and Hood, it was taking
place slowly and also strangely. Hood's original plan—invading the
Volunteer State, defeating the Yankees in detail, then marching to
Virginia to join Lee and destroy Grant—struck Beauregard as oth-
erworldly; but with no alternative and knowing Jefferson Davis's
proclivities, he told Hood to go ahead.[57] Had the forty thousand soldiers of the much-abused Army of Tennessee known of this opium
dream of a war plan, they might never have budged. But they were
going home and had been led to believe there would be no more
wild and crazy combat, so they marched into the state in relatively
good humor. Nathan Bedford Forrest, the expedition's cavalry commander, predicted: "Hood would come out of Tennessee faster than
he entered."[58]

Surprisingly, the initial moves went to Hood, who maneuvered
his army between Schofield and Thomas back in Nashville. But on
the night of November 29, Schofield managed to slip the better part
of two corps past the Confederates and set up in Franklin down the
road. Reverting to type, Hood went after them like an angry bear
and the next day ordered multiple frontal assaults, beating his army
to pieces and taking seven thousand casualties, three times the
Union total. Not satisfied, he followed the Yankees to Nashville and
strung his infantry, now reduced to barely twenty thousand, across
the high ground overlooking the city's defenses, behind which were
now fifty thousand Federal soldiers along with one very patient
Rock of Chickamauga.

That was the problem. As far as Stanton and Grant were concerned, George Thomas was impossibly slow. In the tension-filled

Sherman and his boys, on their best behavior, marching in Savannah. *Library of Congress*

atmosphere of Washington, it seemed as though he were doing nothing. Grant bombarded his subordinate with cables urging action and was ready to relieve him. But nothing would move Thomas off his tectonic pace of preparation. Hood wasn't going anywhere and could not be reinforced, so Thomas took his time and made sure his forces were ready. When the attack finally came on December 15—a feint to Hood's right, followed by a crushing blow to his left—it was such a success that he used it again the next day, this time shattering the Confederates, causing thousands to surrender, and sending the remainder out of Tennessee more of a crowd than an army. Only Forrest, through sheer force of will, prevented complete military evaporation. The Rock had done his job.

Sherman reappeared less than a week after the good news came in from Nashville, setting off a wave of euphoria among Union supporters. His strategic plan had worked perfectly. While Grant remained mired in northern Virginia, Sherman kept coming up with new ways to confound Confederates, beating them at all levels. He arrived on the coast with around ten thousand African Americans, making him the de facto pied piper of emancipation and giving the lie to the Southern claim that their slaves were ultimately satisfied with their condition. Instead, they had voted with their feet, and Sherman was in Savannah to prove it.[59]

This was why the news of what happened at Ebenezer Creek was so troubling to official Washington and the administration. Sherman's reputation in this regard was hardly sacrosanct, and Halleck, always a bellwether, warned him that he was thought by some to "have manifested an almost criminal dislike to the negro."[60]

One of these was probably Secretary of War Stanton, who would arrive in Savannah aboard a revenue cutter on January 11 for a heart-to-heart on race relations with everybody's general du jour.

Sherman had arrived in Savannah in exemplary conqueror mode, driving home his point yet again: Once you give up, you are my fellow citizens. He quickly reached a deal with the mayor that released the abandoned Confederate rice stores to civilians, and by mid-January, boatloads of donated food from the North were coming ashore.[61] Local government would be sanctioned, businesses opened, and citizens encouraged to resume their normal lives. His boys were equally well behaved, and just to make sure, he spent a good deal of time marching them around Savannah's principal streets in a series of reviews. It was also a way of letting the army see for itself what it had become. Sherman himself amazed his ragged warriors by appearing in full-dress uniform. "Uncle Billy's dolled up like a duke," one proclaimed.[62]

You might say he was in costume, the principal player in his own theater of national unification. As usual he was everywhere, attending Christmas services, looking up old acquaintances, paying social calls, even partying with his officers and selected locals, and as always talking to anybody who wanted to talk to him. That included a number of African Americans, who were extremely grateful for what he had done. He treated them graciously and attentively, which proved fortuitous.

Edwin Stanton was not one to be taken lightly. A Democrat, he had reluctantly taken over the War Department from corrupt Simon Cameron in mid-1862 and then, through sheer energy and efficiency, had managed to effectively orchestrate the overall Union war effort, adopting in the process the radical Republican agenda and becoming one of Lincoln's key advisers. He was also notoriously rude and utterly vindictive when crossed.

When he met the secretary, Sherman was not in the best state of mind. Always mercurial, he had been made more so by recent events. He had just learned that his newborn son, Charles, whom he had never seen, had died on December 4 and was already buried. Sherman might also have been feeling the effects of what might easily be termed riotous success. If Grant had a problem with alcohol, Sherman at this point was a bit tipsy on Sherman—a man in full, full of schemes, some of them too clever for their own good.

After some initial sparring over the character of Jefferson Davis (Northern version), Stanton produced newspaper clippings detailing what had transpired at Ebenezer Creek and demanded an explanation. Sherman produced Davis himself, who seems to have put up enough of a defense to mollify the secretary.[63]

But he was far from finished. Next, he told Sherman he wanted to interview a number of black people. On short notice, Sherman managed to put together a roster of around twenty of those he considered "the most intelligent of the negroes." Once they were assembled, Stanton pulled another surprise and told Sherman to leave the room.

But if he thought he had turned the tables, he was mistaken. When he asked the black leaders what they thought of the general and his commitment to their cause, they called Sherman "a friend and gentleman" and told Stanton they "could not be in better hands." Some have attributed this to fear and a wariness of white people; but this seems unfair. In the eyes of these men, Sherman had treated black people kindly and delivered a multitude of their brothers and sisters to freedom. He may not have been the Great Emancipator, but he certainly was an effective one, and they seemed to have recognized that.

It's hard to believe Stanton wasn't pleasantly surprised, as from this perspective, at least, Sherman appeared to be on the side of the angels. Following the meeting, he urged the general to come up with something positive and concrete that could be done for freedmen. Probably Stanton would have been satisfied if Sherman had integrated a few black regiments into his combat elements. Instead, when some arrived by sea, he stripped them of their arms, gave them picks and shovels, and turned them into teamsters and pioneers.[64]

Sherman had something more spectacular in mind for the secretary of war. He dangled the prospect of setting aside for freedmen the abandoned land on the Sea Islands off the coasts of Georgia and South Carolina, and Stanton jumped at it.[65] Together they worked through several drafts of Special Field Orders No. 15, outlining a scheme by which heads of families might enlist and in return eventually receive forty-acre parcels of these lands—on paper, what one historian called the "single most revolutionary act in race relations in the Civil War."[66] But it was also utterly without implementation, beyond appointing a subordinate "Inspector of Settlements and Plantations" (Sherman told President Andrew Johnson in 1866 that he always believed it to be an emergency wartime measure without permanent standing).[67] What the general had managed in No. 15 was a strategist's version of bait and switch, at once a magnetic distraction for black people and sufficiently high-minded to leave the secretary, as he told Ellen, "cured of that Negro nonsense."[68] But as is inevitable with scams, the glitter wore off this one, not soon enough to complicate Sherman's getaway, but later and with shocking results. Edwin Stanton was the wrong man to snooker.

Meanwhile, Sherman was starting to have trouble with his friends. Back in Washington, shouldering Grant's administrative load and sitting on a bad case of hemorrhoids, Henry Halleck couldn't have avoided considering the reversal of fortunes between him and his old rival from Monterey days, the hapless lieutenant William Sherman. There was a picture of the new Sherman, Sherman the conqueror, taken outside Atlanta, ramrod straight aboard a huge black stallion. Halleck probably had not seen it, but he was a military man and knew what years in the field meant in terms of fitness, as opposed to his own physique, ever more potbellied and frog-eyed. He may have performed administrative miracles at a desk, but he knew he was sliding steadily in Washington's pecking order.

This was not a man immune to jealousy. In Sherman's case, it began with backbiting. Compared with his praise for the takedown of Johnston and Atlanta, Halleck was barely lukewarm over the

Sherman tall in the saddle, outside Atlanta. *Library of Congress*

March to the Sea, conceding that "his campaign has been quite a success" while letting it be known privately that he was not happy with Sherman for allowing Hardee's force to escape.[69] There was more to come, for it would end with backstabbing.

Even before he took Savannah, Sherman's biggest problem had become Grant. Unexpectedly, Grant's aide Orville Babcock arrived right after the capture of Fort McAllister, carrying a letter from his boss dated December 6 that ordered Sherman "with the balance of your command to come here by water with all dispatch." There was no mistaking this message: "I want more men to throw at Lee, and I want them fast." And it was exactly the opposite of what his wingman wanted to do, like asking a surfer to kick out of the wave of a lifetime while it's still building.

Sherman spent most of the morning crafting his response; it was long, but also slick. Of course he would come with fifty or sixty thousand infantry, but since it would take a while to accumulate the necessary ships, he might as well do something constructive, like taking Savannah. He also noted that while transport by ship would require four weeks and men are never much good after a long sea voyage, a healthy and vindictive march through Columbia and then on to Raleigh (both state capitals) would take only six and would accomplish so much more. "I do sincerely believe that the whole United States, North and South, would rejoice to have this army turned loose on South Carolina." Finally, to make himself completely clear, he closed with, "I feel a personal dislike to turning northward."[70]

Grant surrendered, pretty much unconditionally. It's easy to imagine him shaking his head and chuckling as he read his friend's reply. "The season was bad, the roads impassable for anything except such an army as he had, and I should not have thought of ordering such a move."[71] But since Sherman suggested it and made the case brilliantly, it was worth doing—by now part of the established routine between the two of them, giving the wingman permission to fly alone.

4

Shortly before Sherman invaded, a Georgia militiaman was confronted by a squad of South Carolinians who asked "what in hell we meant by letting Sherman march through Georgia," to which he replied: "You will have a chance of it in a few days, for he is surely coming, and you will not be able to stop him either."[72] Actually, the move into South Carolina posed dangers and difficulties far greater than its Georgia equivalent; the rivers and adjacent wetlands were swollen with winter rains, potentially enabling small forces to slow his army to a crawl. (Always hedging, Sherman told the navy where on the coast he would be, in case he had to withdraw.)[73] Everything depended on alacrity, moving before the enemy figured out where he was—that and his men's energy and enthusiasm to chew through the swampy terrain and get at the rest of the state.

With admirable ingenuousness, Sherman would later write in his memoirs: "Somehow, our men had got the idea that South Carolina was the cause of all our troubles."[74] Of course, he knew at the time that his men were aching to get at the Palmetto State. "I have never burnt a house down yet," one corporal wrote his sister, "but if we go into South Carolina I will burn som[e] down if I can get the chance."[75] But Sherman also knew it would stop at arson, that he could turn up the heat on the very place they had learned to hate and still trust his army not to go apocalyptic. As usual, they would send exactly the message he wanted to transmit, a vengeful message but not a disgraceful one. For in the end, Sherman was still waging war on the Confederate mind. If South Carolinians "entertained an undue fear of our Western men…had invented such ghostlike stories of our prowess in Georgia, that they were scared by their own inventions…this was a power, and I intended to utilize it."[76]

Barely three weeks after taking Savannah, Sherman recommenced the road show, sending most of two corps into Beaufort, South Carolina, to clear the way for the rest. Operationally, nothing had changed: two wings—the right under Howard, the left under Slocum—each divided into two flanking columns, with Kilpatrick's cavalry screening and roaming.[77] He was also up to his usual tricks. "I will feint on Augusta & Charleston, avoid both and make for Columbia," he told Ellen in confidence.[78]

But before he could do that, he had to get through what must have seemed eternal swamp. Once again, the bridging regiments proved exceedingly useful, but several times the men had to wade through icy water up to their necks to keep moving. Also, the passage of the wagons and artillery demanded that most roads be corduroyed with freshly cut timber, sometimes in several layers to overcome the ooze. This was an enormous job, and many of the infantry pitched in. But it was the African American pioneers who shone, leading one historian to state that the army never would have made it through without them.[79] Unlike intelligence, this was a tangible benefit, something Sherman could see. These men were helping him traverse the swamp at a vital juncture; they were a critical part of his army, the cutting edge. And they punched through in

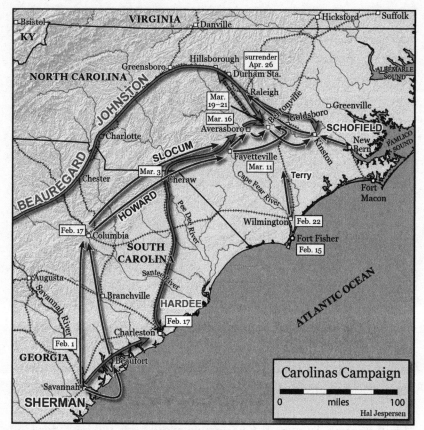

about ten days, reaching the South Carolina railroad, which the army promptly began to tear apart. But this was only a temporary diversion.

South Carolinian conventional wisdom, already jolted that anyone should invade the state at this time of year from this direction, no doubt assumed Charleston would be Sherman's target, given its role at the start of the Civil War. On the other hand, many considered Columbia to be one of the most secure places in the South, with families on the coast stashing their valuables there for safekeeping.[80] They failed to consider that not only was the city a munitions manufacturing center, it was the capital of the first state to secede from the Union. That may previously have been an item of local pride. But if you thought like Sherman and there was a nest of treason to be found, Columbia was in your crosshairs.

"Accidentally on purpose" is hardly a valid concept of historical causation, yet it's awfully tempting to apply it to the demise of Columbia. Actually, it started before the Yankees arrived. To keep them from the invaders, Wade Hampton's retreating Confederate cavalry had torn up and set fire to cotton bales stacked in the city's main streets before they left. Then, as the tough Fifteenth Corps marched in on February 17, 1865, some of the men were heard singing: "Hail, Columbia, happy land. If I don't burn you, I'll be damned."[81] From then on, it became a matter of piling on more incendiary material.

Twelve hundred Northern prisoners of war, all of them officers, had been held in Columbia before being evacuated as Sherman's force neared. But around fifty had managed to hide themselves in the confusion and were now free, very angry, and carrying the addresses of Columbians who had spat on them as captives, along with those of notorious Confederates such as Dr. John Cheves, the inventor of the hated land mines encountered outside of Savannah.[82] To say these men had a short fuse and a strong desire for fire understates the matter.

Then there was the alcohol. As Sherman rode in, a soldier in a long-figured dressing gown and a plug hat greeted him: "I have the honor (hic) to present (hic) you with (hic) the freedom of the (hic) City."[83] Many other soldiers were already similarly inebriated and in nowhere near as good a mood. Throughout the day and into the night, freed slaves would lead the boys in blue to caches of wine and liquor, fueling what was remembered as a cast of thousands, riotous, arson-punctuated drunk.

Finally, there was Mother Nature. A sudden gale whipped up in the night and began to spread the burning tufts of cotton all over the city, fluffy balls of fire adding to what was quickly becoming a flaming disaster. Around three a.m., General John Oliver's brigade, on Sherman's orders, marched into the city to put out the fires and put down the riot, eventually arresting nearly twenty-five hundred soldiers and civilians. But by dawn, a third of the place had burned, including the business district and best residential streets.[84]

Sherman was not about to shoulder the blame. "Your Governor is responsible for this," he told a local minister. "Who ever heard of an evacuated city to be left a depot of liquor for an army to occupy?"[85]

He consigned them five hundred head of cattle so they wouldn't starve and a hundred muskets to maintain order, but that was about the extent of his redress for Columbia. He certainly hadn't ordered it; some Union troops had tried to keep the fires from spreading; and relatively few civilians were actually hurt or killed. But in the end, the cradle of the Confederacy went up in smoke.

Sherman wasn't sorry, nor would he ever be. On the plane he was now waging war, it had been the climactic moment in his horror show for Southern edification, and he later claimed it was the death-blow for the rebellion. "From the moment my army passed Columbia S.C. the war was ended."[86] Not quite, but almost.

From beginning to end, Sherman's boys were hard on the state—burning portions of Gillisonville, Grahamville, Hardeeville, McPhersonville, Springfield, Lawtonville, Barnwell, Blackville, Midway, Orangeburg, and Lexington on the way to Columbia, then torching parts of Camden, Winnsboro, Lancaster, Chesterfield, and Cheraw on their way to the North Carolina border.[87] Explaining his incendiary behavior, one soldier caught the mood of most when he berated a merchant whose store was on fire: "Say, did you and your folks think of this when you hurrahed for secession before the war?"[88] Meanwhile, their procession through the state left a corridor fifty miles wide picked so clean of edibles that a Confederate prisoner maintained "a crow could not fly across it without a haversack."[89]

But in North Carolina the end really was in sight, and that required a different approach. Sherman let it be known he wanted his marchers to "deal as moderately and fairly by the North Carolinians as possible, and fan the flame of discord . . . between them and their proud cousins of South Carolina."[90] Message sent and received: the boys immediately throttled back the destruction. Shortly after reaching Fayetteville on March 11, the marchers regained contact with the outside world. This meant reestablishing a real supply chain in the near future and a halt to living off the land and the people who occupied it.

As always near the end of a war, the operational and strategic picture became increasingly fluid. Overall, Sherman was plainly headed for Grant with the intent of placing Lee in a giant pincer that would

Like many towns in South Carolina, McPhersonville burned when Sherman's boys arrived. *Library of Congress*

force him to withdraw from Petersburg and take his chances in the field. In Sherman's way, or trying to be, was a scratch force of about twenty thousand put together by the yet again renascent Joseph Johnston, now in command in the Carolinas, from Hardee's Savannah evacuees, Hampton's cavalry, and dispirited remnants of Hood's army railroaded east.[91] Johnston didn't have much chance, but his best shot was to try to defeat Sherman in detail before he reached the supply base at Goldsboro and linked up with thirty thousand more Yankees under Schofield and Alfred H. Terry.[92]

On March 16, two of his divisions waged a delaying action against four of Sherman's at Averasborough, learning in the process that the two wings of the Yankee army were separated by at least a dozen miles. Johnston accordingly massed his infantry on the road near Bentonville, directly in the path of Slocum's wing strung out in marching order, putting it in dire jeopardy. Slocum fought ferociously until the next day, March 21, when Sherman arrived with Howard's wing, and the tables were turned. Mower's division easily broke through on Johnston's left but was immediately called back by Sherman, allowing the rebels to retreat into the night.

He later claimed that he was interested primarily in getting to

Goldsboro's supplies and reinforcements;[93] but this was the second time in succession that Sherman had declined to pulverize a Confederate force when he was in a position to do so. Still, this may say less about his merciful side than it does about his entire approach during the March. Implicitly, at least, inflicting defeat was now more about imposing despair than it was about destroying armies.[94]

When Sherman reached Goldsboro the day after Bentonville, he considered the March over as a military operation.[95] It had been a remarkable success, and not just on the psychological level. It stands as one of the most memorable and successful treks in military history—and also one of the last. In a matter of four months, he had brazenly paraded an army of sixty thousand through six hundred miles of enemy territory, taking what was wanted and daring anyone to stop them. When they arrived, they were not only intact as a fighting force—having suffered fewer than four thousand total casualties—but probably healthier and even more confident than when they started.[96] "Splendid legs," Sherman erupted as he watched them marching by, "splendid legs. Would give both of mine for any one of them."[97] They had certainly served him well; but now the context was shifting, and at long last the endgame was at hand.

5

As soon as the railroad could take him, Sherman headed for Grant's headquarters at City Point along the James River in Virginia, arriving on March 27. After about an hour of catching up, Grant informed him that Abraham Lincoln was docked nearby aboard the *River Queen* and that the two of them ought to drop in on him. Just how spontaneous this visit actually was remains open to question, but it's a safe bet that after the results of the 1864 election, Lincoln was more than happy to be reunited with Sherman, who in turn regaled him with stories of the March to the Sea and the exploits of his bummers. More important, they agreed to meet the following day to discuss winding down the war.

The three were to be joined by the generals' old friend from the

Sherman dominating the conversation in G. P. A. Healy's *The Peacemakers. The White House Historical Association (White House Collection)*

swamp David Dixon Porter—who recorded what was said that night—and the confab would be made famous by George Healy's subsequent painting *The Peacemakers.* It may not be great art, but it certainly seems true to character: Sherman facing the others and plainly doing most of the talking, Porter and Grant looking somewhat glazed, and Lincoln leaning forward in rapt attention.

When it came time for the president to speak, he was emphatic about sparing further bloodshed and very willing to give the rebels "the most liberal and honorable terms" for surrender. When the generals demurred that the strategic situation left little choice in the matter, Lincoln, according to Porter, urged them to err on the side of generosity: "I want no one punished; treat them liberally all round."[98] Other things may have been said, but this was certainly the message Sherman took away from the gathering—not coincidentally, one that meshed with his own hard war/soft peace approach.

Just before leaving to rejoin his army, Sherman received a note from Stanton: "God speed you; and . . . shield you from every danger, and crown you with victory, is my earnest prayer."[99] Coming from someone normally as chilly as the secretary of war, this was not only out of character, it was suspiciously effusive, and other men might have taken it as a warning. Not Sherman.

Events came in a cascade in April, which began with Lee's evacuation of Petersburg and the Confederate abandonment of Richmond. Eight days later, Grant received the surrender of the Army of Northern Virginia from Lee, effectively ending the Civil War. Technically, however, all the remaining Confederate forces, including Johnston's, remained at large.[100]

In announcing the surrender at Appomattox, Sherman told his troops: "A little more labor, a little more toil on our part, the great race is won and our Government stands regenerated."[101] Then he sent them to Raleigh, the latest destination on the state capitals tour and Johnston's temporary resting spot. He was gone by the time they arrived, and Sherman immediately held a review—one soldier remembered him standing on the state capital grounds as a "sea of bayonets" passed in what had become Uncle Billy's standard Confederate exorcism.[102]

But it was premature, and he knew it. Sherman was clearly worried about Johnston's army, not for its combat potential, but for the prospect that it might dissolve into a host of guerrillas, as might the other Confederate forces.[103] The possibility that men like Forrest (who somehow survived and subsequently helped found the Ku Klux Klan) would lead them in what amounted to perpetual war was not implausible and preyed on Sherman's mind.[104] He needed to pacify this army and do it quickly.

Actually, Johnston knew he was beaten and had no intention of fostering an insurgency. After conferring with Jefferson Davis, he wrote Sherman on April 14 requesting a suspension of operations so that they could "enter into the needful arrangements to terminate the existing war." It was exactly what Sherman wanted to hear, and they agreed to meet on April 17.

That morning, just as Sherman was about to board the train for the meeting site near Durham, a telegraph operator raced up to inform him of a critical ciphered message. "It was from Mr. Stanton," Sherman later wrote, "announcing the assassination of Mr. Lincoln, the attempt on the life of Mr. Seward . . . and a suspicion that a like fate was designed for General Grant and all the principal officers of the Government."[105] He swore the operator to secrecy and then let the train proceed.

What he was thinking on that short ride will never fully be known. But it's hardly a stretch to assume that this news meshed with Sherman's nightmare scenario of perpetual insurgency. This was a true emergency, and bold action seemed necessary—especially since he had never received Stanton's coded cable to Grant forbidding him to deal with political questions when negotiating with Lee.[106] And Sherman was in no mood to shirk responsibility. He had fought the Civil War from beginning to end to drive the seceding states back into the Union. Once this was accomplished, he had always maintained he would greet them with magnanimity—the kind of magnanimity that would preclude an insurgency. This was Bill Sherman's war, and very suddenly Fate had given him the opportunity to conclude it on that basis. Besides, wasn't generosity what the martyred president had insisted upon the last time he had seen him alive?

Sherman and Johnston had never met, but judging by their close postwar friendship and Sherman's impulsive nature, he probably liked Johnston from the beginning. Once they were alone, Sherman handed Johnston the fated telegram and then watched closely as he broke out into a sweat. Appropriately enough, Johnston denounced the acts as a disgrace and hoped they would not be charged to the Confederate government. Sherman remained skeptical, suggesting that once his men found out, Raleigh's fate might make Columbia's look pale. But Johnston only got more agreeable; he was ready to surrender his entire army immediately, just as Sherman wanted. He even pitched working a deal that would embrace all Confederate forces everywhere, a dazzling proposal that seems to have blinded Sherman to the fact that he was dealing with another cagey strategist.[107] They agreed that Johnston needed civilian approval to negotiate for all rebel armies and then adjourned for the night.

The next day, the Confederate general assured Sherman he had the necessary authority over Southern forces and suggested they be joined by John Breckinridge, the wily former U.S. vice president and currently Confederate secretary of war. Sherman was hesitant, but he agreed. Now he was outnumbered—about to face not one, but two clever interlocutors. Breckinridge arrived with a draft agreement, which Sherman claims to have rejected as "general and verbose." Yet his own final version was, in the words of biographer John Marszalek, "strikingly similar."[108]

If you were a Southerner, it was a sweetheart of a deal. Upon disbanding, Confederate armies were to deposit their weapons at arsenals located in their own capitals. Existing state governments were to be recognized once they swore a loyalty oath and Federal courts had been reestablished. The political rights of all individuals in seceding states were guaranteed, and no one would be punished for activities during the war as long as they maintained the peace. "In general terms—the war to cease; a general amnesty."[109] They might have been instructions on a utensil: "*Status quo ante bellum;* no reconstruction required." As for slavery, since the two Southerners conceded verbally that it "was dead," Sherman saw no reason to mention it.

Earlier, Sherman was described as tipsy on himself; this document reflects serious inebriation. In forwarding it to Halleck, he was happy to announce that it would "prevent Confederate armies from breaking up into guerilla bands" and suggested that the new president, Andrew Johnson, "if possible not... vary the terms at all, for I have considered everything."[110] His own subordinates, Slocum and the politically savvy John Logan, along with Major Henry Hitchcock, the factotum who delivered it, all expected a toxic reception.[111] Grant had to read it just once to know it wouldn't fly, and he passed it forward to Stanton and President Johnson along with a recommendation that the cabinet meet immediately.[112]

These reactions were mild compared with the secretary of war's. He had been diddled once by Sherman in Savannah. Now, like some sort of military dictator, he wanted to impose his own version of the peace, one that made it seem as if the Civil War had never happened. Stanton was a committed abolitionist, wanted the South humbled, and was by nature personally vindictive. This agreement was like pouring gasoline on a blowtorch.

The cabinet met and summarily rejected the terms, with Stanton ticking off the objections on his fingers. He didn't stop there. On April 21, he ordered Grant to proceed immediately to Sherman's headquarters and take over operations.[113] The same day, he wrote Halleck, whom he had just sent to Richmond, that Sherman was throwing "away all the advantages we had gained from the war... afford[ing] Jeff Davis an opportunity to escape with all his money."[114] As if on cue, the general's ancient rival responded that he had learned from reliable local sources that Davis was trying to cut a deal with Sherman to escape with the Confederate treasury, a supposedly huge amount of specie.[115] Then, having assembled his "case," Stanton leaked it. The very next day, *The New York Times* opined that it looked "as if this negotiation was a blind to cover the escape of Jeff Davis and a few of his officials, with the millions of gold they have stolen."[116] The story was everywhere, receiving more newspaper coverage than any event in the Civil War save Lincoln's assassination.[117] Sherman had been slimed by a master—two, actually—but in the end it proved transparently false and stupidly vindictive, especially considering the target.

The first Sherman knew of any of this was on April 24, when Grant arrived unannounced at his camp. He was plainly there in damage control mode, to ease the embarrassment of Sherman's monumental bender. Rather than taking over, he simply told Sherman to reset with Johnston on the same terms that were given Lee, which he did two days later.

Technically, that ended the matter. The war was over, though not Sherman's response. Initially, before he learned of the newspaper campaign, he quickly and revealingly conceded that he had exceeded the role of military strategist in trying to define the purpose of a war, writing Stanton the night after Grant arrived: "I admit my folly in embracing in a military convention any civil matters."[118] But when he ascertained the full extent of his own demonization and, further, learned that Halleck was busy cabling his subordinates not to obey his orders,[119] William Tecumseh Sherman went back on the warpath.

Though the shooting was over, his army was once again on the march and not in a good mood. They might have burned Raleigh after learning of the assassination had it not been for the quick work of John Logan, who got two thousand of them back into camp by threatening them with artillery.[120] They also read the newspapers and were boiling over the way their Uncle Billy had been smeared. To keep them hot, Sherman issued one of his Special Field Orders, announcing, "A most foul attempt made on his fair fame [by] Maj. Gen. Halleck, who as long as our Enemy stood in bold & armed array sat in full security in his Easy chair at Washington."[121] But now he was in Richmond, not just the last of the state capitals and final resting place of the Confederacy, but a great place to get even. That's where they were headed.

If Henry Halleck had been a dog, his tail would have been between his legs, its tip wagging plaintively. On May 9, he had written Sherman apologizing for his letter to Stanton, gushing, "You have not had during this war, nor have you now a warmer friend & admirer than myself."[122] He even offered him a room. Sherman's response couldn't have been colder: The two could no longer "have any friendly intercourse," he wrote, and warned Halleck to stay out of sight when he marched his troops through the city lest "loss of life or violence result."[123] Halleck was on the portico when they passed by his headquarters on May 11, but only to watch as not a single soldier in the multitude saluted him. It was the equivalent of being buried in a mountain of white feathers.

The insult had not only been repaid in full, but the long rivalry between these two exceptionally talented military officers was over. They would never again speak. Halleck had probably done more to foster Sherman's career than to undermine it. He had also performed a key service during the war, developing an administrative interface between civilian authority and the military that was crucial in a conflict this large. But he was no combat soldier, and Sherman was a hero. It was pure folly to take him on at this point. Halleck had made his career in substantial part by knowing his own limitations; but in the end his jealousy betrayed him and he overreached, only to be slapped down, fading inexorably, as his biographer admits, into the national background.[124]

Sherman's star, although momentarily doused, continued to burn brightly all the way to Washington, D.C., the last stop on the grand tour. He had earlier told Salmon Chase that the controversy would probably end his military career,[125] but he arrived to find that the tide of public opinion had shifted decisively in his favor. "Grant and Sherman, the team that won the Civil War": This was plainly to be the enduring message, and carpers beware, especially if your name was Edwin Stanton.

Sherman's squelch here was even more theatric. At the Grand Review riding at the head of the Army of the West, he got off his horse, mounted the reviewing stand, and in front of basically everybody important in the government refused to shake the hand of the secretary of war. Connoisseurs of put-downs would be hard-pressed to find a better one-two combination than this and the one in Richmond.

But that had been Halleck. This was Stanton, a much tougher nut. This sort of West Pointer posturing barely dented his shell. He had an agenda and, as everybody—including the president of the United States—would soon discover, he was not going away. But neither was Sherman. He had weathered the storm and was firmly planted along with Grant at the helm of the U.S. Army. He was a career army officer, and in his view his career was far from over. He had big plans, but to accomplish them, he and the secretary of war would have to reach some kind of accommodation. Fortunately, Grant stood between them.

Sherman had played a key role in winning the Civil War. Without questioning the primacy of Lincoln and Grant, it is possible to say that his fertile imagination allowed him to become uniquely adaptive. The army he led was a remarkable creation—his own as well as its own, since it often found its own solutions—the archetypal American ground force, and he commanded it with just the flair needed in a mass democracy. Overlooked at the time but of considerable significance now, Sherman also managed to thwart a dangerous and extremely well-led insurgency in the Mississippi Valley, though he never fully appreciated the importance of intelligence supplied by African Americans. Still, rather than becoming bogged down by guerrillas, he seized the initiative and leaped on the Southern mind. Sherman was a theatrical person, and he played his role to the hilt, alternating between model conqueror and modern Attila, sowing confusion and fear and in the end breeding despair. During the last stages of the March to the Sea, desertions from the Army of Northern Virginia skyrocketed to the point that Longstreet's corps had more pickets in the rear than in the front, as soldiers bolted to protect their homes or at least find their families.[126] The Confederacy was an idea, and Sherman trampled it relentlessly—its symbols, its institutions, its pride—bled the life out of it, and replaced it with hopelessness. That's the way to win.

Chapter VIII

BANDS OF STEEL

I

WILLIAM TECUMSEH SHERMAN'S central historical importance is derived from his role in the physical consolidation of transcontinental America. But it was chance that tilted him in this direction; his own awareness of his part in the process evolved and intensified only gradually. There exist no fantasy maps drawn during his days at West Point, no sophomoric verse eulogizing westward expansion. In Florida he was little more than an observer, though an acute one. But in California, along with all its frustrations, he seems to have first caught a glimpse of a transcontinental mission and what was required. In 1859, the long report he had composed for his brother John on the possibility of a transcontinental railroad had generated quite a stir in Washington. Then the South seceded, and Sherman waged a four-year vendetta to knock it back into the Union, a defining experience that only intensified his yen for national spaciousness.[1] From this point, he became Manifest Destiny's chief of operations, orchestrating the construction of the four great bands of steel, the transcontinental railroads that would tie everything together coast-to-coast, from sea to shining sea. It was his final act, his culminating achievement, and one he felt did the country more good than his services during the Civil War.[2] But as that conflict ended, Sherman's future was far from assured.

In large part, it was his own professional focus and his disdain for politics that saved him. Sherman had no interest in Reconstruction or its enforcement, and everybody in Washington knew it. His only interest in the brewing battle between Edwin Stanton, the embodiment of the Radicals, and President Johnson was to avoid it. He had his own plan, to a military strategist something far more intellectually challenging, and for the most part he had the good sense to stick to it.

And of course, he had Grant to cover him. Grant was interested in politics—he wanted to be president—but he was also farsighted enough to realize the criticality of the transcontinental project. Who better to oversee it than the most brilliant and reliable of wingmen? The obvious stumbling block was the secretary of war, "as vindictive as old satan," Sherman assumed.[3] But not necessarily. As general of the army, Grant was technically subordinate to Stanton, but in terms of stature he towered over everybody in Washington, and he wanted harmony. Stanton had bigger things to think about, such as trying to carve out a future for African Americans. This was a reasonable solution; if nothing else, it would remove the offending Sherman and send him far to the west. So it was to be that General Orders No. 118 of June 27, 1865, designated Major General W. T. Sherman to command the vast Military Division of the Mississippi, extending out to the crest of the Rockies and north and south from Canada to the Mexican border, to be headquartered at (where else?) St. Louis.[4]

Technically, the program had been under way since July 1, 1862, when Lincoln signed the Pacific Railroad Act, which provided a generous combination of loans and public land grants to finance private construction of a line stretching from Omaha to San Francisco. But the Civil War overwhelmed everything, and in his 1864 message, Lincoln admitted that only a hundred miles on the eastern end had been surveyed, along with twenty miles of track laid in California.[5]

The house that Sherman built (courtesy of local benefactors) at 912 Garrison Avenue, St. Louis, the strategic center of the general's universe. *Archives of the University of Notre Dame*

But peace shot the equivalent of a bolt of adrenaline into the project, and as it gained momentum, it became apparent it would involve a great deal more than just working on the railroad. It was in fact a great national enterprise, combining crony capitalism on a grand scale (Crédit Mobilier), heroic civil engineering, vast labor pools (many of them veterans), a folk migration, an ecological disaster (the buffalo), and a vicious and persistent insurgency that would end with the destruction of an entire way of life. All of it was known at the time as civilization on the move, and Sherman was exactly the man to keep it running.

No doubt the Civil War had gotten him used to a fast-paced life, but even he probably marveled at his change of circumstances: in a matter of months he went from being accused by the secretary of war of virtual treason to an assignment doing exactly what he wanted in exactly the place he'd always wanted to do it. In the summer of 1865, Sherman found himself in a sweet spot, personally and professionally.

Very conveniently, friends in St. Louis passed the hat and gave him a substantial residence in a nice part of town. At last the family was gathered together, residing comfortably at 912 Garrison Avenue.[6] Sherman had finally emerged from the shadow of Thomas Ewing—so had his brother John, whose career in the Senate continued to thrive. They were now the dominant males in the interlocking family directorate. Ellen was definitively his, not Daddy's; so were his children. The brood now numbered five, and two years later another son, P. Tecumseh Sherman, would join them—all destined to survive into adulthood.[7] This was what Sherman had wanted since he'd wed Ellen—togetherness—and if the marriage was already in slow decline, for the moment he gave every indication of enjoying his oft deferred domesticity in the city of his dreams.

If anybody thrived during the Civil War, it was Sherman, and he arrived at his new post in top form, a master of what he now called "grand strategy." At this point, it's conceivable that he understood warfare—at least its terrestrial variety—more profoundly and along more dimensions than any other person then living. The sheer magnitude of what was being attempted fit Sherman to a tee: his massive capacity for detail, his uncanny knowledge and understanding of the terrain, his ease at multitasking and operating at several different levels. This was an era virtually devoid of automated memory and accounting mechanisms; a brain like Sherman's gave him an even greater relative advantage in such a huge and variegated operation than he would have enjoyed in today's electronically aided environment. This was as close as it came to a perfect job fit.

As always, he dove into everything, first studying maps and statistics and then moving immediately to see what they reflected in a series of elongated inspection tours. Out of these, the plan he developed was a masterpiece of economy of force and rigorous prioritization. He then executed it steadfastly for more than a decade in the face of steadily declining resources—exactly the kind of persistence irregular warfare seems to demand.

As he eventually saw it, the problem set contained three interacting variables and one subvariable. First there were the railroads working their way west, initially two strands: one jutting out from Omaha (the Union Pacific) and the other from Kansas City toward Fort Riley (Kansas Pacific). Next there were the American settlers,

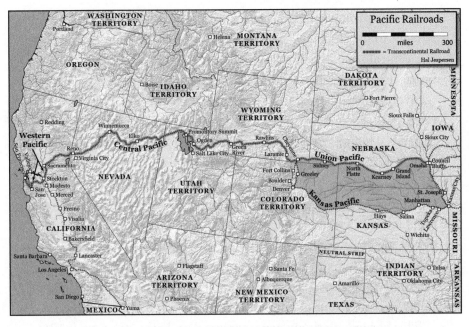

those already established on homesteads and up to a hundred thousand each summer on the three main trails west, all of them stretching like fingers through Indian country.[8] The Indians were the last variable. Of around a quarter million Native Americans living in the western territories, about a hundred thousand belonging to the Sioux, Cheyenne, Arapaho, Kiowa, Comanche, Apache, Nez Percé, Ute, Paiute, and Modoc were actively resisting the great white wave, as well they should have, since both the railroads and the settlers spelled doom for their wandering lifestyle and the millions of buffalo (the subvariable) upon which it depended.[9]

Sherman's solution was as unequivocal as it was ingenious. Not only would the security and uninterrupted construction of the railways receive first priority, but they would also be used as a pivot to address the other variables. He understood that as they progressed westward, the rails would be the ideal instrument to overwhelm the Indians and also foster settlement: first by bringing operational speed and logistical magnitude to the military effort to secure the prairie, and then by providing a lifeline for as many settlers as the land could support. Significantly, Sherman told Grant that he hoped the two tracks would not converge at the hundredth meridian as originally planned, but instead would be brought out in parallel straight to the Rockies.[10] Together, they would form the boundaries of a central zone of security, conceptually a sort of steel fence defining a vast inner domain reserved for white settlement, one that effectively shut out the Indians. Once this was accomplished, the territory north and south could be progressively expanded and protected.[11] This was exactly what occurred. If you were a transcontinentalist, it was brilliant; if you were an Indian or a buffalo, it was a disaster.

Prior to Sherman's coming and for several years after, the Indians fared relatively well in their military struggles. Apaches were superb desert and mountain fighters, while the Sioux and Cheyenne excelled at horsemanship. And many were very well armed, having acquired repeating rifles through illicit arms traders in numbers sometimes sufficient to outgun their blue-coated opponents.[12]

This became glaringly apparent just days before Christmas 1866, when a column of eighty-one men under an impetuous captain, William Fetterman, fell into a false retreat ambush and was wiped out, setting off an avalanche of fear and panicky headlines all across the white settlements. "I do not yet understand how the massacre to . . . Fetterman's part could have been so complete," Sherman wrote Grant. "We must act with vindictive earnestness against the Sioux, even to their extermination, men, women and children. Nothing else will reach the root of this case."[13]

While it's debatable whether he meant this literally, he certainly understood how it could be accomplished and applied the solution ruthlessly. He knew from his days in Florida that for all their tactical panache and guerrilla skills, Indians were fatally flawed as longterm combatants. Unlike the insurgents he'd faced in the Mississippi Valley, these adversaries were tethered to a vulnerable food supply, which could be, and already was being, eliminated.

Pity the poor subvariable: it was the linchpin of his strategy. To say Sherman encouraged buffalo hunting completely understates the case; he declared war on them, orchestrating the killing of roughly five million beasts between 1867 and 1874.[14] Initially, when the slaughter didn't seem sufficient, he proposed to Phil Sheridan that they invite "all the sportsmen of England & America there this fall for a Grand Buffalo hunt and make one grand sweep of them all."[15] The result was inevitable, and he knew it, telling John as early as June 1868 that "it will not be long before all the buffalo are extinct near and between the railroads, and after which the Indians will have no reason to approach them."[16]

However, the settler variable remained a continuing distraction. Sherman's forces were extremely limited, and he needed a core cavalry force to pursue and harass Indian bands. But there was steady and strident pressure to build more forts than necessary, to scatter his forces in a futile effort to provide protection from hit-and-run raids. "There is a general apprehension of danger, though no one seems to have a definite idea of whence it is to come," he wrote in 1866, and that same year he sarcastically replied to the residents of Pueblo, Colorado, that there were more signatures on their petition requesting protection than there were soldiers available at the nearest garrison.[17]

But this was a far different Sherman from the one buried by the Gold Rush in California. He now knew an irresistible wave when he saw one and understood he had to deal with it. So he made sure his many protracted inspection tours of his vast Military Division included civilian stops, especially in Indian-threatened areas, and peppered the locals with his usual blend of acuity and curiosity that both charmed and soothed them. When the citizens of Montana and Colorado formed their own militias and threatened to take the fight to the Indians, Sherman shrugged off the implied threat to his authority and went on with his own business.[18]

And this was ultimately devoted to ramrodding the railroad across the plains. While the story of the transcontinental line's construction has frequently been told in terms of rollicking corruption and free enterprise at its freest, in reality this proved to be a highly militarized operation and therefore very much to Sherman's liking. Conveniently, one of his corps commanders during the Atlanta campaign, Grenville Dodge, was the Union Pacific's chief engineer. Many of the laborers had been soldiers with the Army of the West, so many that cries of "Uncle Billy!" habitually rang out when he walked the tracks. Whom better to hire? Years of breaking up and bending track had thoroughly familiarized these vets with the nuances of construction; they were probably the best railroad workers on the planet.[19]

Sherman marveled at their efficiency, reporting in October 1865 that "a heavy track-laying force was completing one-half mile of road each day."[20] And their pace only accelerated: in 1866, the team out of Omaha nearly doubled that rate, laying over three hundred miles of rails.[21] He was intent on their keeping it up, urging Dodge "by superhuman energy" to reach out to the Rockies and promising to do everything within his power to screen the work gangs from Indian raiding parties.[22] At one point, he told his former general he would push the Bozeman trail to Virginia City in order to "divert the attention of the hostile Sioux from your road."[23] Protect the railway and shield its workers: the self-evident center of gravity pursued by Sherman until it was built and then after to ensure its security.

But was it actually necessary? It's interesting to note that Sherman's policy amounted to protecting his own soldiers, or at least former soldiers. They could have been armed, and many probably already were. These were very good fighters, with recent combat experience. How endangered were they, really? How endangered was the railroad? The Plains Indian lifestyle does not seem compatible with the kinds of activities necessary for serious and persistent railroad wrecking. Perhaps they would have gotten the hang of it, but from an anthropological perspective it's at least debatable. Coexistence was a possibility.

But that was never seriously considered, not by Sherman, not by the engineers, not by the moneymen, not by nationalist politicians. Indian exclusion was from beginning to end the transparent objective. And being at the blunt end of this national bulldozer, Sherman developed exactly the force he needed and also one that could persist even in the face of a hostile and parsimonious environment.

During the Civil War, Sherman had little luck with cavalry or cavalry commanders, and he learned to operate almost as if they did not exist. But this was the prairie, where mobility was everything, and now he had Phil Sheridan to turn to.

Besides Grant and Sherman, nobody on the Union side had emerged with a better military reputation—every bit of it earned. Small and oddly shaped, he compensated with astonishing courage and tenacity. No match intellectually for either Sherman or Grant, he was nonetheless an extraordinarily effective leader and the best cavalry commander at the operational level the Civil War produced. He was also implacable, as destructive in the Shenandoah Valley as Sherman had been in South Carolina. He was exactly what this mission required.

By necessity, the army had always nurtured a core element of experienced Indian fighters—Sheridan learned the trade in the Pacific Northwest, for example. During the Civil War, a number had remained on the frontier, while others fought in the great campaigns and were now available for duty in the West. Sherman had his pick. Even if Washington halved the Mississippi Division's force allotment of twenty-five thousand enlisted men between 1865 and 1866, it simply allowed him to be more selective, to get rid of burnouts.[24]

He needed quality, not quantity. The vastness of the West called for a special breed of garrison troops, men willing and able to man lonely outposts at strategic points over long periods without losing military readiness. It also engendered a particularly tough and versatile brand of cavalry—horse soldiers able to fight on foot, prepared to take full advantage of their repeating weapons, and trained and supplied in a way that rendered them capable of relentless pursuit. This was key: they had to be ready to go at all times, particularly in the winter, when their adversaries were stationary and vulnerable. And as the rail lines moved forward, Sherman came to realize their strategic mobility and advantage would only grow.[25]

The number of troops demanded was not high, in the low thousands. Besides some special logistical considerations, this was an inherently parsimonious mission, one that could be carried through a future of declining military budgets. All that was required was a cadre of competent troops and good leadership willing to use them ruthlessly and with persistence. With the exception of George Armstrong Custer, the campaign was consistently well directed, not just by Sheridan, but by notable irregular warriors such as C. C. Augur, Benjamin Grierson, and George Crook. The outcome was assured. In essence, Sherman had created a perpetual motion machine for destroying a way of life, one perfectly capable of running without him. And it had to, since he had lots of unexpected distractions.

2

In the summer of 1867, Congress saw fit to include William Tecumseh Sherman's name on its list of appointees to the newly created Indian Peace Commission, created to negotiate with the Plains Indians. Although he was hardly thrilled, he agreed with Grant "that the chief use of the Peace Commission is to kill time."[26] Besides, Sherman waged war in all directions, including the home front; he well understood that elite eastern outrage was fueling a reassessment of Indian policy and that he was becoming their bête noire. So into the breach, one filled with pacifists and do-gooders, plunged Sherman.

But clearly with his own agenda. "I don't care about interesting myself too far in the fate of the poor devils of Indians who are doomed from the causes inherent in their nature or from the natural & persistent hostility of the white race," he told Ellen; he just wanted to make his own role clear.[27] This he did.

From Sherman's perspective, the civilians on the Indian Peace Commission, epitomized by Boston abolitionist Samuel F. Tappan, had at least one virtue: They wanted to go out and meet the Indians, examine their situation firsthand. Sherman always loved an expedition, a chance to add more geography to the database. So in August they all took off up the Missouri and by the end of the month had splashed their way to Fort Randall nearly thirteen hundred miles beyond St. Louis. Before they returned, they met with nine of the major Sioux groups. Whatever their personal sympathies, the commissioners as a group offered the same deal the U.S. government had been offering for a long time: "Give up your present habitat and go live on reservations of our choosing."

The civilians may have put a softer face on it, but Sherman addressed one of the Sioux chiefs, Pawnee Killer, with icy realism: "We now give you advice...you cannot stop the locomotive any more than you can stop the sun or moon, and you must submit." They had until November to decide.[28]

Almost immediately, the commission set off on a second swing to Fort Harker, where they met with two thousand Arapaho, Comanche, and Kiowa, convincing the latter two groups, aided by a heaping pile of presents, to give up their lands between the railroads and move to reservations in Oklahoma territory. By November, some (though not all) of the Sioux signed on and relinquished their old hunting grounds in return for promises of U.S. government support in their new reservations in the sacred Black Hills. But support was delayed by Congress, which was caught up in the presidential impeachment crisis, and when it came the following year, with Sherman designated to disburse it, the half a million dollars proved completely inadequate. Yet again, the Indians who submitted got the worst of it, the same old story. Soon enough, many were again on the warpath.

Sherman didn't care. And when Samuel Tappan accused him of cynicism, he admitted to cooperating with the Peace Commission only because he knew it would fail and allow him to use force again.[29] As good as his word, he had been playing for time. By 1868, the rail lines were drawing near the Rockies, flanked by the army, slicing up the prairie into secured segments; the plan was taking on an irresistible momentum. But once again Sherman's attention was diverted by Washington, this time by the president and also by his best professional friend.

The maladroit Andrew Johnson, locked in his perpetual struggle with Stanton and Congress, had clumsily raised the stakes to the point of impeachment. In March 1867, Congress passed the Tenure of Office Act, requiring its own approval for any future cabinet change. The president only pushed in more chips on August 12 by suspending the secretary of war during a congressional recess, and when he was unable to persuade Sherman (whose views on Recon-struction he understood to be close to his own) to take the post, he turned to Grant, assuming Congress wouldn't dare reject him.

Keeping his rank of general of the army, Grant gingerly stepped into a job that entailed writing orders to himself, ostensibly to pro-tect the service from further manipulation, but also because he was deeply involved in Washington politics and wanted to be president—something Sherman couldn't believe.[30] Still, he worried about his friend and also about Johnson's plans for his own future, so he al-lowed himself to get involved.

In December, Congress did what Johnson thought they wouldn't do: they refused to approve Grant as Stanton's replacement. Grant wasn't about to cross Congress for Johnson, so he turned the office, like a hot potato, back to the former secretary of war without even bothering to tell the president, who reacted by dressing him down in a cabinet meeting.

Sherman came to Washington to cover his friend's flank by lever-aging his own and his family's good relations with Johnson. So he pushed a compromise candidate for secretary of war, and when this failed, he was by Grant's side when he met privately with the presi-dent.[31] None of this seems to have done the slightest good. The crisis only deepened, and now Sherman was part of it. Johnson and Stan-ton remained at loggerheads until the president persuaded General Lorenzo Thomas to step in, or at least try to step into the post ad interim, an act of bullheaded defiance that led Congress to vote on articles of impeachment February 24, 1868.

Meanwhile, worried about a military confrontation with the leg-islators, and having been burned by Grant, the president came up with the idea of promoting Sherman on a brevet or temporary basis to full general and creating for him a new military district out of Washington, D.C. It was not hard to see where this was going.

Sherman reacted with horror. When Thomas Ewing, now nearly eighty, suggested he actually accept, his foster son/son-in-law waxed Shakespearean to describe Johnson's motivation: "He is like Lear roaring at the wild storm, bareheaded and helpless. And now he wants me to go with him into the wilderness."[32] In a similar vein, and even more specifically, he told Grant: "I never felt so troubled in my life. Were it an order to go to Sitka, to the devil, to battle with rebels or Indians, I think you would not hear a whimper from me, but it comes in such a questionable form that, like Hamlet's ghost, it curdles my blood and mars my judgment."[33] He begged Johnson to be excused and kept at his command in St. Louis, while in Washington, John was enlisted to fight the poison posting from that angle. Johnson had enough problems and gave up, cabling Sherman on February 19: "As . . . your assignment to a new military division seems so objectionable, you will retain your present command."[34]

Saved. Other than a few tortured days at the impeachment trial that failed to convict Johnson, Sherman was back on task. Free to pursue the strategic agenda with the first of the great bands about to be joined. Fulfilling his transcontinental destiny and having fun with his friends.

3

Grant was running for president, basically on four words: "Let us have peace." Other than that, his campaign managers were happy to keep him out of what was shaping up to be a close race. So nobody objected when he removed himself for a tour of the Far West with Sherman and Sheridan in July 1868.

The three amigos were in high spirits as they picked up the Kansas Pacific and rode west, making frequent stops, posing for photos, and engaging the press (though he hated the press, Sherman was always a good interview). But this was about considerably more than public relations. As one strategist to another, Sherman wanted Grant to see the terrain so he could understand the complications the great enterprise presented. In effect, this was an inspection tour by the high command.

Just how high became apparent when they ran into a personnel problem near Laramie. Thomas Durand, first vice president of the Union Pacific, used their arrival as the occasion for a showdown with Grenville Dodge, accusing him of selecting impossible terrain for

Grant, Sherman, Sheridan, and Dodge, the command staff of the transcontinental railroad, shown together at Fort Sanders. *Archives of the University of Notre Dame*

the remaining construction. Perhaps he did not know Sherman and Dodge were friends or that Dodge had run Grant's intelligence operation at one point during the Civil War. Whatever his motivation, the response he elicited from the general of the army left little doubt who was in charge: "The government expects this railroad to be finished. The government expects the railroad company to meet its obligations. And the government expects General Dodge to remain with the road as its chief engineer until it is completed."[35]

The transcontinental was a great deal more than a company building a railway. It was an act of conquest, a national expansion, and in such matters the military, as the sharp end of the state, had the last say. Grant was really only stating the obvious: construction would proceed from within the context of the overall military strategy. This was the fundamental order of things.

Otherwise the summer tour of the three amigos was significant in that it probably marked the last happy and uncomplicated days of

Sherman's alliance with Grant. Their futures would be wrenched apart beginning in November 1868, when Grant was elected president and underwent what Sherman would undoubtedly have characterized as an unwholesome career change.

It also meant that he too would be drawn to Washington, to occupy Grant's vacated slot as general of the army, a post Sherman would retain through thick and thin for nearly a decade and a half. But he came east expecting a great deal more power than he actually got. If he was certain of one thing initially, it was that Grant would never allow the general of the army to be jerked around the way Stanton and Andrew Johnson had done repeatedly during the impeachment crisis.[36]

And sure enough, on March 5, 1869, the day after the inauguration, General Orders No. 11 subordinated all elements of the department under Sherman and not the secretary of war, as well as placing him directly in the chain of command. To make matters even more cozy, John Schofield, the "missing cadet" and longtime Sherman associate, was the current secretary and not likely to challenge the new order of things. But everything changed in less than a month.

Without warning, Grant replaced Schofield with John Rawlins, his longtime chief of staff and career alter ego. Rawlins thought No. 11 gave Sherman too much power and wanted it withdrawn. Knowing his intent, Sherman wrote Grant on March 26: "It would put me in a most unpleasant dilemma because the Army and country would infer your want of confidence."[37] That same day, Rawlins under his own signature returned power to the secretary as if No. 11 did not exist.

Flummoxed, Sherman rushed to the White House the next morning and confronted what looked to be a very uncomfortable Grant. "Rawlins feels badly about it; it worries him, and he is not well [he was dying of tuberculosis]." "But Grant, ought a public measure that you have advocated for years...be set aside for such a reason?" Grant remained unmoved. "I don't like to give him pain now; so Sherman, you'll have to publish the rescinding order." "But Grant, it's your own order...." "Well, if it's my own order, I can rescind it, can't I?" Sherman stood and bowed: "Yes, Mr. President, you have the power to revoke your own order; you shall be obeyed. Good morning, sir."[38]

Sherman must have left the executive mansion with the shattering realization that his relationship with Grant would never be the same, that they were no longer associates or even necessarily allies under certain circumstances. Grant was president; he had his own agenda.

Sherman was also hurt, but this was in part because he had never really understood Grant. For all his battlefield insensitivity, Grant was a loving individual, particularly to those closest to him—his wife, Julia, was the prime example, but also Rawlins, who had been with him from the beginning in Galena. Sherman, on the other hand, had professional friendships, alliances of like-minded individuals; his relationship with his brother and many foster brothers provided fulfillment of the sort shared by Rawlins and Grant. Therefore, he took as betrayal what was mostly an extravagant gesture of sympathy—finding a friend a good job to die in. Nevertheless, in overall effect Sherman had it right: Grant's track and his own were diverging.

But for the moment, tracks were also converging, east and west, at Promontory Summit, Utah. On May 10, 1869, Sherman had one of his best days as general of the army. Surrounded in the War Office by Sheridan, Rawlins, and assorted members of the army staff, he sat fidgeting by the telegraph, awaiting news from twenty-four hundred miles away. Finally it came, a personal message from Grenville Dodge: "As a steadfast earnest friend of the Pacific Rail Road, I send you greeting the fact at twelve (12) A.M. today the last connection was made, and you can visit your old friends in California overland, all the way by rail."[39]

Symbolically, it was a moment to savor. Shipwrecked twice on the way to California, Sherman had been an advocate of the transcontinental from the beginning. But he also would have been the first to add that the task was far from completed. Much on the strategic agenda remained—the other lines, Indian removal, buffalo extinction—and he would pursue them relentlessly, though the politics only became more murky.

Part of the problem, from Sherman's perspective, was that Grant had a soft spot in his heart for Indians. Prior to his inauguration, he had conferred with a group of eastern philanthropists led by Philadelphian William Welsh, who convinced him to adopt a more humane, less violent program for Native Americans. What Grant produced, his so-called Peace Policy, still called for containment of the tribes on reservations, but it was certainly a softer approach, with an emphasis on education and the treatment of Indians as individuals.[40]

This he followed up by appointing his military secretary, Ely S. Parker, as Indian commissioner. Another crony, but a crony with a difference, Parker was an innovative administrator and a full-blooded Seneca. (At Appomattox, Lee is said to have told him, "I am glad to see one real American here," to which Parker replied: "We are all Americans, sir.") He wanted to split the responsibility, leaving tribes on reservations in the hands of civilians from his own Bureau of Indian Affairs, while those roaming free would come under the jurisdiction of the army.

It seemed like a reasonable plan, a possible blueprint for gradual demilitarization, until late January 1870, when a squadron of U.S. cavalry, with Phil Sheridan's enthusiastic approval, attacked a village of friendly Peigan Indians immobilized in heavy snow, killing more than a hundred, many of them women and children. Sherman jumped to the defense of the army before Congress, and the incident effectively rendered permanent the split between civilian and military conceptions of the Indians' future.[41] By 1871, Parker was gone, ironically brought down by Welsh and the humanitarians.

Sherman stayed, and though his wings were clipped, his strategy ground on. Shortly after the Peigan massacre, he assured C. C. Augur, his commander in Omaha, that nothing had changed: the railroad's protection remained uppermost, and that meant pursuing the other strategic corollaries.[42] The buffalo slaughter soon reached a crescendo, with more than three million bison gunned down by whites between 1872 and 1874; and when Congress passed a law protecting them, Sherman convinced Grant to employ a pocket veto.[43] Meanwhile, the general of the army took every opportunity to pursue the Indian problem.

But it wasn't easy. When Rawlins died in September 1869, Grant turned to Sherman for advice on a new secretary of war, and he recommended William W. Belknap, one of his brigade commanders in the Army of the Tennessee. It was a mistake. Belknap was even hungrier for power than Rawlins, and he quickly filled his plate at Sherman's expense, even interrupting his line authority over units in the West.

The general of the army responded with a series of calculated retreats and hands-on adventures. In the spring of 1871, he took a two-month inspection tour of the Southwest to get a feel for the extent of Indian depredations. At Fort Sill, after conferring with commander Benjamin Grierson, he decided to set a trap for some reservation Indians accused of attacking a supply column, and he would have been caught in a crossfire had not some black soldiers stood them down. Sherman explained the incident in terms of the Indians' "natural propensity to steal horses and kill people," and it only reinforced his opposition to the Peace Policy.[44]

Largely to escape frustration, Sherman jumped at an opportunity to tour Europe and spent most of the next year there. But when he returned, things were no better bureaucratically, and in 1873 he submitted an annual report extraordinary in its brevity: "No part of the Army is under my immediate control, and the existing Army regulations devolve on the Secretary of War the actual command of the military peace establishment, and all responsibility therefore, so that I forbear making any further recommendations or report."[45]

In the spring of 1874, he upped the ante by requesting to move his headquarters to St. Louis, sighting as precedent Winfield Scott's similarly abrupt withdrawal to New York. Belknap was only too happy to get rid of this cantankerous presence, and Grant probably also breathed a sigh of relief, so yet again, Sherman headed for this mecca on the Mississippi. One biographer views his behavior during this period as petulant, but it was also cunning and strategic. Having the general of the army state officially that he had nothing to do had to make an impression. And moving to St. Louis was his best chance to get his hands back around operations in the West. As he left, Belknap reminded him: "No material change shall be made in the stations of troops or commanders without previous approval by this Department."[46] Sherman may have chuckled or simply muttered: "Fat chance!"

He was Uncle Billy Sherman, and his boys were all over the West. Their commanders were some of his closest military friends—O. O. Howard, Edward Ord, and Phil Sheridan—and he had an entire network of other West Pointers involved in every aspect of the huge operation. Belknap had gone to Princeton and was back in Washington, giving parties. Who was likely to get the latest information on military developments? Who would be turned to for advice? Who was in the best position to oversee implementation of the strategic plan? From this perspective, Sherman's seemingly quixotic retreat from the Potomac was simply a rigorous assertion of priorities, focusing on what was really important in a constrained environment. At any rate, Belknap turned out to be on the take, receiving substantial kickbacks through his own wife. When outed he was forced to resign, but he was impeached anyway by an outraged Congress in March 1876—one of the biggest stains on what became an epically bespattered Grant administration. In St. Louis, Sherman remained well clear of the mess.

So too did he avoid exploiting his connections with the railroads for anything more than free rides on his inspection tours. Even if his days as a banker had not soured him on free-for-all enterprise, Sherman probably would have steered clear of peculation; as a strategist, he always viewed himself solely as an agent of the state. It helped that his pay as general of the army was extremely generous,[47] but in an age of unapologetic greed, Sherman remained steadfastly a salaryman.

Meanwhile, his infernal mechanism had continued to clobber the Indians. When a band of Modoc led by "Captain Jack" broke out of their reservation and began waging a guerrilla war that tied up hundreds of U.S. troops, then gunned down the Peace Commission sent to negotiate with them in the spring of 1873, Sherman's instructions could not have been clearer: he ordered attacks "so strong and persistent that their fate may be commensurate with their crime. You will be fully justified in their utter extermination."[48] "Captain Jack" and several warriors were hanged, and the remaining Modoc—no more than 160 individuals—were exiled to Oklahoma.

Of far greater significance were the thousands of Sioux who were gradually being cornered in the Black Hills of Dakota Territory. In 1868, the Fort Laramie Treaty had supposedly exempted the area from all white settlers, but by 1873 enough had trickled in that Sherman, expecting trouble, wanted the final section of the Northern Pacific traversing Sioux country built last.[49] The situation went critical in the summer of 1874, when an expedition under George Armstrong Custer discovered gold in the Black Hills. Rumors swept across the plains that gold-hungry miners by the thousands were about to invade. Sherman, seeking to calm the situation, stated publicly that they would do no such thing.[50] Actually, the summer of 1875 turned out to be notably quiet, and most breathed a sigh of relief.

But not the army, not Sherman. In November, he wrote Phil Sheridan that the situation was explosive, and "in the spring it may result in collision and trouble."[51] In April, Sherman reminded him that he was anxious to "finish this Sioux business, which is about the last of the Indians."

Sheridan took it from there. Grant may have been committed to a policy of peace with the Indians, but when his old cavalry commander told him the army was currently powerless to contain the flood of gold miners that would inevitably arrive in the Black Hills, he listened.[52]

Sheridan's plan to protect the Indians was basically to herd them into a portion of the reservation and try to segregate them from the expected miners. If you were among the assembled thousands of Lakota Sioux, Arapaho, and Northern Cheyenne, this type of operation would have felt a lot like an attack.

Sheridan's version of containment was to seal off the Indians by surrounding them with three converging prongs of cavalry: from the north, Colonel John Gibbon led an element out of Fort Shaw in

Montana; from the south, General George Crook proceeded from the prophetically named Fort Fetterman; and heading west was a substantial infantry-cavalry column commanded by General Alfred Terry. Intelligence was weak, and none of the prongs realized the Indians now numbered some five thousand warriors, many having slipped in from other reservations.[53]

The first nasty surprise came on June 17, 1876, when Crook, a very competent irregular fighter, was severely checked by what he considered an astonishingly large number of Native Americans, forcing him to pull back and regroup. Unaware of Crook's setback, the two other columns proceeded, joining forces in early June.

At this point, the cavalry element, twelve companies under George Custer, was sent ahead for a reconnaissance in force. After weeks on horseback, the impulsive Custer made contact with a large encampment of Sioux. Thinking it much smaller than it was, on June 25 he ordered an attack that was promptly engulfed at Little Bighorn, costing him his own life and those of over 250 members of the Seventh Cavalry—one of the most famous defeats in American history.

The news shocked the nation, a particularly ill omen with the hundredth anniversary of the Declaration of Independence just days away. The Peace Policy was out; Indian blood was in. But Sherman remained calm. The last thing he wanted was some sort of great, disorganized Indian hunt. "Surely in Grand Strategy we ought not to allow savages to beat us," he told Sheridan, "but in this instance they did."[54] Little Bighorn was simply a setback and a chance to apply the relentless pressure the overall strategy demanded.

Crook and Nelson Miles, another relentless fighter, continued operations through the winter, keeping the Indians hungry and continuously under pressure when they were most vulnerable. Then, in the spring, Sheridan unleashed these two dogs of war again in a renewed offensive that caught the Native Americans in a giant vise. On May 6, 1877, Crazy Horse and his entire contingent surrendered, effectively ending Sioux resistance and a process Sherman maintained began at Plymouth Rock.[55]

4

In 1883, shortly before he retired, Sherman undertook a last great western inspection tour aboard a special three-car train of luxury Pullmans, courtesy of the grateful rail barons for whom he had done so much. The West was developing faster than even he had hoped. He marveled in particular at Denver, which had matured almost miraculously: "the peer of any City of the Great West...elegant hotels, thousands of fine brick stores and dwellings, lighted by electricity, with bountiful supply of [the] purest water, and every thing that can make life agreeable."[56]

Everywhere he saw similar progress and proudly attributed it to his own strategy and the influence of the military in general, even believing that the privations and challenges of the Civil War had conditioned veterans to head west in huge numbers, "a potent agency in producing the results we enjoy to-day, in having in so short a time replaced the wild buffaloes by more numerous herds of tame cattle, and by substituting for the useless Indians the intelligent owners of productive farms and cattle-ranches."[57]

But it was the railroads that were transformative, great arteries accelerating and then sustaining settlement, allowing them to branch off into myriad domestic capillaries. And in his last annual report as general of the army, he was able to state that the four great transcontinental trunk lines were complete, "for my agency in which I feel as much pride as for my share in any of the battles in which I took part.... I regard the building of these railroads as the most important event of modern times.... A vast domain, equal to two-thirds of the whole surface of the United States, has thus been made accessible to the immigrant, and, in a military sense our troops may be assembled at strategic points and sent promptly to the places of disturbance, checking disorders in the bud."[58] The great enterprise was concluded. It was an impressive valedictory, and not necessarily exaggerated. Who else had been as relentless and instrumental in binding up transcontinental America? Everywhere he went, the nation had grown—or in the case of the Civil War had been restored to its original size—and this was the final jewel in his crown of national aggrandizement.

But at what cost? Ironically, Sherman, who was taken to task in the twentieth century for being the intellectual instigator of total industrialized war and its extension to the civilian sphere, now stands potentially culpable before a new sensibility horrified by the wanton destruction of wildlife and traditional cultures. There can be no doubt: he stood for what made America big fast, and as general contractor, his building techniques were none too gentle and incredibly wasteful. He shattered the South, bulldozed the Indians, and reduced the buffalo to scraps. He was a general; his modus operandi was war, the most wasteful of human activities. If he wasn't exactly the antithesis of ecological, he came close. And it may be that future generations will heap upon him scorn equivalent to that which he received from the apologists of the Lost Cause. But if so, it will be wrong and hypocritical.

We continue to live here, by now more than three hundred million of us. Nobody is talking seriously about giving the place back. Americans overwhelmingly continue to like living spaciously and abundantly. And on these grounds, limits must be put on any wholesale critique. Sherman's assault on nature and the Indians had been proceeding not simply since the colonization of North America, but in a larger sense since the Neolithic, as agricultural and herding cultures pushed hunter-gatherers back everywhere they encountered them. In this regard, economic history, like time, seems to march in only one direction. And once the myth of the Great American Desert was dispelled and it was realized that the western plains could be profitably exploited, the demise of the buffalo and the hunting cultures that lived off them was assured. Sherman's masterful planning only made it more sudden.

Part II

THE GENERAL
AND HIS ARMY

Chapter IX

THE BOYS

I

IT SEEMS THAT one of the reasons contemporary Americans like learning about the Civil War is that the participants appear so familiar—stripped-down, low-tech versions of us, still very much the same in speech and behavior. Arguably, it was not always so. Americans did not necessarily spring fully formed out of the Declaration of Independence and the U.S. Constitution.

Instead, it appears to have taken a while for the crucible of vast continental possibilities and a style of government salubrious to individual initiative to temper and finalize the national character. Earlier Americans, the revolutionary generation and those that immediately followed, likely would have struck us as more formal—ritualistic and deferential in ways we are not accustomed to. This is not to say that the process that made us who we are was not already at work—the American Revolution itself is a testimony to that—only that it was not yet finished.

This seems to have taken place in the two decades between 1820

and 1840,[1] most intensely in the western portions of the country at
or near the frontier.[2] Frenchman Alexis de Tocqueville toured the
United States in the early 1830s and famously proclaimed the emer-
gence of *Homo democraticus*, a cheeky creature whose passion for
equality and self-interest was tempered only by his ability to join
fellow citizens in all manner of mutual associations for pragmatic
benefit.[3] He may not have approved, but it was obvious to him that
this was something unprecedented. Literary Americans, epitomized
by Walt Whitman, saw it too, though they took a more positive slant.
A new kind of people walked the earth—exuberant, optimistic,
egalitarian, and opinionated—ready to take any situation in hand
and shape it to their own advantage.

This has considerable significance for our story of Sherman, since
he was born in 1820 and his soldiers were in large part members of
the next generation—in other words, the first and second iterations
of the national archetype brought to fruition.

Still, like any new models, they were a bit extreme and untested
by hard use. Democratic enthusiasm remained high among those
who joined the Army of the West; but these were largely rural young
men who had little experience in hierarchical organizations, and
they were about to enter one that was traditionally and intentionally
rigid. Not unexpectedly, sparks would fly. But the process of mutual
accommodation proved unique and remarkable. Other force structures in the Civil War faced similar challenges, but Sherman and his
boys were together longer, faced a broader range of military problems, and were more consistently successful in solving them.[4]

The key was a new kind of military adaptability. Change came
not only top-down from an innovative commander, but bottom-up
from the soldiers themselves. In the process, Sherman and his men
revealed what intellectual historian Joseph Kett has described as a
singular American ability to remain creatively insubordinate within
large organizations and still survive, even thrive.[5] These reinvented
soldiers were what the situation demanded—static firefighters, maneuver troops, amphibious assaulters, combat engineers, and masters of fortification, at once wizards of supply and among history's
greatest foragers. Militarily, they did it all and in doing so provided

a window on the future of U.S. ground forces, the great expeditionary armies that were destined to wage America's battles all over the
globe.

To this day, our fighting edge and ultimate hedge against disaster
remains the adaptability of individual soldiers and noncommissioned officers, a continuing capacity to somehow penetrate or find
a way around the fog of war in the worst of circumstances. Sherman's Army of the West was the first force in U.S. history to give full
vent to the military possibilities of such soldiers. This improvisational essence, warlike democracy's DNA, was passed fatefully forward over the next century and a half—the seeds of many victories
and, under adverse circumstances, inoculation against utter disaster.

Sherman's role in fostering this mind-set, along with the force it
created, is fundamental to his military importance—no biography
should treat it lightly. But it is also the story of individual soldiers. It
has to be: they were the whole point of his army. You can't even say
Sherman created this army, because in many respects, it created itself. Rather, he invented a unique military identity, Uncle Billy, that
epitomized what he wanted from them and mirrored the style and
degree of control he wished to exert. In a real sense, understanding
Sherman means understanding this army. Uncle Billy and his boys,
it's impossible to tell the story of one without the other. This means
more than a few digressions. It demands and will get a separate telling, its own act in the life of this theatrical general. Judging by his
attendance at an endless string of soldier reunions, Sherman would
demand no less. His boys were his military masterpiece, just as he
was theirs.

2

Like most such creations, it was a process as much as a product,
beginning simply with raw material. As we saw, it was only after
Missionary Ridge that a unified entity, the Army of the West,
emerged in the minds of the participants, one united under the
command of a single individual, Uncle Billy Sherman. Before that

transpired a long courtship, which began with neither side much liking the other (or their circumstances, for that matter). Of the two, the soldiers had the most to learn.

They were and always would be "the boys." This was the preferred nomenclature for the entire Civil War, North as well as South, but it seems particularly appropriate for these westerners who joined the Union army in droves during 1861 and early 1862 and would form the bulk of Sherman's forces throughout, reenlisting at a far higher rate than would soldiers in other Federal forces.[6]

We likely would have called them "the Army of the Midwest," since just under 60 percent hailed from Ohio, Indiana, and Illinois.[7] But all over the region, young men (average age about twenty-five)[8] had come in from farms (around 50 percent of the whole)[9] and joined laborers and others in scattered small towns and villages to undergo the rite of passage that was enlistment.

For the most part it was a community affair, with lots of picnics, speeches, and bands playing to accompany their oaths. Some alcohol was consumed, but usually everyone behaved themselves. If he had one, a soon-to-be soldier brought his best girl; if not, maybe he found one, for there were kisses to be stolen and promises to write exchanged—but probably not much else, since there was no great wave of pregnancies reported. Groups of women had gathered to sew intricate regimental flags, which were then presented with the innocence that inevitably precedes war—banners destined to be shot full of holes and stained with blood before this one was over. But for now, it was mostly about good, clean fun.

They joined for a number of reasons. Most were literate and a number were caught up with the cause to abolish slavery, but not that many. A much larger group wanted to restore the Union and "fight to maintain the best government on earth," as the common phrase went.[10] Finally, there were the rest: those who volunteered to join their friends and neighbors, or because they wanted to do something new, or just to get away and see someplace else. For at this point, it must have struck many as a grand adventure, sort of Tom Sawyer and Huck Finn go to war. And in fact both were destined to head south along the Mississippi—only instead of the benign presence of the Nigger Jim, these boys would discover an even darker fellow passenger, one clutching in his bony fingers a scythe fated to cut many of them down.

Death was even a factor organizationally. The basic unit of administration and military identity during the Civil War was the regiment, consisting initially of a little more than one thousand men recruited from a particular state. What's known as "military wastage" (desertion, disease, injury, and death) would eventually reduce a typical combat regiment in Sherman's army to around a third of that total by war's end.[11] But rather than restocking them, states for political reasons continued to create new regiments, until the Union army accumulated more than two thousand, the great majority of them infantry.[12]

Regiments themselves were divided into ten companies of one hundred, each of which was generally formed from the same locality.[13] The net effect was that from the beginning soldiers knew one another and were networked. Later, as different regiments were parceled out to larger elements, this network of common acquaintance grew until it constituted almost a separate nervous system from that of the traditional hierarchy of command—a subtle back channel by which military lessons were communicated and adopted almost unseen by the soldiers themselves. Although the proliferation of regiments was problematic in a number of ways militarily (Sherman certainly objected), it can also be seen as having accidentally generated a multitude of what are called today "battle labs," individual elements each of which approached combat slightly differently and then reported what worked and what didn't. This in theory explains the bottom-up dynamic, how an army of amateurs learned to fight so well in so many different circumstances. But before they could, they had to become soldiers, and that was a killer from the beginning.

Newly formed regiments were brought first to rendezvous points, large training bases such as Camp Fuller in Rockford, Illinois, or Benton Barracks at St. Louis, where Sherman commanded briefly. Here by the thousands they were first exposed to the unending routines of military life, the most leaden being drill.

Because of Winfield Scott's decision to keep the regulars together, drill instructors were at a premium and many officers had to improvise, sometimes interpreting Hardee's or Silas Casey's manual of arms with comical results.[14] Fortunately, most units had some veteran of the Mexican War or immigrant with European service to act as drillmaster and begin beating this human raw material into infantry cogs.[15]

Loading and marching, marching and loading, repeated endlessly—or so it must have seemed to the boys. All of it was done in a progression beginning at the squad level, and as the subjects became more proficient, they moved up the chain of combat formations to company, then regiment, and eventually brigade (four regiments). Troops also learned to form pickets for protection and to skirmish out in front of the lines of battle. All of it consumed much of the day, rain or shine, cold or hot: an ancient routine guaranteed to draw men together, a dance that unified in body and spirit, but also assaulted the individuality of what was a rowdy and spirited bunch of westerners. Sometimes they clowned around, performing pathetically on parade for officers they didn't like; and they hated the abusive punishments that were occasionally inflicted on malefactors (hanging by thumbs was one).[16] But these boys were also volunteers. They wanted to become soldiers, and this was the only process being offered to move them around and get them deployed and shooting. So they drilled and continued to drill until they began to feel the power of the whole, which was the entire point.

It was also a big problem. Most of these boys had arrived in what we would call good shape: lean and physically fit from lives on farms or strenuous work elsewhere, used to walking and being outdoors. But they were weak in ways they never suspected, and living together—sleeping in twelve-man Sibley tents and eating in mass messes—almost immediately revealed their lack of immunity to measles, mumps, and tonsillitis, childhood diseases that soldiers from cities would have already experienced.[17]

These put them down in huge numbers, half or more during their first months of service.[18] So many were sick that Sergeant Spotts of the Eighty-seventh Indiana was shocked to see "only 400 guns (out of a 1000) are stacked at night."[19] Though most recovered, many were weakened for the arrival of real killers, smallpox and the *Streptococcus erysipelas*. Before long, boys were helping to bury their friends and neighbors, casualties of an enemy they couldn't see and hadn't signed up to fight. And it would only get worse when subsequent campaigns led them into skirmishes, then pitched battles with dysentery, typhoid, pneumonia, and that swamp standby, malaria—the Civil War's principal killers, taking two of them for every one done in by rebels.[20] Meanwhile, the camps' primitive hygiene and rudimentary medical care at this stage only compounded matters. Still, the great majority survived these initial encounters with the Reaper and would come to understand it was part of the process that was turning them into soldiers.

On the positive side, they were beginning to look the part. Though the westerners were never as well clad as their eastern equivalents, even at an early stage the Union government was racing to replace aberrant uniforms (those of the Zouaves, for instance) and those of confusing coloration (gray) with the standard dark blue jacket and light blue trousers of the regulars. Depending on the quirks of a supply system that was a work in progress, soldiers also might be issued a cap, a wool flannel shirt, drawers, socks, and a long blue overcoat. And they were provided shoes, a really bad pair of foot maimers (not shaped for left or right) known with absolutely no affection as "gunboats."[21] Boys on the march soon learned the shoes were prone to falling apart, a painful prospect for an army destined to walk more than two thousand miles and one of Sherman's biggest supply problems.

The guns they got initially were not a lot better. Prior to mid-1862, most troops were issued inherently inaccurate smoothbore muskets, either the .69-caliber 1842 Federal issue or an imported Belgian gun with an enormous cheek piece. "I don't believe one could hit the broadside of a barn with them," complained one recruit.[22] These boys were used to firearms, and he probably knew what he was talking about. But the style of warfare they were being trained for and expected was not about accuracy so much as it was about rate of fire, making this a moot point—at least for a while.

Nor can it be said that the boys at this stage were well led. Democratically led they were, though, since among the common initial activities at camp was the election of officers—lieutenants and captains by the men; majors and colonels by those at company grade.[23] Noncommissioned officers, sergeants and corporals, were similarly chosen.

While the practice went on in the East and even among Confederates, it was most heartily embraced by the westerners. The elevation of men for reasons of popularity and not necessarily military competence struck regulars like Sherman as lunacy,[24] but leadership elections reflected a deeply held sense of equality among these volunteers. Officers and men of the Army of the West got along notably well together, and in good measure it was because they viewed themselves as the same.[25] In large part they were. Eventually, over 90 percent of the lieutenants and 50 percent of the captains had prior service as enlisted men.[26] "Rank is not royalty in Sherman's Army,"[27] one sergeant wrote his mother.

But neither did it signify proficiency at this stage. Amateurs leading amateurs was closer to the truth. The newly elevated struggled to interpret tactical manuals, were often required to attend night schools conducted by superiors,[28] and pumped regulars they could find for guidance; but in general this was a very green group by the end of the training cycle. Yet many had been elected because they were known at home as bright and capable individuals. They too wanted to learn, to be respected and relied upon by their men and their superiors. They would make numerous rookie mistakes, some of them fatal, but they were also largely unburdened by much of the conventional military wisdom that proved dysfunctional in the fluid tactical and technical environment of the Civil War. They remained ready to adapt, just like their men, all of them acting like Americans.

Still, the transition from training to active duty was a shock. Men found themselves packed in railway cars and steamships or simply marched toward the periphery of the South's western defenses. Staggering under fifty or sixty pounds of equipment over all sorts of terrain was a far cry from the drill field and proved exhausting. "We have been doing our first real soldiering and its no fun," wrote an

Indiana soldier, and soon enough boys "began to throw away things and there were blankets[,] books[,] overcoats and underwear scattered all along."[29] But even freed of nonessentials, they remained heavily laden, ill shod, and obliged to keep up the pace day after day. At the end of an eighteen-mile march that began at two in the morning—one that killed two and left eighteen of his company sick from heat exhaustion—another Hoosier infantryman wrote "a soldier's life[,] the worst lie a man ever seen."[30]

Even given their rural background, being outdoors all the time, subject to nature's whims, proved a miserable experience for most. Off the road, camp living was hardly better than on the road. The disease-incubating Sibleys were soon replaced by the two-man dog tent—a rudimentary affair erected by buttoning together the half sheets carried by each occupant and then propped at the ends by their guns with bayonets fixed and stuck in the ground.[31] They were light and easy to pitch, but far from weatherproof.

The soaking reality of "rained all night" literally washed over them. Sergeant Rice Bull echoed the experience of many when he recalled: "In our ignorance we did not ditch around our tents so were washed out of house and home."[32] Remembering a similar predicament, another soldier wrote: "It rained so hard that we had to stand up a considerable part of the time to let the water run off."[33] Still another summed up the experience laconically: "It still rains and it is an auful wet rain too."[34]

Nobody starved, but some occasionally went hungry as the Union logistics tail stretched as they moved. And the food they got from supply trains remained consistently horrible. The sustenance of Sherman's troopers quickly evolved around three dietary pillars— coffee, hardtack (cracker baked from flour and water), and salt pork. This culinary pyramid could be combined in at least two ways: "skillygallee" (soaked hardtack browned in pork fat and seasoned with coffee) or, for those on the move, fatback between hardtack for a nourishing lard sandwich.[35]

Occasionally, food could be purchased from locals if the soldiers had any money; mothers sent care packages that sometimes reached them; and later, foraging provided much better dietary alternatives.

But early in the war and on the road, the boys were stuck with what amounted to mean cuisine. To stave off scurvy, soldiers got lime juice and pickles and here and there could pick blackberries, which was an excellent preventive. But the Union commissariat's efforts in the direction of a more balanced diet—desiccated vegetables and concentrated milk—were typically scorned as "desecrated vegetables and consecrated milk."[36] Instead, the boys stuck mostly to the basics. "I have got so I can drink out of mud puddles and eat raw pork. Dear me, what are we coming to?" one soldier wrote his mother.[37] But slowly, those still on their feet came to agree with an Indiana private who surmised that it was part of a "hardening process which soldiers very much need in order to get them ready."[38]

As far as recreation went, there wasn't much. But this was, after all, a giant camping trip, and in the constant presence of one another, soldiers developed friendships that deepened over time, particularly at the lowest or squad level—an ancient process by which through propinquity and eating together, men were welded into little bands of brothers who would one day risk their lives, even throw them away, to help and protect one another.

These were young men full of sexual desire, but outlets were and remained scarce. There is little evidence of homosexual activity or even veiled reference to it. Meanwhile, contact with available women remained rare, rarer than in other Federal forces.[39] With the exception of stints in Memphis, Chattanooga, and Savannah, where there were lots of whores, the Army of the West stuck mostly to the countryside, and their lower rates of infection (about a quarter that of the Union army as a whole)[40] reflected it. They certainly drank when they could get alcohol, but this too was episodic (most notably in Columbia, South Carolina) and inherently limited by their itinerary. The boys played cards a lot—poker, which they called "bluff," twenty-one, and faro—and when they had money, they gambled, by reputation, at least, more than other armies.[41]

But most of all they wrote letters, and this was true everywhere. In the fall of 1861, one civilian who had firsthand knowledge of many units reported that some regiments mailed an average of six hundred letters per day.[42] Most were sent to home and family, but the boys also kept track of relatives and friends stationed with other elements. This was highly significant, since it helps explain how soldiers would communicate combat experiences and tips on how to stay alive—paper messengers traversing the sub-rosa soldier network and providing information for change and adaptation. Combat would land them in a place beyond horrible, and they would need all the help they could get.

They called it "seeing the elephant," and though a huge thing, they found it much more elusive and difficult to comprehend than they ever imagined. At this stage, tactical intelligence extended not much farther than pickets and skirmishers could see. Making contact with the enemy, especially on favorable terms, proved extremely difficult, a matter of fits and starts. "We went out about three miles but did not find any Cavelry but did find some chickens that looked good,"[43] a sort of consolation prize for one Indiana boy.

There were also numerous false alarms. "We had quite a scare last night," reported the same soldier. At two in the morning, word had come that rebels were crossing a river about four miles away. "We hastily got out of our warm beds, fell in line and were told to load our guns. I don't know wether it was because I was cold getting up so suddenly or what but I shivered so I could hardly load my gun and a good many of the boys seemed to be affected the same way."[44] If they were frightened, they need not have worried; yet again, the elephant slipped away.

Eventually, though, the elephant burst out of the thicket. Like First Bull Run, early battles in the West—Wilson's Creek and Belmont—were confused affairs subject to wild swings of fortune as virginal combatants staggered between fight and flight. Some fought bravely, some ran away, some did both, and for a relative few[45] it was their last day on earth. While disease would kill many more Yanks than bullets, combat was what war was all about. And once they had seen it, the boys realized it was another reality entirely, one in which men could turn into killing machines, and if you were unlucky, writhing, soon-to-be dead meat. It was a sobering experience. One member of the Twenty-fourth Ohio allowed that he "had seen the elephant several times, and did not care about seeing him again unless necessary."[46] It would be. The future would feature whole herds of the gray giants.

3

A thousand miles to the east, William Tecumseh Sherman viewed the maturation process of the volunteers with the deepest skepticism from the beginning. And after the humiliation of Bull Run, being chased off the battlefield and all the way back to Washington, his view of them hardened into studied contempt. Several weeks after his famous encounter with the president and the recalcitrant captain he had threatened to shoot, some two hundred of his volunteers went on strike—and met with similar results: he lined up three companies of regulars with guns leveled and arrested the diehards.[47] As far as Sherman was concerned, "this is a bad class of men to depend on to fight. They may eat their rations and go on Parade, but when danger comes they will be sure to show the white feather."[48] Not unexpectedly, his disdain was reciprocated. According to one volunteer captain in the Sixty-ninth New York, Sherman was remembered as "a rude and envenomed martinet" who was "hated by the regiment."[49] For what would become a memorable military romance, this was one rocky start.

Nevertheless, there were already many sides of Sherman that would one day endear him to these grumbling volunteers. It would take time for him to gain confidence, to find a comfortable place under Grant's wing and evolve into a strategic wizard; but he was already an accomplished warrior—cool in combat, a natural and charismatic leader who possessed an extraordinary toolbox of military skills.

One day, his men would marvel at his almost supernatural understanding of terrain and direction. Vast armies would follow him blindly and with utter confidence that he knew where he was going. His capacious mind also had plenty of room for the myriad logistical details that would get them fed, plus the imagination to cut them loose on the countryside to get their own. Your best bet for not starving was to stick with Sherman. And also for not getting killed. Later in the war, no one was more parsimonious with his soldiers' lives, a quality guaranteed to endear.

But eventually they came to worship him because he was Sherman—or, more precisely, Uncle Billy. His manic energy was infectious, and his iron constitution made his personal invincibility seem their own. Uncle Billy also defined the perfect distance between them, avuncular, not patriarchal—gave them room to grow and adapt under his tutelage, not an iron hand.

It worked most of all because Sherman was by nature theatrical. He constructed Uncle Billy, and though the process seems to have been unconscious and instinctive, it resulted in as good an example of what John Keegan called "the Mask of Command" as ever existed. The first glimmerings may have come in Louisiana with his military cadets gathered around him. His uniform became almost a costume—rumpled but sourced from Brooks Brothers, topped with an assortment of straw hats.[50] His extreme gregariousness came across for the most part as a friendly interest in everybody he encountered, including the lowliest private. But he could impose his mood on any situation, which is a necessity in battle—a key quality of successful commanders.

Like Napoleon, he dominated the script of war, and not just through sheer volume. He matched Grant, even surpassed him, in his capacity for the memorable phrase, the strategic one-liner, once again critical in operations since you want subordinates to remember what you told them to do. But it also welded him to his men, who reveled in his rhetoric and traded his aphorisms across their soldier network until they all believed they knew him. That combined with his capacity for the grand gesture: jumping nude in the river with the rest of the boys to wash off months of campaign grime accumulated from chasing Joe Johnston and John Bell Hood. "Great chance for the boys to get cleaned up for Atlanta," he proclaimed. One soldier spoke for all when he turned to a friend and whispered: "I'd follow Uncle Billy to hell."[51]

4

That journey had begun at Shiloh on April 6, 1862, when he and the boys found themselves facing a gray wall of howling Confederates bearing down on them with the energy of a tsunami. This first gathering of what became the Army of the West was also its first monumental exposure to combat, a full helping of killing and being killed, of agony beyond measure. With the exception of Antietam and Cold Harbor, the Civil War never got worse than this.

Although the Southern plan was to roll the Yankees up along the Tennessee River, the battle quickly devolved into something more primeval, a pattern repeated in a number of the most desperate battles in military history—one army attempting to drive the other into a body of water. For the force on the defensive, nothing could be more elemental. There was no escape: failure to hold meant annihilation.

On the Confederate side, those rebel yells were true yelps of rage at being invaded, their land violated by these arrogant Northerners, and they were determined to throw them out. They were also for the most part—like the Yankees—combat virgins, and what they experienced transported them to a place barely imagined, a hell on earth. Many on both sides ran, but most stayed and fought with a rage never felt before, one that altered perceptions and caused them to do things both desperate and heroic, all in a kind of trance. Shiloh was a stand-up fight, literally. The great majority of the participants, both blue and gray, were still armed with smoothbore guns, so it was possible for each side to blaze away at the other out in the open for extended periods. It produced horrific results. Yet the twenty-four thousand casualties marked the barest outline of what was experienced.

For that, we need to see Shiloh through the eyes of a participant, one of the boys—in this case a seventeen-year-old drummer, John Cockerill. He had arrived at Pittsburg Landing convalescing from a serious illness under the care of his father, who commanded one of Sherman's regiments, the Seventieth Ohio. When shots rang out

Sunday morning, the father mounted his horse to take command of his regiment, leaving his son, who was part of another unit in Buell's army, basically on his own. Cockerill grabbed a gun, and there ensued a mind-bending combat odyssey, one that Sherman himself considered the truest rendering of what happened that day and the next.[52]

At first Cockerill was just an observer, taking refuge in the Shiloh church, marveling from afar as Confederate units deployed, half-obscured by the smoke from their own firing. He could see Sherman ("erect in the saddle...a veritable war eagle") and his staff racing from one emergency to another. Then the fighting neared and he was driven from the church.

For a while, he helped carry a wounded officer and found the rear chaotic. Then he fell in with a brigade wearing Scotch caps, one he discovered dancing nervously to tunes supplied by a regimental band before going into battle. Cockerill decided to join them. A kind lieutenant took his name and wrote it down "in case anything should happen to me." On the way to the front, the unit was ordered to screen several batteries of artillery and was severely shelled, all hugging the ground and scattering for cover from the exploding projectiles. "Everything looked weird and unnatural. The very leaves on the trees, though scarcely out of the bud, seemed greener....The faces of the men about me looked like no faces that I had ever seen on earth. Actions took on the grotesque forms of nightmares....The wounded and butchered men who came up out of the blue smoke in front of us...seemed like bleeding messengers come to tell us of the fate that awaited us."[53]

They were. The brigade was pushed over to the extreme left flank and waited as the volleys rolled toward them. Then a nervous shot revealed their presence and brought forth a torrent of shrieking bullets. As Cockerill delivered his second shot, a ball shattered a bush and threw splinters in his face. Suddenly the dry leaves in front of him were burning. Men were falling, including the kind lieutenant, shot dead while waving his sword. The storm of fire drove them into a ravine for cover. Cockerill kept firing until he was out of cartridges, then everybody ran.

As they raced away, a soldier next to him, perhaps three years older, was hit in the leg. He begged for help, and Cockerill threw away his gun and half dragged him along until he could no longer stand. Cockerill propped him under a tree and helplessly watched him bleed to death in a few minutes.

Now out of range, he wandered back toward the river. He took a drink from the canteen of a soldier sitting on a stump and drained it to the last drop, suddenly aware of an insatiable thirst. He saw a man he recognized from the Seventieth Ohio, who told him he had seen his father shot dead from his horse. "This intelligence filled me with dismay," and his retreat slid into withdrawal. He rode an ambulance past cavalry trying to herd skulkers back toward the fighting. He passed a temporary field hospital, where hundreds of wounded men were being unloaded and where "their arms and legs were being cut off and thrown out to form gory, ghastly heaps."[54]

On foot again, he moved within sight of the river and saw a mass of wagons, mule teams, disabled artillery, and "thousands of panic-stricken men." Then he saw Grant, surrounded by bodyguards, ride to the landing and beg them to make one more effort, promising that reinforcements were on the way and then threatening them with cavalry. The cavalry came and went, and most of the skulkers filtered back.

Across the Tennessee, he saw a horseman brandishing a white flag with a square in the middle and realized he constituted the leading edge of Buell's army—the one to which his own unit, the Twenty-fourth Ohio, belonged. Reinforcements were on the way. He found his brother, who was one of the regiment's company commanders, and told him of their father's death. His brother gave him some fried chicken, and once again Cockerill, a drumstick in each hand, started marching toward battle; but then his sibling ordered him back. Within minutes, he watched them all disappear toward the smoke and potential oblivion of battle. It was almost nightfall; the sun went down and the roar of small arms finally ceased.

That night, Cockerill found another member of his father's regiment, Silcott, who told him "nearly all his friends and acquaintances figured as corpses."[55] Together they sat on a bale of hay, drenched by an unrelenting downpour. Finally, they curled up in the mud and slept fitfully, awakened every few minutes by gunboat broadsides, the endless storm's thunder, and the general commotion caused as Buell's army continued to unload from across the river and sloshed off toward the front, their canteens rattling against their bayonet scabbards.

As dawn approached, the band of the Fifteenth Regulars struck up a selection from *Il Trovatore* and Cockerill took heart. In the midst of what had now become a hailstorm, he headed yet again for the fight, which he could hear starting. Thousands of others joined him. Lew Wallace's division had also finally arrived. Someone gave him a shot of commissary whiskey. He saw a crowd of Confederate prisoners, and when one was asked to identify himself, he responded: "Company Q, of the Southern Invincibles, and be damned to you!"[56] The tide was plainly turning.

The Union lines were now moving steadily forward, and as Cockerill followed, he saw what battle had done—great trees shattered, the underbrush mowed down by bullets, and the ground full of corpses "so thick that I could step from one to the other....All the bodies had been stripped of their valuables and scarcely a pair of boots or shoes could be found upon the feet of the dead."[57] He broke into tears upon noticing a beautiful blond Confederate boy about his age, who looked as if he had fallen asleep. "The blue and the gray were mingled together. This peculiarity I observed all over the field."[58]

Cockerill never caught up with the fighting, but eventually he found himself back at the Shiloh church where his terrible walkabout had begun. He found the camp of the Seventieth Ohio and learned they had been sent with Sherman to pursue the rebels as they headed toward Corinth. He found his father's bullet-riddled tent and discovered the contents exchanged for ragged Confederate equivalents. There he stayed through the day and late into the evening, when the regiment finally returned. At its head rode Cockerill's father, unscathed. After "the most affectionate embrace that my life had ever known," the two spent the rest of the night talking over what had happened to them. Whether they put it into words or not, it boiled down to one thing: They were both alive, still on the right side of the dirt.

Cockerill's experience is worth recounting precisely because battle is all about survival (he lived to become editor of the *New York Herald*). Those who managed to get through the first great test had a significantly better chance of living through future encounters. Those still standing got to move on; the dead got picked clean before the fighting was even over. At Shiloh, the boys learned when to keep their heads down and also when they had to fight—corporately, the Army of the West had seen the elephant, looked him in the eye. From now on, they at least knew what to expect from the great gray beast.

So did Sherman. Shiloh marked the last time he emerged from battle winged and bleeding. There would be other near misses, many of them, but he too learned to sense danger approaching and get out of the way. He too was a survivor.

The next day, Sherman visited the Seventieth Ohio, and Cockerill had the pleasure of hearing him tell his father: "Colonel, you have been worth your weight in gold to me."[59] Hardly memorable words, but any compliment from this odd, jumpy general was coming to mean a great deal. As he returned to the battlefield from his pursuit and first encounter with Forrest, great roars of approval had erupted, "rolling down the line," brigade after brigade.[60] It was not just the troops he had brought to Pittsburg Landing. Buell's army, Kentucky soldiers who had once disliked him, now broke into cheers whenever they saw Sherman—"such shouting you have never heard."[61] It was true everywhere he went. Not long after, they began calling him Uncle Billy. This was still Grant's army, but these were becoming his boys.

5

But the war in the West was not fought simply at the conventional level. Sherman and his troops quickly discovered they were surrounded by an insurgency; that the countryside of southwestern Tennessee and northern Mississippi was against them. And this presented an entirely different set of military challenges. As we have seen, Sherman's own reprisal-based approach only added fuel to the fire, nor did he seem to fully understand the potential danger he and the Union invasion force faced if things got out of hand. For once Uncle Billy was clueless, or nearly so.

Without guidance from above, the boys were on their own— many scattered in small garrisons, guarding supply lines—left to cope with boredom, loneliness, and a deceptively peaceful environment that could turn lethal in an instant. Tactically, insurgencies are intensely personal, a style of warfare built on terror and surprise aimed at undermining the psyche of its victims and inducing passivity and helplessness. Its target is the individual soldier. At an elemental level, the issue is reduced to whether he copes or doesn't; is alert or isn't; is tricked or sees through the ruse. This is why it makes sense to view the insurgency from ground level, again through the prism of a single participant.

There had always been Union supporters in the South, those who did not agree with secession. Through bitter experience, they had learned to keep their heads down. But when Federal forces established themselves deep in the Mississippi Valley, these people could be expected to take heart and align themselves with the invaders. This seemed normal and natural to young Theodore Upson, whose unit, the One Hundredth Indiana, was stationed near Collierville, just east of Memphis.

"We had got acquainted with a young man and his wife on a plantation about 1½ miles East of our stockade. He claimed to be loyal and we had some very pleasant visits at their house. He told us that a flock of wild turkeys staid in a swamp near his place and...if one of us would bring his rifle and stay all night so as to be there early in the morning he might get one easily."[62] It seemed to Upson like an ideal opportunity to get to know this attractive couple, "Bud Raymond and his little wife," sleep in a bed for the first time since he left home, and then bag supper. The next morning, he and Bud awoke early and went down by the swamp, where "Raymond told him to stand by a tree and he would go a little to one side and call up some turkeys."

Instead, two gray-clad cavalry came galloping out of the brush, and in a desperate instant Upson realized he was the designated turkey. Many soldiers, even veterans, might have frozen and then died at the hands of these manhunters. But Raymond and his Confederates had cornered the wrong boy. Upson jumped behind the tree, shot the first horseman, then threw down his rifle, pulled a revolver, and fired so close to the second that he fell off his horse. Finally, he whirled and shot Raymond in the arm as he raced up the hill brandishing his own revolver. Upson had disarmed all three when the boys arrived from the stockade, having heard shots. Some wanted to hang Raymond, but instead they marched him back to the stockade and then to the guardhouse in Collierville, from which he quickly escaped. Soon after, the plantation house was burned and Raymond's wife went south. Upson would be decorated for bravery, but he told his friends that "he was so mad to think how he had been tricked that he never thought of the danger."[63]

There was an epilogue. In October 1863, as Sherman's train headed toward Chattanooga, it was ambushed at the Collierville station by a substantial number of Confederate cavalry. Upson's unit, the One Hundredth Indiana, was marching close behind and raced over to save him. They arrived just as the rebel horsemen withdrew, having inflicted some casualties, but not on Sherman. The next morning, Upson went out to look at the dead and found among them Bud Raymond in a captain's uniform—shot through the head—and his father-in-law, McGee, dressed as a civilian: "They will be good Johnnys now sure," concluded Upson.[64] Home, family, now his own life: Bud Raymond had given it all for what was supposed to be a turkey shoot. Insurgency was a snake among wars and could turn and strike in any direction.

But not Upson's. He proved to be an exemplary soldier, possibly one of Sherman's best. In today's army, it's likely he would have found his way to the Special Forces. He had all the qualities—not simply courage, lethality, and exceptional endurance; Upson adapted to emergencies with lightning acuity, and he never took more chances than he had to. He was a natural, especially if you were looking for one.

Henry Hall was. Hall was also a member of the One Hundredth Indiana, a local merchant from Upson's hometown who, after failing to be elected lieutenant, took to scouting the countryside around the regiment, often in disguise, sometimes as a Confederate officer.[65] This was exceedingly risky, since military custom dictated that spies in the opposite uniform be summarily executed. But Hall was a good mimic and apparently could pass as a rebel.

It was also clear he was tapping other sources. "I find that Hall gets a good share of his information from the Negros," wrote Upson. "They seem to know every thing and are pretty shrewd too. One of them told us where two field guns were hid.... In the same way we captured several boxes of Enfield rifles that had never been un-packed. Such things have given Hall a reputation as a scout."[66] It also exemplified the way things were happening in the Army of the West. Intelligence in this environment was plainly critical, and what amounted to a freelancer found a way to get it. This did not long go unnoticed at the top.

Hall's dark network informed him that Union gunboats were on the way up the Tennessee, and he made sure the information went directly to Sherman, who wanted to cross without delay. Soon after, Hall learned that a group of Confederates were holed up in a house about fifteen miles away and with a party of five captured the lot of them—four officers, including a lieutenant colonel and fourteen en-listed.

Sherman's reaction was characteristic. Almost instinctively, he re-warded initiative and success. As a commander, he was as much fa-cilitator as dictator, and he was every bit as improvisational as his men. In this case, he ordered a detail of a hundred men to serve under Hall as "scouts"—instant anti-insurgents.

This was not necessarily good news for Theodore Upson. Hall had been after him for some time, knowing he was exactly what he needed for irregular warfare. But Upson hesitated; Hall's schemes were all high-risk. "He told me what he was going to do when he got his 100 men and said he wanted them all to be brave men who would go anywhere and do anything he told them to do and that he thought I was just the one he wanted."[67] There was no escaping Hall, it seemed. But that proved only temporary. Within days, he learned Hall had been ambushed by rebels armed with shotguns and mortally wounded. "And so this is the end of all his great ambitions. He was a good soldier, brave but reckless of danger," Upson concluded, speaking like a true survivor.[68]

6

Shiloh changed everything for Sherman. Once he knew these volunteers would and could fight, he never again viewed them with contempt. In the aftermath of the battle, he continued to drill his division intensively. Yet by the end of May 1862, he was telling Ellen that "our army is now composed of all the best troops & men in the West and if we cannot conquer here we might as well give it up."[69]

This, however, would demand many more military skills than could be learned on the parade ground. Besides, the variety of missions they would undertake precluded turning them into any one thing. So he became a guiding hand, presenting them with a series of challenges and basically letting them figure out how to meet them. Yet he never lost contact; he was always among them, completely approachable. "Every soldier of my command comes into my presence as easy as the highest officer....They see me daily[,] nightly[,] hourly."[70]

This was exactly how he led them into the swamps around Vicksburg. First he loaded them onto riverboats with names like *Forest Queen, Ohio Belle, Prairie Rose,* and *Polar Star,* either freezing on deck or packed below, where "the air [was] stinking and unfit to breath[e]."[71] Then he deposited them at Chickasaw Bluffs and the Arkansas Post and expected them to conduct what amounted to amphibious assaults, excruciatingly difficult tactical operations. They didn't always win, but they gave a good account of themselves and also learned that Sherman wasn't careless with their lives. They didn't blame him when Grant wasted their time trying to dig their way around Vicksburg with canals that only flooded. Instead, they followed Sherman into the Yazoo Delta, sometimes marching in water up to their hips, and learned that he never seemed to get lost; they rescued Porter at Steele's Bayou that way, all of them.

Sherman didn't want Grant to take them inland, cutting their supply lines and circling in behind Vicksburg. He worried they might starve, considered it all too risky. Instead, the boys took to foraging, as he later said, "like ducks to water."[72] Next, they all became combat engineers, surrounding Vicksburg with trenches and besieging it till it fell on that fateful July 4, 1863.

It seemed for a while they would all get some rest. But then came news of Chickamauga, little Willy died, and they found themselves on the road to Chattanooga. Not exactly dancing lessons from God, but if ever an army had an opportunity to march through thick and thin, it was during this campaign, one that after the heroics of Missionary Ridge drove them all together—a unified Army of the West under the auspices of Uncle Billy Sherman, at last. But there was still more marching to be done—six days virtually nonstop over frigid mountainous terrain—to relieve Burnside at Knoxville, only to find him eating a turkey dinner. As they trudged their icy way back, hundreds of soldiers were entirely barefoot.[73] When Sherman finally brought them back to winter quarters, their uniforms in tatters, their equipment bent and broken, they had become underneath a true all-weather, all-terrain vehicle, a prodigy of foot power. Their road-ready spirit was caught around this time by some of Sherman's troops watching another army pass by:

" 'Good marching that,' said one.

" 'Yes,' said another, 'but them fellers's been fed on pate de foie gras, and there's too much paper shirt-collar for me.'

" 'Twenty-six inches to the step,' said another, 'seventy steps to the minute; we'd beat 'em twenty steps a minute in a march, which would be more'n a half a mile an hour, and them havin' such good shoes on, too.' "[74]

7

There was something else. Something very important. They were doing it all in the midst of a firepower revolution. By the spring of 1862, both sides were largely equipped with rifles, not smoothbores, nearly identical weapons—the .58-caliber Springfield Model 1861 on the Federal side and the British-made .577 Enfield for the Confederates.[75] The key to these guns was a dramatically improved bullet, the so-called minié ball, with a deep cavity at its base that filled with hot gas upon firing, expanding the edges to form a tight seal with the bore, one that caused it to follow the twisted grooves, or rifling, of the gun. Whereas slugs shot by smoothbores bounced up the barrel, these new projectiles emerged straight and with accuracy-enhancing spin. Prior to shooting, however, minié balls could still be loaded as fast and easily from the muzzle as their smoothbore cousins—faster, actually, since the new rifles also employed all-weather percussion caps to ignite the charge, rather than the previous era's cumbersome flintlocks, which were all but useless in heavy rain.[76]

But firing at up to three shots per minute was the least of it. The accurate range of these guns was now extended to four hundred yards, roughly triple that of their smoothbore predecessors. At the tactical level, this shifted the dynamics of the battlefield suddenly and dramatically. Following Napoleonic precedent, American officers fighting the Mexican War had enjoyed great success by moving artillery forward with infantry to blow holes in enemy lines and soften them up for a final charge.[77] Now, however, the accurate range of rifled small arms exceeded that of cannon (which mostly remained smoothbores), allowing infantry to slaughter artillery crews should they attempt to unlimber at close range out in the open.

The impact was even more devastating on cavalry, which traditionally had been used to break wavering infantry or to swoop down on artillery before they set up. Now, with the new rifles, a cavalry charge became tantamount to suicide. Early in the war, infantry had regularly practiced forming squares with bayonets fixed, the standard anticavalry maneuver—Sherman had employed one at First Bull Run. Now nobody bothered. Cavalry who wanted to survive stuck to reconnaissance and raiding, and if they chose to fight, they got off their horses and deployed like infantry.

But if everything now turned on the foot soldier, adaptation at this level was also difficult. Officers, particularly the professionals, had been trained in traditional open-field, close-range infantry tactics at West Point, and many of the key leaders on both sides of the Civil War had fought in Mexico, where it had worked brilliantly. With smoothbores, such stand-up firefighting made sense; but these new guns facilitated engagement very early, inflicting casualties for much longer periods as the lines closed. With increasing regularity, frontal assaults became occasions for slaughter; yet mainstream commanders, typified by Grant and Lee, had great trouble understanding what was happening and continued to throw their men at one another.[78]

Sherman, who had not fought in Mexico, proved more circumspect. His tendency to break off combat when it appeared hopeless, along with his penchant for operational and strategic maneuver over sheer confrontation, pointed to a kind of instinctive understanding that the lethal dimensions of battle had grown far wider. Yet he could still be provoked into a frontal assault, as he would be at Kennesaw Mountain. Nor is it possible to cite any statement on his part that the new Springfields had made any difference, much less all the difference.

Sherman and his West Point brothers had grown up in a period that looked back on centuries of stability in weapons technology. The idea that the future was to be one of constant and revolutionary innovation, sometimes leading to huge disasters such as the western front, would have struck them as bizarre. On a case-by-case basis—adopting rifled small arms, exploiting the possibilities of railroads—they were not necessarily regressive technologically, but they missed the implications almost entirely, the second- and third-order effects. Their cognitive filters were simply not set up to receive such a message. Besides, they were in the midst of a great war.

The reaction of the soldiers themselves, the users and the targets, was a lot faster and more direct—individually, they lay low and sought cover whenever they could. But it was also complicated. Basically, the boys liked firepower. A number had complained bitterly over the early guns issued, and Federal troops universally greeted the new Springfields as a great improvement, regarding them with pride and affection.[79]

And these western boys very likely knew how to use them, most having come from a rural background where early exposure to guns and hunting was part of growing up. The myth of the frontier marksman was no myth. The boys really could shoot.

But for most there was also a great deal of difference between picking off a squirrel, a deer, or even a bear and willfully gunning down a member of one's own species. Strong, though definitely rescindable, human inhibitions against killing our own have been well documented.[80] Yet this was bound to vary among individuals—inherently and also subject to differences in training and experience.

Some killed easily, some never could, and accurate small arms facilitated both. The days of bladed weapons, cutting and puncturing an adversary, were pretty much over—the bayonet played almost no role in Civil War death dealing.[81] Instead, it now went on at increasingly longer ranges, making it easier physically and especially psychologically. For those who were good at it, this meant a great leap in lethality. For those who couldn't do it at all, there were many reasons for missing. And then there was everybody in between.

Despite the huge amount of evidence and firsthand battle commentary, there is not a lot of reliable accounting as to how these differences played out: how the true shooters were recognized and their effect maximized, and also what everybody else did. For the most part, the men were reticent about killing. Even Upson, who was extremely efficient, never actually admits to taking another life.

Still, the way firing patterns developed among units under attack—less at the beginning and more as the aggressors got closer—suggests that those known to be the best shots were continuously fed loaded rifles until putting up a storm of lead became paramount, and then everybody picked up a gun and shot fast and blindly through a cloud of gun smoke at the advancing line. This is known to have happened, but how much remains an open question.[82] Most didn't want to be remembered as killers, but neither did they want to be known to posterity as loaders.

One thing is certain: If at all possible, they wanted to do it from behind cover. Vicksburg's last chapter was the first major action in the Civil War to be fought from trenches. It was a siege, of course, but it was also prophetic. The new climate of lethality, though only vaguely comprehended in letters home, was changing behavior quickly.[83]

Very suddenly, the boys became combat engineers. This was not the result of a command decision. The officers had nothing to do with it; the boys themselves had reacted, and their intent shot out across their soldier network until everybody was digging and piling on for dear life. "Troops, halting for the night or for battle," Sherman later observed, "stacked arms, gathered logs, stumps, fence rails, anything that would stop a bullet; piled these to their front, and digging a ditch behind, threw the dirt forward, and made a parapet."[84] Other observers were amazed at how fast and skillfully they worked, yet they were also willing to dig deep into the night, anything for cover.[85]

This happened on both sides: the rebels too were going to ground. To the consternation of their officers, they also had reacted to the new guns and now much preferred to fight on the defensive. This implied gridlock—something that actually happened on the western front during World War I courtesy of the machine gun and high-explosive powered artillery—but at this stage there were alternatives. Operational maneuver was certainly possible, and it became Sherman's preference; but it often ended with both sides simply occupying a new set of field fortifications.[86]

Since officers remained in charge, attacks could be and were mounted—though it quickly became a rule of thumb that a three-to-one numerical advantage was needed for a decent shot at success.[87] The boys had not lost their aggressiveness. Far from it: when ordered, they remained ready to go forward and attack with determination. Out here, if not yet no-man's-land, it was certainly danger land, and they had to adjust. Formations loosened, and men advanced in spurts, taking advantage of any cover the ground might offer.[88] Above all, they stayed low. "When advancing or retiring," George Cram of the 105th Illinois told his mother, "they either lie flat to load or simply raise up on their knees."[89] And well they should have. The days of high, inaccurate fire were over. The Confederates with their Enfields were every bit as lethal as they were. Cram spoke for all in observing that "a terrible sheet of lead bridged the air above us and leaden hail flew threw our ranks…little leaden messengers."[90]

Combat out here under this volume of fire became more and more a matter of chance. Practically everybody had some close call to report—most dramatic, a shell shredding a knapsack, a shot stopped by a belt buckle, or a uniform grazed; but usually it was simply a near miss, an angry buzzing just a few inches away, sure to unnerve the most hardened veteran.[91] Yet even under the worst of circumstances, the majority emerged unscathed to wonder at their good fortune…and also at the bad luck of others. It was said that it took a man's weight in lead to produce a shot that would actually kill; but for some it just took one.

Death could come with stunning suddenness. Survivors repeatedly marveled at comrades next to them, firing one moment and then slumped dead the next. Before it was over, they would become connoisseurs of death: "This one was shot through the lungs and had been dead all night; this one was shot through the bowels and died hard, he kicked a great hole in the dirt and snow."[92]

But frequently the first indication of a bullet finding its mark was an eruption of profanity.[93] "When a ball strikes a man in full force…the instant pain is not so great as that would be from a light stroke of a carriage whip," wrote John King from the Chickamauga battlefield.[94] "The pain comes on gradually," and kept coming, he might have added, until it became a screaming omnipresence.

An ounce of lead traveling at between seven and eight hundred miles per hour caused terrible wounds, worse even than later high-velocity, low-mass, steel-jacketed rounds, which generally went right through the body. Minié balls plowed in and lodged—pulverizing organs, crushing bones, and shredding arteries. In an era not yet aware of antiseptics, amputation was the only answer for shattered limbs if gangrene and tetanus were to be avoided. Wounds to the torso were worse; gut shots were generally fatal, as there was no prevention of peritonitis, and hits to the lungs frequently ended in terminal pneumonia.[95] Around one in seven died from their wounds (the figure was one in four hundred during the Vietnam conflict a century later).[96]

Some received no care, the worst prospect of all. Many hundreds of the boys lay unattended in the rain the first night of Shiloh and even after the battle. The ambulance corps improved, but there was always the prospect of casualties being trapped behind enemy lines. This was what happened to Rice Bull, one of the easterners who joined the Army of the West after Chickamauga: "By May 8th our wounds had all festered and were hot with fever; our clothing which came into contact with them was so filthy and stiff from the dried blood that it gravely aggravated our condition. Many wounds developed gangrene and blood poisoning; lockjaw caused suffering and death. While the stench from nearby dead horses and men was sickening it was not worse than that from the living who lay in their own filth. Finally, not the least of our troubles were the millions of flies that filled the air and covered blood saturated clothing."[97] Bull lay like that for nine days before being evacuated in a prisoner exchange. After a long convalescence at home in New York State, he departed, his wounds not fully healed, and rejoined his unit in Tennessee.

As always, the boys made do. But in the case of medical care, it was the folks at home who rushed into the breach and helped them cope. All over the North, Sanitary Commissions sprang up, and a legion of civilians, many of them women, descended on the camps and hospitals to ease suffering and push for improvements.

In the West, the effort was spearheaded by the formidable Mary Ann Bickerdyke, who became a perpetual thorn in the side of lax practitioners and an eternal champion of the enlisted men, who dubbed her "Mother" Bickerdyke. Sherman wasn't exactly enamored with the "Sanitaries," whom he groused evacuated lightly wounded men and generally got in the way. But he recognized a kindred spirit in this vitriolic angel of mercy. When his staff complained about the insubordinate nurse who ignored red tape and army procedures, he gave them a verbal cold shoulder: "She ranks me. I can't do a thing."[98] And he didn't. She was the only woman he permitted in his advanced base hospitals,[99] his agent free to raise hell, Sherman-like, until things got better for the boys. Meanwhile, he made sure that the ambulances got springs, the surgeons were better organized and as competent as possible, and medical supplies flowed promptly to the front. Change came from the top and the bottom, everybody working together in the unlikeliest combinations.

This was true of all the other skills they would need to accumulate, the military odds and ends that kept an army going. Boys at all levels took initiative. Quietly, in obscurity, the Fifty-eighth Indiana and the First Missouri Engineers learned to work their bridging equipment, set and anchor the canvas boats, lay the beams to keep them together, and stabilize the planking—all potentially in fast-flowing streams. This required intensive and realistic practice, and these pontoniers took it upon themselves to get very good. When called upon, they would be ready.[100]

As we have seen, the boys became virtuosos at wrecking railroads. Sherman wanted the job to last: "Let the destruction be so thorough that not a rail or tie can be used again," he told his corps commanders.[101] The boys responded en masse: heaving up track in sections the length of a regiment, breaking up the rails, heating them until they glowed with bonfires made from the ties, then twisting them around trees so they were useless without remilling—"Sherman's neckties," they would be called.[102] One day, many would apply these skills productively and help build the transcontinental railroad; but for now they were into deconstruction, and it worked because everybody pitched in.

Meanwhile, teamsters by the thousands—wagon drivers and mule skinners—kept supplies flowing from railheads to the troops and learned to keep up with an army on the move through the roughest terrain. Out ahead, pioneers cleared the way, waging their own campaign against forest and swamp, chopping and corduroying so those behind might keep moving, and also blazing a path for African Americans, who largely took over this role in Sherman's epic assault on the South Carolina lowlands.

And it was all set to music, the way Americans have always liked it. Regimental bands had it hard in Sherman's army; instruments were hardly portable, and there were plenty of other things to do besides practicing the piccolo. Yet beat up and dented like practically everything else traveling with Uncle Billy, the bands persevered, striking up a tune impromptu as troops marched by, playing in the camps at night or at daybreak—serving up the patriotic mood music that fed the boys' souls on their long journey through hostile territory.

It all got done because an individual picked up not just a gun, but a rein, an ax, a rail, or a clarinet and made it happen. So it was that the Army of the West, commanded by William Tecumseh Sherman, had by the beginning of 1864 become the best fighting force that currently walked the face of the earth. He had helped, but they had made themselves the first truly archetypal American ground force. Now it was time to show what they really could do together.

Chapter X

ROAD WARRIORS

I

IT WAS AS IF the Army of the West collectively gritted its teeth. The Mississippi River had been taken back and the South cut in two, but still the Confederates refused to quit. With Grant, Uncle Billy had devised a strategy for a harder war. But the boys also seemed to intuitively grasp its necessity. "The prevailing feeling among the men," Rice Bull later wrote, "was a desire to finish the job...they were intelligent and could see that the Rebellion was nearing its end, so were willing and anxious to meet quickly any privation or danger that would bring the speedy end to the war."[1] Even among those whose three-year term was over, more than half chose to stay.[2] Home and family certainly called, but seeing this to an end was now paramount. The Army of the West was welded together with a sense of purpose and finality. Like their commander, they would first resort to pure violence; but when this didn't work, they too had the capacity to shift the paradigm and begin waging war on the mind of the South.

For they were not simply Sherman's sword, they were a multitude of swords, each autonomously directed, all in sync. As one eastern officer told a superior: "Sherman's appears to be an army of independent commands, each individual being a 'command.'"[3] This versatility was the reward of its democratic constituents and their painful self-evolution, more Swiss Army knife than sword, really. Whatever their configuration, they fit the hand of their commander with uncanny precision, enabling him to do to the South anything his protean military imagination could conjure up to inflict defeat.

At first the objective—at Grant's urging, as part of the Grand Plan—was simply to obliterate Joe Johnston's Army of Tennessee. Sherman's boys were better, and there were more of them. "No man ever saw all of Sherman's army in one day," wrote Sergeant John King of the Ninety-second Illinois from Adairsville, Georgia, in mid-May 1864. "The road was full all day, four men abreast as close as they could walk, occasionally interspersed with artillery, and it took from early morn till long after dark for this vast army of three corps to pass, all moving on a steady walk."[4] Ninety-eight thousand they numbered, a five-to-three advantage over the Confederates, whom they dared to come out and dance so they could lock them in a death's embrace. But Johnston was no fool: he kept his boys behind fortifications, and there ensued a war of maneuver.

Looking back, Sherman made it sound like a strategic matchup between cat and mouse, the routine being "to leave one part exposed inviting an attack by the enemy ... while the rest of the army is moving to some exposed and vital object or line of retreat to the enemy. The whole movement from Chattanooga to Atlanta was composed of different phases of the 'Game.'"[5] But the sterility of this description was belied by its reality: tough going and increasingly vicious fighting.

"A look at the map will give you little idea of the country we are passing through," wrote one soldier.[6] The 120-mile route to Atlanta was a roller coaster of rumpled Appalachian mountain spurs, cut by deep river valleys and covered with thick forest vegetation.[7] No great battles developed initially, but as the forces maneuvered from one set of fortifications to another over such terrain, there was constant small-unit contact along their leading edges. Because of limited visibility, the fighting was sudden, at close quarters, and often desperate. Rather than orgies of death, casualties accumulated in small doses, marked, Major James Connolly told his wife, by "the hundreds of little mounds that are rising by the wayside day by day, as if to mark the footprints of the God of War."[8] Meanwhile, a number of the boys were packing still more firepower, which in the end only complicated matters.

2

As the Civil War commenced, there were already available in the North two guns whose potential lethality far surpassed that of the Springfields. Both the Spencer and the Henry rifles employed self-contained rim-fire cartridges (the copper base holding the powder expanded to form the bore seal), enabling true mechanical loading and a seven-shot and sixteen-shot capacity, respectively. Rather than two to three aimed shots per minute, these guns were theoretically capable of over twenty. Even better, they could be fired and reloaded lying down or from behind almost any sort of cover. While Lincoln liked the repeaters and ordered them acquired, the armament authorities in Washington dragged their feet, considering them an excuse to waste ammunition. This may have been true of recruits, but in the hands of veterans, who knew how to hold their fire, these guns constituted a breakthrough in deadliness.[9]

The boys loved them—most preferred the Spencer, which shot a heavier slug; but the Henry also had its advocates, including Theodore Upson, who liked having sixteen shots at the ready[10]—and they set about acquiring them with their usual pragmatism. Thousands of individual soldiers appear to have spent $48 each to purchase repeaters.[11] Meanwhile, a number of commanders, on their own initiative, managed to equip their units with the new guns. One of them, Colonel J. G. Wilder, had turned the Ninety-second Illinois into mounted infantry and issued them Spencers, making them instantly what Sergeant John King described as a "boss" regiment.[12] His recounting of their subsequent adventures makes exceptionally clear the impact of these new guns.

After an initial successful skirmish, it became apparent "the 92nd would be placed where rebels were easy to get at and we would have an opportunity to use our superior guns."[13] With supreme confidence, in late January 1864 the Ninety-second took on an entire brigade of Confederate cavalry and "poured it into them until every horseman was either killed, wounded, or over the hill and out of sight."[14]

Eager for more combat, and feeling invincible, the unit almost immediately got into another firefight near Sweet Water, Alabama, one in which King found himself the point man. Concealed by a fence, he took aim at the corner of a house behind which there was a squad of Confederates who took turns jumping out and shooting. As they did, King fired six "splendid" shots in rapid succession before ducking when a rebel put a bullet into the rail in front of him. After the fight was over, King "had a curiosity to see how things looked at the corner of the house...and to my astonishment five men lay there, three dead and two mortally wounded.... One of the wounded rebels I really felt sorry for....He was shot through the lower part of the abdomen...tearing the intestines and leaving an opening through which they protruded." Faced with the results of his remarkable killing mechanism, King added: "I hoped that it was not a ball from my gun that hit him. There were so many of us shooting that no one could tell who did the execution."[15]

Three months later, the Ninety-second found themselves in the rough country near Ringgold, Georgia, at the very beginning of the Atlanta campaign. Sixty-two of the men had drawn picket duty and were guarding Nickajack Gap when, at four in the morning, they realized a large force of Confederates was lined up and ready to attack them. "There was no time for reflection and no plan for retreat was made, but every man prepared for fight, getting in good position behind stumps." The vegetation enabled the Confederates to get within thirty feet before the Yankees' Spencers barked out, halting them only momentarily. The Ninety-second was completely outnumbered and had to scatter; in the dark and under such conditions,

their repeaters did them little good. Something else happened—
three of those captured, Willie Hill, Joural O'Connor, and William
Cattanach, were summarily executed by the rebels.[16] This was highly
unusual, and one reason may have been the Ninety-second's guns.

"I think the Johnny's are getting rattled," wrote an Indiana sergeant from another unit; "they are afraid of our repeating rifles.
They say we are not fair, that we have guns that we load up on Sun-
days and shoot all the rest of the week."[17] Humorous from his perspective, but another matter entirely if you were on the receiving
end. The Confederates were confounded by such guns. They
couldn't fabricate them, and even captured repeaters were useless
since they didn't have the copper to make the ammunition casings.
So they simply had to take it and strike out when they could.

Still, theirs was only a temporary condition. Soon enough, all
armies would be similarly equipped with repeating firearms of
vastly increased power, along with a whole lot more, and the net effect would be millions gunned down in the most random fashion.
Firepower was not just a fickle mistress; it was the real enemy. And
this should have become apparent as the boys charged up Kennesaw
Mountain, a battle fought with hardly any Spencers at all.

3

In the end, an army is a tyranny, and a general is a dictator who
orders his men to go kill and die. For all its democratic inspiration,
this remained true of the Army of the West: its members were subject to the whims of their commander. "Uncle Billy" was a convenient and useful mask for all of them, but in the end William
Tecumseh Sherman was their absolute master. This can go to the
head of the best commanders. On the level of grand strategy, it's all
too easy to let individual lives fade into numbers and to let ego shade
military necessity. Something like that seems to have happened to
Sherman as he looked up at Kennesaw Mountain and considered his
options. Grant wanted the Army of Tennessee destroyed and was
taking terrific losses in the East. Once the rains stopped, Sherman

could continue maneuvering and probably force the Confederates out of their entrenchments here. Or he could pull a fast one: attack and confound their belief that "flanking alone was my game." He chose the latter, and his men suffered the consequences.

Thanks in large part to a stark and remarkable reconstruction by historian Charles Royster, we have a good idea of what transpired on June 27, 1864.[18] The army and corps commanders had been told the plan several days in advance, and John Logan, for one, didn't like it. Neither did other officers as word cascaded down. General John Harker, who would lead one of the attacking brigades, told a reporter the night before the attack: "They are powerful works; we can never take them; I will do my best though." One of his captains was even more pointed: "Received orders to be in readiness to march tomorrow morning at sunrise with sixty rounds of cartridges. (Hell expected)."[19]

There were always rumors, but most enlisted men probably had little idea what was in store until they were moved into position and lined up in battle formations. Veterans reported worrying about combat far less between encounters; but at moments like this, the presence of the elephant was felt just as intensely as when they were callow inductees.[20] From their location in the thickly wooded terrain, it was impossible to get even a glimpse of the Confederate works three hundred feet above. The only thing that seemed clear was that it would be a steaming hot day. A Union artillery barrage boomed out for an hour, until it seemed to Theodore Upson that "everything must have been smashed to smithereens."[21]

No such luck. In the first major attack, elements of the Fifteenth Corps had to fight their way through skirmishers even to get a clear view of the rebel lines, only to discover they were caught in a crossfire. "We mowed them down like hay," one Confederate soldier wrote his sister.[22] But they were stubborn, and their withdrawal, Royster explained, came gradually, with an accelerating shift from men going forward to men going backward, until they were all headed downhill.[23] Those who could move, that is. Many lay dead or dying. "Heads, arms & [et]c were blown off & scattered over the earth."[24]

About a mile and a half south, the main attack against what was thought to be the weakest point in the rebel line got a like reception. The brigades of Wagner, Harker, Kimball, and Mitchell were all similarly thwarted. A few made it to the outer face of the rebel line, but most were pinned down by the withering fire. Harker saw this happening and rode forward, waving his hat: "Forward, men, and take those works." All those who stood to follow him were shot down, and then he was hit through the body, his spine severed. His brigade was the first to break, followed by the others.

It went no better for Dan McCook—one of Sherman's law partners back in Leavenworth—or for his brigade. Just before the assault, one veteran was heard to whisper to a friend: "Aye! God, Jim, that hill going to be worse'n Pea Ridge. We'll catch hell over'n them woods."[25] It got even worse when they broke into the open and found themselves in the converging fire of two Confederate brigades. Regiment by regiment, they charged into this wedge of flying lead. McCook actually reached the rebel trenches and was yelling, "Come on, boys, the day is won!" when he was shot fatally through the right lung—the sixth in his immediate family to be killed in the Civil War.

By this time, everybody had gone to ground. "We were in a bad fix," Theodore Upson later wrote. "We could not go ahead and could not get back."[26] Union boys worked their way into depressions thirty to sixty yards short of Confederate trenches, below their line of sight, and began digging furiously with their bayonets and tin cups, throwing up an earthwork, clawing for cover. Some caught in between made it to their friends behind the dirt, others were shot trying, and many remained pinned down in the face of unrelenting rebel fire.

For the Johnnys were as desperate as they were. If their line broke, Johnston's entire army would be cut in two and might be pushed into the Chattahoochee, another battle in which a river defined military oblivion. In the intense heat of the day, they kept firing until little balls of melted lead rolled out of their muzzles after each shot and the barrels became too hot to hold. The continuous concussive fire left men bleeding from the nose and ears. Others were covered with the blood of wounded and dead comrades. Finally, as it became apparent they would hold, many rebels slumped to the ground in exhaustion and began vomiting.[27] But it was worse for the Yankees. Captain James Hall of the Ninth Tennessee looked out over the parapet in front of him and saw "a frightful and disgusting scene of death and destruction" and would later remember never in four years of war having seen "the ground so completely strewn with dead bodies."[28]

Mercifully, with his generals in agreement and his men wanting no more, Sherman called a halt to the folly by midafternoon. The next day, a truce was called to bury the bodies, already blackened, stinking, and covered with flies. Union officers shared their whiskey with rebel generals Maney, Cheatham, and Hindman, while the enlisted swapped coffee for tobacco with Southern boys and even got autographs from the Confederate commanders. When the digging was done, the men headed back to their trenches, a shot was fired, and after a pregnant moment the war was on again.

Meanwhile, the medical corps had been hard at work, under orders to get the wounded to the rear within twenty-four hours. Every available wagon and ambulance was loaded with wounded and driven six miles over rutted roads to the tracks of the Western and Atlantic. There, trains picked up almost two thousand injured men and headed back toward Chattanooga. Evacuation was now swift and routine; this much, at least, had changed since Shiloh. But in terms of firepower, the dangers confronting the boys were much worse, especially if they were sent directly in its face.

Sherman was never much for apologies. It took him two decades to admit: "McCook was my law partner, and *I* caused his death."[29] But in the immediate aftermath of Kennesaw, it was plain that he got its message. He might rationalize to Thomas that "our loss is small, compared with some of those East," but actions spoke, and he went back to flanking. He soon had Johnston off Kennesaw and back across the Chattahoochee.

There was plenty of hard fighting ahead, but in the future he would keep his boys under cover whenever possible, on the tactical defensive. Courtesy of John Bell Hood, they would have a profusion of targets, and in the three great battles around Atlanta that led to the city's investment, Sherman's boys essentially shattered the Army of Tennessee in a hail of gunfire. The combat was as bitter as ever, perhaps more so. At Jonesboro a month later, a brigade of Sherman's Fourteenth Corps poured rifle shot into Confederate troops trying to surrender, even bayoneting some before obeying the third call to "cease fire!" The Army of the West was now a true killing machine. But it was not enough. Atlanta was doomed, but the Confederacy persisted.

4

The Atlanta campaign and the March to the Sea were enormously complicated undertakings, and even with Sherman's huge capacity for detail, he needed help—subordinates to lead his boys in the field and staff to plan their way and supply them. In both regards, Sherman accumulated people as needed and only as needed.

"The great retinues of staff-officers with which some of our earlier generals began the war were simply ridiculous,"[30] Sherman wrote later. Instead, he grudgingly and progressively assembled a tiny group of functionaries, the key members being Orlando Poe, chief of engineers; L. C. Easton, quartermaster; Amos Beckwith, commissary chief; Edward D. Kittoe, medical director; and John M. Corse, inspector general. In addition, he had three personal aides: McCoy, Dayton, and Captain Joseph C. Audenried[31]—the last serving as social emissary, traveling companion, and husband of heiress Mary Audenried, with whom Sherman would later have a liaison.

Grenville Dodge had run intelligence for Grant and picked up that function for Sherman. But when he was shot in the head outside of Atlanta and forced into a long convalescence, Sherman apparently did not replace him.[32] Instead, perhaps in consideration of his incendiary future, he picked up a mouthpiece just before his March to the Sea: Henry Hitchcock, a prominent St. Louis (where else?) attorney who was anxious to join the war effort before it left him behind and whose diaries and letters would provide an important

William Tecumseh Sherman and staff, probably by Mathew Brady. *Library of Congress*

window on his boss's thinking during the campaign. Finally, there was foster brother Charley Ewing—bent on heroics—whom Sherman probably included to try to make sure he didn't get killed. That was it: a staff stripped down to the basics, utterly portable and completely devoted to the needs of a chief who would rather do everything himself if he only could.

It was much the same with the command element: true subordinates and mostly mediocrities, assembled by Sherman simply as implements of his will. The two with real military talent, Frank Blair and John Logan, were volunteers and career politicians, so he never trusted them and kept them on a tight leash. As for the rest—Howard, Slocum, Schofield, Mower, even the much-mourned McPherson and the Rock himself, George Thomas—they could be trusted not to have ideas of their own. Some seemed to be facets of the larger Sherman. Thus Jefferson C. Davis and Judson Kilpatrick appear to have been brought on board for their nastiness—Bad Sherman—and Howard for his rectitude—"a Christian, elegant gentleman, and conscientious soldier."[33] Not a great one, certainly (his corps had collapsed at Chancellorsville and Gettysburg), but a sincere abolitionist who had lost an arm fighting for the Union— Good Sherman. In the end, as long as they were competent, that was good enough. It was not about Sherman and his generals, not at this stage; it was between him and his men. They would win this campaign because they would fight it the way he wanted, as the actors in the psychodrama he designed.

5

The boys were all in. They supported Lincoln over McClellan overwhelmingly in 1864 because he could be trusted to pursue the war to a victorious conclusion. Renewal of the Union was uppermost in their minds at the time of the March,[34] but their thinking on why they were fighting was undergoing a significant evolution.

Like Sherman, the boys had come to believe that the planter class had led the South to secession and was perpetuating the war. Emancipation struck directly at them, undermined everything they stood for, and was therefore popular in the units.[35] "My government has decided to wipe out slavery, and I am for the government," Major James Connolly wrote home.[36] Most of these midwestern boys still had little personal experience with black people and were conditioned by negative racial stereotypes; but increasing familiarity on the March would erode that. As they observed with their own eyes the cruelty of slavery and got to know African Americans, who uniformly left no doubt whose side they were on, attitudes softened toward them and hardened still further toward the Confederacy.[37]

Of course, this all just sort of happened, another path taken by an improvisational army. Situations presented themselves, and they reacted. At the beginning of the March, most officers and enlisted had barely any idea where they were going, only that they had been weeded out and chosen for something special. Few were worried. "We are in fine shape," wrote Upson, "and I think I could go anywhere Uncle Billy would lead."[38] They felt invincible, up to any challenge, and the fact that it turned into a kind of grand adventure and movable picnic at the South's expense was simply a bonus.

But this was still war, a serious and deadly business. Everybody understood that the whites whose country they were marching through hated them, that they were dogged by lethally aroused rebel cavalry, and that being taken prisoner could well prove fatal. The relative absence of battle was certainly a relief. But when it came at Griswoldville, they settled into their formations almost reflexively, then gunned down the inexperienced Confederates with a hail of Spencer fire. They were not again challenged on the field until they reached North Carolina.

In the meantime, mostly they marched—in huge, corps-sized columns, great snakes of men, wagons, and artillery five to eight miles long and moving forward at about fifteen miles a day through farmland, pine forests, swamps, and whatever else they encountered, halting only to camp briefly and then moving relentlessly onward.[39] But if this was the central thrust of their mission, sending a great force unhindered through the heart of the South, all the action was at the edges.

Without a supply chain, survival depended on the success of their foragers, who fanned out daily from the columns to comb the countryside for edibles. They were everywhere, or so it seemed to a combat surgeon, Dr. Edward Duncan, who was heard to exclaim: "Damn the bummers they are always bumming around when they are not wanted."[40] After this, they were seldom called anything else, though hardly in a pejorative sense. The bummers were brilliantly successful, and not just in the enormity of foodstuffs they collected. As befitted the Army of the West, they developed a swagger and style of operations that enabled them to both protect themselves and screen larger formations.

Being a bummer wasn't for everyone. This was difficult and dangerous work, the kind that normally appeals to outliers in the military behavior bell curve. At least one authority believes virtually everybody in Sherman's army tried his hand at bumming; but a more realistic estimate is about three thousand daily, or around 5 percent of the whole—most likely many of the same 5 percent of risk takers repeatedly.[41]

They were the featured players in Uncle Billy's dark extravaganza. Many whites fled, but those who stayed would most likely have encountered and later remembered the bummers, Sherman's personal emissaries of bad tidings. Like their commander, they came in costume, the more outlandish and unmilitary the better—Civil War trick-or-treaters who, if you didn't cooperate, might burn your house down. But not more.

In his memoirs, Sherman provides a sanitized version of how foraging was accomplished, one featuring officer supervision and details of about fifty men moving together.[42] In many cases, this was not how it was done. Instead, bummers broke up into much smaller parties, fanning out to different farms and plantations simultaneously. Men at war do terrible things to civilians in such situations. Not the bummers. They might have stripped you clean of livestock, food, and occasionally the family jewels, but they didn't rape your wife and daughter or shoot your family. Besides gathering calories, their job was to scare you out of the Confederacy, and they stuck to it.

But being strung out all over the countryside left them vulnerable. Sherman's army recovered the bodies of sixty-four foragers in Georgia and at least a hundred more in the Carolinas, all hanged, shot at close range, or with throats slit.[43] Overall, though, casualties remained low—around fourteen a day in Georgia, probably somewhat higher in South Carolina.[44] For the bummers had ways to defend themselves. Even spread out in tiny parties, they were networked and ready to swarm to their own defense.

Sergeant Lyman Widney described how this worked when, on a lark, he and a messmate went foraging one day, heard several shots, and saw two bummers racing toward them. "We now considered ourselves in a predicament.... Looking over their shoulders, they saw not a relief column, but scattered clumps of men—other foraging parties like themselves. A bit of frantic signaling brought many to them on the run; before very long there were fifty or more soldiers on hand... and without any officers present, moved aggressively into the woods.... With the danger removed the impromptu formation dissolved as the soldiers picked up where they had left off."[45]

Bummers also formed a mobile shield around and between the main force's columns. Mounted on "liberated" horses and heavily armed, they rapidly concentrated to fend off flank attacks and on occasion reached out ahead to seize towns and railroad junctions, leaving Sherman himself to marvel at their acuity and aggressiveness.[46] "Your foragers were the most efficient cavalry ever known," Joe Johnston told Sherman after the war. "They covered your flanks so completely that I never could penetrate through them far enough to feel your columns."[47] Along with feeding their army, these bummers had picked up the art of reconnaissance in force on their own because it worked.

The main columns, where the great bulk of the boys remained, were far more isolated from the countryside. But they too were becoming familiar with the inhabitants—in fact, they were bringing some along. The boys never intended to become a dagger in the heart of slavery; but shortly after they left Atlanta and continuing throughout, escaped slaves were drawn to the advancing columns like iron filings to a magnet until they had gathered by the thousands. One member of a Wisconsin regiment remembered what happened when one caught up with them: "'Mass,' he said, 'I'se gwine 'long with uns.' His expression made it clear that the topic was not open for discussion."[48] But of course the boys didn't have to let these refugees join them. It was a matter of choice. A friendly invitation shouted out from the mass of blue shirts to a few blacks standing by the side of the road, a moment of decision, then: "I're off."[49]

They made themselves useful, eager to work for their getaway. At the very least, they could carry a gun and a haversack, making it a lot easier to do that daily fifteen miles. Crowds of women and children came to follow close behind, and at night they cooked and helped out, and some probably traded sex for food—though this doesn't seem to have been rampant or even prevalent. Meanwhile, the black males, especially big ones, gravitated to the teamsters and pioneers. Most of the boys remained unwilling to fight alongside freedmen, but they were ready to have them join their ranks in this capacity. So gradually, by a process of human osmosis, these elements became blacker and blacker.

Sherman, intent on keeping his columns moving as fast as possible, objected, viewing the crowd of refugees as a serious impediment. Though he did not give the orders, it was in this spirit that the disgraceful episode at Ebenezer Creek occurred. Then in Savannah, when he was given a few black regiments to integrate into his combat elements, he took their guns away and provided axes.

Clearly, neither Uncle Billy nor his boys were equal opportunity employers. But they were employers; they did incorporate what likely amounted to several thousand former slaves into their army, along with becoming the pied pipers of freedom for a great many more. It may have been demeaning, but it was also vital. These pioneers were soon to become the buzz saw of the avenging army, chopping their way through the Carolina swamps, a feat many, including Joe Johnston, thought impossible.[50] They were an integral part of the March. Sherman for one did not forget them.

There were other gestures of magnanimity along with civility. Even as they stripped the countryside of foodstuffs, there were many times the boys shared their rations with hungry whites, especially poor ones. Sherman was kind and generous to Savannah, and so were the boys, acting more like tourists than conquerors—besides marching in review, traipsing out to the beaches to marvel at the Atlantic, and paying for what they got. On Christmas Day, a captain and ninety of his men loaded several wagons full of food and went back to the pine barrens they so recently had given the locust treatment, to distribute it to the needy—converting their mules to reindeer by tying branches to their heads.[51]

It was a good stay. But they were still a mean army and about to enter South Carolina. By this time, many of the boys had become personally familiar with the South's "peculiar" institution: seen the scars from the whippings, observed the gradations in skin color among African Americans, and gradually realized that ownership often included sexual license—things that outraged them and turned them still further against the Confederacy and what it symbolized.[52]

That wasn't all. Substantial numbers of Sherman's soldiers had been taken prisoner during the Atlanta campaign and ended up in Andersonville and other hellholes. As the March progressed, some escapees managed to find their way back to Union columns, where they told eager ears details not just of the horrible conditions in the camps, but of rebel attempts to track them down and of black people who risked their lives to conceal them.[53] Back in Georgia during a two-day rest in Millen, many in the Fourteenth and Twentieth Corps had personally inspected nearby Camp Lawton and found that it lived up to the stories. "Everyone who visited this place came away with a feeling of hardness toward the Southern Confederacy he had never felt before," wrote one officer.[54]

Yet there was little they could do. Rebel authorities repeatedly demonstrated an ability to evacuate the camps before Sherman's troops, even cavalry, could reach them. So they shot dogs instead, having been filled with stories of "trackhounds" being used to hunt fugitive slaves and escaped Union prisoners. Any pooch that crossed the path of Sherman's army was more than likely to end the day paws up.[55] Yet not their masters.

Theirs was and remained a controlled fury. Even drunk and temporarily out from under military supervision in Columbia, Sherman's boys never lost track of the difference between property and people, never cast aside Sherman's central point: These were their fellow Americans, however misguided.

Their mood then is best described as incendiary. As far as infrastructure, the pattern was premeditated from the beginning and epitomized by an Ohio diarist: "Burned many cotton mills and presses, took dinner at Buckhead station[,] burned the station."[56] Government buildings, facilities associated with the war effort, the mansions of prominent Confederates—all were torched in Georgia.

But the flames—metaphorically, at least—turned into a firestorm in South Carolina, where virtually everything was a candidate for rapid oxidation. James Connolly predicted: "If we don't purify South

Carolina it will be because we can't get a light."[57] This was not a problem, as columns of smoke sprang up wherever Sherman's boys went. Whether your house was burned now became a matter of whim—witness the Ohio lieutenant who entered an abandoned residence near Orangeburg, sat down to play the piano, and was promptly burned out by someone who started a blaze in an adjacent room; or the bugler who had just finished telling a family that Union soldiers did not torch inhabited structures, only to notice that the back of the house was already on fire.[58] "I can hardly describe the appearance of Winnsboro when we left," wrote Rice Bull; "it was deplorable."[59] So it was for town after town, until they left the state and a charred path behind them.

The boys may have been free spirits and at times freelancers, but they were never freebooters, and when Sherman told them to turn down the blowtorch at the North Carolina border, they did so immediately. "The people around here are very poor as a general thing but very kind and hospitable. There is none of the treachery we have found in other places," wrote Theodore Upson in a better mood that reflected the army's.[60] They would soon be in Goldsboro, linked to the Union supply chain, and able to stop bumming. They understood the war was ending; that they had already played their essential role in the vast drama.

So did Sherman. When Joe Johnston hit them at Averasborough, then harder at Bentonville, Sherman could have obliterated the rebels, but he cut his losses and moved on instead. A victory in the field would have been beside the point and waste boys he had come to love. A few days later, he wrote Ellen: "I could have time to run to Washington, but prefer to stay with my troops. . . . I really do think they would miss me, if I were to go away even for a week. . . . My army is dirty, ragged and saucy. . . . Strange to say we are all in fine health and condition, only a little blackened by the pine smoke from our camp fires." Then he added, beaming with pride: "I would like to march this army through New York just as it appears today, with its wagons, pack mules, cattle, niggers and bummers."[61] Sherman's road show would never make it to Broadway, but soon he would have the chance to wow the nation's capital.

6

The boys swaggered into Washington in the same refractory mood as their commander, who announced to Grant: "The Vandal Sherman is encamped near the canal bridge....Though in disgrace he is untamed and unconquered."[62] Exactly their attitude—Uncle Billy's reputation had been slimed by Stanton and Halleck, and it was the Army of the West, not that spit-and-polish battering ram the Army of the Potomac, that had broken the Confederacy.[63] Predictably, this did not go over well with certain eastern colleagues. "The affair at Willard's Hotel was a small affair," Sherman wrote Grant, explaining the ensuing brawl, "arising from a heated discussion between a few officers in liquor, late at night, and unobserved save by the few who were up late."[64]

Enlisted men were kept under tighter wraps in the camps, but soon many were filtering through Washington in a similarly rambunctious mood. To some, it seemed their experience in the South had not simply rubbed off but become indelible: thus an article in the *Chicago Times* reported that many of Sherman's soldiers "seem to regard themselves as having some kind of right to appropriate articles for their own use."[65] This must have seemed glaringly apparent after members of the Fifteenth Corps "captured" the Fourteenth Street Railroad and began using it for their own convenience, or when some of the boys appropriated the horse and buggy of the captain of the Capital Police.[66]

But this was all done in fun, and besides, most folks were happy to put up with a few high jinks from these newcomers. The Army of the Potomac had been around for four years, they were old hat; Sherman's boys were a novelty, they had star power. Everybody wanted to talk to a bummer and hear about his adventures.

Suddenly and unexpectedly, Theodore Upson found himself a celebrity. "Take charge of this man, look after him carefully," the provost marshal of D.C. ordered one of his officers. "He is a *'Genus Homo,'* in fact one of the famous *'Bummers'* we have heard so much about. We cannot have him long, so make the most of him."[67] That night, Upson was the guest of honor at a hotel reception and regaled fifty officers with stories of the March to the Sea. They gave him a tour of the city; nobody let him pay for a thing.

The next morning the officers had him back for a further recounting, and the subject turned to sharpshooting. Upson began talking about some of the shots he had made with his Henry repeater and his certainty of hitting a man at five hundred yards. Some in attendance must have rolled their eyes as Upson reiterated that he could put half the shots in his magazine into a target that size at that distance. "Well to make a long story short we went out to a Shooting Range as they call it, and I took of[f] my coat and put 12 shots, one after another, into thier target and did not half try. Those fellows opened thier eyes; said they had no idea such shooting could be done."[68] These westerners were plainly more than just stories and tall tales, and very soon they would have the opportunity to provide a public demonstration—not of their marksmanship, but of what got them there, strutting their stuff.

On May 23, the first day of the Grand Review of the Armies, led by the dour George Meade, the Army of the Potomac—decked out in new uniforms, polished brass, even noncommissioned officers wearing sabers—paraded through the capital in impressive fashion, passing in review before the president and his cabinet. "Meade," Sherman told him, "I am afraid my poor tatterdemalion corps will make a poor appearance to-morrow when contrasted with yours."[69] Basking in the moment and not recognizing a sandbagging, Meade told him not to worry.

He wasn't. Uncle Billy had something more comprehensive in mind: street theater. That night, he met with his commanders and they lined up a cavalcade just like the one he had outlined to Ellen— wagons, ambulances, pontoons, a little livestock, and some of the African Americans who had joined them down south. But this wasn't meant to be a crowd scene. He also made it clear he wanted his legions to march better than the easterners.

It filtered down to the troops in simplified fashion: "Boys remember its 'Sherman' against the 'Potomac'—the west against the east today." The boys reluctantly exchanged tattered pants and shirts for new ones but still wore anything that wasn't falling apart,[70] knowing he didn't necessarily want them to "put on any extra style," but to perform, to leave no doubt that they were not simply an army in every sense of the word, but a brilliant one. And so they came forth, marching with a precision few in the crowd had expected and many thought exceeded that of the Potomac—the central attraction, but far from the only one, in Uncle Billy's street spectacle.

Being Sherman, he would also settle old debts and old scores in the most public way. He knew John Logan deserved more than he had given him, should have been made commander of the Army of the Tennessee; so on this day, he asked Howard to step aside and Logan to lead them. Always the Christian gentleman, Howard generously agreed, meekly requesting to join Sherman's staff. "No Howard, you shall ride with me."[71] And so they did, side by side down Pennsylvania Avenue before the gathered thousands— symbolizing, you might say, Good Sherman.

On the way, he spotted Secretary of State William Seward, still recovering from wounds received the night of Lincoln's assassination, turned his horse, rode over to the second-story window, and bowed deep in the saddle.[72] "When I reached the Treasury-building, and looked back, the sight was simply magnificent. The column was compact, and the glittering muskets looked like a solid mass of steel, moving with the regularity of a pendulum."[73] The show was unfolding exactly as he wanted—great rectangles of men marching past buildings festooned with banners proclaiming the day: "We Welcome Our Western Boys, Shiloh, Vicksburg, Atlanta, Stones River, Savannah, and Raleigh."[74]

Soon he neared his destination, the main reviewing stand, an island in a sea of people. It was Sherman's moment, the struggles of a lifetime focused on that single gathering of dignitaries and loved ones, and as he swung down from his Kentucky Thoroughbred and mounted the platform, it's possible to wonder if Rome could have engineered any sweeter triumph for one of its victorious consuls.

First in line was the new president, Andrew Johnson, who had earlier told him: "General Sherman, I am very glad to see you— very glad to see you—and I mean what I say"[75]—signaling clearly

The Army of the West steals the show at the Grand Review.
General Henry W. Slocum and staff passing onto Pennsylvania
Avenue. *Library of Congress*

that the aborted peace with Joe Johnston was forgotten. Then there
was Ellen and her father, the still formidable Thomas Ewing, drink-
ing in a scene that shouted he, Cump Sherman, was the family alpha
male, at last worthy of his own wife. Grant was also there to greet
him, smiling warmly and perhaps slightly amused at how his theatrical wingman had set this up. Then there was the proffered hand of
Edwin Stanton. Sherman remained characteristically proud of not
shaking it,[76] but he could have easily afforded magnanimity. Still, it
would have done little good to remind him that revenge is a dish
best served cold; for he was plainly on fire, amped to the max with
excitement.

And it was in this hyperaware state that he would have watched
the rest of the review, his eagle eyes fastened on the Army of the
West, thousands of whom he had spoken to individually, whose
names he knew. Probably he would have caught Mary Ann Bickerdyke, the original "Big Nurse" and avenging angel of the wounded,
at Sherman's orders riding with Logan's staff.[77] Unlike the newspa-

pers, he did not confuse the black folks who walked along to symbolize the army's emancipation mission with his African American pioneers proudly marching with picks and shovels at the head of each division, "abreast in double ranks, keeping perfect dress and step," he remembered.[78] "Significant frontispiece," noted one eastern officer[79]—Sherman's chain saw enabled him to cut into the Carolinas, and he hadn't forgotten.

As precisely as the army marched, there were delays. Marking time, some regiments turned to the crowd and began to go through the routinized motions of loading drill, executed with such precision that spontaneous applause erupted on at least one occasion. Perhaps their old drillmaster on the reviewing stand heard rifle butts hitting the pavement simultaneously, but certainly as the marching resumed he saw their regimental battle flags, once sewn with such loving care, now tattered and bullet riddled, many on their second and third iteration, prima facie evidence of what they had all been through. The blocks of men must have seemed endless; six hours had passed by the time the Fourteenth Corps's last regiment departed Capitol Hill.

Then it was over. Sherman left the reviewing stand with as many flowers as he could hold under one arm, shaking hands with the other, trying to reach his horse. The well-wishers quickly exceeded his patience, and soon it was, "Damn you, get out of the way! Get out of the way!" until the crowd parted and he rode off alone.[80] Likely this was more than a Shermanic display of grouchiness, for in his moment of glory, he must suddenly have realized that professionally, the relationship of a lifetime was at an end.

The Army of the West had just over a month longer to live, when on May 30 Sherman issued Special Field Order No. 76: "The general commanding announces to the Armies of the Tennessee and Georgia that the time has come for us to part....

"Little more than a year ago, we were gathered about the cliffs of Lookout Mountain, and all the future was wrapped in doubt and uncertainty....Three armies had come together from distant fields, with separate histories, yet bound by one common cause—the union of our country...fought four hard battles for the possession of the citadel of Atlanta. That was the crisis of our history...but we solved the problem, destroyed Atlanta, struck boldly across the State of Georgia...and our Government stands vindicated before the world....

"Your general now bids you farewell, with the full belief that, as in war you have been good soldiers, so in peace you will make good citizens; and if, unfortunately, new war should arise in our country, 'Sherman's army' will be the first to buckle on its old armor, and come forth to defend and maintain the Government of our inheritance."[81]

Brave words uttered in the face of time and the human condition. Bent on defying them, the boys met yearly in great reunions inevitably chaired by their redoubtable Uncle Billy. But in the end, the Reaper they had first met almost upon enlistment got them all—physically, at least, the Army of the West ceased to exist.

Yet a good case can be made that its spirit, its organizational DNA, survived to become the seminal element behind the evolution of subsequent U.S. ground forces. If it is true that Americans have a peculiar ability to remain creatively disobedient within large and otherwise rigid organizations, then this quality was certainly given full vent in Sherman's army, where challenges were met and adaptations made from both the bottom and the top.

Being full of Americans, the Army of the Potomac must have developed a certain amount of this same ethos. But there were significant differences. Becoming locked in great battles of attrition, the eastern force never had the chance to move long distances and face all manner of terrain and combat problems. Instead, it took huge casualties frequently in losing efforts, keeping the number of veterans low and never really developing a victorious spirit. If it had a legacy, it was the western front.

Things were different out west. There were bloodbaths like Shiloh and Chickamauga, but most of the boys survived, moving and gaining experience, until by the time Sherman took over, they had developed a real combat style—almost instinctively flanking to deliver fire at the edges. The boys loved firepower and they loved to move; that was their signature. Arguably, this was the last truly great marching army. But it's a good bet most would have gladly ridden in a truck or flown in a jet, and not simply because it was easier. You could go farther faster, something American armies have always been ready to do. As long as they had good guns and a plenitude of kinetic energy to deliver, they were willing to face any environment and remain alert, connected, and able to adapt.

Sherman and his boys were a violent bunch, but they were also decent, idealistic, and inherently magnanimous, reflexively holding out a hand to defeated Southerners. This was easier because almost all believed they were fellow Americans. Yet it would remain true of subsequent American armies in some very far-off places where the people were decidedly not fellow Americans—that is, when they weren't making the rubble bounce. Alternately devastating and benevolent, that's us, or at least our spear tip, and has been since Uncle Billy and his boys scared the hell out of the Confederacy.

Part III

THE MAN AND
HIS FAMILIES

Chapter XI

CUMP

I

OUTSIDE OF HIS HOUSE, gathered with his brothers and sisters in June 1829, nine-year-old Cump Sherman was in the midst of the worst day in his young life. Earlier, a neighbor had quietly entered their classroom and whispered something to the teacher, who quickly sent them all home, where their grandmother Stoddard had told them their father was deathly ill in Lebanon, Ohio. Lebanon was about ninety miles to the west, but they wouldn't have known that, only that he was far away and this was bad. They'd watched as their mother had frantically packed and then left to try to get to him. Instead she'd come back alone within hours, white as a ghost, and had to be put to bed. It was then that Grandmother had told them their father, Charles Sherman, was dead and soon after shooed them into the yard.[1]

Besides the older boys, Charles and James (one away at Ohio University and the other clerking in Cincinnati) and the three infants still inside, the six remaining Sherman children—ranging from

Elizabeth, who was sixteen, to John, who was six—were left to consider their fate, doubtless amid tears, confusion, and an awful sense that suddenly nothing was certain.

It was not supposed to turn out this way. The Shermans were a family of substance—Connecticut people, attorneys and legislators. Roger Sherman, a distant relative, had signed both the Declaration of Independence and the U.S. Constitution. Charles had been born in Norwalk, graduated from Dartmouth College, and then studied for the bar in his father's law office. He was admitted in 1810, and that year he also married Mary Hoyt, the daughter of a prominent business clan. But instead of settling down and practicing, that summer he headed west to the so-called fire lands of northern Ohio (reserved by Connecticut for the benefit of families whose property had been burned by the British during the Revolutionary War).

Charles arrived to find the local tribes, inspired by the eloquent and charismatic Shawnee Tecumseh, violently determined to prevent further white encroachment. It certainly caught his attention: one day he would name his third son after the Indian leader. But for the moment, he made tracks south along Zane's Trace for safer territory and in the process found himself in the thriving and lawyer-dominated community of Lancaster. He apparently fit right in, and as winter approached, he returned to Connecticut to fetch his bride.

Back in Norwalk, Mary bore him his first son and namesake in February 1811, but this only slowed him down. By early summer, the little family was ready for the nearly six-hundred-mile trek on horseback through the wilderness. It took twenty-one days to reach their destination, alternately carrying the baby on the front of their saddles[2]—yuppie pioneers, we might call them.

It seems to have been worth the ride. The couple settled in for nearly two decades and became pillars of the community. But although they certainly multiplied, the fruitful part remained problematic. Charles's legal career plainly lived up to expectations, but paradoxically, prosperity eluded him. He had played a minor role in the militia during the War of 1812, and the next year James Madison appointed him collector of internal revenue for the Third District of Ohio, apparently as a reward.[3]

Charles Sherman, the natural father of the son he named Tecumseh. Attorney and transplant from Connecticut to Ohio, he was destined to live a short life full of rectitude and debt. *Archives of the University of Notre Dame*

It proved a kind of hair shirt instead. Taxes had traditionally been paid in local banknotes, the only readily available currency in Ohio. But in April 1816, in a response to inflationary pressure, the national government suddenly announced that only bills from the recently chartered Bank of the United States would be accepted after February 1817.[4] The immediate effect was to leave large quantities of now worthless local notes in the hands of Charles Sherman's deputies. He could have hung them all out to dry or declared bankruptcy, but instead he assumed the debt himself and spent the rest of his life trying to pay it off.[5] This left him mortgaged to the hilt, but also with a statewide reputation for honesty and fairness, which bore fruit in 1823 with an appointment by the state legislature to the Ohio Supreme Court.[6]

Still rich in rectitude but weak in revenue, Charles Sherman was now defunct, leaving Mary little besides the debt and eleven children. Just how much Cump understood is hard to know, but he

Thomas Ewing's imposing home in Lancaster, Ohio, where Cump Sherman would spend his formative years. *Archives of the University of Notre Dame*

would soon find out, and it would leave him with a lifelong fear and hatred of debt, but also with his father's Pyrrhic scrupulousness in this regard. Meanwhile, the immediate implications couldn't be more apparent: the family would be broken up. Mary kept the youngest ones; the oldest, including Elizabeth, who would soon be married, made their own way; and the rest were sent out to live with friends and relatives.

Thomas Ewing, Charles Sherman's best friend in Lancaster and fellow rider on the Ohio legal circuit, offered to take one—"You must give me the brightest of the lot, and I will make a man of him"—and his sister Elizabeth had designated Cump.[7] So it was that young Sherman found himself walking up the hill, his hand enfolded in the massive paw of his towering neighbor, headed toward his equally imposing mansion.

But almost as soon as he arrived, Cump ran into a "my way or the highway" demand. Ewing's wife, Maria, a hyperdevout Catholic, wanted him baptized as a condition of his staying.[8] Since Dominicans came once a month to Lancaster offering Mass, it was not long before Cump was in the front parlor receiving the first sacrament and a new name—the initial shots in a lifelong campaign by the

Mother Church, at least as Sherman came to see it. Mary Sherman, a Presbyterian, had been consulted and given permission (how could she refuse?) but significantly did not attend. Meanwhile, the appellation "Tecumseh" proved problematic, there being no such saint, at least not in the Catholic Church. Since the day commemorated Saint William, the priest acted accordingly and anointed the suitably dampened redhead "William Tecumseh," but not Ewing; he was and would forever remain Sherman.

But everybody in the Ewing family continued to call him Cump. This was characteristic. They really did want to make him feel at home. He was embraced—indeed, enveloped—by Ewings, the start of what would prove to be the most important personal relationship, or rather nest of relationships, in his life.

Sad and disoriented he may have been, but the childhood version of one of history's greatest strategists was unlikely to have missed the positive aspects of the transfer. His style of life had abruptly improved; the house was filled with books, musical instruments, and elegant furniture. The Ewings were highly social, and elevated conversation and interesting guests were often the order of the day. Meanwhile, he was surrounded by familiar faces—Philemon (Phil), less than a year younger, was already his best friend, and since the families had always played together, he would have known Ellen, then five and his future wife, along with three-year-old Hugh and infant Tom Jr. (Charles and Theresa would follow in 1835 and 1837). Although his real mother remained just down the street, his new mom had been a foster child herself and likely understood his predicament.[9] Maria Ewing, in addition to being very Catholic, was also very Irish, attractive, highly intelligent, and an excellent parent. In this regard, though, as in almost everything else, she took her cues from her impressive (indeed, virtually monumental) husband.

Thomas Ewing had been born in 1789, the son of an impoverished Revolutionary War officer in what is now West Virginia. From the beginning, he seems to have been prodigious in both body and mind—he read the Bible when he was eight, and at twelve he walked forty miles to obtain a translation of the *Aeneid*, the opening parts of which he then committed to memory.[10] By age nineteen he was six feet tall, well on the way to filling out a frame that one day would weigh 260 pounds—massive in the head and shoulders and already locally famous for his feats of strength. He would need every bit of it, since he was determined to invent a future for himself first by boiling salt.

The Ewing family was now located in the Hocking Valley of Ohio, a place that at this point had no indigenous salt wells, or "salines," necessitating transport from sources in the mountains far to the east. Having come from the area, Thomas Ewing knew of the Kanawha salt works and also that there was good money to be made there. So, with permission from his impecunious father, he set out on the two-hundred-mile journey to a future of twenty-hour days of unending labor—drawing brine to the surface, tending the giant salt kettles, cutting trees, and dragging them to fires beneath to keep the kettles boiling.

The first summer, he earned $80 and wanted to use it for higher education; but he ended up giving it all to his father. The next spring, he was back in Kanawha. Toughened and much better at his job, he earned $400, of which the senior Ewing tithed only $60. Thomas spent the rest in Athens, studying for three months at the newly established Ohio University, "by way of testing my capacity."[11] For six years, he bounced between the books and the vats, earning in the process the sobriquet "Salt Boiler" and in 1815 a baccalaureate, Charles Sherman having served on the granting committee.[12]

Although Ewing during this period demonstrated an eclectic love of learning, teaching himself French and Latin and easily mastering higher math, he found his true calling when, after delivering a keelboat full of salt to Marietta, Ohio, he wandered into its courthouse to observe a case being argued. Hooked by the rival attorneys' oratory and wit, he sat transfixed and returned to Kanawha determined to boil enough salt to finance legal training.[13]

One hundred and fifty dollars richer from a four-week saline blitz, Ewing, possibly at the urging of Charles Sherman, rode into Lancaster in the summer of 1815 and quickly established himself at the office of Philemon Beecher, who was dean of the bar and a state legislator. For thirteen months of sixteen-hour days, he read law and then more law, emerging not just a full-fledged attorney, but a formidable one. Although still in his twenties, there was nothing callow or the least bit salty in Ewing's courtroom demeanor. He was solemn, circumspect, and determined, speaking slowly and arguing his cases with a relentless logic that left his opponents disarmed but also admiring. From the beginning he inspired trust: people naturally and comfortably deferred to him. "Grandeur sat upon him," wrote a contemporary journalist, summing up his aura.[14]

Predictably, Ewing's career built momentum quickly, accelerating even beyond the talented Charles Sherman's to the national level in 1828, when he was admitted to practice before the U.S. Supreme Court.[15] He was plainly the local young man on the rise, yet he antagonized very few—not Sherman, not his colleagues, not his neighbors.

Ewing's perceived solidity stemmed in part from his deep roots and loyalties. He never forgot where he came from, and in essence, at least, he stayed there. He married a local girl, Maria Boyle, who was the ward of his legal mentor, Philemon Beecher. He built his dream house in Lancaster, and it remained his domestic focal point for the rest of his life. Nor did he lose track of his career bedrock: with the proceeds of his growing caseload, he launched the Chauncey Salt Works near the Hocking River in Athens County, a lifelong enthusiasm and, eventually, a recurring son-in-law trap.

Curiously for such a sober individual, one thing Thomas Ewing did not develop was much of a religious sensibility. He was nominally Protestant, with the emphasis on nominal. He sometimes accompanied Maria to Mass, but more to please her than from any perceptible fervor, just as she went with him on long carriage rides to watch salt being boiled. They were a compatible couple, their Catholicism and skepticism mutually coexistent.

At the point when Cump entered the household, Thomas Ewing's career was taking off. A nationalist and a westerner, he had a natural affinity for Henry Clay's American system (national bank, protective tariff, and internal improvements). Indeed, Whig politics fit over his massive pate as if made for him. Accordingly, a string of important pols—including Clay himself, along with Daniel Webster and William Henry Harrison—eventually found their way to the mansion on the hill to pay court and size him up.[16] They liked what they saw, as did the state legislature, which in 1830 elected him to the U.S. Senate, thereby initiating a pattern of long absences from Lancaster during which Maria would be in charge.

Technically, at least. Shortly after arriving in Washington, Ewing sent his wife an exacting letter of instructions on parenting, emphasizing the development of reading skills. But then he thought to add: "And there is Cumpy too—he is disposed to be bashful, not quite at home. Endeavor to inspire him with confidence and make him feel one of the family."[17] This was typical of the paternal Ewing: despite everything going on in his life, he didn't miss much.

Reflecting later on Cump's childhood, Ewing noted: "I never knew so young a boy who would do an errand so correctly and promptly as he did. He was transparently honest, faithful and reliable, studious and correct in his habits."[18] Trying too hard, in other words. Sherman's extraordinary adaptability plausibly had its origins in his move to live with the Ewings, but there were likely to have been early rough spots, and they probably left their mark.

Foster children are known to suffer from a host of emotional problems, but also there was the history of depression in the Sherman clan. When brother John—also destined for a stellar career— returned to Lancaster from an initial foster placement in Mansfield, he was plainly angry, fighting frequently with peers, punching one of his teachers in the face, and hitting another with an inkstand.[19] Cump wasn't belligerent, but he was unusually sensitive about his personal appearance, at one point responding to his foster brother's taunts of "Red-haired Woodpecker" by dyeing the offending mane green with a concoction of available chemicals.[20]

Ewing was probably wise in insisting on the smartest Sherman. As parents, he and Maria were extremely ambitious for their own children and saw their way forward in terms of education. This was, and would remain, a family preoccupation. All of them were bright, and if a newcomer was to survive, he had better be able to keep up. For Cump, this would never be a problem, and to the Ewings' credit, they gave him equal access to a wealth of instruction. Charles Sherman and Thomas Ewing had been instrumental in establishing Lancaster's first school, and in 1832 the highly competent Howe brothers took it over, instituting a rigorous curriculum that included Latin, Greek, history, and modern literature. For a time, Cump and the Ewing children also received additional instruction at night, and at one point they attended what Ellen later described as "a select & quite expensive French school."[21]

Being proctor and Catholic tiger-mom, Maria Ewing also made sure there was no dearth of religious edification. When the once-a-month priest descended on Lancaster, Mass for the kids was mandatory, along with personalized instruction in the second-floor bedroom set aside at the Ewings' for visiting clerics. Possibly the brood welcomed the opportunity, at least in comparison with the ecclesiastical boot camp Maria ran on off-Sundays.

Promptly at nine, she herded her charges into the dining room and then commenced an elongated litany—prayers, Bible verses, favorite passages from Butler's *Lives of the Saints* and Gobinet's *Instruction of Youth,* followed by more prayers. Then they all said the rosary, after which they settled into an extended question-and-answer session from the catechism.[22] Nobody left before everything was completed. How many hours this took is anybody's guess.

The children all may have squirmed, but from Maria Ewing's perspective, the process had its intended effect—Phil, Ellen, Hugh, and later Charley and Theresa all emerged intensely religious, with only Tom Jr. mirroring his father's skepticism. As for Cump Sherman, mandatory Catholicism came to be viewed as a continuing assault—one that had to be endured as part of a lifelong Ewing immersion. He would become only vaguely and generally Christian. "I cannot with due reflection, attribute to minor points of doctrine or form the importance usually attached to them," he would later write Ellen, "I believe in good works rather than faith."[23] From a theological standpoint, this likely boiled down to Sherman's last word on the subject. But, of course, with Ellen, when it came to religion there was never a last word.

Life with the Ewings was not just about hitting the books and the beads. Lancaster was a small (population about one thousand) but lively place, safe but interesting enough for growing boys. He saw his mother frequently and sometimes brought Phil along for supper. For someone as curious as Sherman, the rhythms and details of the town itself must have held his attention for a long time.

Meanwhile, the surrounding vastness also beckoned—ponds for fishing, swimming, and (in the winter) skating, horses to ride, endless woods full of game, paths to follow to who knew where, with the near memory of Indian massacres to spice things up. A relative encouraged Cump and Phil to raise and sell watermelons, and they rode the produce wagon underneath the stars on the way to market.[24] Another time, the budding capitalists tried to turn sumac into shoe dye and unload it on the local cobbler, with absolutely no success.[25] It's hard to say how happy or unhappy Sherman was from age nine to sixteen, but all the basic ingredients of a kind of mythic nineteenth-century boyhood were there, including lots of brothers and sisters, though this implied some divided loyalties.

Cump always thought of himself as a Sherman, but with the exception of John, whom he saw and grew close to during his temporary return to Lancaster, and older sister Elizabeth, whom they later found it necessary to support, he remained distant from the other offspring of Charles and Mary. Instead, the Ewing children became his siblings, and he forged particularly strong bonds with the three eldest. Phil, close in age, was a natural companion, and Sherman also seems to have taken it upon himself to keep an eye on the impulsive, high-risk little Hugh.

Then there was Ellen. She appears to have been vivacious and engaging from the outset. Tiny, mirthful, extraordinarily bright, but utterly credulous, she seemed put on earth to be her father's genetic counterpoint: together they were the yin and yang of Ewing and worshipped each other accordingly.

But if she was and would forever be Daddy's girl, Ellen also liked Cump—apparently from the beginning. She remembered his arrival and baptism vividly for the rest of her life as a welcome addition to the family.[26] He and Phil let her and Hugh tag along on some of their milder escapades. The two also were charged with reading aloud to the children as part of the Ewing curriculum, a duty bound to impress. Later, Cump made a special effort to help Ellen with her homework when she entered the Howe school and also her religious lessons—something he may have subsequently regretted.

Gradually, the stringy redhead took on the role of defender and champion in the eyes of the bright and fervent little girl. Meanwhile, he was maturing, hitting a growth spurt at thirteen that left him towering over the Ewing children. The next year, Cump was one of four boys chosen from the Howe school to work as a rod man for a party surveying a lateral extension of the great Ohio Canal down to Lancaster. "His being called to start out on business or to work before daylight made a great impression on me," Ellen later recalled.[27] It would have been hard to miss.

This is not the sort of thing people write about in letters, but neither is it hard to imagine Maria and Thomas alone, late at night, asking themselves the pregnant question "What are we going to do about Ellen and Cump?" These were intelligent and perceptive people, and this was potentially an explosive situation. But they were also kind and oblique and would act accordingly.

"Tell Cumpy I want him to learn fast that he may be ready to go to West Point or college soon," Ewing had written his wife in December 1833.[28] This could have been the first the boy heard of the scheme, and he may have brushed it off. But Ewing was nothing if not relentless. He was also politic and never obviously self-serving, so when he wrote Secretary of War Lewis Cass inquiring about an appointment to the United States Military Academy for Cump, he couched the request in terms of Charles Sherman's wish that his son "receive an education which would fit him for the public service in the army or navy."[29] The elder Sherman had a brief association with the militia, but there was nothing else remotely military about him; he sprang instead from a family full of lawyers. More likely this was a Ewing-inspired view of Cump's future, veiled in characteristic misdirection.

At any rate, the request had arrived past the yearly deadline for application, and Cass pigeonholed it. But Ewing was back early in 1836, well within the time limit, and less than a month later, William Tecumseh Sherman received an appointment to West Point, at age sixteen a young cadet indeed.[30] It seems Ewing had managed to boil down a knotty family problem into a free college education for his ward and a convenient six-hundred-mile separation from Ellen, now twelve and nearing puberty. Just how anxious her father was to get Cump out of the house may have been reflected in a letter he sent in May, scolding the boy for not specifying his travel plans to West Point, and one to which Sherman replied somewhat testily that "to show that I attended to it faithfully I will state now what I did from the time of the appointment until now," signing it "Your most obedient servant."[31] This was characteristic, feelings may have been rumpled, but in the Ewing family everyone remained civil and in the end operated for the mutual benefit of one and all. But it was also apparent that Cump Sherman's boyhood was now officially over.

2

If Thomas Ewing's intent was to nip Cump and Ellen's relationship in the bud, ironically, sending him to West Point had the opposite effect. By placing him in what amounted to a military monastery, he more or less froze Cump in place, while allowing Ellen to grow slowly and comfortably into the relationship as she matured. But for Thomas Ewing's later elaborate schemes to keep his daughter by his side, you might even think he had planned this to bring them together.

From the time he left, Ellen proved, Cump told her father, "my best Lancaster correspondent."[32] Nevertheless, only a limited number of his replies survive, and the early ones remain decidedly brotherly. In one he thanks her for the candy she sent him and describes a cadet ball he did not attend. Significantly, perhaps, he concludes by looking forward to the following June, "when I expect to have the extreme pleasure of visiting Lancaster."[33] Meanwhile, in another letter he describes to her his brief furlough in New York, staying at the house of his uncle Charles Hoyt in Brooklyn Heights, "the handsomest place" he had ever seen and touring the city's parks, museums, gardens, colleges, and the Park Theatre—the start of his love affair with the stage.[34] All pretty tame stuff, yet there was more.

One incident he relates not to her but to Phil, in a letter the next day. It concerns an evening spent at Castle Garden, an entertainment area in what is now Battery Park, ostensibly to watch fireworks. "But what astonished me most was to meet A. Pitcher formerly of Lancaster with a great big whore (I expect) on his arm." While Cump is careful to stipulate that "I left him as soon as common politeness would admit of," his shocked innocence has the ring more of social convention than of sincerity.[35] Alternately, prostitution thrived in the city. He was seventeen years old, alone, and free briefly from an all-male environment, likely with enough money...the young Sherman, like many a youthful warrior, came packed with sexual energy, and if you had to date the loss of his virginity, it might as well be here. The reasoning may be convoluted, but the point is not. Sherman had reached the stage that his relationship with Ellen, if it continued, could no longer remain fraternal.

The next move was hers, and it took place during the long-anticipated furlough to Lancaster in the early summer of 1838. Cump found the visit disappointing, but Ellen, nearly fourteen, seemed transformed the minute he climbed down from the stagecoach, later telling her children how strong and straight, clear-eyed and bright he seemed and how "very grand" he looked in his uniform—the words of a girl smitten.[36]

How her father, who had not been reelected to the Senate and was back in Ohio, reacted to the visit goes unrecorded; but when Cump returned to West Point and almost immediately invited Ellen to the cadet ball, she was not allowed to attend.[37] It came up again in May of the next year, when Cump heard there was a chance of Ellen visiting West Point with her father. "I am delighted with the probability of your coming here during coming summer, and why shouldn't you?"[38] The reason was Thomas Ewing, who changed his mind and took Ellen instead to Washington and a new school, the Georgetown Visitation Convent, where Maria wanted her.

But the relationship continued to deepen. When she sent him a pair of slippers, he told her they were too elegant to wear: "It would be a sacrilege."[39] He now spoke to her as an adult and confidante, raising the most basic of family issues: "Indeed I often feel that your father and mother have usurped the place which nature has allotted to parents alone, and that their children [are now] those of brothers and sisters, with regard to myself."[40] Who am I? Who are you? Doesn't nature decide that? Ellen was very bright; she wouldn't have missed the message.

Cump graduated on July 1, 1840, and then visited Ellen at the convent school in Georgetown, before they both headed to Lancaster for the rest of the summer. The Ewing household was full of visiting Whigs, including presidential candidate William Henry Harrison, strategizing the approaching fall campaign, so Cump stayed down the street with Mary Sherman. He was now twenty and cut an impressive figure, even to eleven-year-old Jimmy Blaine, a Ewing relative and playmate of Tommy's destined to become the famous politician James G. Blaine: "a tall and very slender young man, straight as an arrow, with a sharp face and a full suit of red hair."[41] One night Ellen, now sixteen, gave "a fancy dress party" and Cump arrived not his usual disheveled self, but in full uniform as a second lieutenant of the U.S. Army, and he soon became the life of the party when he managed to chase an intruding bat from the ball. "General Sherman's first battle,"[42] they called it, no doubt to Ellen's delight. For at that moment, her favorite soldier must have looked awfully good.

But it would prove not nearly that simple. If Thomas Ewing really was intent on keeping Cump away from Ellen on a long-term basis, he couldn't have chosen a better profession for him than the military. But instead he wanted Sherman to resign his commission and become a civil engineer; Ellen wanted him to do the same and become a lawyer. But he had already told her otherwise: "Indeed, the nearer we come to ... graduation day, the higher opinion I conceive of the duties and life of an officer of the United States Army, and the more confirmed in the wish of spending my life in the service of my country. Think of that!"[43]

The Ewings chronically underestimated the power the military bonding experience held over Sherman. It wasn't simply that he liked being a soldier; this young man of multiple families had found a new one, forged by drill and discipline and united in ways nearly impenetrable to civilians. Asking him to leave the army always implied much more than they understood.

So the Cump/Ellen/Salt Boiler triangle lurched forward eccentrically, made lopsided by mixed and ambiguous motives, plenty of misunderstanding, and three extraordinarily willful individuals. But it never broke, because all were held together by love and admiration. If these had been ancient Greeks, they would have been at one another's throats; eyes would have been poked out. But they were nineteenth-century Americans bent on epic achievement and very much aware of the power of leverage and teamwork. Cump may have been thwarted by Thomas Ewing—about to be elevated to his first cabinet post, secretary of the treasury, in 1841—but he still held him in the highest esteem, the ultimate measure of his own success. Ewing, for his part, seemed truly proud of his foster son, did what he could to help him, and never overtly objected to his relationship with Ellen. Finally, Ellen worshipped them both, but she wanted them both Catholic.

The courtship took a decade and proceeded at long distance as Cump bounced from assignment to assignment. In the first few years, when their romantic attachment had yet to become explicit, his letters to Ellen freely describe his social life and the attractive young women he encountered, but he always stipulated that they were illiterate or at least not very bright, he implied, in comparison with her.[44]

Later photographs and George Healy's midlife portrait probably don't do justice to the youthful Ellen. She was plainly no beauty, but neither was she unattractive, with thick black hair, large expressive eyes, and good skin, though prone to boils. She was also tiny, under five feet tall,[45] an advantage in that it accentuated her larger-than-life personality. Her endless pious pronouncements in correspondence might leave the impression of a dour individual, but Ellen in person was the opposite—a mirthful, joking presence, whip smart and magnetic, she was plainly the spark plug of the Ewing clan. She may have been self-indulgent, yet she had also inherited her moth-

Ellen Sherman in her early forties. This portrait by
G. P. A. Healy captures her determination, if not her
warmth and energy.

er's generosity of spirit. She truly cared about others—not just Ewings, but everybody she deemed virtuous—and gave of herself
instinctively as well because she was Catholic.

This was the Ellen who captivated Cump, qualities he never really found in any other women, certainly not at this point. She was
his match in the ways that most mattered—she was strong and determined and could stand up to him intellectually. But she was also
utterly devoted, with an endless capacity to hear and consider his
problems, frequently providing sage advice, his best-ever confidante.
Nor would it appear that the relationship lacked passion. Given
Sherman's amorous nature, it is possible to say with some confidence
that he never would have gotten this deeply involved with a woman
he did not love physically. Meanwhile, as religious as she became,
it's worth noting that nobody seems to have suggested a career in the

nunnery for Ellen. Letters show Sherman to be spare with terms of endearment, but Ellen was warm, affectionate, and at times even horny. They may have shared a destiny, but as with a pair of unusually intricate jigsaw puzzle pieces, fitting them together proved no simple matter.

It took until August 1843 for the relationship to go critical. For the first time in three years, Sherman returned to Lancaster on a five-month furlough. Ellen was nineteen and very much the young woman. He had earlier written her that when he came home, "the first thing I will expect of you will be to mount the wildest horse and charge over the hills and plains."[46] And that's exactly what she did. With him following close behind, the two fell into a pattern of long rides beginning at dawn and traversing the countryside until hunger drove them back to town.[47] At night, Cump joined the Ewings around the piano, where Ellen charmed him with her singing and especially her newfound skill on the harp. It was plain to everyone: they were in love.

Shortly after, doubtless with some trepidation, Cump asked Thomas Ewing for his daughter's hand. If he was expecting an explosion, he didn't get it. Ewing reacted cautiously and characteristically, hesitating briefly over the potentially scandalous implications of such a union, weighing his options, then giving his consent, hedged by an expectation that Cump would quit the army and find a real job capable of supporting a wife who liked to shop.[48] Ellen followed suit, accepting his proposal, but on condition of his becoming both a Catholic and a civilian. Sherman had no such intentions on either count. Everybody said "yes," everybody said "no"; it amounted to a hair ball of mixed intentions that would string out the courtship for another six years.

There was another irritant. The Ewing boys were reaching maturity and also making career choices. Their father wanted them to become lawyers, and Phil, Tom Jr., and eventually Charley obediently followed the legal path. But Hugh had other ideas: he had grown up idolizing Cump and now wanted to go to West Point, too. Sherman always considered him impulsive and therefore probably not a good candidate, but he did give Hugh some encouragement.

He also wrote Thomas Ewing, telling him of Hugh's aspirations, indicating that he personally thought it was a bad fit, but offering to smooth the boy's way should he enter the academy.[49] This only angered Ewing, especially after Hugh insisted on joining the long gray line in June 1844. To make matters worse, it proved to be an unhappy stay. Tagged with the mocking moniker "Monk" for his piety, Hugh struggled through four years near the bottom of his class and was not allowed to graduate[50]—a Ewing family scandal that was bound to reflect negatively on Cump's already suspect career choice.

Meanwhile, time favored the patriarch. The long-distance engagement went transcontinental and in superslow motion (letters took up to six months by packet), with Cump marooned in California, Ellen growing older in the East, and the two of them sifting through the same issues over and over—she angling for Catholicism, conversion, and his return to Lancaster, and he sticking to his guns and his uniform despite a self-perceived career tailspin after missing the Mexican War. To add angst to what must have been some pretty frayed emotions, he kept peppering her with tales of other women—"whores and whore dances" in Valparaiso, living with Doña Augustias in Monterey, not to mention the many dusk-to-dawn fandangos he attended, where señoritas broke eggshells filled with cologne and spangles over the heads of their *novios*.[51]

The betrothal gave every sign of wearing thin. Sherman was exceedingly depressed much of the time, and Ellen's tone turned motherly, then darker. By early 1849, she was nearing old maid territory by the breeding standards of the day and living in Washington, where Thomas Ewing had just been installed as the first secretary of the interior. Besides nearly drowning at a social outing, Ellen's health, never robust, took a mysterious (though temporary) turn for the worse, and she fell into despair over the relationship: "I do not hope ever to make a wife, dear Cumpy, therefore if you think any of the girls out there can make you a companion do not let a thought of me prevent your marrying."[52] By mid-May, she was abject: "I have almost despaired of hearing from you again dearest Cump.... Nothing could induce me to serve you so. I must and will under any circumstances treat you as one whom I love, whom I have loved from my childhood."[53]

But then the clouds that hung over the couple suddenly began to dissipate. Within days, she received a letter from Cump assuring her of his affection. Tom Jr., who was now Zachary Taylor's private secretary, and her father were working on a furlough that would bring Cump east, and abruptly in January 1850, after four years of separation, she heard his footsteps approaching the Blair House greenhouse, where she was bathing her canary, and she ran into his arms. The wait was over.

None of the issues that had hitherto separated them were settled, but the couple nonetheless set the date of the wedding, appropriately enough, for May Day. Over the years, they had picked up something useful, a key to their subsequent marriage. Both were mulishly obstinate and utterly opinionated, but they had learned to set belligerence aside, build fences around disagreement, and relate at a more pleasant level. In part, this may be a function of the evidence, as their correspondence bounces from subject to subject, mood to mood, from angry rejoinder to lighthearted banter, all in the space of a few paragraphs. But the Sherman offspring, especially little Cumpy Jr., also left a similar impression—upbeat repartee, fast-paced gamesmanship, instant mood changes, but essentially happy combatants. There were very likely angry outbursts, but both had grown up in the imperturbable Ewing household, and that must have set some limits. Certainly there was never a hint of domestic violence.

Tongue-in-cheek, Sherman wrote Ellen that spring promising "to assume the high trust of your Guardian and Master. I will not promise to be the kindest hearted loving man in the world nor will I profess myself a Bluebeard.... You shall be my Adjutant and Chief Counselor and I'll show you how to steer clear of the real and imaginary troubles of this world."[54] When she was with him, this was about how it went; but as far as becoming full-time Guardian and Master, he had another think coming.

In part 1, we checked in briefly at the wedding—the happy groom surrounded that night by Washington's power elite—and considered the career-enhancing aspects of now being locked into the Ewing clan. But this was also personal. After a long and arduous campaign, Cump had won the hand of Ellen—had her to himself, or so it must have seemed in the candlelit glow of the moment. Yet if so, he had entirely miscalculated the guile and determination of the father of the bride. As far as the Salt Boiler was concerned, the battle for Ellen was just getting started.

3

The honeymoon proved to be a portent of marital bliss Ewing style—Tom Jr. chaperoned the couple on the first leg to New York City and Niagara Falls, after which they spent a month in Lancaster with Phil, who was now married and living down the street from the mansion on the hill.[55] The newlyweds returned to Washington just in time for the Fourth of July ceremonies that ended up killing Zachary Taylor and leading to a cabinet reshuffle that brought Thomas Ewing once again to the Senate and his base of operations back to Lancaster.

Meanwhile, Ellen discovered she was pregnant and Cump discovered this had given Thomas Ewing the leverage to reel his daughter back to the comfort and security of home as she awaited birth, this one and potentially others. Likely the term *confinement* had more than one meaning to Sherman as he stalked off to St. Louis and his next assignment without his wife. This marked the beginning of a fifteen-year tug-of-war. Those seeking to explain Sherman's eventual virtuosity as a military strategist might pause to consider that he cut his strategic teeth on a long and complex domestic struggle with two crafty and exceedingly resourceful adversaries, in some respects the match of anyone he would meet later.

Ellen gave birth to their first child, Minnie, at the end of January and wanted to stay the winter. Sherman's riposte was operational surprise: he descended on Lancaster at the beginning of March, snatched wife and child before the father, delayed in Congress, could return, and left only a note apologizing for what "might be construed into a disregard for your known wishes," adding bluntly, "I want Ellen with me in St. Louis."[56]

He had her only temporarily. By May 1852, she was pregnant again and back with Minnie in Lancaster. "She has been too much in Lancaster since our marriage," he fumed from St. Louis, "and it is full time for her to be weaned." Yet he could not bring himself to confront Thomas Ewing directly: "I cannot help feeling sometimes a degree of dislike for that very...name of Lancaster."[57]

The place, and Ohio in general, became Sherman's whipping boy for the family patriarch. This being a contest waged by Ewings, it remained contained and oblique, hostilities reduced to a matter of location—not only Ellen's, but his own. "At Lancaster I can only be Cump Sherman," he would write his father/father-in-law at his career nadir.[58] Implicitly, to win Ellen and remove her from Lancaster, Cump had to be the match of Thomas Ewing and truly a successful man in the larger world.

The death of his biological mother, Mary, in September only further welded Sherman to the Ewings as he headed down the Mississippi alone to his next assignment in New Orleans.[59] It wouldn't last long. He did succeed in drawing Ellen back to him once she delivered their second child, Lizzie, but her servant-heavy, extravagant lifestyle was clearly too much for Sherman's army salary. Meanwhile, he must have realized that she would soon be pregnant again and reeled back to Lancaster and Daddy.

Then in December, Henry Turner, his friend from his Monterey days and St. Louis, raised the possibility of California and banking, and the strategic Sherman saw an opening, a path to victory through escalation. It promised not only the respectability and big bucks to truly impress Thomas Ewing, but a destination so distant that "confinement" in Lancaster became, at the very least, far-fetched.

It was also a tremendous gamble for Sherman, who instinctively liked to calculate his risks. Besides the uncertainties involved in the move itself and the potential for failure in a field in which he had no real experience, it meant leaving the army, his other adopted family—all of this a measure of just how committed he was to the contest. But so were his fellow contestants. By arranging a six-month leave of absence for Sherman, Turner cleverly eased the transition out of the army, but Cump himself would seriously underestimate both Ellen's and her father's capacity for equivalent escalation.

He took the Isthmian route, and besides befriending a young woman who later turned out to be a whore headed west,[60] the voyage north along the Pacific coast proved uneventful until his steamship neared San Francisco and ran aground in the fog. Sherman managed to hitch a ride on a lumber schooner, only to have it capsize and dump him momentarily in the frigid waters off Sausalito. Two shipwrecks in one day: Those searching for the emotional origins of Sherman's enthusiasm for a transcontinental rail link need look no further.[61]

He remembered San Francisco in its initial Gold Rush days as a mud-soaked village, but in just five years it had ballooned into America's boomtown, boasting a population of almost fifty thousand, with wharves reaching a mile out into the bay and new construction of every shape and variety. "This most extraordinary place on earth," he called it, but he also noted that "it wears the appearance of a mushroom of rapid growth and rapid decay."[62]

Henry Turner had already opened the branch when Sherman arrived and was ready to turn it over to him and return to St. Louis. But the replacement didn't like what he saw. He quickly recognized that San Francisco was floating on a river of gold, and should its flow be interrupted even temporarily, the whole economy could dry up. Banking practices only compounded the risk: the standard lending rate of 3 percent a month (36 percent a year) was one sign of exposure; insufficient levels of collateral was another. Everybody was leveraged to the max. For his part, Sherman refused to play in this game without much higher levels of capitalization than he had been promised. "Without it," he wrote John, "I stick to Uncle Sam emphatically."[63] But this was a matter only the St. Louis moneyman James Lucas could decide; so back east Sherman went.

In St. Louis, things went extremely well. Lucas quickly agreed to double the stake to $200,000 cash, with additional credit available

James Lucas, Sherman's moneyman in St. Louis. *The State Historical Society of Missouri*

from the New York branch, and also told Sherman to go ahead with a new bank building budgeted at $50,000.[64] It was a substantial commitment, a vote of confidence by any measure. Sherman reacted accordingly and formally resigned his commission. Seventeen years after he'd first walked up the hill to West Point, he was a civilian and a banker.

Thomas and Maria were aghast upon learning of Sherman's intention to take Ellen and the children to San Francisco; they had assumed he would leave them in Ohio.[65] Ellen was hardly more enthusiastic. In the end, the Salt Boiler demonstrated just how tough a negotiator he could be, pulling a strategic surprise of his own: Family approval of the move would come at the cost of leaving little Minnie with them—a hostage to the basic Ewing objective of living in Lancaster.[66] Since his daughter was similarly inclined, Cump found himself outflanked and outvoted, but he did succeed in making off with his wife and one offspring, no small victory given the

Maria Ewing with Minnie, their hostage in Lancaster when Cump absconded with Ellen to California. *Archives of the University of Notre Dame*

caliber of the competition. The fractured family reached San Francisco without major incident, and as the year 1854 began, William Tecumseh Sherman was open for business.

During this period and later, Sherman liked to portray his mate as a sybaritic couch potato. Ellen Sherman did not exactly thrive on privation, but her husband's view was greatly exaggerated. Besides riding, she seems to have loathed exercise. Still, she managed to travel widely all her life, much of it under truly primitive conditions. Hence, on the initial voyage to California, we find her sidesaddle crossing the isthmus: "I wore out a pair of gloves and a huge stick in a vain effort to get my mule out of a walk.... Really the mule-ride, although twelve miles in length was a great relief after the monotony and weariness on ship board."[67] In this instance and others, Ellen Sherman was every bit the yuppie pioneer of the previous generation.

Clear sailing lasted less than a year. By December, Sherman and other financial cognoscenti were beginning to detect signs of weakness—declining sales, increasing numbers of business failures, squirrelly creditors. Soon thereafter, "Honest Harry" Meiggs, the city's biggest speculator, sailed for South America, leaving $800,000 in unpaid debts and equivalent pressure on the bankers.[68]

Then, on February 17, 1855, word arrived that Page, Bacon & Company, the other big bank in St. Louis, had failed. A full-scale run began, first on its San Francisco branch, taking it down, and then spreading to the others. Six days later, it hit Lucas, Turner, & Company, but unlike many of the others, Sherman was ready with hard cash to cover his bets. He was and always would be a conservative and calculating risk taker, and now as a banker he had avoided leveraging, so there was cash in the till for panicked depositors. Not quite enough—he had to race around the city shoring up his positions— but sufficient in the end to carry the bank through the lines of frazzled creditors to safety. In the wake of the disaster—seven of nineteen banks failed outright—Sherman's conduct won him broad respect among the city's power brokers as a man who could handle himself in a crisis.[69] Unfortunately, it also marked the peak of his career as a banker.

The situation was equivalently shaky at home. Ellen hated the Golden State from the outset, and Cump's efforts to provide her with a Ewing-appropriate lifestyle drained his bank account. She told her brother that for "all the gold in California, I would rather live near my home poor than to be a millionaire away from it."[70] As far as Sherman was concerned, she certainly lived like one.

Ellen found the first two houses they occupied insufficient, so Sherman borrowed $7,000 to build an impressive place on tony Rincon Hill. Although he blamed Ellen for the general cash hemorrhage, it's clear Sherman also thought his position necessitated living large. They entertained lavishly, holding frequent dinner parties for influential locals and a string of West Pointers, including his old roommate George Thomas. Three servants, several horses, and a carriage also came with the package, one that precluded putting much, if anything, aside.

At home and at the bank, Sherman worried constantly about cash flow, and in the process his asthma flared badly. For months at a time, he spent his nights sitting up in bed, breathing potassium nitrate smoke and grumbling "that the climate will sooner or later kill me dead as a herring."[71] Ellen complained constantly about her own health but still managed to bear two boys, Willy and Tom, during their time on the west coast—the former, a particularly sturdy red-head, was Sherman's namesake and the apple of his father's eye. Although there were no "confinements" back in Ohio, this can hardly be seen as a vindication of far-off places, since Ellen escalated by decamping for Lancaster in May 1855, leaving Cump to take care of Willy and Lizzie and suffering a shipwreck in the process.[72]

Letters back were not reassuring. Ellen told her husband that they might never recover Minnie[73] and was vague about her return. "I feel that I must devote myself to Father during my visit whatever may be its length and wherever he chooses to go....He is determined to keep me as long as possible regrets the children but says that considering your feeling on the subject I did perfectly right in leaving."[74] The stay stretched to seven months, during which time Ellen worried that her mate might "seek pleasure" that he "would not otherwise think of" and promised "to give more evidence of love" in the future.[75]

She may have known her man or suspected as much, but probably Cump was not in a frisky mood. Likely his escalating asthma attacks were brought on not only by the climate, but by the stress and anxiety involved in the losing battle to keep his bank afloat, the humiliating episode with the vigilantes, and one very complicated set of familial expectations. Ellen openly wanted the bank to fail, Thomas Ewing remained as dominant as ever, and Cump's Golden State gamble ground inexorably toward a dejected return east.

Word soon came that Lucas had decided to shut down the San Francisco branch and open one in New York, with Sherman in charge.[76] Sherman was shocked but also compelled to make the best of it. Closing a bank in these circumstances was tricky: if word got out prematurely, it could provoke a run. Sherman quietly accumulated cash and declined new loans until by April he was ready to pay off his depositors.[77] The strategy worked, and it proved to be an orderly shutdown. Only delinquent debtors, some San Francisco real estate now of questionable value, and a trust fund that held the investments of a number of Sherman's military friends remained on the books, to be disposed of later. He was free to leave. Ellen couldn't have been happier to see the last of the place. Not unexpectedly, she and the family would return to Lancaster while Sherman tested the financial waters in New York. By mid-May 1857, they were gone.

But things just got worse. Sherman bounced from possibility to possibility, only to see each one turn to dust, often but not always through no fault of his own. His banking career with Lucas sputtered to an end in New York. Then Ewing arranged for him to join Hugh and Tom Jr.'s law office in Leavenworth, Kansas. This was a low point for Sherman. Originally planning only to manage property, he had changed his mind and had been admitted to the bar "on the grounds of general intelligence." Back in Charleston at Fort Moultrie, to please Ellen he had read Blackstone on the common law and later Vattel's *Law of Nations;* but this was about the extent of his legal education. He appeared in court exactly twice and lost both times—in the latter instance buried beneath an avalanche of precedents by his opponent. "That little bow-legged gnat beat me slick and clean and came near taking my boots," he remembered.[78] From California came word from a mutual friend that "Halleck & myself had a good laugh at your turning lawyer."[79]

Hugh and especially Tom were competent attorneys, but the firm did not thrive. Sherman described the situation as one of "little paying business and plenty of lawyers," but he also blamed Tom for being more concerned with antislavery politics than with practicing law. At least when Tom decided to leave town for the winter he offered Sherman the use of his house, allowing him to send for Ellen and the children.

It was a short stay. She arrived proclaiming homesickness no longer a problem. Became ill. Got pregnant. Began longing for Lancaster. Was encouraged by her father to return. And was gone by March 1859. Sherman had seen it all before, but it only served to drag his mood further into deficit territory.

During this period, Sherman was deeply concerned about money, and his correspondence reflects constant bickering with Ellen over her resolute spending. It does seem his personal finances hit a low in Leavenworth, particularly when compared with what he had been making in San Francisco. Still, he speaks as if they were on the edge of destitution, which was plainly not the case. Ellen actually had a firmer grip on financial reality; the Ewings remained exceedingly wealthy and influential. Sherman spoke from the perspective of making it alone, when in fact he was part of the family enterprise. With the law practice drying up, there was another Ewing project—opening a farm on a large tract in Shawnee County for a nephew to settle—waiting in the wings. It was humiliating, but an undeniable safety net.

Duly enmeshed, Sherman found himself alone, forty miles west of Leavenworth on "the Pampas of Kansas." This was not a good setting for someone who was already feeling bad about his career prospects. The job this time was constructing farm buildings, fencing, and shelter for seven thousand bushels of corn he and Thomas Ewing planned to sell to the wagon trains heading west in the spring (four thousand would go unsold).[80] But the weather was slow to warm, holding up construction. The howling frigid wind reminded Sherman of his passage around Cape Horn, and the nights left plenty of time to ruminate. His hands full of splinters, he wrote Ellen in apparent despair: "I look upon myself as a dead cock in the pit, not worthy of further notice."[81] He may have been "pitiless in his self-appraisal," as one historian put it, but he was also exaggerating.[82]

The sole bright spot was Cump's remarkable relationship with his full brother John. The Sherman offspring remained scattered, yet these two middle sons bonded inexorably, but also pragmatically, since they were by far the most talented.

As noted earlier, John's career rocketed past Cump's, and at this point he was an important member of the U.S. House of Representatives. Yet there was no trumpeting or condescension, and he still thought enough of his brother's abilities to encourage and circulate his report on the transcontinental railroad and ask his advice on international military affairs. Meanwhile, the proud and depressed

Sherman's cabin on "the Pampas of Kansas," where his self-esteem hit rock-bottom. *Archives of the University of Notre Dame*

Sherman showed not the slightest trace of jealousy toward his younger sibling's success, nor would John later when Cump became Uncle Billy. Their natures were as complementary as Ellen's and her father's—fire and ice—Cump's volatility repeatedly contained by John's careful calculation of the possible. Meanwhile, given Cump's relationship with the Ewings and John's political nature, it was probably inevitable that John too would be drawn steadily into the family's orbit, an addition that eventually would have a major effect on the domestic balance of power.

Back in Lancaster, Ellen and her father were inventing an alternative life plan for Cump, supported by faith and a bed of salt. By this time, Ellen was not simply devout and observant in every detail, she was aggressively and expansively Catholic, marking her husband *numerus unus* on her list of potential converts and never missing an opportunity to suggest a quick embrace of the Mother Church. Cump did what he could to fend her off, but he came to realize that

Ellen had conflated a life for them in Ohio with a kind of saintly, half-otherworldly existence—"divine domesticity," as one historian put it.[83] Indeed, one factor that may have kept Cump's relationship with the Salt Boiler from exploding was the older man's religious skepticism. At least he could count on no ecclesiastical encouragement from this quarter during Ellen's endless visits to Lancaster.

But otherwise his wife was relentless in feathering her Catholic nest back home. When Cump insisted that the children be placed in public rather than parochial schools, Ellen responded with lurid tales of Lancaster academics—a teacher dismissed "owing to his habits of intimacy & familiarity" with the older girls; a seatmate who had "made the most indecent exposure of his person" to Minnie; and a pack of boys who "make holes in the fence and wet on the girls as they pass to the necessary."[84] Not unexpectedly, the children soon would be enrolled in Catholic schools. Ellen subsequently strategized a religious-based education for them that would surround Cump with pious offspring and one day nearly break up the family.

Yet if the fantasy life Ellen envisioned in Ohio was deeply devout, so was it salty, and this was the contribution of her father. Over the years, Thomas Ewing held on to the Chauncey Salt Works, presumably as a souvenir of his own grit and determination; but now it promised to become a means of keeping Ellen permanently close.

A career in salt had been initially suggested to the groom shortly before the wedding, but it was only after Cump's humiliating return from California that Thomas Ewing began his campaign in earnest, proposing that Sherman take over the works on three separate occasions, each time following a severe career setback.[85] Though at times in sheer dejection Sherman was tempted, he always made it clear he saw no future in salt and moved on to something else.[86] But the Salt Boiler persisted in his offers, ones he never made to any of his natural sons—the equivalent of rubbing the substance into open wounds.

It's not hard to posit a certain amount of hostility here; nor is it much of a stretch to have expected some reciprocal animosity on Cump's part. Yet blinded by his own sense of failure, he also failed to see that events were beginning to turn in his favor. His move to the Louisiana military seminary marked a return to his natural and

preferred career path, and the political crisis he did his best to ignore would soon erupt into the Civil War and, among other things,
an utter reversal in Sherman-Ewing family dynamics.

4

What became Team Ewing/Sherman was ultimately fueled—
intoxicated, really—by a vision of success that was based primarily
on achieving high office and public distinction in a burgeoning
America. Up to this point, the Ewing way (John's, too) was the legal-
legislative way; but very suddenly this had changed. War and warriors were now the focus of everybody's attention, and the family
resolutely set about making their mark on this new terrain by
achieving, first of all, high rank.

Cump, who briefly played Hamlet in St. Louis, was the obvious
focus of the campaign—he was the professional soldier, leader of
men, plainly capable in their eyes of great things. In mid-January
1861, Ellen wrote: "I have been convinced for sometime past that
you will never be happy again unless you go into the Army. General
Scott is high in favor and influence in Washington and will get your
proper rank for you."[87]

Team Ewing/Sherman was more than ready to lend a hand; in
fact, they invaded the capital. John arranged the inconclusive but
likely memorable meeting with Lincoln described earlier. Meanwhile, Tom Jr. stalked the halls of Washington, buttonholing and
cajoling every general and cabinet member he could find on behalf
of a command for Cump.[88] Even Charles Taylor Sherman, Cump's
eldest full brother and John's law partner, was enlisted in the campaign.[89] In early April, John managed to convince Montgomery Blair
to offer his brother the chief clerkship in the War Department, only
to have him reject it. Still the team soldiered on. On May 7, the day
before Cump wrote Secretary of War Cameron to officially offer his
services, all three sat down with Lincoln, who professed a high opinion of Sherman, then merely "said he would *second* your appointment to a high place," Tom Jr. explained.[90] John took the hint and

spoke directly to Cameron, who then offered the rank of colonel commanding regulars, which Cump wanted but never really got. Yet he could hardly blame the team: they had done their job.

Or at least part of it. If this war was to be a family affair, there were other commands to secure. Phil's health was not good, so he remained in Lancaster; but Hugh had been to West Point, and though he had never gone on active duty, he knew plenty about the military and was an obvious candidate in an experience-starved Union officer corps. Although the team's fingerprints are less evident, the results spoke for themselves. In April 1861, Ohio governor William Dennison appointed Hugh brigade inspector of volunteers, and a year and a half later Hugh was a brigadier general. Then there was little Charley, now in his midtwenties and spoiling for a fight; he too would quickly receive a commission and eventually end up a general. Tom Jr. soon followed the same path back in Kansas, and with the same results.

As helpful as it all may have been, Sherman himself viewed the campaign with some sense of derision. He not only had his own connections within the army, he was part of a brotherhood probably understood only by Hugh within the family—and certainly not by Ellen, who as the war progressed inveigled her husband relentlessly with inappropriate demands for her brothers' promotion. When it came to war, Cump proved coldly impartial. Tom made his own way, but the others proved more needy and dependent when they gravitated under his command. It's not that he viewed Hugh and Charley as bad soldiers; they were just impulsive and required some seasoning. Sherman did what he could to help and advise both, but he refused to advance them over those with superior military accomplishments, no matter how loudly or frequently his wife complained.[91]

But if Ellen was annoying, so was she stalwart, throwing herself into the career breach when Sherman imploded in Kentucky; rallying the family defenses at a time when the press was calling him "INSANE." Her letter of protest to Lincoln and subsequent meeting with him probably did not do a great deal of good, since the president was already sympathetic. But she had stood by her man in the

Except for Phil, all of Thomas Ewing's sons jumped into uniform. Pictured here are Hugh, Philemon, Thomas Jr., and Charley. *Archives of the University of Notre Dame*

most demonstrative way, and the crestfallen Sherman was almost pathetically grateful: "I ought to get on my Knees and implore your pardon for the anxiety & Shame I have caused you.... May you rest assured that the devotion & affection that you have exhibited in the past winter has endeared you more than ever."[92] Emotionally, at least, it may have marked the high point of the marriage.

For in Lancaster, family tectonics had begun to shift. On the face of it, nothing had changed: Ellen was back in Daddy's house, "confined" with Rachel (born in July 1861), and Cump was apologizing to the senior Ewing for the Kentucky meltdown and being labeled crazy: "You will be mortified beyond measure at the disgrace which has befallen me."[93]

But then with the team's help and under the guiding hand of

Henry Halleck, Cump's military potential began to unfold, at first slowly and then, after Shiloh, in a spectacular fashion. In reporting the battle, he still wanted to impress the Salt Boiler, noting that at its most intense phase, "many even of our Generals...hung round me for orders." But his tone is no longer obsequious, nor does he accept Ewing's and Ellen's assertions that he took unnecessary risks. This was a much more confident Cump, and he lets the old man know it: "I am not in search of Glory or Fame, for I know I can take what position I choose among my Peers."[94]

These themes were only reinforced after Vicksburg: "I can better judge of where balls are likely to strike than a mere looker on.... I now enclose you a short dispatch Just received, which will I know give you real pleasure. The Commission as Brig. Genl. In the Regular Army is a high honor, and to have it date July 4, places my name next to Grants as an actor in the most complete Act of the war this far."[95] He was not just a success, he was a star, and far from finished hammering it home to Ewing.

Meanwhile, Cump's added gravitas began to draw Ellen decisively into his orbit. Her letters, always sympathetic, become almost worshipful in terms of his accomplishments, never failing to heap praise and report favorable comments—for instance, "Father writes that Secretary Stanton told him you were 'by far the best General we have—administrative & in the field'—So do not provoke me again by putting yourself below McClellan."[96] His fame became her passion, and along with John, she repeatedly advised him to nurture rather than blowtorch the press: "If you give them a little kindness, they will prove your best friends."[97] Although her father and particularly her mother were in declining health, a newly independent Ellen still found time to help organize "Sanitary Fairs" and benefits for the troops.[98] More to the point, in September 1862 she announced her desire to move out of her parents' home and into Mary Sherman's old house down the hill.[99] Then in November, over her parents' and even Cump's objections, Ellen brought the children down the Mississippi to visit him in Memphis, a month-long sojourn everybody enjoyed, including little Willy, who was made an honorary corporal in the Thirteenth Regulars.[100]

Yet whatever her allegiance in the family triangle, Ellen remained Ellen, vociferous, impulsive, and adamantly Catholic. The lethal uncertainties of battle—especially since Cump kept reminding her he probably would not survive the war—only sharpened Ellen's concern over her husband's disinclination to consider the religious implications of getting shot dead. "Do not go into the battle as a heathen would with no prayer for another world to which you may be hurried," she reminded him shortly after Shiloh. Without conversion, there would be no Cump in heaven, a thought that preyed on her no less than his lingering refusal to embrace the faith.[101] Yet death would strike where she least expected it.

Cump had written to Ellen inviting her to visit during the summer after Vicksburg.[102] Ellen brought the family, and it proved to be an idyllic interlude along the Big Black River. Hugh and Charley, both attached to Sherman's vast armies, were there, and sons Willy and Tommy bunked in the latter's tent. Minnie and Lizzie slept separately, while Cump and Ellen shared two hospital tents pitched together, accommodations apparently to her liking, since she left pregnant.

And there were plenty of other amusements—socializing with the Grants and McPherson, military bands to provide background music, a former slave, "Old Shady," to serenade them after dinner, and even a priest from Notre Dame (installed in the command by Hugh) handy to say Mass.[103] But if this was Ellen's kind of vacation, no one seemed to enjoy it more than nine-year-old Willy. Having mastered the rudiments of drill, the Thirteenth Regulars—Sherman's favorite regiment—made him an honorary sergeant and had sewn for him a little uniform. In it, he rode proudly next to his father as he reviewed the troops, becoming in short order the camp mascot.[104]

Then with star-crossed suddenness word had come of Chickamauga. Grant ordered Sherman to relieve Rosecrans and come to Chattanooga, and the family found itself decamped and on a riverboat to Memphis. Ellen and Minnie were already running fevers, but Willy, only flushed when he came aboard, got much worse. A regimental surgeon diagnosed dysentery and malaria; it may have

William T. Sherman

Little Willy, the doomed favorite of
both Cump and Ellen. *Archives of the
University of Notre Dame*

been typhoid, and the boy died in the Gayoso Hotel shortly after
reaching Memphis.[105]

It was the worst moment in the marriage, numbed perhaps only
by the necessity of parting company almost immediately, forestall-
ing at least recriminations over bringing the family down to such a
pestilent venue. But other than this, nothing softened the blow.
Cump idolized the boy as a little redheaded version of himself—his
alter ego, gregarious, afraid of nothing, and fascinated by all things
military: "Of all my children he seemed the most precious."[106] As a
father, he would never get over the loss. How could he? It was a
shared burden. Ellen in her Catholic way mourned Willy just as
deeply (decades later, a grandchild found his sergeant's uniform
folded neatly beneath her pillow),[107] and his memory, as historian
Michael Fellman points out, forged a bond between the couple over
the years, literally till death did them part.[108] Yet it was as much a

Little Willy's tombstone, now in St. Louis next to his parents'. *Archives of the University of Notre Dame*

manacle as it was a connection, for shared pain is still pain and seldom makes a marriage any happier.

Meanwhile, there was more Civil War to be fought, and Sherman, though saddened, was not through impressing Thomas Ewing. This was complicated, because the old man took genuine pride in Cump's exploits, moved to tears at one point when a ceremonial sword presented to him found its way to Lancaster. After some initial speed bumps, Sherman had brought nothing but fame and honor to the House of Ewing—exactly the Salt Boiler's mission in life. But so too had the elder Ewing always been the standard by which Cump measured himself. This was far more than a competition just for Ellen; it was a matter of ultimate validation among ambitious people, one that had been building over the course of a lifetime. So in the midst of everything else, Cump v. Salt Boiler continued . . . though at times subtly.

In November, barely a month after Willy's death, Sherman took an unusual interest in the prospective marriage of Ellen's only sister to Clement Steele, a colonel invalided out of the army: "I approve highly Theresa's hurrying at once, tell her so. When parties are agreed the Sooner they consummate the marriage the better for all concerned."[109] This was a vigorous endorsement, particularly coming from someone who almost never approved of anybody leaving the front. But the fact that Steele had agreed to take over management of the Chauncey Salt Works helps to clarify the urgency.[110] Even at this point, it was apparently reassuring that other than the shaker on the table, there would be no more salt in Cump Sherman's future.

Instead there were additional victories to savor and also to proclaim to the old man. After taking Atlanta, Sherman wrote him: "You have often Said that Napoleon had no subordinate to whom he was willing to entrust an hundred thousand men & yet have lived to See the little readheaded urchin not only handle an hundred thousand men, smoothly & easily, but fight them in masses of tens and fifty thousands at a distance of hundreds of miles from his arsenals and sources of supply."[111] All true, all doubtless appreciated by Ewing, but also rubbing it in.

Yet there also appears to have been real sincerity in his desire for Ewing's approval. After reaching Savannah, he wrote: "Of course I feel a just pride in the satisfaction you express and would rather please and gratify you than all the world beside." But then he had to add: "I know full well that I enjoy the unlimited confidence of the President and Commander in Chief, and better Still of my own Army."[112]

So it went until they reached the final act in Washington. The Grand Review took place in an atmosphere of extreme controversy—Lincoln's assassination was barely a month past, and the brouhaha surrounding Sherman's initial peace terms was second only to that in the press coverage. Team Ewing/Sherman, by now a well-oiled publicity mechanism, had moved quickly to his defense with a barrage of countering articles and a coordinated advance on official

Washington. It appeared to be working, yet the situation remained touch and go.

Nevertheless, Cump continued to pursue essentially his own agenda, not just Uncle Billy's extravaganza featuring the Army of the West, not simply his chance to get even with Stanton, but also a ceremony of the most profound familial significance. Ellen as his wife was on the reviewing stand as a matter of course, but Sherman made sure Thomas Ewing was also included, the triangle complete. No doubt he was proud to have him, as was Ewing honored to be there. Yet there must have been something else, something that hour upon hour of troops marching by—all of them dedicated to the proposition of Uncle Billy—had to hammer home indisputably: Although Thomas Ewing was certainly an important person, Cump Sherman was by now a great man. The contest was over. For better or worse, Ellen was at last his. Everything had changed.

Chapter XII

BIG TIME

I

IF ANYBODY CAN BE SAID to have emerged from the Civil War with a pat hand, it was William Tecumseh Sherman. Only Grant was more widely revered and respected; but he was not satisfied, and that proved his undoing. Sherman held the same set of cards into a happy retirement; he tinkered with them, burnished them, rearranged them, but never lost track of who he was and what he had become. For all his fame, he retained a healthy sense of his own limitations and his good fortune. He had been through the grinder—personally, from a career perspective, and simply in terms of survival. Yet he had come out intact. It's safe to say that war is bad for most people, but for a fortunate few, almost always the victors, it is invigorating. That was Sherman at forty-five—his narrow, slant-shouldered, nearly six-foot frame packed with vitality, destined to carry him easily into a ripe old age. Physically, professionally, and emotionally, Cump Sherman had found his sweet spot, and he was determined to stay in it.

To an amazing degree, he succeeded. There were certainly some setbacks—son Tom's defection to the priesthood was the worst—but for the most part, the latter portion of Sherman's life was for him the happiest, the part he plainly enjoyed. We remember him today because of what he did in the Civil War, and he realized this would be true, that his most momentous days had passed. Yet he was always extraordinarily adaptable, and now he used those skills to position himself so that he could finally begin to live life on his own terms. In essence, he believed that America owed him a living (or at least a good-paying job more or less in perpetuity) for his heroics, and this was exactly what he got. He may have groused and retreated to St. Louis, but it was basically a good thing to be general of the army, and he wore the rank like a bespoke suit through much of what we call the Gilded Age.

Sherman also discovered that he liked being famous—buoyed by a sea of newsprint, recognized everywhere, the chance to meet anybody and everybody—the stuff of modern celebrity. Ever gregarious, he thrived on it, came to crave it. But more significant, he figured out how to keep it, turning the Army of the West's Uncle Billy into a national icon—a prototype for a line of larger-than-life characters that stretches to the present. Which is ironic, really, since as he aged Sherman became rather more patriarchal.

Certainly, he was now head of the amalgamated family. In fact, the center of gravity had swung wildly in his favor: Team Ewing/Sherman had become de facto Team Sherman/Ewing. For if John's star was not as bright as Cump's, it still shone prominently in national politics virtually until the twentieth century—secretary of the treasury, secretary of state, principal author of the Sherman Antitrust Act—a career every bit as distinguished as the senior Ewing's, probably more so. Meanwhile, the younger Ewing boys, while capable, remained at another level entirely and in the future would come to depend on Sherman patronage.

This reversal in gravitas was also reflected on the home front, but here Cump's dominance was far from stable or complete. Ellen had been his prize for decades, but now that he had her, he came to realize just what that meant. From the beginning, their romantic rela-

Family gathering on the now dominant Sherman wing of the family team, August 1886. Standing (from left to right): Charles W. Moulton; Francis "Fanny" Sherman Moulton; Elizabeth Sherman Reese; Babcock, secretary of John Sherman; Cecelia Stewart Sherman; her husband, John Sherman; Lampson Sherman; General William T. Sherman; Sarah Sherman; Hoyt Sherman; Ellen Ewing Sherman; Kate Willock. Seated (from left to right): Mary Sherman; P. Tecumseh Sherman; Minnie Moulton; and Addie Sherman. *Archives of the University of Notre Dame*

tionship had been framed by long absences. That had become the pattern of their marriage. Yet neither realized it. The intent had always been to settle down, sink into a stable domestic setting. Sherman's success in the Civil War made this possible, pretty much on his terms, mostly in St. Louis. Yet it never worked like that.

These two were like gunpowder and gasoline, packed with unspent energy, best stored separately. The children mostly remembered the family environment during this period as happy, if frenetic, which it likely was on the surface. Yet all the same differences remained, and these were two supremely willful individuals, so the whole family edifice was more or less built on a foundation of unresolved tensions.

No soldier likes to be surrounded, and as Sherman surveyed the family circle, he could plainly see that Ellen, like her mother before her, had packed it with Catholics. Whatever hopes he'd had for the children's secular education were postponed to the college years. Ellen maintained an iron grip around the children's instruction, and it would be strictly parochial—a string of Catholic day schools and cloistered academies. Also like Maria, Ellen brought religious instruction into the home, suffusing it with a regimen of rosaries, catechism, and prayer, in the process creating a line of highly religious little Shermans. Then Thomas Ewing himself had a deathbed conversion in 1871 that sent his daughter into paroxysms of joy and left his foster son/son-in-law speechless, barely eulogizing the old man or even mentioning him in the years that followed.[1] All this was irreversible, Cump understood—Ellen had controlled the home front for too long—but it gradually came to infuriate him, fed by a lifetime of sacerdotal interventions.

Differences over money persisted, as did his horror of debt. "As a rule don't borrow. 'Tis more honest to steal," he admonished Ellen near the end of the Civil War, plainly worried about his wife's spendthrift ways.[2] This proved alarmist, to put it mildly. By 1869, a grateful nation, or at least some of its most prosperous citizens, had come forward with gifts of money and property totaling nearly $150,000, a financial mother lode in an era when congressmen earned $5,000 yearly.[3] Added to this was a salary that ballooned to $19,000 when he became general of the army. Though it was later cut to $15,000, it remained twice what a Supreme Court justice made.[4] It was good money that ended up lasting a lifetime, yet Sherman persisted in portraying the family as hemorrhaging funds and Ellen as bleeder in chief.

Reality reflects a different picture. Sherman had earned a place for himself and his family in the front ranks of American society, and almost by definition hobnobbing is costly. When eldest daughter Minnie was married in 1874, a thousand guests attended the reception and the *New York Herald* called it "the most sumptuous wedding America had known in a generation."[5] Such events will drain any bank account, and in Sherman's case it was flanked by a host of other costly social obligations—eventually what amounted to keeping up with Carnegies.[6]

Ellen ran a good upper-class household, making sure it was well supplied and efficiently staffed. But this was inherently expensive, as was moving everything back and forth from St. Louis to Washington and eventually to New York at her husband's beck and call. But somehow Sherman found a way to blame the costs mostly on Ellen. He was hardly a penny-pincher himself, as demonstrated by his generosity to his children and just about any hard-up Civil War vet he ran into; yet in his eyes Ellen was the culprit, the family's fiscal fire hose. In part this was true, but it speaks well for her, though it cycles back to the central issue of Catholicism. Ellen Sherman took Christian charity not just seriously, but literally: giving away the entirety of the small fortune she inherited from Thomas Ewing before she died, much of it to the Little Sisters of the Poor.[7] Although Cump made no attempt to control Ellen's personal finances, they left him fuming.

There was more. Ellen had never liked to exercise, and now in her forties she began to put on weight—145 pounds and eventually 165 pounds on a five-foot frame. Ever lean and fit, Cump blamed it on indolence, a lifetime of being waited upon. There may have been some truth to this, but there was also the matter of her health. "Cump says I have been complaining all my life and never was sick an hour, that it is pure imagination whenever I complain & if I chose I could always be well," Ellen wrote her father in 1868.[8] In fact, she had never been robust but had nevertheless borne him eight children, the last, P. Tecumseh (Cumpy), coming in 1867—a string of pregnancies bound to have worn down any woman. However Sherman might delude himself, his wife's health problems were real. Her heart was not strong; she was in decline.

This had clear implications for their sex life. Apparently, Cump remained as amorous as ever. "I think he missed his calling when he took a civilized wife, as nature made him the spouse of a squaw," Ellen complained in the same angry letter to her father. She was a warm person and may still have been interested in marital sex; but given her health issues and the chances, albeit diminishing, of becoming pregnant, it is plausible that Ellen was inclined to give their love life a break.

Ellen Ewing, with son Tom, in the 1860s. *Archives of the University of Notre Dame*

In most respects, the concept of a break served the larger interests of the marriage. These two power-packed people needed time away from each other, lots of time. So they reverted to form: marriage at a distance, a kind of domestic-punctuated equilibrium that served the interests of both. Ellen had long stretches of peace and quiet and Catholicism, and Cump was granted his freedom for further adventures. It never quite stabilized the marriage, but it allowed Sherman to live the life he wanted, his rank entitled, and the world expected—the big time, in other words.

2

In part 1, it was noted that as a military strategist, Sherman always thought of himself as an agent of the state, by definition an employee. He was a professional military officer and never truly wanted to be anything else, especially not at this stage. When he assumed the rank of general of the army in March 1870, he became exactly what he wanted to be.

Much is made of his substantial political failings in the Washington arena—especially the battering that the service took at the hands of John Logan, the subordinate he did not promote and who now, as House Military Affairs chair, was dedicated to the smallest possible army led by the fewest possible West Pointers. Sherman hated politics, and his tendency was to withdraw when it wasn't going his way. But as we saw earlier, he had a larger transcontinental strategic agenda and could afford to overlook issues of budget and force size as long as he had enough to accomplish what he wanted to do. In a letter to John in December 1875, he admitted as much: "As to the army, I agree that it is entirely too costly. Twenty-five thousand soldiers with a due proportion of officers ought to be maintained at less than present estimates, which I see are stated at forty and also fifty-five missions."[9]

Yet all of this also misses the sheer pleasure Sherman took in living the life of general of the army, the spirit in which he performed his duties. He was concerned about the fate of the force, but he was also sanguine about the future. The nation, in the form of the volunteer armies it put together, and also Sherman himself, had recently demonstrated awesome capabilities; now he looked upon both as essentially in repose.

This was another adaptation, a recycled Sherman at the helm of the same sort of professional army he had grown up with—more hierarchical, but also more relaxed. It suited him perfectly. Feeling patriarchal in general, he morphed from Uncle Billy to what amounted to paterfamilias of the U.S. Army. Thus, when a young officer informed Sherman of his intent to wed, he told him to tell the betrothed "that I the Father welcome her into the Great Army family."[10] Greetings from the patriarch, but also a relatively laid-back one.

Sherman approached his job as first soldier in the spirit of a man who knew what a supreme effort meant and cost and therefore was comfortable cutting back in less demanding times. When he was in

Sherman Entering the Capitol

Sherman entering the Capitol, dressed as usual in civilian clothes. *Library of Congress*

Washington, he arrived at his third-floor office in the War Department between nine and ten, seldom wearing a uniform but brimming with energy and purpose. He immediately took to his large rolltop desk backed up against a wall in his spare, shadowy, map-laden lair. There he would bellow the last names of his various staff officers, by now a veteran group used to the drill—a recitation of daily reports, items of interest, and the progress of longer-term projects. He knew all of these men well, and while he peppered them with questions, conversations were filled with digression and storytelling—businesslike, but hardly formal or rushed. Visitors were ushered in and parked on one of two converging lines of cane chairs forming a V facing his desk. Some simply sat there watching the general of the army work until he turned to discover they were there, generally offering a hearty welcome, inevitably chomping on a cigar.[11] Sometimes he wandered the outer offices, chatting with whoever piqued his interest. Around one, everybody broke for lunch, usually sandwiches and a glass of whiskey. After this, he might stay as late as four if he had a meeting, but otherwise the general called it a day and resumed acting out his various other roles, public and private.

Despite the easy pace, Sherman remained an extremely efficient administrator with an enormous capacity to store and use information; he got things done during his tenure, but on a limited scope that was appropriate for the army's situation. As the years passed, his affection for West Point grew, and addressing graduating cadets became an annual and sentimental ritual. But he also maintained a consistent interest in the academics, trying to move the curriculum in the direction of military education and away from engineering.[12] Similarly, he established an advanced school for infantry and cavalry officers at Fort Leavenworth, designed to embody and impart the state of the art in active campaigning—but also, he admitted, as "a safety valve for those who are resolved to escape from the drudgery of Garrison life at small Posts."[13] Moreover, he encouraged individuals, supporting intellectually inclined officers, whether it was Emory Upton studying the German military or Richard Irving Dodge publishing a book on Indian policy. Sherman understood that weapons technology was racing ahead in Europe, and although he remained largely blind to the revolutionary tactical implications, he made sure the army knew what was happening and, to the degree possible, was modernized accordingly.[14]

In the end, he steered the army wisely through times when its mission and its detractors demanded that it keep a low profile but still retain a vital core that might be built upon in times of national emergency. Sounding like the father of a son who never quite lived up to expectations but still remained game, Sherman wrote: "Our little army is over worked and I do not believe the officers and soldiers of any army . . . work as hard and take as many risks of life as this little army of ours. In what we call peace I am proud of them."[15] This was not a judgment from afar. He knew exactly what they faced, because he was with them every chance he got—out of the office, on the road, a traveling man.

If Cump and Ellen's marriage was best served by long intermissions, his interpretation of what the general of the army did admirably served this purpose. If Grant and the bureaucrats stripped the office of its administrative power, all the more reason to get out of town and be with the troops. Sherman reveled in these jaunts; they constituted another state of being with another of his families, army brothers (officers) and children (enlisted), doing what he liked to do best, wander around and suck up geography. "Our plains resemble your seas," he wrote his friend from the Civil War, now admiral David Dixon Porter, "and it will take some years of cruising for me to familiarize myself with all the interests and localities. I do not regret this for I naturally get tired of any single place."[16]

During the first portion of his postwar career, these trips related to military operations in support of the transcontinental project. But as time moved forward and the Plains Indians were moved out of the way, they evolved into protracted camping trips and triumphal railroad tours of every corner of the West. Meanwhile, each feature on the map was being transformed into a mental image in his now vast topographical database, his compulsion to turn lines on a map into reality fed by a succession of majestic vistas.[17]

Sherman was seldom happier, living the life of a soldier among soldiers, telling war stories and sipping whiskey deep into the night, sleeping a few hours under the stars, then up first at dawn for more of the same. "He threw off all reserve," recalled Colonel James Rusling of Sherman's visit to Fort Garland, Colorado, and "entered fully into the life of the pioneer and Indian. He asked a thousand questions of everybody and was never at a loss for a story or a joke, and added to the effect of these by the twinkle of his eye, the toss of his head, and the serio-comic twitch of his many-wrinkled features."[18]

But he was also happy to venture still farther afield, to leave the boys behind and strike out with his faithful aide Joseph Audenried and Grant's son Fred for a grand tour of the Old World—Europe, Russia, and the Middle East—one that began barely two weeks after Thomas Ewing's deathbed conversion and stretched on for ten months to mid-September 1872. It turned out to be a sort of backward version of Oscar Wilde's famous trip to the American West.

Rather than the sophisticate thrust among chauvinists, Uncle Billy reversed the role. In both cases, they played to boffo reviews.

As he bounced from place to place, he inevitably applied the standard of home. Thus he found Cairo "a hard looking old adobe town," something Mexicans might build; and Madrid lacking in "comforts that every house in the United States possesses." Only "Switzerland seemed more like our country."[19]

Yet he hardly played the Ugly American. He seems to have charmed, or at least impressed, pretty much everyone he encountered.[20] And he encountered almost everyone in the power structure: King Amadeus of Spain, Victor Emmanuel II of Italy, Turkey's sultan Abdülaziz, Russian czar Alexander II, Austro-Hungarian emperor Franz Joseph, two successive presidents of the French Republic (Adolph Thiers and Marshal Mac-Mahon), plus Queen Victoria and her son the future Edward VII. The sultan insisted he travel on the royal yacht, and Ismail Pasha, the khedive of Egypt, liked him enough to send daughter Minnie a diamond necklace wedding present so valuable that it provoked a family quarrel.[21] He also appears to have had a pleasant encounter with Helmuth von Moltke, Europe's premier strategist, fresh from his Cannae-like engulfment of the French army in the Franco-Prussian War of 1870. The two canniest soldiers in the world apparently stuck to superficials, but it's hard not to be intrigued by the pairing of such seminal figures, each one the formative architect of military systems—Moltke with his *Großer Generalstab* and Sherman with his democracy-fueled legions—destined to clash in two world wars.

There was also a religious aspect to the trip. Sherman had an audience with Pope Pius IX, absolutely the most important man in this world according to Ellen Sherman. As they waited to be received, Audenried, upon learning they were expected to go to their knees, blurted out that he "would kneel to no man." Sherman simply shrugged and replied he was going to "follow regulations."[22] This visit was mandatory as far as he was concerned, obligatory if he was not to provoke a tempest of recriminations from his wife. Biographer Stanley Hirshson dates the increasing friction between the two over religion to Thomas Ewing's deathbed conversion and cites as an example Sherman's angry disinclination to visit the Catholic archbishop when he reached England, informing Ellen that he had recently told a fellow American: "I was not a Catholic, and from the nature of my mental organization could not be, but that my family were, and I did not or could not shake their faith."[23] In the Sherman household, those constituted fighting words.

3

The general's positive reception in the Old World only confirmed what his countrymen had long since decided—that William Tecumseh Sherman was a unique and appealing presence whose pronouncements on almost anything would hold their interest. Yet here there was none of the patriarch about him. Instead he retained the image earned during the Civil War: reliably Uncle Billy in the eyes of an admiring public, the curmudgeon savant, the man who never minced words.

As suggested earlier, Uncle Billy was not exactly a conscious creation, nor did he plot its perpetuation with the calculated steadfastness of modern celebrity. Sherman had a reputation to protect, and he guarded it fiercely and reflexively. Yet he did it in a way that almost never failed to draw attention to himself and in doing so only reinforced the image. Inadvertently, he had hit upon the elixir of fame in a mass media environment—continuing controversy—and for Sherman, as for a line of combative celebrities, it proved a veritable fountain of youth. Ironically, the hated press became his enablers, if not his allies. He never stopped abusing them, but they continued to hang on his heels and his pronouncements, knowing that despite everything else, he was always good copy.

As far as Sherman and the public were concerned, the controversies were serious, since the Civil War continued to cast a long shadow over America for nearly three decades after the last shot was fired. For Sherman, it really began when he published his memoirs in 1875, particularly since he was the first of the major military figures to do so. "We the victors must stamp on all history that we were right and they were wrong—that we beat them in Battle as well as in argument," he later wrote a friend.[24] Composed largely during his nineteen-month bureaucratic retreat to St. Louis, it proved to be a reflection of the man—wordy, filled with all manner of documentation, at times trenchant and memorable, but always defensive and ready to cast blame where he thought it was due.

Initially, the fire he drew came from the blue side of the former conflict, and in one notable instance it appeared to have some official support. Henry Van Ness Boynton, a journalist and Medal of Honor winner, published a book-length response, *Sherman's Historical Raid: The Memoirs in Light of the Record,* plainly based on documents only the War Department could have provided (Sherman thought the culprit was William Belknap, but it turned out to be Orville Babcock, Grant's private secretary).[25] It was also a calculated and specious slam, giving Sherman no credit for anything, including the March to the Sea, which Boynton attributed to Grant.[26]

Initially Sherman tried to ignore Boynton's book, but turning the other cheek was never a strongpoint. In the end, he organized a furious counterattack, one that characteristically enlisted literate members of his network of family and army connections to provide appropriately slashing defenses in print. Then, in early 1876, Grant put in writing what he had already told Sherman: "I will repeat that I do not believe a more correct history can be given of the events recorded by you in the 'Memoirs.'"[27]

The president of the United States had weighed in on the matter, yet still Sherman was not satisfied. Four years hence, in an interview with the *Cleveland Leader,* he remained eager to provide a character assessment of Boynton: "You could hire him to do anything for money. Why, for a thousand dollars he would slander his own mother."[28] When Boynton confronted him about the quote, Sherman did not back down: "This is a hard thing to say of any man, but I believe it of you."[29] Boynton, needless to say, went public— demanding that the general of the army be court-martialed for conduct unbecoming an officer. Sherman wanted the matter pursued in civil courts instead. All of it played out gloriously in newsprint across the nation. As every comedian who has an appreciation for

Jack Benny knows, continued success is often a matter of making the most of your material, and for Uncle Billy controversy just seemed to breed more controversy.

So it was with the presidency. Reliably, at the approach of every presidential contest between 1868 and 1892, some group with some degree of political clout—almost always Republican—attempted to launch a Sherman candidacy. All to no avail; in fact, it was an absurd proposition. Not only did their man truly hate politics, but he had likely retained his horror of being ultimately in charge. As Grant's wingman, Sherman had seen what the office had done to his former boss. "If forced to choose between the penitentiary and the White House for four years," he wrote Halleck late in the war, "...I would say the penitentiary, thank you, sir."[30]

Nor did he keep this to himself. Nobody with his chances of being elected ever so bluntly and loudly turned down the possibility.[31] He spent over a decade working on the same basic message[32] until he got it right in 1884, when the Republicans were particularly desperate for a viable candidate: "I will not accept if nominated and will not serve if elected."[33] It was classic Uncle Billy and one of the most famous squelches in American political history, but it still didn't get the job done. Yet again, Sherman had stumbled upon another dynamic of celebrity: Hold a part of yourself back and the public will want more. So the pols continued badgering him virtually to death's door, offering up what he least desired.

Meanwhile, something more fundamental was happening: the political ground was shifting. The Democrats, fortified by reinstated Southerners, were staging a comeback, by 1878 capturing the House of Representatives and in 1884 electing Grover Cleveland president. Sherman gradually came to realize that this revival turned on a radical reinterpretation of the Civil War and its intended impact; the disenfranchisement of African Americans was making the solid South possible.[34] "What the Union armies conquered in war," he wrote John, "the South conquered in politics." Besides the unlikely prospect of scaling down Southern representation in Congress and the electoral college, there was only one solution: "The Republican Party which gave the negro the vote, must make that vote good."[35]

This was more than a political calculation; he was ready to re-think his own prejudice—though from the perspective of Uncle Billy. In October 1888, the *North American Review* published his re-membrance of the escaped slave who had serenaded the family along the Big Black when Willy had died. "Old Shady, with a Moral," the piece was called. The moral was that Shady's virtues were those of his people: "they are a kindly and inoffensive race," one that was "gaining in experience and intelligence every day." On this basis, he urged white Southerners to do the right thing, recognize their value by giving them the vote. "I would far prefer Old Shady as a voter than any of the Bohemians who reach Castle Garden by the thou-sands every day of the year." Leaving aside the condescension—not to mention the feelings of Bohemians—this still constituted an ac-ceptance of African Americans fully as fellow citizens and deserving of a better future. "Let us freely accord to the Negro his fair share of influence and power, trusting the perpetuity of our institutions to the everlasting principles of human nature which tolerate all races and all colors, leaving each human being to seek in his own sphere, the enjoyment of life, liberty and happiness."[36] This was seventy-seven years before the Voting Rights Act. The author may not have been politically correct, but he was plainly ahead of his time.

Of course, Uncle Billy wasn't simply about the issues. He was a personality, a continuing presence, a role played to a seemingly endless string of packed houses, commemorations, and reunions. His postwar speeches numbered in the thousands, and in the process of giving them, he became a master of the spoken word. Though considered one of the Gilded Age's most sought-after and popular dinner speakers, Sherman was truly in his element back among the boys at the vast reunions dedicated to his former commands, par-ticularly the Army of the Tennessee. Largely forgotten today, Civil War veterans organizations were a politically potent and visible fea-ture of the American scene—in 1890, the Grand Army of the Re-public numbered 490,000—and their gatherings drew reporters from all over the country.

Uncle Billy Sherman was always the star attraction, and these en-campments were his stage. He seldom missed an opportunity to at-

Sherman at the center of yet another Civil War veterans' reunion, circa 1884.
Library of Congress

tend, no matter how far or inconvenient. No other place allowed for the full range of Uncle Billy—ringmaster, spellbinder, and spiritual medium back to the bad old days—"the old army feeling of unity," he called it.[37]

The "bummer meetings" were the best, open sessions in which favorites' names would be called out for a speech, until Sherman cut them short with a couple of stories of his own, then back to the audience—a sort of militarized version of Billy Crystal at the Oscars. They dragged on forever, but the reporters left with a story and everybody had a good time.

Never more so than on August 11, 1880, at the Grand Army of the Republic's encampment at what is now Franklin Park in Columbus, Ohio. The president, Rutherford B. Hayes, spoke first, and as he began, rain started to pelt the crowd of between five and ten thousand. Before long, shouts began to ring out for Sherman, who went to the rostrum as usual with nothing prepared, then delivered a command performance. He joked about the rain. He said he was just the president's escort; had come to see them and to "let the boys look at old Billy again. We are to each other all in all as man and wife, and every soldier here today knows that Uncle Billy loves him as his own flesh and blood." He didn't have to tell them about war. "You all know this is not soldiering here. There is many a boy here to-day who looks on war as all glory, but, boys, it is all hell." But before sitting down, he added: "I look upon war with horror; but if it has to come I am here."[38]

He didn't think he had said anything memorable, and, of course, what he had said would be distilled and remembered simply as "war is hell." Yet the power of the statement and the authenticity of the speaker were really nested in the longer version. For a public gathering, it was astonishingly intimate—"as man and wife"—and that was exactly his point. They had been through everything together, and war really was hell; they knew it, he knew it. But they had somehow survived and endured, and he remained, as he always was, Uncle Billy, a hedge against bad times. No one else could have said these things without sounding ridiculous. Yet he was utterly believable, bulletproof. So Uncle Billy persisted, ultimately to the day William Tecumseh Sherman died. For the two were separate: Uncle Billy was a role, albeit a brilliant one; the man was entirely more complex.

4

On a trip together soon after the war, Grant asked Sherman what kind of hobby he was planning to take up. Sherman hadn't even thought about it, and he wondered what difference it made. Grant told him he had to have a hobby or the press would make one up, probably something that would make him look bad. Being Grant, he planned to indulge his passion for horses. Sherman thought about it: "Let me see—let me see; what shall it be? I have it! You may drive your fast horses, and I will kiss all the pretty girls. Ha! ha! that shall be my fad."[39] He may have been laughing, but he wasn't kidding.

Before time closed in on him, he would do a great deal of kissing and a good deal more.

Sherman's first significant encounter with Vinnie Ream was on Valentine's Day 1873 in the Senate chamber where she and several other sculptors were displaying plaster renderings of Admiral David Farragut as part of a competition the Senate was holding for a major bronze outdoor statue.[40] He was impressed with Vinnie's entry, but a lot more with Vinnie. Like Ellen, she was small, barely five feet tall, brimming with energy and ambition. But Vinnie was twenty-six, a pixielike presence with cascading curls and possessing an utterly beguiling personality. She invited him to see her studio. The outcome was predictable. Within days, the two were lovers. Subsequently, Sherman would move heaven and hell to make sure Vinnie got the Farragut commission, enlisting John and even Ellen in the successful cause. But this amounted to a lot more than a quid pro quo; besides Ellen, Vinnie Ream was Sherman's most significant romantic attachment, and as such she gives us an unexpected window (she never burned his letters, as instructed) on what he had become, the man in full.

She was born in 1847 in Madison, Wisconsin, along what was the frontier, but during the Civil War the family found its way east to Washington, D.C. Vinnie at fifteen found work clerking at the U.S. Post Office and soon drew the attention of a number of important men. One of them, Missouri congressman James Rollins, took her to visit the prominent sculptor Clark Mills at his studio in the Capitol building, and Vinnie found her calling, apparently blurting out the equivalent of: "I can do that!" Laughingly, Mills let her try, and within hours she had produced a credible clay medallion of an Indian chief's head.

Mills was hooked, and from that point Vinnie spent every spare minute away from the post office under his tutelage, chipping, modeling, and studying with a ferocious outburst of energy. She proved amazingly precocious and before long was producing portrait busts for a number of congressmen and public figures, including George Custer.

Vinnie Ream, Sherman's plucky lover, busy on her bust of Lincoln. *Library of Congress*

Friends of Vinnie's—perhaps intimate friends—eventually went to Lincoln, suggesting a bust. At first he refused, but then, learning of her humble western origins, he relented. She spent five months near the end of his life in half-hour daily sittings and wrote that she was "still under the spell of his kind eyes and genial presence"[41] when he was assassinated.

Vinnie-like, she was seized with a passion to stretch her well-received bust into a full-sized marble statue and petitioned Congress for the funds. In the summer of 1866, legislators responded with a $10,000 contract. She was eighteen, the first woman ever to receive such a federal commission.⁴² There was some controversy. Mary Todd Lincoln didn't like the idea, and there was talk of "feminine wiles" having been involved; but Vinnie wisely took the money and ran.

To Europe for a two-year residence in Rome, armed with a letter of introduction from Secretary of State Seward, she charmed just about everybody she met. George Healy and George Caleb Bingham both painted her, while she did busts of Cardinal Giacomo Antonelli and Franz Liszt, all the while forging ahead with "the Project," turning her block of the purest white Carrara marble into Lincoln. "There was the very devil of a rush and Forward! March! About her, always in a hurry," wrote the Danish critic Georg Brandes, whom she twisted around her little finger as she continued chipping away.⁴³

In 1871, the finished work was publicly unveiled in the Capitol rotunda, where it still stands, head bent slightly forward, the right hand grasping the Emancipation Proclamation. "Of this statue, as a mere work of art, I am no judge," noted Senator Matthew Carpenter of Vinnie's native Wisconsin, "...but I am able to say, in the presence of this vast and brilliant assembly, that it is Abraham Lincoln all over."⁴⁴ Besides being politic, this was not a bad critique. Vinnie had talent, enormous energy, and drive, but she would never be a great artist. She was instead a great American story, the kind we have always loved—obscure individuals who on their own initiative overcome all odds to achieve success, pluck *über alles*.

She was made for Sherman. Vinnie Ream was exactly the kind of person he liked and was like—a sexy version of Mary Ann Bickerdyke, the "Big Nurse"—an independent individual who had earned a place in the world. Had there been no physical attraction, they probably would have been friends. Since there was, however, she became, in his words, "a special friend."⁴⁵

Sherman was fifty-three, and given his increasingly patriarchal propensity in all but his public image, he naturally slipped into a fatherly role with Vinnie, a sort of super-paterfamilias. On the one hand, he called her "my foolish little pet" and talked of "toying with your long tresses, and comforting your imaginary distresses";⁴⁶ on the other hand, he waxed inspirational: "With each award the critics will be silenced of the charge that your success is due to your pretty face and childish grace.... If in your hard struggle for fame, you can keep a loving woman's breast you will have a double claim to the respect of true and brave men."[47]

These weren't sex-addled empty words. Sherman wasn't possessive; he would leave for St. Louis in the fall of 1874 and recognized that Vinnie would soon have other men. He continued to see her when he was in Washington, but gradually the physical relationship cooled. Not the friendship or the sponsorship—both John Sherman and Grant sat for busts—and not even the possibility of matchmaking.

In 1878, Vinnie announced plans to wed Lieutenant Richard Hoxie, a West Point graduate and member of the elite Army Corps of Engineers, whom she had met while casting the Farragut statue in the Washington Navy Yard. Sherman reacted by telling her he was "prepared to act as your Father to give you away in marriage."[48] It's not clear if he did, but he certainly attended the gala affair, as did Grant and most of the Senate. At her husband's insistence, Vinnie took a long hiatus from sculpting and settled into domestic respectability in a house located, appropriately, on Farragut Square, where she became one of the city's leading hostesses—the happy ending part of this American dream. Ellen never found out about Vinnie ("she thinks you are wedded to your marble statues"),[49] yet despite this, the situation along Sherman's own home front continued to move in a direction that left him feeling like a stranger.

As always, the crux of the matter was religion, and as usual Cump Sherman would find himself outmaneuvered, outprepared, and ultimately flummoxed. Even given his continued long absences, he spent significantly more time with his family than before the Civil War, and as befitted his age and mood, he took more interest in parenting. But on the central issue, it proved stunningly too little, too late. By this time, all were well on the way to becoming devout Catholics—a veritable nest of Papists, from his perspective. Sherman harbored plans for a counterstrike, but in the end it would be shattered.

He was far from a terrible parent. When he was home, mealtime

Vinnie Ream's statue of Admiral Farragut, a commission that her "special friend" William Tecumseh Sherman helped engineer. © *iStock.com/Rostislavv*

conversation remained as lively and inclusive as it had been at the Ewings'. Evenings were spent singing around the piano or listening to him read from Dickens and Shakespeare; in the summer, there were long rides in the family coach at twilight.

But Sherman was a man of his age, and that implied a double standard. With his girls, he was attentive, supportive, and never too demanding—typically advising Minnie, "When you are done with your books let your mind run free."[50] He was also extremely generous, unfailingly indulging their Ellen-derived passion for fashion and jewelry, along with contributing substantially to their support once married.[51] Minnie, Lizzie, Elly, and Rachel all reciprocated with love and affection, viewing him as virtually the ideal father (their sole reservations being his lack of Catholicism).

Meanwhile, Sherman mapped an entirely more rigorous path for his boys, one cluttered with responsibility and self-sufficiency. Much of this fell on Tommy. Earlier, he had witnessed his father shamelessly favor the more bluff and venturesome Willy as the key to the family's future; but then, within weeks of his brother's untimely death, he felt the load shift to his own shoulders. "You are now our only Boy, and must take Poor Willy's place, to take care of your Sisters, and to fill my Place when I too am gone."[52] He worried about the boy's exclusively Catholic education,[53] but in this regard he viewed his wife as tactician and himself as grand strategist. "When you get old Enough [you] can choose for yourself whether to be a Soldier or Lawyer, Doctor or Farmer," he advised his eight-year-old putative successor of his options, and then he immediately narrowed the boy's choices: "I don't want you to be a Soldier or a Priest but a good useful Man."[54]

Useful, he left no doubt as Tommy grew older, had to do with shouldering the family finances. The Shermans were certainly prosperous, but they also lived an expensive life and had accumulated no vast, generation-sustaining amounts of capital. Future survival in the eyes of the economically wary father demanded professional success and the money that came with it from the son. Consequently, he continued to discourage a military career for Tommy, and in 1873, when Grant offered Tommy an appointment to West Point, Sherman convinced him to decline.[55] What he had in mind instead amounted to an educational counterattack.

"Logic, mathematics & the actual exact sciences embrace knowledge of things and of law as they actually exist....The next period will be suited to men who think and work the foundations [of] positive knowledge," he told Tommy, by then in his teens and enrolled at the Jesuit academy linked to Georgetown University. The classics and moral education he was currently receiving were things of the past; science was the future, and "I am not satisfied that Georgetown [has] professors skilled in teaching modern science."[56] Sherman therefore recommended an alternative, the brand-new Sheffield Scientific School at Yale University, thoroughly up-to-date, unquestionably at the forefront of learning, and not Georgetown. It seemed a brilliant gambit. Tommy may have been devout, but he was also

Sherman and young son Tom, already staring
each other down. *Archives of the University of
Notre Dame*

very bright and plainly relished the intellectual challenge. For once,
Ellen failed to mount much of a defense, and in 1874 Tommy enrolled at New Haven.

The plan proceeded smoothly. Tom proved a diligent and adept
student, gobbling up the curriculum and graduating ahead of schedule in 1876—the commencement exercise Sherman fled to be later
found sharing his Havana cigars with a black man recently released
from the workhouse.[57] Whatever advice on obeying the law the elder
Sherman may have received during this interlude, he had already
decided on a legal career for the son, the traditional family fallback
and next step in the training and deprogramming process.

He even chose the site of Tom's legal trajectory, Washington University School of Law in (no surprise here) St. Louis, after which he
would settle into a designated slot at the local firm of Henry Hitchcock, Sherman's mouthpiece and factotum from the Georgia campaign. This was career engineering worthy of a master strategist.

And Tom gave every indication that it was working. Not only did he sail through law school in two years, but he took over management of Sherman's considerable real estate holdings in the city, reporting back in great detail much as Cump had done for Thomas Ewing.[58] He even joked with his father over his supposed interest in a local belle.[59]

May 13, 1878, the day Tom graduated from law school, must have been a happy time for Sherman, the culmination of everything he had been building. Now the future was assured. Tom would be waiting when he returned to retire, by this time part of the St. Louis establishment and ready for a smooth handoff of the Sherman family financial future. Or so it seemed for a little over a week, at which point William Tecumseh Sherman received his worst surprise since Shiloh.

It came in the form of a letter from his son, announcing in no uncertain terms: "I do not intend to become a lawyer. I have chosen another profession—in one word I desire to become a priest—a Catholic priest."[60] He had been considering it since Georgetown and planned on joining the Jesuits. He had gone to Yale and law school simply out of respect, telling no one in the family of his aspiration, informing his mother of his decision only a week earlier—needless to say, she approved.

Sherman was shattered. In a few moments, he saw his meticulously wrought future flattened by an avalanche of Catholicism, a tactical and strategic surprise that brought forth a lifetime's worth of rage and resentment. His initial letters to Tom and Ellen were so bitter that the family subsequently destroyed them and left Ellen talking about taking shelter in a convent.[61] Nevertheless, she wrote back a sincere denial of meddling, while jumping to the defense of her son: "Tom's act was not a 'disgrace' but...an honor—not...a 'defection' but a heroic response to a call from the Lord."[62]

As far as Sherman was concerned, his son was guilty of dereliction of duty, desertion of the family, and utter self-absorption, and he told him so: "I tried coaxing, persuasion, threats, demands ..."[63] He enlisted the aid of John, Tom Ewing Jr., and Charley, all of whom were against the idea. Tom did his best to defend his decision point by point, Sherman demanded a public letter of apology for wasting a first-rate education, and the two finally agreed to let New York cardinal John McCloskey decide whether Tom could join the Jesuits. This only reflected the general's bad bargaining position, and by summer, his son was in England, a neophyte seminarian.

The imbroglio left Sherman not only "an enemy [of Catholicism] so bitter that written words can convey no meaning,"[64] but also profoundly depressed. "I saw him cast down but twice," remembered military aide John Tourtellotte, "once after the publication of his Memoirs when some persons insisted he had been unjust; and once, when he thought Tom had deceived him in choosing a profession."[65] Even this probably understates his combination of rage and pain. Despite cutting Tom out of his will and refusing to write, Sherman told one friend, "I can hardly stand it because I miss Tom."[66] "He was the keystone of my arch," he wrote another, "and his going away lets down the whole structure with a crash."[67]

Sherman plainly felt disaffected from his immediate family, even disassociated. During most of the episode, Ellen and the children hung back in St. Louis while he performed his official duties in Washington and moved about among the army's far-flung units— domestic intermissions as a way of life. When Ellen came east, she took the children to Baltimore with the intention of enrolling them in Catholic schools and taking up residence. Culminating with the grim Christmas of 1878, which found Cump alone in Washington and his wife and children celebrating the holidays forty miles north, the family seemed to be coming apart.[68]

But it didn't. Just as he had in war, Sherman knew when he was beaten, backed off, and proceeded with the overall plan. Ellen, generous in victory, quickly agreed to bring the children and resume residence in Washington. Once his domestic environment was restored, the shaken patriarch's mood started to improve. By spring 1880, he was again exchanging letters with Tom, and that summer they had an emotional reunion: "With a cry my father threw his arms around him," reported youngest daughter, Rachel.[69] Sherman loved Tom, but he never really forgave him or showed the slightest understanding why he would "subject himself to such an absolute

Cumpy with Tom, when he was at Yale, in
1875. *Archives of the University of Notre Dame*

and worn out order of Priests."[70] That was how things went in the
Sherman household: on one level, good relations and placid interac-
tions were restored, but on another, the war continued.

The strategic Sherman saw one shot left in his reproductive revolver—P. Tecumseh ("Cumpy"), now in his early teens. For Cumpy,
he had exactly the same plan with precisely the same objective. This
time, though, he managed the process with considerably more vigilance, and as opposed to Tom, who was always withdrawn and secre-
tive, Cumpy had been an open little boy and much more anxious to
please. Ellen made sure his preliminary education remained suitably parochial; but from this point, it would be Yale University, secular studies, then the law and the yoke of family finance, which was
exactly what resulted.

Dutiful Cumpy grew smoothly into a moderately successful New
York labor attorney and diligently supervised the family's assets. Yet
he never married or reproduced. Not surprisingly, neither did Tom,
but his fate was sadder: chronically depressed and ineffective as a

priest, he left the Jesuit order and spent the next two decades in a solitary existence split between aimless travel and a little house in Santa Barbara, before dying in a Catholic nursing home in 1933.[71] It's hard to miss the implications. It's never easy growing up the son of a famous father, not to mention two such willful parents; but over the years, undercurrents of anger had built up between Cump and Ellen that really were corrosive and could well have had a negative impact on the reproductive prospects of these two sons, from whom so much else was expected.

The depth of this acrimony was never more apparent than when Mary Audenried slipped into the family drama. She was the socially prominent and independently wealthy wife of Sherman's faithful military aide Joseph Audenried, who sickened and died in 1880. "Poor Mrs. Audenried is so dumb founded—so stunned, poor little lady that I feel deeply for her...I have acted as a father to her."[72]

Of the super-paterfamilias variety, it turned out. She may have had her eye on him all along. "Even in the hey-day of your young married life you told me you liked me better than Audenried," he later wrote her, "that was not exactly proper, but no man dislikes such a compliment."[73] Certainly not Sherman. Though he doesn't necessarily seem the aggressor in the affair, and did consistently urge her to find a new mate or at least a more appropriate "special friend," he quickly succumbed to Mary's considerable charms and availability.

Because of his former relationship with her husband, it was hardly inappropriate for the general of the army to continue associating with the widow Audenried, who was genuinely depressed and in need of support. He was helpful. He even took her annoying teenage daughter, Florence, off her hands for a while, bringing her and his own child Rachel along on a tour of the West out to the Pacific with President Hayes.[74] For his troubles, of course, Sherman was bathed in endorphins and showered with expensive gifts. He was over sixty; she was in her midthirties. And it was an easy relationship to per-petuate. Mary had a house in Washington and was rich and independent enough to meet him anywhere, anytime, as long as they remained discreet. So it stretched on for over three years, at which point he thought it would end, since he was retiring from the army and moving back to St. Louis.

But almost as soon as he arrived, he was seized with a strong urge to bring her to him and wrote he was "ready to carry you bodily (willingly if possible—violently if necessary) to St. Louis, Missouri, where your friends demand your presence.... You can have the guest room right over my office and though somewhat jealous of my rights, I think I will let you have a pretty free range of my sanctum."[75] This was not only reckless, it amounted to flaunting his mistress in front of Ellen on the flimsy grounds that she was a friend of the family, the cruelest sort of insult to a faithful wife of more than thirty years.

Ellen had overlooked a great deal, but this was too much, and she exploded along with daughter Lizzie, ostensibly over Mary's comment that a Protestant convent might be as good as a Catholic one for wayward Florence. That did it. Sherman soon wrote Mary that she was on Ellen's enemies-of-the-church list and there would be no more friendly intercourse, at least not with the rest of the family.

He remained on board—in fact, this made Mary more attractive, since she now afforded him a sympathetic receptacle for his rage: "Mrs Sherman is not a Roman Catholic, but an Irish Catholic and [prefers] an Irish drayman who gets drunk six times a week and belabors his wife and children—yet who has kept the true faith and goes to Church on Sunday—as a higher type of manhood than a patriot soldier at the head of a victorious army."[76]

The situation degenerated further five months after Mary's visit, when Ellen read one of her letters. She (or perhaps he in self-defense) burned the rest, and then he had the gall to lecture her "that no lady is willing to have her letters read by another."[77] And he made it stick, telling Mary not to hesitate to write since "Mrs. Sherman will not open my letters more." This was a matter of power and reveals the man at his coldest and most vindictive, taking cover behind Victorian conventions, much as he had spouted the law of war to Hood after Atlanta. Ellen had no choice. Her health was bad, and she had given away all her money; she was utterly dependent on him. So the affair continued.

Yet so did the marriage, and more than in just a pro forma way. For people of their station in this era, divorce was really not an option; but there is no evidence they even considered it. In spite of the beating it took over the years, Cump and Ellen's relationship still allowed them to thoroughly compartmentalize and hermetically seal the bitterest of disputes for the moment and get on with family business.

Publicly, Ellen remained her husband's biggest booster, manicuring his reputation and fiercely defending the turf against all attacks and intrusions.[78] She also continued as Team Sherman/Ewing spark plug, regularly dunning her husband and John in favor of her brothers' careers. They did well enough—Phil became a highly regarded Ohio judge; Tom Jr. more than held his own with two terms in Congress; Charley had a successful Washington legal career; Hugh became U.S. minister to The Hague—but it was the two family giants who provided the impetus. Thus, when Ewing relative James G. Blaine wanted Hugh recalled because he was "acting badly" and replaced with Charley, Ellen made sure that Cump got to Grant, and that was the end of it. The networking never stopped. The clan was destined for political obscurity in the next generation, but the team endured as a force virtually to the doorstep of the twentieth century and the deaths of the two Sherman brothers.

Closer to home, as always, things never really stabilized; but they did persist. The facade of domesticity held. The Sherman daughters basically grew into happy, sociable young ladies and, with the exception of the devout, dutiful Lizzie, would marry and have children. Elly and vivacious Rachel also put in considerable duty as designated social companions for the general of the army, since Ellen dropped out of society and narrowed her range of contacts after Tom joined the priesthood.

While the hypersocial Sherman grumpily got used to the arrangement, he also seemed to have attributed it to a general withdrawal on the part of his wife, which was far from true. In fact, she had cast aside her social obligations largely so she could remain active in her work with the Catholic Church, which continued nearly unabated. As always, she traveled regularly, not as regularly or epi-

Ellen Sherman (center), with children and grandchildren, on the disastrous Maryland vacation in which two of Minnie's offspring died suddenly. *Archives of the University of Notre Dame*

cally as her husband, but still a good many miles for a woman of her age and physical condition—principally to Catholic functions from the Midwest to the east coast and a range of tony resorts. One such vacation had catastrophic consequences. In 1882, Ellen decided to rent a summer place in Maryland's Allegheny Mountains large enough for the family, including Minnie and her five children. But even faster than little Willy on the Big Black, Minnie's two youngest developed dysentery and died.[79]

The episode can't have done Ellen's health any good, nor did the move to St. Louis, which was full of soot and pollution from burning brown coal. Her weight continued to mount, as did her lassitude and aversion to exercise. She developed respiratory problems and attributed them to asthma like her husband's, perhaps expecting some sympathy.[80] She didn't get much, as he stubbornly continued to think of her as simply too fat. But he wasn't much happier in the Queen City.

St. Louis's most prominent citizen complained about the water service and what he deemed confiscatory taxes on the Garrison Street house, which he had been given in the first place. As usual, he found his way into the newspapers, a figure of controversy even here. Minnie, who had been living nearby on a farm he had given her, decamped to Pittsburgh when her husband's business failed. Cumpy was about to enter Yale, and Sherman was determined to keep a close watch on his progress. All signs pointed to a move east, not the nation's capital, but Gotham. For in the end, he left St. Louis for the same reason he had always left St. Louis. "In New York he will be amused," noted a perceptive acquaintance. "Here he is bored."[81]

5

Despite having lived longer and remained in better health than he'd ever expected, Sherman recognized that his life was winding down, that it was a time of reckoning. After his retirement on November 1, 1883—exactly one century after Washington's[82]—the former general of the army showed little further interest in military developments. He did remain intensely concerned with his professional and historical legacy—and also Grant's. His friend had been brought low and was at the end, as were many other contemporaries, including Ellen. He did what he could to settle old scores and make amends, but on his own terms. He remained to the end Uncle Billy—indeed, like many old people, he became more like himself...Broadway Billy, even Diamond Billy. For although the road was ending, there was still considerable fun to be had along the Great White Way.

Yet responsibility and reconciliation came first. Sherman had been deeply hurt when Grant favored John Rawlins in the jurisdictional dispute over who controlled the War Department, then watched cheerlessly as his administration sank into scandal. He never understood why Grant wanted to be president, and he concluded, Sherman-like, "I believe he is a mystery to himself."[83] As befitted the two, very little was ever said directly. They remained cordial, but a cloud hung over the relationship. Then came Grant's annus horribilis, 1884, when he learned in rapid succession that he had been swindled out of all his money and that a lifetime of cigars was going to end with throat cancer.

Just as he might have in wartime, Grant's wingman flew to his aid, visiting him in New York repeatedly and trying to help restructure his debts and at least preserve his personal possessions.[84] He also encouraged "what he should have done in 1868–9—compiling his Memoirs," realizing how lucid the otherwise stolid Grant could be. But he concluded sadly that his hopes to save wife, Julia, from poverty with the proceeds were bound to be dashed when he "discovered that the publishers take 90 per cent."[85] In fact, their mutual friend and publisher, Mark Twain, worked out a much better deal that eventually left Julia around $450,000 on 350,000 copies sold.[86] And the product was better, too—probably the best military commentaries written by a commanding general since Caesar. Grant struggled heroically to finish, delivering the last of it just days before he passed away on July 23, 1885; yet the quality never suffered, and the prose flows smoothly from beginning to end.

Just a few days after the president's death, Grant's son Fred told Sherman that not only would the forthcoming book give him full credit for conceiving the March to the Sea, but "in his later days his father was more and more recognizant of the truth that I had been his most loyal friend throughout his military career."[87] This may have overlooked what had happened later, but to Sherman it constituted closure.

Grant was far from alone. By the mid-1880s, Sherman had seen Civil War luminaries, some a decade younger, fall one after another—Meade, 1872; Hooker, 1879; Burnside, 1881; Logan, 1886; Sheridan, 1888—and for each there would be a mass memorial service and later probably the dedication of a statue, all of which William Tecumseh Sherman would be expected to attend. Sherman still loved a good ceremony, but this plainly started to bring him down. "Will attend my own funeral, but must be excused from others," he advised Ellen, who may have found this foreboding.[88]

She was not in good shape. The final move to New York in 1886 had not gone well for her. Cump installed them at the Fifth Avenue Hotel—he knew it well, having met Mary there—and she blamed the place for her continued breathing problems (not without reason, since the city's air quality was not likely to have been much better than it was in St. Louis). She retreated to lodgings in less polluted New Jersey, and yet again the couple lived apart, much to Sherman's chagrin, who blamed it on "fat about the heart," not New York. "We should be together for better or worse, and I know of no better place *now* than the Fifth Avenue Hotel."[89]

She returned, and predictably her health did not improve, despite her husband's protestations to the contrary. "I am extremely weak," she told brother Phil in the spring of 1888, "I certainly am not robust as Cump reports."[90] Nevertheless, she decided to spend the summer in rural Woodstock, Maryland, where Tom was attached to a Jesuit center. To reel her back, Sherman finally gave up on the hotel gambit and in a whirlwind of acquisition purchased and furnished a new four-story brownstone near Central Park. Ellen took the bait. By late September, the place was ready and the family moved in, all hoping that Ellen soon would be feeling better, though she could not walk up the steps and had to be carried to her room.

She only got worse. And Sherman remained in denial. Tom Ewing Jr. recommended that they bring in a specialist from Philadelphia. He agreed but insisted there was no cause for alarm: "Her father was exactly so for twenty years and lived to 83 yrs."[91] Ellen was likely suffering from congestive heart failure and accompanying pulmonary edema; at any rate, nothing helped. On November 27, Cump finally faced up to reality, wiring John: "The doctors pronounce Ellen in a most precarious situation and I am forced to the same conclusion."[92] The next day, while reading downstairs, he heard the nurse call out that Ellen was dying. He raced up the steps: "Wait for me Ellen, no one ever loved you as I loved you."[93]

She was no woman to keep God waiting, so he missed her passing but had already cut to the heart of the matter. They had been bonded in a way few humans ever are—first brother and sister, then man and wife—enmeshed for a lifetime by a twisted skein of affection, attraction, frustration, and antagonism, one that had been stretched to the horizon but had never broke. Both were fierce and determined, under normal circumstances almost certainly incompatible; but their circumstances were not normal, so they remained mated, paired like squawking geese until death intervened.

He went mechanically about the business of burying her, journeying to St. Louis, where she was laid to rest next to little Willy. It was only when he returned and walked into the empty house that it hit him: she was gone forever. He tried to busy himself answering the wave of condolences that included Presidents Hayes and Harrison and Vinnie Ream and her husband. A steady stream of visitors tried to cheer him, but his mood remained leaden and he spoke of suicide. On one occasion, either Cumpy or Tom found him in his office, sitting speechless and pointing to his throat, which asthma had almost totally closed. On another, he failed to cut off an extinguished gas jet, risking asphyxiation.[94]

Yet, catatonic Sherman was not—not once the initial shock of Ellen's death wore off and the lure of the outside world began to reassert itself. This was, after all, New York City, and soon Uncle Billy was out and about, again living the life he had been sliding into even before the final move to the city—a life of entertainment and, above all, the theater. He had seen his first play long before in New York and now caught every one he could—savoring them by halves over two nights, frequently getting a standing ovation from the audience as he entered, then sauntering backstage to chat with the cast. This was not a subtle era, and the productions were staged to draw the widest possible audience—flashy costuming, massive sets, dumbed-down dialogue—as much spectacle as theater. As a general who favored unorthodox garb and lots of special effects, Sherman never complained. Melodramas, comedies, romances: He liked them all.[95]

And also the participants. He was drawn to theater people, whether it was Buffalo Bill Cody or impresarios like Augustin Daly, as kindred spirits and compatriots. He frequently dined with them and socialized, becoming a founding member of the aptly named Players Club. For theatrical connections also provided entrée to actresses, women often unattached, charismatic, and independent, just the sort Sherman liked. How many—if any—such liaisons actually existed is impossible to know, but he did befriend a number and the opportunities were there.[96]

But he was also nearly seventy, romance now more a matter of memory than possibility. He was free to marry Mary Audenried but instead chose to let her drift out of his life, seeing her at the last as an enabler of her out-of-control daughter and almost as spoiled and self-indulgent.[97] As much as anything, it was anger at Ellen that had driven this affair, and now that she was gone it ran out of energy, replaced perhaps by regret.

Not so with Vinnie Ream. He retained his affection and respect for his plucky past paramour and continued corresponding, in 1887 telling her: "You have a sick husband and I a sick wife....I sometimes think the Mormons are right and that a man should have the right to change— Tell Hoxie I will swap with him." Yet when Vinnie answered back, apparently with some expectation of at least a visit, he replied, "Dear Vinnie, the old times *never* come back...we change."[98] They continued corresponding to his death, but he never saw her again.

There was one more woman in his life: Mary Draper, the socially prominent widow of pro-Sherman historian John W. Draper. However, she appears to have been not a lover, but a designated dinner companion. For if Uncle Billy's ardor had cooled, he remained a highly social creature and the invitations kept coming.

Never really a relic, he continued as a bridge to the past, after Grant's death the last true embodiment of the Northern victory. "You've been a landmark to me all my life," one young man told him, much to his annoyance.[99] In New York City, that translated into numerous ceremonies and banquets. He became a fixture, a necessary attendee at the full range of social rituals, but particularly at those of the very wealthy—Astors, Vanderbilts, and Carnegies all looked to Sherman to round out a repast, wedding, or reception, and he seldom disappointed. In the winter of 1891, he was still averaging four public or private dinner parties a week, attending the theater regularly, and splitting the remainder of his time visiting friends or exchanging gossip at the Union League Club.[100] "Indeed for a 71 year old colt," he told one friend, "I manage to get a good deal of fun."[101]

Yet he knew it was temporary, that the tide of history and biology had turned against him. The South was again solid—back in the Union, but anchored now on condition of their black citizens' disenfranchisement and legalized subordination. Meanwhile, those of like mind sought to turn the Southern version of the Civil War into a noble enterprise and William Tecumseh Sherman into what one historian called "Demon of the Lost Cause."[102] As long as he could hold a pen or give a speech, he beat them back—as well as anybody else who challenged his reputation. But it was simply a matter of time: "fleet[ing] by with race horse speed," he told Mary Draper.[103]

"I feel it coming sometimes," he told another friend, "when I get home from an entertainment or banquet, especially these winter nights. I feel death reaching out for me, as it were. I'll take cold some night and go to bed never to get up again."[104]

He called it almost exactly. His two favorite diversions sent him into the final dive. On February 4, 1891, he attended the theater and awoke the next morning with a severe cold, despite which he insisted on attending a wedding the next day. By the time he returned home, he was sick enough to call off a dinner with actor Lawrence Barrett at the Union League Club.

Physicians were called, and he remained in bed for the next week. But the cold severely aggravated his asthma, and he was having increasing trouble breathing as his lungs filled with fluid. The family gathered, and a local priest stopped by and told Minnie that "he would give Papa conditional absolution if we would let him see him. Indeed he would gladly give him Extreme Unction."[105]

Between February 11 and 13, he rallied and regained full consciousness. Yet he remained in the deadly grip of pneumonia, and when he resumed his slide that night, Lizzie and Minnie decided to call the priest. They asked the attending physician if he had any medical objections to the sacraments being administered. "The Dr. said No," Minnie remembered. "Nothing will make any difference now."[106] So Ellen had her way at the last. Surrounded by meticulously Catholicized offspring, William Tecumseh Sherman was delivered unconscious into the arms of the Church. He died quietly the next day at around two in the afternoon.

They brought him back west, but not before parading him through New York City, where tens of thousands lined the curbs and housetops as the procession, which numbered thirty thousand soldiers, turned onto Fifth Avenue and proceeded slowly to the end of Manhattan, where a ferry awaited to deliver him to New Jersey and a special eight-car train. It was winter, and the wind was blowing. One of the honorary pallbearers was Joe Johnston, just turned eighty-four. "General, put on your hat, you will take cold," suggested Elly's husband, Alexander Thackara. But the old man would have none of it: "If I were in his place and he standing here in mine he would not put on his hat."[107] That was probably true, but he still caught pneumonia and died barely a month later.

Not unexpectedly, Sherman's final destination was St. Louis. The train sped across the country, stopping only to change engines; yet huge crowds gathered in Pittsburgh and Columbus. When it arrived at the Gateway to the West, the ceremonies and throngs of mourners rivaled those in New York. Tom delivered the funeral Mass ("It's a comfort to the children," John Sherman explained),[108] and he was buried next to Ellen and Willy in Calvary Cemetery, a permanent resident at last.

But he was America's. He played a significant role in defining us—dimensionally, in the nature and spirit of our fighting forces, and our ethos, or at least the celebrity version of it. Historically, he was one of the ingredients for what we became. A continent for the taking brought forth people like Sherman, and they in turn produced us. Their energy, ambition, optimism, and pragmatism serves to explain our own, but so does their self-righteousness and proclivity for violence.

Sherman was all of these things, a mixture of good and bad, but still a familiar and comfortable presence. It's hard to imagine a more American man than Sherman. And although he died over 120 years ago, it's a safe bet that should Uncle Billy be brought back to life tomorrow, after a short orientation with the requisite hardware and software, he'd find himself right at home.

In the end, it amounted to a lot of Sherman, years of thinking, wondering… obsessing. It seems to be a common affliction among those who write about him, maybe all biographers. He didn't just move in to take over large slices of my daily consciousness; he turned me into a long-distance walker, then into a ventriloquist's dummy mouthing tales of his exploits to anyone who would listen, and finally—inevitably—into a pilgrim.

Monumentally speaking, there was really only one place to go. His body may still be in St. Louis, but if his spirit is anywhere, it's at Fifth Avenue and Fifty-ninth near the entrance to Central Park, manifested in a king-sized equestrian statue.

Augustus Saint-Gaudens, at the time America's foremost sculptor, had become fascinated with Sherman in 1887 when he had been persuaded to sit for a bust—a very good one, as it turned out. Four years later, he swooped in to do a death mask and a month later took a commission from the New York Chamber of Commerce to execute a statue commemorating the general. Saint-Gaudens wanted to produce a great piece of art, one worthy of the subject, and he didn't

Augustus Saint-Gaudens became fascinated with Sherman and angled for the chance to produce a monumental equestrian rendition, which took him eleven years to complete (unveiled 1903). *Library of Congress*

care how long it took him, which eventually amounted to eleven years.

Unveiled before thousands on Memorial Day 1903, perched on a twenty-foot granite base, it consisted of a bronze cast group featuring a caped Sherman atop a spirited Thoroughbred, closely following an allegorical representation of Victory (the model for her head was probably Sherman's beautiful niece and Henry Adams's unrequited love, Elizabeth Cameron), all covered with gold leaf. It appears to have been an immediate success. "She is an American Victory, as this is an American man on an American horse," wrote Saint-Gaudens's friend and fellow artist Kenyon Cox in *The Nation*. At any rate, it's been there ever since.

You can see it from several blocks off: it's big and certainly reflects the bright noontime sunlight. When I saw it up close, I must admit my first thought was, That's Uncle Billy, forever on the heels of a pretty girl. My art credentials are nonexistent, but I don't think Sherman looks good in gilt, certainly no better than C-3PO. In fact, the whole thing looks a little like a giant hood ornament for some overwrought 1920s limousine.

But that didn't seem to bother the small crowd gathered at the base and in the surrounding plaza, many eating their lunch. Uncle Billy—just across from Bergdorf's and the Plaza—still has lots of visitors, unlike Grant, whose much grander mausoleum in Morningside Heights remains deserted—a state of affairs weirdly paralleling their respective careers. Sherman always enjoyed company, and I began wondering what, besides their sandwiches, might have drawn the people there to this spot—a dangerous thought. My wife, the victim of way too much Sherman, could see it coming and backed off, plainly trying to pretend she didn't know me. I was about to break a fundamental New York taboo, commit a cardinal New York sin: I was about to start talking to strangers.

It probably turned out better than I deserved. Everybody responded. I really only wanted to know if they knew whose statue this was. About half didn't, but most of those seemed to recognize the name when I brought it up. One said he had been eating there at noon for a decade and never looked up. "Helped Grant win the Civil War," went another apt summary. A well-dressed financial type knew quite a lot and actually seemed to want to talk serious Sherman. But my wife could see he was humoring me and got me out of there. My polling day was over.

It was sort of a lonely moment for a historian, even if it was expected. Never a historically minded people, Americans seem even less interested in the past these days. Meanwhile, it remains unclear what history can do, whom it should serve, what it should be. Academics continue to doggedly address these issues, but in the process they produce much that is unreadable. Popular history is easier to consume but varies wildly in quality; the genre is largely the province of journalists, who often lack the background to see deep trends and long-term causation. The path forward remains cluttered with question marks.

But amid the confusion, the past itself remains replete with interesting and instructive life stories. To me, that much remains clear. I think my time with Uncle Billy was well spent. I liked him, he was never dull, and he grew into my make-believe friend, sitting in a recliner in his rumpled uniform, watching me compose, accompanying me on long walks—but never saying a word. That's the past for you: a pale echo of what actually happened, a bunch of factual remains of what were once human lives, and for that reason always subject to reinterpretation. So if you don't like this Sherman, wait a while, there's bound to be another. He's too important to forget.

Acknowledgments

Having been a recent visitor to the tribe of Civil War historians, I want to thank two members in particular for their kindness and hospitality. Early in the project, John Marszalek at Mississippi State University helped me get oriented, while his extraordinary scholarship served as a guide throughout. At the University of Virginia, Gary Gallagher provided valuable advice and was kind enough to read and critique my early efforts. Also at Virginia, both Joe Kett and Peter Onuf shared with me ideas that proved extremely useful.

I owe an intellectual debt to Victor Davis Hanson, whose chapter in *The Soul of Battle* on Sherman's army first caused me to wonder how it became so versatile. In addition, at the Naval Postgraduate School, I want to thank John Arquilla for helping me clarify the campaign along the Mississippi by applying a filter of irregular warfare. Also at NPS, thanks to Hy Rothstein and Michael Freeman, both of whom gave the manuscript extraordinarily perceptive reads. In New Haven, I want to thank Stacey Maples for helping me interpret topographical images of the Atlanta campaign from the Yale

University Library Map Collection. Hal Jespersen was my cartographer, and a fine one he proved to be. Thanks, Hal.

Thanks also to friends and family members—Sterling Deal, Si Becker, Nick Taylor, Katherine and Jack MacKinnon—all of whom read the manuscript and made valuable suggestions.

Even in this electronic age it's hard to write history without good libraries. During my time with Sherman, I was fortunate enough to have the support of the staffs of two excellent ones at the Naval Postgraduate School and the Alderman Library of the University of Virginia. Thank you for having the books and materials I needed, getting them when necessary, and even occasionally bending the rules to help me.

At Random House, I want to particularly thank my editor, Jonathan Jao. Not only did he initially point me toward Sherman, but once the book was written, he performed some significant cosmetic surgery. I'm pretty sure nobody in the medical profession does cuts and transplants more cleanly and with less blood than Jonathan.

Finally, I want to thank my agent, Carl Brandt; but regrettably I must do it postmortem. A fellow client once described Carl as "a great solace." This pretty much encapsulated it. For nearly a quarter of a century he was my champion and wise counsel, always ready to lend an ear to my complaints and to shut me down when I got ridiculous. For those of us who knew him, things will never be the same.

Notes

Chapter I: Tyro

1. James L. Morrison Jr., *The Best School in the World: West Point, the Pre–Civil War Years, 1833–1866* (Kent, OH: Kent State University Press, 1986), 63.
2. W. T. Sherman, *Memoirs of General William T. Sherman,* 2 vols. (New York: D. Appleton, 1904), I, 14; Josiah Bunting III, *Ulysses S. Grant* (New York: Times Books, 2004), 15–16.
3. Robert P. Broadwater, *General George H. Thomas* (Jefferson, NC: McFarland, 2009), 8.
4. Morrison, *Best School in the World,* 4.
5. Ibid., 101.
6. John F. Marszalek, *Sherman: A Soldier's Passion for Order* (New York: Free Press, 1993), 20.
7. M. A. DeWolfe Howe, ed., *Home Letters of General Sherman* (New York: Charles Scribner's Sons, 1909), 24.
8. Morrison, *Best School in the World,* 94–95; James M. McPherson, *Battle Cry of Freedom: The Civil War Era* (New York: Oxford University Press, 1988), 331; Robert M. Utley, *Frontiersmen in Blue: The United States Army and the Indians: 1848–1865* (Lincoln: University of Nebraska Press, 1991), 33.
9. Michael Korda, *Ulysses S. Grant: The Unlikely Hero* (New York: Atlas Books, 2004), 24.
10. Bunting, *Ulysses S. Grant,* 15.
11. Michael Fellman, *Citizen Sherman: A Life of William Tecumseh Sherman* (New York: Random House, 1995), 12; Morrison, *Best School in the World,* 100.
12. W. T. Sherman to Hugh Ewing, January 25, 1844, cited in Marszalek, *Sherman,* 19.
13. Morrison, *Best School in the World,* 100.
14. Cited in Pierre Gaxotte, *Frederick the Great,* trans. R. A. Bell (New Haven: Yale University Press, 1942), 104.

15. W. H. McNeill, *The Pursuit of Power: Technology, Armed Force, and Society Since A.D. 1000* (Chicago: University of Chicago Press, 1982), 131; see also W. H. McNeill, *Keeping Together in Time: Dance and Drill in Human History* (Cambridge, MA: Harvard University Press, 1995).

16. Comte de Saint-Germain, *Memoirs* (En Suisse: Chez les libraires associés, 1779), 178.

17. Morrison, *Best School in the World*, 54.

18. Marszalek, *Sherman*, 21; Morrison, *Best School in the World*, 59.

19. Marszalek, *Sherman*, 24.

20. Sherman, *Memoirs*, I, 17.

21. John F. Marszalek, *Commander of All Lincoln's Armies: A Life of General Henry W. Halleck* (Cambridge, MA: Harvard University Press, 2004), 25.

22. Ibid., 19.

23. Korda, *Ulysses S. Grant*, 26.

24. Victor Davis Hanson, *The Soul of Battle: From Ancient Times to the Present Day; How Three Great Liberators Vanquished Tyranny* (New York: Free Press, 1999), 216; Marszalek, *Sherman*, 23.

25. Morrison, *Best School in the World*, 81.

26. Ibid.

27. Marszalek, *Sherman*, 23; Lloyd Lewis, *Sherman: Fighting Prophet* (New York: Harcourt, Brace & Co., 1958), 57–58; Russell F. Weigley, *History of the United States Army* (Bloomington: Indiana University Press, 1984), 597.

28. Fellman, *Citizen Sherman*, 62.

29. Ryan C. Agee, "Deterrence Theory and Localism in Surfing," student paper, August 11, 2011, Naval Postgraduate School, 3.

30. Fellman, *Citizen Sherman*, 118; Bell Irvin Wiley, *The Life of Billy Yank: The Common Soldier of the Union* (Garden City, NY: Doubleday, 1971), 69.

31. *The Seven Military Classics of Ancient China*, trans. Ralph D. Sawyer (Boulder, CO: Westview Press, 1993), 17.

32. Morrison, *Best School in the World*, 7.

33. Jane F. Lancaster, "William Tecumseh Sherman's Introduction to War, 1840–1842," *Florida Historical Quarterly* 72, no. 1 (July 1993): 57.

34. Sherman, *Memoirs*, I, 18–19.

35. Marszalek, *Sherman*, 34.

36. Lancaster, "William Tecumseh Sherman's Introduction to War," 64.

37. Sherman, *Memoirs*, I, 20.

38. Ibid., 20–21.

39. Ibid., 22.

40. Cited in Marszalek, *Sherman*, 34.

41. W. T. Sherman to Phil Ewing, April 10, 1841, in P. B. Ewing Papers, Notre Dame.

42. Marszalek, *Sherman*, 35.

43. Lancaster, "William Tecumseh Sherman's Introduction to War," 62; W. T. Sherman to sister, January 16, 1841, cited in James Merrill, *William Tecumseh Sherman* (Chicago: Rand McNally, 1971), 47.

44. Lancaster, "William Tecumseh Sherman's Introduction to War," 67, 68–69.

45. W. T. Sherman to Phil Ewing, November 1, 1841, cited in ibid., 69.

46. Powhatan Clarke to Leroy Boyd, May 21, 1903, in Sherman Family Papers, Notre Dame.

47. Erasmus D. Keyes, *Fifty Years' Observation of Men and Events, Civil and Military* (New York: Charles Scribner's Sons, 1884), 163.

48. Sherman, *Memoirs,* I, 26.

49. Marszalek, *Sherman,* 42.

50. William T. Sherman, "General Sherman's Last Speech: The Old Army…31 Jan., 1891," *Century* (June 1891): 191.

51. W. T. Sherman to Ellen Ewing, November 28, 1842, in Sherman Family Papers, Notre Dame.

52. W. T. Sherman to Phil Ewing, November 5, 1842, cited in Marszalek, *Sherman,* 43; W. T. Sherman to Elizabeth Sherman, March 12, 1843, in Sherman Family Papers, Notre Dame.

53. Marszalek, *Sherman,* 45.

54. W. T. Sherman to Elizabeth Sherman, September 17, 1844, in Howe, *Home Letters,* 26.

55. W. T. Sherman to Phil Ewing, November 5, 1842, cited in Marszalek, *Sherman,* 42.

56. Marszalek, *Sherman,* 44.

57. Charles Royster, *The Destructive War: William Tecumseh Sherman, Stonewall Jackson, and the Americans* (New York: Alfred A. Knopf, 1991), 142.

58. W. T. Sherman to John Sherman, February 1, 1861, in Brooks D. Simpson and Jean V. Berlin, eds., *Sherman's Civil War: Selected Correspondence of William T. Sherman, 1860– 65* (Chapel Hill: University of North Carolina Press, 1999), 221.

59. Royster, *The Destructive War,* 139–41.

60. W. T. Sherman to Henry Halleck, July 16, 1862, in *OR,* vol. XVII, pt. 2, 100.

61. W. T. Sherman, diary, March 3, 16–23, 1844, in Sherman Family Papers, Notre Dame.

62. W. T. Sherman to Adjutant General's Office, December 19, 1845, in Sherman Family Papers, Notre Dame; January 15, 1845, cited in Lee Kennett, *Sherman: A Soldier's Life* (New York: HarperCollins, 2001), 37.

Chapter II: The Golden State

1. Sherman, *Memoirs,* I, 38.

2. E. O. C. Ord to W. T. Sherman, June 18, 1846, cited in Marszalek, *Sherman,* 53.

3. Ibid., 38–40.

4. Marszalek, *Commander of All Lincoln's Armies,* 30, 42.

5. W. T. Sherman to Ellen Sherman, July 12, 1846, in Howe, *Home Letters,* 36–38.

6. W. T. Sherman to Thomas Ewing, May 3, 1862, cited in Joseph H. Ewing, "Sherman Bashes the Press," *American Heritage* 38 (July–August 1987): 30.

7. Marszalek, *Sherman,* 60.

8. Sherman, *Memoirs,* I, 45.

9. Ibid., 46.

10. Kennett, *Sherman: A Soldier's Life,* 39.

11. Sherman, *Memoirs,* I, 48–49.

12. Marszalek, *Sherman,* 62–63.

13. Cited in Marszalek, *Commander of All Lincoln's Armies,* 53–54.

14. W. T. Sherman to Ellen Ewing, August 28, 1848, in Sherman Family Papers, Notre Dame.

15. W. T. Sherman to Ellen Ewing, January 25, 1847, in ibid.

16. Fellman, *Citzen Sherman,* 25.

17. W. T. Sherman to Ellen Ewing, March 12, 1847, in Howe, *Home Letters,* 93–94.

18. Timothy D. Johnson, *Winfield Scott: The Quest for Military Glory* (Lawrence: University Press of Kansas, 1998), 181.

19. W. T. Sherman to Ellen Ewing, July 11, 1847, in Howe, *Home Letters,* 107–08.

20. Cited in Marszalek, *Commander of All Lincoln's Armies,* 55–56.

21. Ibid., 57–60.
22. W. T. Sherman to Ellen Ewing, November 10, 1847, in Sherman Family Papers, Notre Dame.
23. Sherman, *Memoirs,* I, 58–59, 64–66.
24. W. T. Sherman to Elizabeth Sherman, February 3, 1848, in Sherman Family Papers, Notre Dame.
25. Sherman, *Memoirs,* I, 70.
26. Ibid., 85–86.
27. McPherson, *Battle Cry of Freedom,* 64.
28. Sherman, *Memoirs,* I, 100.
29. Ibid., 98–100.
30. Ibid., 94.
31. Marszalek, *Sherman,* 74.
32. W. T. Sherman to Ellen Ewing, March 5, 1849, in Sherman Family Papers, Notre Dame.
33. W. T. Sherman to J. D. Stevenson, August 26, 1848, UCLA collection, cited in Marszalek, *Sherman,* 71.
34. H. W. Halleck, "Report on the Laws and Regulations Relative to Grants or Sales of Public Lands in California," March 1, 1849, Serial No. 557, 120–183.
35. W. T. Sherman to Hugh Ewing, April 15, 1860, cited in Fellman, *Citizen Sherman,* 25.
36. McPherson, *Battle Cry of Freedom,* 3–4.
37. Sherman, *Memoirs,* I, 111.
38. Endorsement by Winfield Scott, February 8, 1850, cited in Marszalek, *Sherman,* 71.
39. Cited in Marszalek, *Sherman,* 78.
40. Sherman, *Memoirs,* I, 111.
41. Thomas Ewing Sr. to Ellen Ewing, February 13, 1865, Thomas Ewing Papers, Library of Congress, cited in Fellman, *Citizen Sherman,* 6.
42. Theodore Burton, *John Sherman* (Boston: Houghton Mifflin & Co., 1906), 5–6.
43. Marszalek, *Sherman,* 81.
44. Sherman, *Memoirs,* I, 113–14.
45. W. T. Sherman to Ellen Sherman, October 23, 1850, in Sherman Family Papers, Notre Dame.
46. Ellen Sherman to Hugh Ewing, May 18, 1851, cited in Marszalek, *Sherman,* 87.
47. W. T. Sherman to Ellen Sherman, September 24 and 25, 1850, in Sherman Family Papers, Notre Dame.
48. W. T. Sherman to Thomas Ewing Jr., August 30, 1852, cited in Marszalek, *Sherman,* 89.
49. Lewis, *Sherman: Fighting Prophet,* 88.
50. Cited in Marszalek, *Sherman,* 88.
51. Kennett, *Sherman: A Soldier's Life,* 88.
52. James G. Blaine, "Some Personal Traits of General Sherman," in Sherman, *Memoirs,* II, appendix.
53. W. T. Sherman to John Sherman, November 18, 1852, in W. T. Sherman Papers, Library of Congress.
54. Henry S. Turner to W. T. Sherman, December 7, 1852, in W. T. Sherman Manuscripts, Library of Congress.
55. Fellman, *Citizen Sherman,* 39.
56. W. T. Sherman to John Sherman, March 24, 1853, W. T. Sherman Manuscripts, Library of Congress, cited in Kennett, *Sherman: A Soldier's Life,* 61.
57. McPherson, *Battle Cry of Freedom,* 12.

58. Henry Halleck to Frederick Billings, September 18, 1852, cited in Marszalek, *Commander of All Lincoln's Armies*, 78.

59. Marszalek, *Commander of All Lincoln's Armies*, 96.

60. Marszalek, *Sherman*, 105.

61. Kennett, *Sherman: A Soldier's Life*, 68.

62. W. T. Sherman to Thomas Ewing, June 16, 1856, cited in Marszalek, *Sherman*, 107.

63. Sherman, *Memoirs*, I, 156–57.

64. *Daily Evening Bulletin*, June 5, 1856.

65. Marszalek, *Commander of All Lincoln's Armies*, 100.

66. *Alta California*, June 4, 1856.

67. W. T. Sherman to S. S. L'Hommedieu, July 7, 1862, in Simpson and Berlin, *Sherman's Civil War*, 246.

68. Kennett, *Sherman: A Soldier's Life*, 70–71.

69. Sherman, *Memoirs*, I, 159; Royster, *The Destructive War*, 137–38; Marszalek, *Sherman*, 108.

Chapter III: Into the Gloom

1. Sherman, *Memoirs*, I, 165.

2. W. T. Sherman to John Sherman, September 4, 1857, and W. T. Sherman to John Sherman, November 5, 1857, in W. T. Sherman Papers, Library of Congress.

3. *New York Times*, September 10, 1885.

4. Henry Turner to W. T. Sherman, August 12, 1858, in W. T. Sherman Papers, Library of Congress.

5. W. T. Sherman to John Sherman, April 8, 1861, in Simpson and Berlin, *Sherman's Civil War*, 66–67.

6. Marszalek, *Sherman*, 112–13; Fellman, *Citizen Sherman*, 54, 56.

7. W. T. Sherman to Thomas Ewing, April 15, 1858, in Thomas Ewing Papers, Library of Congress.

8. W. T. Sherman to Ellen Sherman, September 18, 1858, in Howe, *Home Letters*, 153–55.

9. Fellman, *Citizen Sherman*, 67.

10. W. T. Sherman to Thomas Ewing Jr., September 18, 1858, cited in Marszalek, *Sherman*, 117.

11. Marszalek, *Sherman*, 119.

12. W. T. Sherman to John Sherman, May 27, 1859, in Rachel Sherman Thorndike, ed., *The Sherman Letters: Correspondence Between General Sherman and Senator Sherman from 1837 to 1891* (New York: Charles Scribner's Sons, 1894), 70–71.

13. W. T. Sherman to Don Carlos Buell, June 11, 1859, and Don Carlos Buell to W. T. Sherman, June 17, 1859, in W. T. Sherman Papers, Library of Congress.

14. Kennett, *Sherman: A Soldier's Life*, 85.

15. W. T. Sherman to John Sherman, August 20, 1859, in W. T. Sherman Papers, Library of Congress.

16. See, for example, Lewis, *Sherman: Fighting Prophet*, 129.

17. McPherson, *Battle Cry of Freedom*, 8–9, 39, 195. See also Royster, *The Destructive War*, 191.

18. U. S. Grant to Charles W. Ford, December 10, 1860, cited in William S. McFeely, *Grant: A Biography* (New York: Norton, 1981), 79.

19. W. T. Sherman to John Sherman, April 30, 1859, in Thorndike, *Sherman Letters*, 69–70.

20. Richard Ned Lebow, *Between Peace and War: The Nature of International Crisis* (Balti-

more: Johns Hopkins University Press, 1981), 107; see especially Irving L. Janis and Leon Mann, *Decision Making: A Psychological Analysis of Conflict, Choice, and Commitment* (New York: Free Press, 1977).

21. Lebow, *Between Peace and War*, 102–03; see also Robert Jervis, *Perceptions and Misperceptions in International Politics* (Princeton, NJ: Princeton University Press, 1976).

22. W. T. Sherman to Ellen Sherman, November 12, 1859, in Sherman Family Papers, Notre Dame.

23. Sherman, *Memoirs*, I, 174–75.

24. Marszalek, *Sherman*, 129.

25. David French Boyd, "General W. T. Sherman as a College President," *American College* 2 (April 1910): 6, 3.

26. John Sherman to W. T. Sherman, December 24, 1859, in W. T. Sherman Papers, Library of Congress.

27. Sherman, *Memoirs*, I, 177

28. Marszalek, *Sherman*, 130.

29. Sherman, *Memoirs*, I, 178.

30. D. F. Boyd to P. T. Sherman, December 7, 1892, in Sherman Family Papers, Notre Dame.

31. Cited in Lewis, *Sherman: Fighting Prophet*, 138.

32. Sherman, *Memoirs*, I, 183.

33. W. T. Sherman to Governor Thomas O. Moore, January 18, 1861, in Sherman, *Memoirs*, I, 183–84.

34. Two years later, upon learning of Moore's capture, Sherman suggested that a successful trial for treason might undermine the South's justification for secession and establishing the Confederacy. W. T. Sherman to T. Ewing, June 14, 1863, in Simpson and Berlin, *Sherman's Civil War*, 482.

35. Royster, *The Destructive War*, 119.

36. W. T. Sherman to John Sherman, February 1860, in Thorndike, *Sherman Letters*, 80.

37. Marszalek, *Sherman*, xvi.

38. Sherman, *Memoirs*, I, 196.

39. Wesley Moody, *Demon of the Lost Cause: Sherman and Civil War History* (Columbia: University of Missouri Press, 1999), 11; Simpson and Berlin, *Sherman's Civil War*, 59.

40. W. T. Sherman to John Sherman, April 1861, in Thorndike, *Sherman Letters*, 111–12.

41. Cited in Marszalek, *Sherman*, 143.

42. W. T. Sherman to John Sherman, March 22, 1861, in Simpson and Berlin, *Sherman's Civil War*, 64; W. T. Sherman to John Sherman, April 22, 1861, in ibid., 71.

43. W. T. Sherman to Montgomery Blair, April 8, 1861, cited in Sherman, *Memoirs*, I, 198–99; Fellman, *Citizen Sherman*, 87.

44. Sherman, *Memoirs*, I, 199.

45. McPherson, *Battle Cry of Freedom*, 291.

46. Sherman, *Memoirs*, I, 201–02.

47. W. T. Sherman to John Sherman, April 18, 1861, in Simpson and Berlin, *Sherman's Civil War*, 69–70.

48. Fellman, *Citizen Sherman*, 84.

Chapter IV: The Black Hole

1. Charles Winslow Elliot, *Winfield Scott: The Soldier and the Man* (New York: Macmillan, 1937), 698.

2. Timothy D. Johnson, *Winfield Scott: The Quest for Military Glory* (Lawrence: University of Kansas Press, 1998), 227.

3. The key elements of Scott's strategy are put forth in two letters to George McClellan (May 3 and 21, 1861), in *OR*, 51, pt. I, 369–70, 387.

4. McPherson, *Battle Cry of Freedom*, 327–28; Wiley, *Billy Yank*, 26.

5. Marszalek, *Sherman*, 147.

6. Ibid.

7. W. T. Sherman to Ellen Sherman, August 3, 1861, in Simpson and Berlin, *Sherman's Civil War*, 127–28.

8. Korda, *Ulysses S. Grant: The Unlikely Hero*, 63.

9. T. Harry Williams, *Lincoln and His Generals* (New York: Alfred A. Knopf, 1952), 21.

10. McPherson, *Battle Cry of Freedom*, 335, 339–42, 344; Bell Irvin Wiley, *The Life of Johnny Reb: The Common Soldier of the Confederacy* (Garden City, NY: Doubleday, 1971), 71–72.

11. Marszalek, *Sherman*, 150.

12. Simpson and Berlin, *Sherman's Civil War*, 112; Fellman, *Citizen Sherman*, 89.

13. W. T. Sherman to Ellen Sherman, July 28, 1861, in Simpson and Berlin, *Sherman's Civil War*, 122.

14. W. T. Sherman to Adjutant General, July 22, 1861, *OR*, I, 2, 755; McPherson, *Battle Cry of Freedom*, 344–45, fn. 4.

15. McPherson, *Battle Cry of Freedom*, 347. He also notes that because of incomplete and inaccurate reporting, such figures must remain approximate.

16. W. T. Sherman to Ellen Sherman, July 24, 1861, in Sherman Family Papers, Notre Dame; Simpson and Berlin, *Sherman's Civil War*, 121–22.

17. W. T. Sherman to John Sherman, December 24, 1861, in W. T. Sherman Papers, Library of Congress.

18. Kennett, *Sherman: A Soldier's Life*, 121–25.

19. Cited in Marszalek, *Sherman*, 151.

20. Sherman, *Memoirs*, I, 216–18.

21. Cited in Kennett, *Sherman: A Soldier's Life*, 123.

22. W. T. Sherman to Ellen Sherman, August 3, 1861, in Howe, *Home Letters*, 211–12.

23. Sherman, *Memoirs*, I, 221.

24. Cited in Aaron Astor, "Bluegrass Blues and Grays," *New York Times*, May 7, 2011.

25. Moody, *Demon of the Lost Cause*, 13–14.

26. McPherson, *Battle Cry of Freedom*, 293–95.

27. Cited in Edward Conrad Smith, *The Borderland in the Civil War* (New York: Macmillan, 1927), 301.

28. Moody, *Demon of the Lost Cause*, 14.

29. W. T. Sherman to John Sherman, September 9, 1861, in W. T. Sherman Papers, Library of Congress; W. T. Sherman to John Sherman, October 5, 1861, in ibid.

30. Sherman, *Memoirs*, I, 227.

31. Royster, *The Destructive War*, 97–98.

32. Marszalek, *Sherman*, 157, 158.

33. William F. G. Shanks, *Personal Recollections of Distinguished Generals* (New York: Harper, 1866), 17–18, 22, 25–26.

34. Sherman, *Memoirs*, I, 230. The other source for the Cameron meeting is Lorenzo Thomas to Simon Cameron, October 21, 1861, in *OR*, I, 3, 548–49, which was reprinted widely in newspapers at the time.

35. Sherman, *Memoirs*, I, 231; Marszalek, *Sherman*, 161.

36. W. T. Sherman to John Sherman, January 8, 1862, in McPherson, *Battle Cry of Freedom*, 305.

37. Cited in Royster, *The Destructive War*, 97.

38. Cited in Marszalek, *Sherman,* 163.

39. John Sherman to Ellen Sherman, December 14, 1861, in Sherman Family Papers, Notre Dame.

40. Cited in Marszalek, *Sherman,* 163.

41. Ellen Sherman to John Sherman, November 10, 1861, in W. T. Sherman Papers, Library of Congress.

42. Ibid.

43. Marszalek, *Commander of All Lincoln's Armies,* 107–08.

44. McPherson, *Battle Cry of Freedom,* 352.

45. Marszalek, *Commander of All Lincoln's Armies,* 110.

46. Ibid.

47. W. T. Sherman to John Sherman, January 4, 1862, in Simpson and Berlin, *Sherman's Civil War,* 174.

48. Cited in Royster, *The Destructive War,* 99.

49. Henry Halleck to George McClellan, December 2, 1861, in *OR,* I, 52, I, 198.

50. Hugh Ewing to W. T. Sherman, December 23, 1861, in Sherman Family Papers, Notre Dame.

51. Simpson and Berlin, *Sherman's Civil War,* 188; Marszalek, *Sherman,* 168.

52. Fellman, *Citizen Sherman,* 105.

53. Ibid., 133; Royster, *The Destructive War,* 100.

54. W. T. Sherman to Thomas Ewing, December 12, 1861, in Simpson and Berlin, *Sherman's Civil War,* 161–64.

55. W. T. Sherman to Henry Halleck, December 12, 1861, in ibid., 165.

56. Halleck to Phil Ewing, December 17, 1861, in *OR,* I, 8, 441–42.

57. Fellman, *Citizen Sherman,* 102.

58. Marszalek, *Commander of All Lincoln's Armies,* 115.

59. Sherman, *Memoirs,* I, 247–48.

60. U. S. Grant, *Ulysses S. Grant: Memoirs and Selected Letters* (New York: Library of America, 1990), 190.

61. *OR,* I, vol. 7, 125.

62. Cited in McPherson, *Battle Cry of Freedom,* 402.

63. Sherman, *Memoirs,* I, 249.

64. Henry Halleck to George McClellan, March 3, 1862, in *OR,* I, 7, 679–80.

65. George McClellan to Henry Halleck, March 3, 1862, in ibid., 680.

66. T. Harry Williams, *McClellan, Sherman and Grant* (New Brunswick, NJ: Rutgers University Press, 1962), 46.

67. Marszalek, *Sherman,* 173–74.

68. Sherman, *Memoirs,* I, 256.

69. *OR,* I, vol. 10, pt. 1, 396–97; James Lee McDonough, *Shiloh: In Hell Before Night* (Knoxville: University of Tennessee Press, 1977), 81.

70. Simpson and Berlin, *Sherman's Civil War,* 16–18.

71. Cited in Marszalek, *Sherman,* 176.

72. Cited in McPherson, *Battle Cry of Freedom,* 408.

73. Ibid., 409.

74. W. T. Sherman to Thomas Ewing, April 27, 1862, in Simpson and Berlin, *Sherman's Civil War,* 212; Royster, *The Destructive War,* 103.

75. W. T. Sherman to Henry Coppee, June 13, 1864, cited in Marszalek, *Sherman,* 180.

76. Robert Selph Henry, *First with the Most: Nathan Bedford Forrest* (Indianapolis: Bobbs-Merrill, 1944), 79.

77. Thomas Jordan, "Notes of a Confederate Staff-Officer at Shiloh," in Robert Underwood Johnson and Clarence Clough Buell, *Battles and Leaders of the Civil War: Opening Battles*, vol. 1 (New York: Century, 1887), 603.

78. Brian Steel Wills, *A Battle from the Start: The Life of Nathan Bedford Forrest* (New York: HarperCollins, 1992), 70.

79. Lyman S. Widney, "Campaigning with 'Uncle Billy,'" *Neals Monthly* 2 (August 1913): 133.

80. W. T. Sherman to Ellen Sherman, April 11, 1862, in Howe, *Home Letters*, 222.

81. Ibid.

82. Royster, *The Destructive War*, 106; Marszalek, *Sherman*, 183.

83. McPherson, *Battle Cry of Freedom*, 415.

84. Marszalek, *Commander of All Lincoln's Armies*, 122.

85. Marszalek, *Sherman*, 183; W. T. Sherman to Ellen Sherman, October 14, 1863, in Howe, *Home Letters*, 277–78.

86. Marszalek, *Commander of All Lincoln's Armies*, 126. "A rather course title, but I am satisfied with it," Halleck noted at the time.

87. Sherman, *Memoirs*, I, 279; McPherson, *Battle Cry of Freedom*, 416.

88. Marszalek, *Commander of All Lincoln's Armies*, 126.

89. Ibid., 129, 135, 137.

Chapter V: Swamped

1. For an example of Sherman's press "supervision," see W. T. Sherman to Samuel Sawyer (editor of the *Union Appeal*), July 24, 1862, in Sherman, *Memoirs*, I, 297–98.

2. Marszalek, *Sherman*, 197.

3. Fellman, *Citizen Sherman*, 151; Sherman, *Memoirs*, I, 293; see also W. T. Sherman to Ellen Sherman, May 26, 1862, in Simpson and Berlin, *Sherman's Civil War*, 226.

4. McPherson, *Battle Cry of Freedom*, 620.

5. W. T. Sherman to Salmon P. Chase, August 11, 1862, in Sherman, *Memoirs*, I, 295.

6. Marszalek, *Sherman*, 193.

7. Royster, *The Destructive War*, 107.

8. Wills, *A Battle from the Start*, 14–20.

9. Jack Hurst, *Nathan Bedford Forrest: A Biography* (New York: Alfred A. Knopf, 1993), 139.

10. When Liddell-Hart sent his friend T. E. Lawrence (Lawrence of Arabia and a master of insurgent warfare) his newly completed biography of Sherman, he showed little interest but wanted to know more about Forrest.

11. Wills, *A Battle from the Start*, 113.

12. Ibid., 71–72.

13. John Arquilla, *Insurgents, Raiders, and Bandits: How Masters of Irregular Warfare Have Shaped Our World* (Chicago: Ivan Dee, 2011), 104.

14. Fellman, *Citizen Sherman*, 140.

15. Moody, *Demon of the Lost Cause*, 18–19; Marszalek, *Sherman*, 195.

16. See, for example, Emer de Vattel, *The Law of Nations: Or, Principles of the Law of Nature, Applied to the Conduct and Affairs of Nations and Sovereigns* (London: J. Coote, reprint 1759; originally published 1758), 9, 125–28, 351.

17. It took Robert E. Lee until May 1863 to realize that "the chief source of information to the enemy, is through our negroes." Even then, few others paid much attention, including Jefferson Davis, whose servant Mary Elizabeth Bowser was a spy in the Confederate president's mansion until the end of the war.

18. McPherson, *Battle Cry of Freedom*, 283, 303.

19. Marszalek, *Commander of All Lincoln's Armies*, 139; McPherson, *Battle Cry of Freedom*, 577.

20. Marszalek, *Sherman*, 203.

21. McPherson, *Battle Cry of Freedom*, 578.

22. David Dixon Porter, *Incidents and Anecdotes of the Civil War* (New York: Google Books, reprint 2007; originally published 1885), 126–27.

23. Korda, *Ulysses S. Grant: The Unlikely Hero*, 84.

24. McPherson, *Battle Cry of Freedom*, 579; Sherman, *Memoirs*, I, 320–21.

25. He wrote his brother the night they left, "I admit slowly we are getting a better army." W. T. Sherman to John Sherman, December 20, 1862, in Simpson and Berlin, *Sherman's Civil War*, 348–49.

26. Porter, *Incidents and Anecdotes*, 130–31.

27. Marszalek, *Sherman*, 208.

28. Marszalek, *Commander of All Lincoln's Armies*, 162.

29. McPherson, *Battle Cry of Freedom*, 582.

30. Marszalek, *Sherman*, 215.

31. Porter, *Incidents and Anecdotes*, 168.

32. Royster, *The Destructive War*, 239; see, for example, W. T. Sherman to Ellen Sherman, April 14, 1862, and June 6, 1862, and W. T. Sherman to John Sherman, February 12, 1863, in Simpson and Berlin, *Sherman's Civil War*, 396.

33. John F. Marszalek, *Sherman's Other War: The General and the Civil War Press* (Memphis: Memphis State University Press, 1981), 121.

34. Marszalek, *Sherman*, 213.

35. Ellen Sherman to W. T. Sherman, January 28, 1863, in Simpson and Berlin, *Sherman's Civil War*, 394, fn. 1.

36. McPherson, *Battle Cry of Freedom*, 589.

37. Sherman, *Memoirs*, I, 342–43.

38. W. T. Sherman to Ellen Sherman, April 23, 1863, in Howe, *Home Letters*, 254. See also W. T. Sherman to Ellen Sherman, April 10, 1863, in Simpson and Berlin, *Sherman's Civil War*, 445.

39. Porter, *Incidents and Anecdotes*, 177.

40. U. S. Grant to W. T. Sherman, April 27, 1863, in *OR*, Navy, I, 24, 591.

41. Marszalek, *Sherman*, 222.

42. Cited in ibid., 229.

43. Ibid.

44. Marszalek, *Commander of All Lincoln's Armies*, 177.

45. W. T. Sherman to Ellen Sherman, June 11, 1863, in Simpson and Berlin, *Sherman's Civil War*, 478.

46. *OR*, ser. I, vol. 24, pt. 1, 227.

47. McPherson, *Battle Cry of Freedom*, 637.

48. Roy C. Basler, ed., *The Collected Works of Abraham Lincoln*, vol. 6 (New Brunswick, NJ: Rutgers University Press, 1952–1955), 409.

49. This description of Chickamauga is derived largely from James McPherson's *Battle Cry of Freedom*, 669–74.

50. Fellman, *Citizen Sherman*, 189.

51. McPherson, *Battle Cry of Freedom*, 675.

52. Tyler Dennett, ed., *Lincoln and the Civil War in the Diaries and Letters of John Hay* (New York: Dodd, Mead, 1939), 106.

53. Marszalek, *Commander of All Lincoln's Armies*, 187

54. Marszalek, *Sherman,* 237.

55. W. T. Sherman to U. S. Grant, October 4, 1863, in John Y. Simon, ed., *The Papers of Ulysses S. Grant,* vol. 9 (Carbondale: Southern Illinois University Press, 1982), 274–75.

56. Marszalek, *Sherman,* 239; Theodore Upson, *With Sherman to the Sea: The Civil War Letters, Diaries & Reminiscences of Theodore F. Upson,* ed. Oscar Osburn Winther (Bloomington: Indiana University Press, 1958), 71–72.

57. P. J. Carmody, "The Battle of Collierville," Society of Army of Tennessee, November 3, 4, 1909.

58. Oliver Otis Howard, *The Autobiography of Oliver Otis Howard,* vol. 1 (New York: Baker & Taylor, 1907), 473–74.

59. Sherman, *Memoirs,* I, 390.

60. Ibid., 389.

61. Ibid.

62. Cited in Marszalek, *Sherman,* 245.

63. Ibid.

64. Cited in McPherson, *Battle Cry of Freedom,* 680.

65. Ibid., 680–81.

66. James A. Connolly, *Three Years in the Army of the Cumberland: The Letters and Diary of Major James A. Connolly,* ed. Paul M. Angle (Bloomington: Indiana University Press, 1959), 158.

67. W. T. Sherman to John Sherman, December 29, 1863, in Simpson and Berlin, *Sherman's Civil War,* 576.

68. Memorandum W. T. Sherman to U. S. Grant, December 19, 1863, cited in Sherman, *Memoirs,* I, 411.

Chapter VI: Atlanta

1. Marszalek, *Commander of All Lincoln's Armies,* 187.

2. W. T. Sherman to Ellen Sherman, March 12, 1864, in Simpson and Berlin, *Sherman's Civil War,* 609.

3. Marszalek, *Sherman,* 259.

4. Korda, *Ulysses S. Grant: The Unlikely Hero,* 95.

5. Marszalek, *Commander of All Lincoln's Armies,* 203.

6. W. T. Sherman to Ellen Sherman, June 12, 1864, in Howe, *Home Letters,* 296–97.

7. Sherman, *Memoirs,* I, 417. "I explained to him personally the nature of Forrest as a man, and of his peculiar force; told him he was sure to encounter Forrest, who always attacked with a vehemence for which he must be prepared....He must in turn assume the most determined offensive, overwhelm him and utterly destroy his whole force."

8. Marszalek, *Sherman,* 252–53.

9. Ibid., 254.

10. Andre Noah Trudeau, *Southern Storm: Sherman's March to the Sea* (New York: HarperCollins, 2008), 47.

11. McPherson, *Battle Cry of Freedom,* 744.

12. Royster, *The Destructive War,* 325.

13. W. T. Sherman to Ellen Sherman, July 9, 1864, in Simpson and Berlin, *Sherman's Civil War,* 675.

14. Jack K. Overmyer, *A Stupendous Effort: The 87th Indiana in the War of the Rebellion* (Bloomington: Indiana University Press, 1997), 143.

15. Marszalek, *Sherman,* 267.

16. Sherman, *Memoirs*, II, 8.

17. Royster, *The Destructive War*, 325.

18. Overmyer, *A Stupendous Effort*, 143.

19. Cited in Marszalek, *Sherman*, 261.

20. W. T. Sherman to Ellen Sherman, May 22, 1864, in Howe, *Home Letters*, 291.

21. James B. Swan, *Chicago's Irish Legion: The 90th Illinois Volunteers in the Civil War* (Carbondale: Southern Illinois University Press, 2009), 132–33.

22. Cited in Lewis, *Sherman: Fighting Prophet*, 357.

23. Sherman, *Memoirs*, II, 42.

24. McPherson, *Battle Cry of Freedom*, 747.

25. Marszalek, *Sherman*, 268.

26. For examples, see Sherman, *Memoirs*, II, 46.

27. Marszalek, *Sherman*, 268.

28. W. T. Sherman to Ellen Sherman, June 1, 1864, in Sherman Family Papers, Notre Dame.

29. W. T. Sherman to U. S. Grant, June 18, 1864, in *OR*, I, 38, IV, 507.

30. McPherson, *Battle Cry of Freedom*, 719; Marszalek, *Sherman*, 269.

31. Wills, *A Battle from the Start*, 178.

32. W. T. Sherman to Thomas Ewing, April 18, 1864, in Simpson and Berlin, *Sherman's Civil War*, 622.

33. W. T. Sherman to Ellen Sherman, April 27, 1864, in ibid., 631–32.

34. W. T. Sherman to Edwin Stanton, June 15, 1864, 6:30 p.m., in *OR*, ser. I, vol. 39, pt. 2, 121.

35. Cited in Wills, *A Battle from the Start*, 224.

36. Ibid., 231.

37. *OR*, ser. I, vol. 46, pt. 1, 20.

38. Cited in Marszalek, *Commander of All Lincoln's Armies*, 203.

39. McPherson, *Battle Cry of Freedom*, 771.

40. Simpson and Berlin, *Sherman's Civil War*, 644, fn. 1; W. T. Sherman to Henry Halleck, June 5, 1864, in *OR*, ser. 1, vol. 38, pt. 1, 68; W. T. Sherman to Henry Halleck, September 15, 1864, in *OR*, ser. 1, vol. 38, pt. 1, 68, cited in Royster, *The Destructive War*, 301.

41. Marszalek, *Sherman*, 273.

42. W. T. Sherman to Ellen Sherman, June 30, 1864, in Sherman Family Papers, Notre Dame.

43. Freeman Cleaves, *Rock of Chickamauga: The Life of General George H. Thomas* (Norman: University of Oklahoma Press, 1948), 225.

44. Royster, *The Destructive War*, 319.

45. W. T. Sherman to John Sherman, July 13, 1864, in Simpson and Berlin, *Sherman's Civil War*, 667.

46. McPherson, *Battle Cry of Freedom*, 751.

47. Marszalek, *Sherman*, 275.

48. Connolly, *Three Years in the Army of the Cumberland*, 234.

49. McPherson, *Battle Cry of Freedom*, 752.

50. *OR*, ser. I, vol. 38, pt. 5, 879.

51. Ibid., 882–83.

52. Sherman, *Memoirs*, II, 72.

53. David Nevin, *Sherman's March: Atlanta to the Sea* (Alexandria: Time-Life Books, 1986), 18.

54. Overmyer, *A Stupendous Effort*, 147.

55. Ibid., 148; McPherson, *Battle Cry of Freedom*, 754.

56. "Testimonial of Willard Warner, February 22, 1876," in Sherman, *Memoirs*, II, 512.

57. Connolly, *Three Years in the Army of the Cumberland*, 248.

58. Sherman, *Memoirs*, II, 90; Overmyer, *A Stupendous Effort*, 148; McPherson, *Battle Cry of Freedom*, 755.

59. John M. King, *Three Years with the 92nd Illinois: The Civil War Diary of John M. King*, ed. Claire E. Swedberg (Mechanicsburg, PA: Stackpole Books, 1999), 223; W. T. Sherman to Thomas Ewing, August 11, 1864, in Simpson and Berlin, *Sherman's Civil War*, 691.

60. McPherson, *Battle Cry of Freedom*, 755.

61. Cited in Hoehling, *Last Train from Atlanta* (New York: Yoseloff, 1958), 325.

62. Sherman, *Memoirs*, II, 98.

63. William Bluffton Millert, diary, Indiana Historical Society, cited in Royster, *The Destructive War*, 277.

64. W. T. Sherman to Henry Halleck, September 3, 1864, in Simpson and Berlin, *Sherman's Civil War*, 695.

65. Moody (*Demon of the Lost Cause*, 33) notes, "The vast majority of historians credit Sherman's capture of Atlanta with Lincoln's reelection in 1864."

66. Henry Halleck to W. T. Sherman, September 16, 1864, in *OR*, ser. I, vol. 38, pt. 5, 856.

67. McPherson, *Battle Cry of Freedom*, 775.

Chapter VII: The March

1. Nevin, *Sherman's March*, 18.

2. Trudeau, *Southern Storm*, 7–8.

3. Dunbar Rowland, *Jefferson Davis, Constitutionalist: His Letters, Papers, and Speeches*, vol. 6 (Jackson, MS: Mississippi Department of Archives and History, 1923), 341–42, 353.

4. Horace Porter, *Campaigning with Grant* (New York: Century, 1897), 313.

5. Marszalek, *Sherman*, 289–90.

6. *OR*, ser. I, vol. 39, pt. 3, 162; W. T. Sherman to U. S. Grant, September 20, 1864, in Sherman, *Memoirs*, II, 113.

7. W. T. Sherman to U. S. Grant, November 6, 1864, in *OR*, ser. I, vol. 39, pt. 3, 658–61.

8. Simpson and Berlin, *Sherman's Civil War*, 733, fn. 1.

9. Sherman, *Memoirs*, II, 145.

10. *OR*, ser. I, vol. 39, pt. 3, 222.

11. Ibid., 239–40.

12. Rice C. Bull, *Soldiering: The Civil War Diary of Rice C. Bull, 123 New York Volunteer Infantry*, ed. K. Jack Bauer (San Rafael, CA: Presidio Press, 1977), 171.

13. Joseph T. Glatthaar, *The March to the Sea and Beyond: Sherman's Troops in the Savannah and Carolinas Campaign* (New York: New York University Press, 1985), 20.

14. Abraham Lincoln to W. T. Sherman, July 18, 1864, cited in Fellman, *Citizen Sherman*, 158.

15. W. T. Sherman to John A. Spooner, July 30, 1864, in *OR*, ser. I, vol. 38, pt. 3, 305–06.

16. W. T. Sherman to Edwin Stanton, October 25, 1864, in *OR*, ser. I, vol. 39, pt. 3, 428–29.

17. Trudeau, *Southern Storm*, 56.

18. Stanley P. Hirshson, *The White Tecumseh: A Biography of General William T. Sherman* (New York: John Wiley & Sons, 1997), 251–52.

19. Ibid., 52.

20. Ibid., 41.

21. Cited in Nevin, *Sherman's March*, 50.

22. Glatthaar, *March to the Sea*, 158–59.

23. Marszalek, *Sherman,* 297.

24. Ibid., 285.

25. W. T. Sherman to J. B. Hood, September 10, 1864, in Simpson and Berlin, *Sherman's Civil War,* 705–06.

26. W. T. Sherman to James M. Calhoun, Mayor, et al., September 12, 1864, in Sherman, *Memoirs.*

27. W. T. Sherman to Orlando Poe, November 7, 1864, in *OR,* ser. I, vol. 39, pt. 3, 680.

28. Marszalek, *Sherman,* 299–300.

29. Sherman, *Memoirs,* II, 178–79.

30. Trudeau, *Southern Storm,* 272; Marszalek, *Sherman,* 301; Sherman, *Memoirs,* II, 388.

31. Trudeau, *Southern Storm,* 115, 122.

32. Field Orders No. 120, November 9, 1864, in Sherman, *Memoirs,* II, 174–76.

33. Cited in Hanson, *The Soul of Battle,* 141.

34. Glatthaar, *March to the Sea,* 161.

35. Cited in Trudeau, *Southern Storm,* 218.

36. Marszalek, *Sherman,* 304–05.

37. Trudeau, *Southern Storm,* 226, 314.

38. Ibid., 255.

39. Ibid., 270, 272.

40. Cited in ibid., 284.

41. Henry Hitchcock, diary, November 17, 1864, in Henry Hitchcock, *Marching with Sherman: Passages from the Letters and Campaign Diaries of Henry Hitchcock, Major and Assistant Adjutant General of Volunteers, November 1864–May 1865* (New Haven: Yale University Press, 1927), 66.

42. Trudeau, *Southern Storm,* 381.

43. Connolly, *Three Years in the Army of the Cumberland,* 367 (diary entry December 18, 1864), 373.

44. Nevin, *Sherman's March,* 146–47; Trudeau, *Southern Storm,* 400.

45. Swan, *Chicago's Irish Legion,* 177.

46. Signals cited in Trudeau, *Southern Storm,* 432.

47. Marszalek, *Sherman,* 307.

48. Cited in Nevin, *Sherman's March,* 150.

49. Henry Hitchcock to wife, December 16, 1864, in Hitchcock, *Marching with Sherman,* 195.

50. Trudeau, *Southern Storm,* 473.

51. Upson, *With Sherman to the Sea,* 142.

52. W. T. Sherman to Thomas Ewing, December 31, 1864, in Howe, *Home Letters,* 320.

53. Cited in Trudeau, *Southern Storm,* 508.

54. Cited in Marszalek, *Sherman,* 306.

55. Cited in Nevin, *Sherman's March,* 147.

56. Colonel Mackland, "Lincoln's Message: The Heartfelt Blessing He Sent General Sherman and His Army," *New York Times,* March 22, 1885.

57. Nevin, *Sherman's March,* 33–34; McPherson, *Battle Cry of Freedom,* 811.

58. Royster, *The Destructive War,* 77.

59. Glatthaar, *March to the Sea,* 54.

60. Henry Halleck to W. T. Sherman, December 30, 1864, in Marszalek, *Sherman,* 313–14.

61. Trudeau, *Southern Storm,* 510–11.

62. Ibid., 515.

63. Sherman, *Memoirs,* II, 244–45.

64. Fellman, *Citizen Sherman*, 162.

65. Sherman, *Memoirs*, II, 249–50.

66. Marszalek, *Sherman*, 165.

67. Ibid.

68. W. T. Sherman to Ellen Sherman, January 15, 1865, in Sherman Family Papers, Notre Dame.

69. Marszalek, *Commander of All Lincoln's Armies*, 220.

70. W. T. Sherman to U. S. Grant, December 18, 1864, in Sherman, *Memoirs*, II, 207–13.

71. Grant cited in Trudeau, *Southern Storm*, 460.

72. Cited in Trudeau, *Southern Storm*, 529.

73. Royster, *The Destructive War*, 330.

74. Sherman, *Memoirs*, II, 254.

75. Cited in Glatthaar, *March to the Sea*, 79.

76. Sherman, *Memoirs*, II, 254.

77. Marszalek, *Sherman*, 318.

78. W. T. Sherman to Ellen Sherman, January 15, 1865, in Simpson and Berlin, *Sherman's Civil War*, 797.

79. Hanson, *The Soul of Battle*, 196.

80. Royster, *The Destructive War*, 6.

81. James Pickett Jones, *Black Jack: John A. Logan and Southern Illinois in the Civil War Era* (Tallahassee: Florida State University Press, 1967), 250.

82. Royster, *The Destructive War*, 21.

83. Upson, *With Sherman to the Sea*, 152.

84. Fellman, *Citizen Sherman*, 227; Royster, *The Destructive War*, 29.

85. Cited in Royster, *The Destructive War*, 27.

86. W. T. Sherman to John W. Draper, in Sherman Family Papers, Library of Congress; Royster, *The Destructive War*, 331.

87. Glatthaar, *March to the Sea*, 142, 146.

88. Cited in Royster, *The Destructive War*, 22.

89. Glatthaar, *March to the Sea*, 119.

90. W. T. Sherman to Judson Kilpatrick, March 7, 1865, in *OR*, ser. I, vol. 47, pt. 2, 721.

91. McPherson, *Battle Cry of Freedom*, 828.

92. Simpson and Berlin, *Sherman's Civil War*, 821.

93. Sherman, *Memoirs*, 304.

94. Fellman, *Citizen Sherman*, 236.

95. Marszalek, *Sherman*, 331.

96. W. T. Sherman to U. S. Grant, March 12, 1865, in Simpson and Berlin, *Sherman's Civil War*, 822.

97. Cited in Marszalek, *Sherman*, 331.

98. Porter, *Incidents and Anecdotes*, 314–15.

99. Edwin Stanton to W. T. Sherman, March 28, 1865, in *OR*, ser. I, vol. 47, pt. 3, 42.

100. Marszalek, *Sherman*, 340.

101. Special Field Orders No. 54, April 12, 1865, in Sherman, *Memoirs*, II, 344.

102. Upson, *With Sherman to the Sea*, 166.

103. W. T. Sherman to Ellen Sherman, April 9, 1865, and W. T. Sherman to Phil Ewing, April 9, 1865, in Howe, *Home Letters*, 342.

104. W. T. Sherman to U. S. Grant, April 25, 1865, in Sherman, *Memoirs*, II, 360.

105. Sherman, *Memoirs*, II, 347–48.

106. Swan, *Chicago's Irish Legion*, 226.

107. Sherman, *Memoirs*, II, 349–50.

108. Marszalek, *Sherman*, 344.

109. Simpson and Berlin, *Sherman's Civil War*, 864–65; "Synopsis of Agreement," cited in Marszalek, *Sherman*, 345.

110. W. T. Sherman to Henry Halleck, April 18, 1865, in Simpson and Berlin, *Sherman's Civil War*, 866.

111. Marszalek, *Sherman*, 346; letter aboard dispatch boat, M. Martin, April 22, 1865, in Hitchcock, *Marching with Sherman*, 304.

112. Simpson and Berlin, *Sherman's Civil War*, 857.

113. Ibid., 878, fn. 2.

114. Edwin Stanton to Henry Halleck, April 21, 1865, in *OR*, ser. I, vol. 47, pt. 3, 263–64.

115. Henry Halleck to Edwin Stanton, April 22, 1865, in ibid., 277–78.

116. *New York Times*, April 23, 1865.

117. Moody, *Demon of the Lost Cause*, 543.

118. W. T. Sherman to Edwin Stanton, April 25, 1865, in Sherman, *Memoirs*, II, 362.

119. Thorndike, *Sherman Letters*, 246; Marszalek, *Commander of All Lincoln's Armies*, 223–24.

120. Marszalek, *Sherman*, 343–44.

121. Special Field Orders No. 69, May 6, 1865, in Simpson and Berlin, *Sherman's Civil War*, 891, fn. 3.

122. Simpson and Berlin, *Sherman's Civil War*, 895, fn. 1.

123. W. T. Sherman to Henry Halleck, May 10, 1865, in Simpson and Berlin, *Sherman's Civil War*, 895.

124. Marszalek, *Commander of All Lincoln's Armies*, 227.

125. W. T. Sherman to Salmon Chase, May 6, 1865, in Simpson and Berlin, *Sherman's Civil War*, 890.

126. Royster, *Southern Storm*, 347.

Chapter VIII: Bands of Steel

1. See, for example, W. T. Sherman to F. A. P. Barard, Coast Survey Office, September 4, 1863, in Simpson and Berlin, *Sherman's Civil War*, 532.

2. W. T. Sherman to Ellen Sherman, September 16, 1883, in Howe, *Home Letters*, 391.

3. W. T. Sherman to Ellen Sherman, July 16, 1865, in Sherman Family Papers, Notre Dame.

4. Sherman, *Memoirs*, II, 410; Robert G. Athearn, *William Tecumseh Sherman and the Settlement of the West* (Norman: University of Oklahoma Press, 1956), 10.

5. McPherson, *Battle Cry of Freedom*, 451, 818.

6. Athearn, *Sherman and the Settlement of the West*, 8,10.

7. Marszalek, *Sherman*, 404.

8. Athearn, *Sherman and the Settlement of the West*, 43.

9. Ibid., 381.

10. W. T. Sherman to U. S. Grant, May 14, 1866, cited in Athearn, *Sherman and the Settlement of the West*, 48.

11. Athearn, *Sherman and the Settlement of the West*, 223.

12. Arquilla, *Insurgents, Raiders, and Bandits*, 115.

13. W. T. Sherman to U. S. Grant, December 28, 1866, cited in Athearn, *Sherman and the Settlement of the West*, 99.

14. Estimate based on figures provided in Stefan Bechtel, *Mr. Hornaday's War: How a Peculiar Victorian Zookeeper Waged a Lonely Crusade for Wildlife That Changed the World* (Boston: Beacon Press, 2012), 62.

15. W. T. Sherman to Philip Sheridan, May 10, 1868, in Sherman–Sheridan Correspondence, vol. 1, Sheridan Papers, Library of Congress.

16. W. T. Sherman to John Sherman, June 17, 1868, in W. T. Sherman Papers, Library of Congress.

17. W. T. Sherman to J. S. Rawlins, August 22, 1866, in Division of the Mississippi, Letters Sent, U.S. National Archives, 65–66; Royster, *The Destructive War,* 394.

18. Athearn, *Sherman and the Settlement of the West,* 133, 141–42, 144.

19. Marszalek, *Sherman,* 392.

20. W. T. Sherman to J. S. Rawlins, October 23, 1865, in Division of the Mississippi, Letters Sent, U.S. National Archives.

21. Athearn, *Sherman and the Settlement of the West,* 102.

22. W. T. Sherman to Grenville M. Dodge, January 5, 1866, in Dodge Papers, vol. 14, State Historical Society of Iowa.

23. W. T. Sherman to Grenville M. Dodge, January 5, 1867, in ibid.

24. Athearn, *Sherman and the Settlement of the West,* 29.

25. Wayne R. Kime, ed., *The Sherman Tour Journals of Colonel Richard Irving Dodge* (Norman: University of Oklahoma Press, 2002), 40.

26. Cited in Fellman, *Citizen Sherman,* 268.

27. W. T. Sherman to Ellen Sherman, September 7, 1867, in Sherman Family Papers, Notre Dame.

28. *Daily Rocky Mountain News,* September 23, 1867; *New York Times,* September 27, 1867.

29. Marszalek, *Sherman,* 391.

30. Ibid., 374.

31. Ibid.

32. W. T. Sherman to Thomas Ewing, February 14, 1868, in Howe, *Home Letters,* 371–72.

33. W. T. Sherman to U. S. Grant, February 14, 1868, in Sherman, *Memoirs,* II, 430–31.

34. Cable: Washington, D.C., 2:00 p.m., February 19, 1868, Lieutenant-General W. T. Sherman, St. Louis, Missouri, in Sherman, *Memoirs,* II, 433.

35. Cited in Jacob Randolph Perkins, *Trails, Rails and War: Life of General G. M. Dodge* (Indianapolis: Bobbs-Merrill, 1929), 221–22.

36. Marszalek, *Sherman,* 384.

37. W. T. Sherman to U. S. Grant, March 26, 1869, in W. T. Sherman Papers, Library of Congress.

38. Manning F. Force, *General Sherman* (New York: D. Appleton, 1899; reprint 2007), 325–26.

39. Grenville M. Dodge to W. T. Sherman, May 10, 1869, in W. T. Sherman Papers, vol. 26, Library of Congress.

40. Bunting, *Ulysses S. Grant,* 119; McFeely, *Grant: A Biography,* 308–09.

41. Marszalek, *Sherman,* 383.

42. W. T. Sherman to General C. C. Augur, June 9, 1870, in Augur Papers, Illinois State Historical Society.

43. Bechtel, *Mr. Hornaday's War,* 64–65, 68.

44. Marszalek, *Sherman,* 396.

45. "Report of the General of the Army," November 1873, U.S. Serial Set, No. 1597.

46. W. W. Belknap to W. T. Sherman, May 11, 1874, in W. T. Sherman Papers, Library of Congress.

47. Marszalek, *Sherman,* 402, 430.

48. *New York Times,* April 16, 1873.

49. Athearn, *Sherman and the Settlement of the West,* 305.

50. Ibid., 306.

51. W. T. Sherman to Phil Sheridan, November 20, 1875, in Sherman–Sheridan Correspondence, vol. 1, Library of Congress.

52. Jean Edward Smith, *Grant* (New York: Simon & Schuster, 2001); Bunting, *Ulysses S. Grant*, 121.

53. Arquilla, *Insurgents, Raiders, and Bandits*, 124.

54. W. T. Sherman to Phil Sheridan, February 17, 1877, in Sherman–Sheridan Correspondence, vol. 1, Library of Congress.

55. W. T. Sherman to Robert Clarke, February 29, 1880, cited in Marszalek, *Sherman*, 399.

56. Kime, *Sherman Tour Journals*, 83.

57. Sherman, *Memoirs*, II, 413–14.

58. Report of W. T. Sherman, October 27, 1883, Annual Report of the Secretary of War, 48th Congress, House Executive Document No. 1 (Serial 2182), 46.

Chapter IX: The Boys

1. This concept came in part from a conversation with American cultural and intellectual historian Richard Slotkin.

2. The debate over Frederick Jackson Turner's famed "The Significance of the Frontier in American History" has reached the stage that about the only point of agreement is that he and it were very influential. Still, that influence and the evidence argue that the basic point—inclinations associated with democracy were felt most intensely in the West—seems to contain a kernel of truth.

3. Alexis de Tocqueville, *Democracy in America* (London: Penguin, 2003; originally published 1835).

4. The theme of Sherman's army exemplifying its democratic origins was earlier explored by Victor Davis Hanson in *The Soul of Battle*. He, however, focused on the March and treated the army and its relationship with Sherman as accomplished facts; I am more interested in their development.

5. Based on a series of conversations in the fall of 2010 and winter of 2011.

6. Wiley, *Billy Yank*, 20; McPherson, *Battle Cry of Freedom*, 321–22, 348, 326. Glatthaar (*March to the Sea*, 27–28) notes that approximately 50 percent of Sherman's soldiers reenlisted for a second three-year term, compared with one in fifteen for Union armies as a whole.

7. Figures derived from Glatthaar, *March to the Sea*, 189.

8. Benjamin Apthorp Gould, *Investigations in the Military and Anthropological Statistics of American Soldiers* (New York: Hurd & Houghton, 1869), 86–88, computed these figures for the Union army as a whole.

9. Wiley, *Billy Yank*, 304.

10. Cited in McPherson, *Battle Cry of Freedom*, 309–510; Glatthaar, *March to the Sea*, 40.

11. This is a highly impressionistic figure based on numbers given for the 87th and 100th Indiana, the 90th, 105th, and 123rd Illinois, and the 123rd New York, which had transferred west. Admittedly this is a small sample, but it seems to track with Sherman's comments and those of other participants.

12. According to Wiley (*Billy Yank*, 319), the total was 1,696 infantry regiments, 272 cavalry, and 78 artillery.

13. Overmyer, *A Stupendous Effort*, 5.

14. McPherson, *Battle Cry of Freedom*, 327–28.

15. Wiley, *Billy Yank*, 25.

16. Glatthaar, *March to the Sea*, 25.

17. McPherson, *Battle Cry of Freedom*, 487–88; Wiley, *Billy Yank*, 132; Overmyer, *A Stupendous Effort*, 42.

18. Wiley, *Johnny Reb*, 244.

19. Overmyer, *A Stupendous Effort*, 42.

20. McPherson, *Battle Cry of Freedom*, 485.

21. Wiley, *Billy Yank*, 59; Overmyer, *A Stupendous Effort*, 60–61.

22. Upson, *With Sherman to the Sea*, 27–28.

23. Wiley, *Billy Yank*, 24; King, *Three Years with the 92nd Illinois*, 6; Upson, *With Sherman to the Sea*, 22.

24. McPherson, *Battle Cry of Freedom*, 326.

25. Glatthaar, *March to the Sea*, 26.

26. Ibid., 21.

27. Ibid., 26.

28. Wiley, *Billy Yank*, 50.

29. Upson, *With Sherman to the Sea*, 36.

30. Overmyer, *A Stupendous Effort*, 33.

31. Wiley, *Billy Yank*, 56.

32. Bull, *Soldiering*, 11.

33. King, *Three Years with the 92nd Illinois*, 65.

34. Upson, *With Sherman to the Sea*, 39.

35. Wiley, *Billy Yank*, 237, 239.

36. Sherman, *Memoirs*, II, 391.

37. George F. Cram, *Soldiering with Sherman: Civil War Letters of George F. Cram*, ed. Jennifer Cain Bohrnstedt (DeKalb: Northern Illinois University Press, 2000), 13.

38. Cited in Overmyer, *A Stupendous Effort*, 34.

39. Wiley, *Billy Yank*, 261.

40. Glatthaar, *March to the Sea*, 94.

41. Wiley, *Billy Yank*, 250; Glatthaar, *March to the Sea*, 94.

42. Wiley, *Billy Yank*, 183.

43. Upson, *With Sherman to the Sea*, 32.

44. Ibid., 30.

45. Early battles were comparatively low in casualties for Union forces in the West. Wilson's Creek accounted for around 1,300 wounded and 250 dead, while Belmont cost Federal forces 120 fatalities and 400 wounded.

46. Cited in Wiley, *Billy Yank*, 69.

47. Marszalek, *Sherman*, 153; W. T. Sherman to Ellen Sherman, August 19, 1861, in Simpson and Berlin, *Sherman's Civil War*, 132.

48. Ibid.

49. Cited in Athearn, *Sherman and the Settlement of the West*, 133.

50. W. T. Sherman to Ellen Sherman, June 27, 1862, in Simpson and Berlin, *Sherman's Civil War*, 246.

51. Cited in Corydon Edward Foote and Olive Deane Hormel, *With Sherman to the Sea: A Drummer's Story of the Civil War* (New York: John Day, 1960), 189–90.

52. Royster, *The Destructive War*, 274.

53. John A. Cockerill, "A Boy at Shiloh," in *Sketches of War History: 1861–1865*, eds. Theodore Allen, Edward McKee, and J. G. Taylor (Cincinnati: Monfort & Co., 1908), 14.

54. Ibid., 25.

55. Ibid., 28.

56. Ibid., 31.

57. Ibid., 31–32.

58. Ibid., 32.

59. Ibid., 34.

60. Widney, "Campaigning with 'Uncle Billy,'" *Neals Monthly*, 133.

61. W. T. Sherman to Ellen Sherman, April 11, 1862, in Howe, *Home Letters*, 222.

62. Upson, *With Sherman to the Sea,* 50.

63. Ibid., 52.

64. Ibid., 72.

65. Ibid., 54.

66. Ibid., 73.

67. Ibid., 75–76.

68. Ibid., 78.

69. W. T. Sherman to Thomas Ewing Sr., April 27, 1862, and W. T. Sherman to Ellen Sherman, May 23, 1862, in Simpson and Berlin, *Sherman's Civil War,* 224.

70. W. T. Sherman to Thomas Ewing Sr., February 17, 1863, in Simpson and Berlin, *Sherman's Civil War,* 400.

71. Cited in Marszalek, *Sherman,* 209.

72. W. T. Sherman to Ellen Sherman, October 26, 1864, in Howe, *Home Letters,* 313–14.

73. Wiley, *Billy Yank,* 62.

74. Porter, *Incidents and Anecdotes of the Civil War,* 219–20.

75. Grady McWhiney and Perry D. Jamieson, "No Myth! The Rifle Revolution in the Civil War," *North & South: The Magazine of Civil War Conflict* 1, no. 5 (1998): 23.

76. Paddy Griffith, "The Myth of the Rifle Revolution in the Civil War," ibid., 17.

77. McPherson, *Battle Cry of Freedom,* 472–73.

78. Robert L. O'Connell, *Of Arms and Men: A History of War, Weapons and Aggression* (New York: Oxford University Press, 1989), 197–98; see also Grady McWhiney and Perry D. Jamieson, *Attack and Die: Civil War Military Tactics and the Southern Heritage* (Tuscaloosa: University of Alabama Press, 1984).

79. Wiley, *Billy Yank,* 623.

80. Irenäus Eibl-Eibesfeldt, *Human Ethology* (New York: Aldine De Gruyter, 1989), 405; Dave Grossman, *On Killing: The Psychological Cost of Learning to Kill in War and Society* (Boston: Little, Brown & Co., 1995), xxix.

81. McWhiney and Jamieson, "No Myth!," 26–27.

82. See, for example, Nevin, *Sherman's March,* 116.

83. Wiley, *Billy Yank,* 85.

84. W. T. Sherman, "The Grand Strategy of the Last Years of the War," in R. U. Johnson and C. C. Buel, eds., *Battles and Leaders of the Civil War,* 4 vols. (New York: Century Company, 1884), vol. 4, 248.

85. Glatthaar, *March to the Sea,* 158; Bull, *Soldiering,* 106.

86. Sherman, *Memoirs,* II, 394.

87. McPherson, *Battle Cry of Freedom,* 476; McWhiney and Jamieson, "No Myth!," 23.

88. McPherson, *Battle Cry of Freedom,* 475–76.

89. George Cram to mother, June 25, 1864, in Cram, *Soldiering with Sherman,* 116.

90. Cram, *Soldiering with Sherman,* 99–100; Cram to mother, May 27, 1864, in ibid., xxii.

91. Glatthaar, *March to the Sea,* 164–65.

92. Burial party conversation cited in King, *Three Years with the 92nd Illinois,* February 1863, 47–48.

93. Wiley, *Billy Yank,* 72.

94. King, *Three Years with the 92nd Illinois,* 126.

95. Wiley, *Billy Yank,* 148; McPherson, *Battle Cry of Freedom,* 486.

96. McPherson, *Battle Cry of Freedom,* 485.

97. Bull, *Soldiering,* 81.

98. Adele DeLeeuw, *Nurses Who Led the Way: Real Life Stories of Courageous Women in an Exciting Profession* (New York: Whitman Publishing, 1961), 27.

99. McPherson, *Battle Cry of Freedom*, 483.

100. Trudeau, *Southern Storm*, 120.

101. Cited in Fellman, *Citizen Sherman*, 177.

102. Sherman, *Memoirs*, II, 105; Fellman, *Citizen Sherman*, 177.

Chapter X: Road Warriors

1. Glatthaar, *March to the Sea*, 42, 46; Bull, *Soldiering*, 196.

2. Glatthaar, *March to the Sea*, 27.

3. A. Ames to General P. B. Black, March 28, 1865, in William H. Noble Papers, Duke University.

4. King, *Three Years with the 92nd Illinois*, 212.

5. W. T. Sherman notes in S. M. Bowman and R. B. Irwin, *Sherman and His Campaigns: A Military Biography* (New York: C. V. Richardson, 1865), in Jared W. Young's Sherman Collection, Northwestern University.

6. James Connolly, *Three Years in the Army of the Cumberland: The Letters and Diary of Major James A. Connolly*, ed. Paul M. Angle (Bloomington: Indiana University Press, 1959), 209.

7. Overmyer, *A Stupendous Effort*, 143.

8. Connolly, *Three Years in the Army of the Cumberland*, 209.

9. Glatthaar, *March to the Sea*, 157.

10. Upson, *With Sherman to the Sea*, 107.

11. Glatthaar, *March to the Sea*, 157.

12. King, *Three Years with the 92nd Illinois*, 105.

13. Ibid., 153–54.

14. Ibid., 172.

15. Ibid., 173.

16. Ibid., 195.

17. Cited in Glatthaar, *March to the Sea*, 157.

18. Royster, *The Destructive War*, chapter 7, "The Battle of Kennesaw Mountain."

19. Harker and John W. Tuttle of the Third Kentucky both cited in Royster, *The Destructive War*, 303.

20. George Cram to mother, May 27, 1864, in Cram, *Soldiering with Sherman*, 99.

21. Upson, *With Sherman to the Sea*, 115.

22. Royster, *The Destructive War*, 309.

23. Ibid.

24. Ibid.

25. Royster, *The Destructive War*, 313.

26. Upson, *With Sherman to the Sea*, 116.

27. Royster, *The Destructive War*, 314–15.

28. Ibid., 314.

29. Ibid., 307.

30. Sherman, *Memoirs*, II, 402.

31. Ibid., 22–23.

32. Central Intelligence Agency, "Intelligence in the Civil War," https://www.cia.gov/library/publications/additional-publications/civil-war/index. html, 22–23; Hirshson, *White Tecumseh*, 239.

33. W. T. Sherman to Henry Halleck, September 4, 1864, in Simpson and Berlin, *Sherman's Civil War*, 698.

34. Glatthaar, *March to the Sea*, 40.

35. Gary Gallagher, *The Union War* (Cambridge, MA: Harvard University Press, 2011), 110.

36. James Connolly to Mary Connolly, May 18, 1863, in Connolly, *Three Years in the Army of the Cumberland,* 57–58.

37. Wiley, *Billy Yank,* 43–44.

38. Upson, *With Sherman to the Sea,* 133; Marszalek, *Sherman,* 398.

39. Bull, *Soldiering,* 175.

40. Trudeau, *Southern Storm,* 265.

41. Glatthaar, *March to the Sea,* 121; Trudeau, *Southern Storm,* 543.

42. Sherman, *Memoirs,* II, 182.

43. Glatthaar, *March to the Sea,* 128.

44. Trudeau, *Southern Storm,* 543.

45. Widney cited in ibid., 318.

46. Glatthaar, *March to the Sea,* 123.

47. Cited in Marzalek, *Sherman,* 322.

48. Cited in Trudeau, *Southern Storm,* 117–18.

49. Ibid., 124.

50. McPherson, *Battle Cry of Freedom,* 827–28.

51. Glatthaar, *March to the Sea,* 74.

52. Ibid., 41–42, 67; see also Connolly diary, November 18, 1864, in Connolly, *Three Years in the Army of the Cumberland,* 310.

53. Glatthaar, *March to the Sea,* 63.

54. Cited in Nevin, *Sherman's March,* 67–68.

55. Marszalek, *Sherman,* 305.

56. Cited in Trudeau, *Southern Storm,* 144.

57. James Connolly to Mary Connolly, January 1864, in Connolly, *Three Years in the Army of the Cumberland,* 375.

58. Glatthaar, *March to the Sea,* 141–42.

59. Bull, *Soldiering,* 214.

60. Upson, *With Sherman to the Sea,* 162.

61. W. T. Sherman to Ellen Sherman, March 23, 1865, in Howe, *Home Letters,* 334–36.

62. Simpson and Berlin, *Sherman's Civil War,* 901–02.

63. Royster, *The Destructive War,* 405–06.

64. W. T. Sherman to U. S. Grant, May 28, 1865, in Simpson and Berlin, *Sherman's Civil War,* 904.

65. Swan, *Chicago's Irish Legion,* 363.

66. William B. Hazen, *A Narrative of Military Service* (Boston: Ticknor, 1885), 378.

67. Upson, *With Sherman to the Sea,* 171.

68. Ibid., 173.

69. Cited in Marszalek, *Sherman,* 355.

70. Glatthaar, *March to the Sea,* 181.

71. Cited in Gallagher, *The Union War,* 14.

72. Royster, *The Destructive War,* 411.

73. Sherman, *Memoirs,* II, 376–77.

74. Royster, *The Destructive War,* 406.

75. Henry Hitchcock to wife, May 26, 1865, in Hitchcock, *Marching with Sherman,* 319–20.

76. Sherman, *Memoirs,* II, 377.

77. Royster, *The Destructive War,* 409.

78. Gallagher, *The Union War*, 19; Sherman, *Memoirs*, II, 378.

79. Royster, *The Destructive War*, 413.

80. Ibid., 417.

81. Special Field Orders No. 76, Sherman, *Memoirs*, II, 379.

Chapter XI: Cump

1. Lewis, *Sherman: Fighting Prophet*, 30–31.

2. Marszalek, *Sherman*, 2.

3. Hirshson, *White Tecumseh*, 4.

4. Marszalek, *Sherman*, 3–4.

5. John J. Patrick, "John Sherman: The Early Years, 1823–1865," PhD dissertation, Kent State University, 1982, 6–7.

6. Hershson, *White Tecumseh*, 6.

7. Cited in Lewis, *Sherman: Fighting Prophet*, 32.

8. Marszalek, *Sherman*, 9.

9. Lewis, *Sherman: Fighting Prophet*, 23.

10. Marszalek, *Sherman*, 7.

11. Cited in Lewis, *Sherman: Fighting Prophet*, 15.

12. Marszalek, *Sherman*, 7.

13. Lewis, *Sherman: Fighting Prophet*, 15.

14. Ibid., 33.

15. Marszalek, *Sherman*, 8.

16. Ibid., 9; Anna McAllister, *Ellen Ewing: Wife of General Sherman* (New York: Benziger Brothers, 1936), 12.

17. Thomas Ewing to Maria Ewing, December 9, 1831, Ewing Family Papers, Library of Congress, cited in Lewis, *Sherman: Fighting Prophet*, 39–40.

18. Cited in *New York Herald*, February 13, 1891.

19. Lewis, *Sherman: Fighting Prophet*, 46.

20. Marszalek, *Sherman*, 13; Lewis, *Sherman: Fighting Prophet*, 36.

21. Ellen Sherman, "Recollections for My Children," 3–4, cited in Hirshson, *White Tecumseh*, 8.

22. Hugh Boyle Ewing, "Autobiography," Ohio Historical Society, Columbus, 6–7; Marszalek, *Sherman*, 14.

23. W. T. Sherman to Ellen Ewing, April 7, 1842, in Howe, *Home Letters*, 17–20.

24. Lewis, *Sherman: Fighting Prophet*, 35.

25. Ibid., 35–36.

26. McAllister, *Ellen Ewing*, 10.

27. Sherman, *Memoirs*, I, 14; Sherman, "Recollections for My Children," 3–4.

28. Thomas Ewing to Maria Ewing, December 22, 1833, in Thomas Ewing Papers, Library of Congress.

29. Thomas Ewing to Lewis Cass, August 1, 1835, Sherman Family Papers, Notre Dame, cited in Marszalek, *Sherman*, 16.

30. Ibid., 17.

31. W. T. Sherman to Thomas Ewing, May 5, 1836, in Thomas Ewing Papers, Library of Congress.

32. Cited in Lewis, *Sherman: Fighting Prophet*, 59.

33. W. T. Sherman to Ellen Ewing, August 20, 1837, in Howe, *Home Letters*, 4.

34. W. T. Sherman to Ellen Ewing, July 10, 1837, in W. T. Sherman Papers, Library of Congress.

35. W. T. Sherman to Phil Ewing, July 11, 1837, cited in Fellman, *Citizen Sherman*, 15.

36. Marszalek, *Sherman*, 26; Lewis, *Sherman: Fighting Prophet*, 59; McAllister, *Ellen Ewing*, 17.

37. Marszalek, *Sherman*, 26.

38. W. T. Sherman to Ellen Sherman, May 4, 1839, in Howe, *Home Letters*, 6.

39. W. T. Sherman to Ellen Sherman, November 1, 1839, cited in Kennett, *Sherman: A Soldier's Life*, 22.

40. W. T. Sherman to Ellen Sherman, August 21, 1839, in Howe, *Home Letters*, 10.

41. Gail Hamilton, *Biography of James G. Blaine* (Norwich, CT: Henry Bill, 1895), 582.

42. Cited in Marszalek, *Sherman*, 31.

43. Cited in Lewis, *Sherman: Fighting Prophet*, 61–62.

44. W. T. Sherman to Ellen Ewing, January 13, 1842, and April, 7, 1842, in Howe, *Home Letters*, 17–18, 19–21.

45. There is no actual record of Ellen Sherman's stature. However, a Sherman family photograph taken in August 1886 shows the couple standing and clearly reveals Ellen to be at least a foot shorter than her husband, who was just a shade under six feet tall.

46. W. T. Sherman to Ellen Ewing, September 7, 1841, in Howe, *Home Letters*, 16.

47. McAllister, *Ellen Ewing*, 36.

48. Marszalek, *Sherman*, 48; W. T. Sherman to Ellen Ewing, February 8, 1844, in Howe, *Home Letters*, 24.

49. W. T. Sherman to Thomas Ewing, January 20, 1844, in Ewing Family Papers, Library of Congress; Fellman, *Citizen Sherman*, 9.

50. Hirshson, *White Tecumseh*, 24.

51. W. T. Sherman to Ellen Ewing, January, 25, 1847; W. T. Sherman to Ellen Ewing, August 28, 1848; and W. T. Sherman to Ellen Ewing, March 12, 1847, in Sherman Family Papers, Notre Dame.

52. Ellen Sherman to W. T. Sherman, February 1849, cited in McAllister, *Ellen Ewing*, 56.

53. Ellen Sherman to W. T. Sherman, May 19, 1849, cited in ibid., 58–59.

54. W. T. Sherman to Ellen Ewing, March 27, 1850, in Sherman Family Papers, Notre Dame.

55. McAllister, *Ellen Ewing*, 64, 68.

56. W. T. Sherman to Thomas Ewing, March 11, 1851, in Ewing Family Papers, Library of Congress.

57. W. T. Sherman to Thomas Ewing Jr., September 7 and August 30, 1852, cited in Marszalek, *Sherman*, 89.

58. W. T. Sherman to Thomas Ewing, April 15, 1858, in Thomas Ewing Papers, Library of Congress.

59. Fellman, *Citizen Sherman*, 39.

60. Sherman, *Memoirs*, I, 122–23.

61. Ibid., 126.

62. W. T. Sherman to John Sherman, June 3, 1853, in W. T. Sherman Papers, Library of Congress; W. T. Sherman to Ellen Sherman, June 30, 1853, in Sherman Family Papers, Notre Dame; Marszalek, *Sherman*, 94.

63. W. T. Sherman to John Sherman, June 1853, in Thorndike, *Sherman Letters*, 124.

64. Marszalek, *Sherman*, 95.

65. Ibid.

66. Thomas Ewing Sr. to W. T. Sherman, February 1, 1853, and Maria Ewing to Ellen Sherman, February 27, 1853, cited in Marszalek, *Sherman*, 95–96.

67. Cited in McAllister, *Ellen Ewing*, 92.

68. Sherman, *Memoirs,* I, 134; Royster, *The Destructive War,* 132.

69. Marszalek, *Sherman,* 101.

70. Ellen Sherman to Hugh B. Ewing, April 3, 1854, cited in Fellman, *Citizen Sherman,* 42.

71. W. T. Sherman to Henry Turner, September 29, 1854, cited in Kennett, *Sherman: A Soldier's Life,* 74.

72. Marszalek, *Sherman,* 102–03; McAllister, *Ellen Ewing,* chapter 9, "Shipwreck of 'Golden Age.'"

73. Ellen Sherman to W. T. Sherman, May 13, 1855, in Sherman Family Papers, Notre Dame.

74. Ellen Sherman to W. T. Sherman, May 23, 1855, cited in Hirshson, *White Tecumseh,* 45.

75. Cited in Marszalek, *Sherman,* 103.

76. W. T. Sherman to Henry Turner, December 18, 1856, in Sherman Family Papers, Notre Dame.

77. Kennett, *Sherman: A Soldier's Life,* 79–80.

78. Ibid.

79. Charles Welch to W. T. Sherman, December 12, 1858, cited in Marszalek, *Commander of All Lincoln's Armies,* 96.

80. Fellman, *Citizen Sherman,* 67–68.

81. W. T. Sherman to Ellen Sherman, April 15, 1859, in Sherman Family Papers, Notre Dame.

82. Kennett, *Sherman: A Soldier's Life,* 83.

83. Fellman, *Citizen Sherman,* 48.

84. Ellen Sherman to W. T. Sherman, October 24, 1860, and November 21, 1860, in Sherman Family Papers, Notre Dame.

85. Marszalek, *Sherman,* 80, 121; Sherman, *Memoirs,* I, 167–68.

86. W. T. Sherman to John Sherman, March 6, 1861, in Simpson and Berlin, *Sherman's Civil War,* 61.

87. Ellen Sherman to W. T. Sherman, January 16, 1861, cited in McAllister, *Ellen Ewing,* 178.

88. Marszalek, *Sherman,* 144.

89. Hirshson, *White Tecumseh,* 84.

90. Thomas Ewing Jr. to W. T. Sherman, May 8, 1861, in Ewing Family Papers, Library of Congress; Hirshson, *White Tecumseh,* 84.

91. For instance, W. T. Sherman to Ellen Sherman, June 27, 1863, in Simpson and Berlin, *Sherman's Civil War,* 489; W. T. Sherman to Ellen Sherman, October 19, 1864, in ibid., 737; W. T. Sherman to Phil Ewing, January 29, 1865, in ibid., 810–14.

92. W. T. Sherman to Ellen Sherman, February 21 and March 12, 1862, in ibid., 192, 196.

93. W. T. Sherman to Thomas Ewing Sr., December 12, 1861, in Thomas Ewing Papers, Library of Congress.

94. W. T. Sherman to Thomas Ewing Sr., April 27 and May 3, 1862, in Simpson and Berlin, *Sherman's Civil War,* 212–13.

95. W. T. Sherman to Thomas Ewing Sr., August 13, 1863, in ibid., 521.

96. Ellen Sherman to W. T. Sherman, December 23, 1862, Sherman Family Papers, Notre Dame, cited in Hirshson, *White Tecumseh,* 137.

97. Ellen Sherman to W. T. Sherman, May 1862, cited in McAllister, *Ellen Ewing,* 224.

98. Kennett, *Sherman: A Soldier's Life,* 154.

99. W. T. Sherman to Ellen Sherman, September 25, 1862, and Ellen Sherman to W. T. Sherman, September 28, 1862, in Sherman Family Papers, Notre Dame; Hirshson, *White Tecumseh,* 135.

100. Marszalek, *Sherman,* 197–98.

101. W. T. Sherman to Ellen Sherman, April 11, 1862, and July 26, 1864, in Simpson and Berlin, *Sherman's Civil War,* 202, 671.

102. W. T. Sherman to John Sherman, August 3, 1863, in Rachel Sherman Thorndike, ed., *The Sherman Letters: Correspondence Between General Sherman and Senator Sherman from 1837 to 1891* (New York: Da Capo Press, 1969), 214.

103. Marszalek, *Sherman,* 234.

104. Fellman, *Citizen Sherman,* 199.

105. Marszalek, *Sherman,* 237; Hirshson, *White Tecumseh,* 165.

106. Sherman, *Memoirs,* I, 376.

107. McAllister, *Ellen Ewing,* 360.

108. Fellman, *Citizen Sherman,* 200–06.

109. W. T. Sherman to Ellen Sherman, November 17, 1863, in Simpson and Berlin, *Sherman's Civil War,* 572; McAllister, *Ellen Ewing,* 274–75.

110. Simpson and Berlin, *Sherman's Civil War,* 573, fn. 2.

111. W. T. Sherman to Thomas Ewing Sr., September 15, 1864, in ibid., 711.

112. W. T. Sherman to Thomas Ewing Sr., December 31, 1864, in ibid., 782.

Chapter XII: Big Time

1. McAllister, *Ellen Ewing,* 331; Marszalek, *Sherman,* 407–08.

2. W. T. Sherman to Ellen Sherman, April 9, 1865, in Howe, *Home Letters,* 342.

3. Marszalek, *Sherman,* 402.

4. Ibid., 430–31.

5. *New York Herald,* October 2, 1874.

6. Fellman, *Citizen Sherman,* 401.

7. Hirshson, *White Tecumseh,* 392.

8. Ellen Sherman to Thomas Ewing Sr., March 10, 1868, in Sherman Family Papers, Notre Dame.

9. W. T. Sherman to John Sherman, December 29, 1875, in Thorndike, *Sherman Letters,* 345.

10. W. T. Sherman to Lieutenant J. C. Scantling, April 15, 1879, cited in Fellman, *Citizen Sherman,* 288; Thorndike, *Sherman Letters,* 405.

11. Marszalek, *Sherman,* 425; Kime, *Sherman Tour Journals,* 9–10.

12. Kime, *Sherman Tour Journals,* 66.

13. Royster, *The Destructive War,* 389; W. T. Sherman to Philip Sheridan, July 31, 1881, in Sheridan Papers, Library of Congress.

14. Sherman, *Memoirs,* II, 394–95.

15. W. T. Sherman to McCrary from Fort Ellis, August 19, 1877, "Report of Inspection Made in the Summer of 1877," 33–34.

16. W. T. Sherman to David Dixon Porter, November 24, 1865, cited in Athearn, *Sherman and the Settlement of the West,* 13.

17. Athearn, *Sherman and the Settlement of the West,* 45.

18. James S. Rusling, *Men and Things I Saw in Civil War Days* (New York: Eaton & Maions, 1899), 139–40.

19. W. T. Sherman to Ellen Sherman, March 24, 1872; W. T. Sherman to Ellen Sherman, January 6, 1872; and W. T. Sherman to George Bancroft, July 11, 1872, cited in Fellman, *Citizen Sherman,* 307.

20. Marszalek, *Sherman,* 363.

21. Ibid., 415–16.

22. Ibid., 363.

23. Hirshson, *White Tecumseh,* 350; W. T. Sherman to Ellen Sherman, July 7, 1872, in Sherman Family Papers, Notre Dame.

24. W. T. Sherman to Willard Warner, February 9, 1888, cited in Marszalek, *Sherman,* 461.

25. Fellman, *Citizen Sherman,* 325.

26. Marszalek, *Sherman,* 465.

27. U. S. Grant to W. T. Sherman, January 29, 1876, in W. T. Sherman Papers, Library of Congress.

28. Cited in Marszalek, *Sherman,* 466.

29. W. T. Sherman to Henry Van Ness Boynton, January 16, 1880, in W. T. Sherman Papers, Library of Congress.

30. W. T. Sherman to Henry Halleck, September 4, 1864, in Simpson and Berlin, *Sherman's Civil War,* 698.

31. Royster, *The Destructive War,* 375.

32. John Marszalek (*Sherman,* 449) points out that in 1871, Sherman sent the following message: "If nominated by either party, I should peremptorily decline, and even if unanimously elected, I should decline to serve."

33. W. T. Sherman to J. B. Henderson, June 5, 1884, in Sherman, *Memoirs,* II, 466.

34. Fellman, *Citizen Sherman,* 407.

35. W. T. Sherman to John Sherman, September 15 and December 22, 1885, cited in Fellman, *Citizen Sherman,* 408.

36. W. T. Sherman, "Old Shady with a Moral," *North American Review* 147 (October 1888): 361–68.

37. Royster, *The Destructive War,* 375.

38. *Ohio State Journal,* August 12, 1880; *New York Times,* August 19, 1880; Marszalek, *Sherman,* 476; Hirshson, *White Tecumseh,* 372.

39. S. H. M. Byers, *Twenty Years in Europe ... with Letters from General Sherman* (New York: Neale Publishing, 1900), 281.

40. Fellman, *Citizen Sherman,* 355.

41. Vinnie Ream Hoxie, Arlington National Cemetery website, www.arlington cemetery.net/vrhoxie.htm.

42. Ibid.

43. Ibid.; R. L. Hoxie, *Vinnie Ream* (Washington, D.C.: 1908), 11.

44. Vinnie Ream Hoxie, Arlington National Cemetery website, www.arlington cemetery.net/vrhoxie.htm.

45. He uses the term in letters to Vinnie and also to Mary Audenried, another lover. See Fellman, *Citizen Sherman,* 357, 365.

46. W. T. Sherman to Vinnie Ream, April 19, 1873, and May 6, 1874, Vinnie Ream Hoxie Papers, Library of Congress, cited in Marszalek, *Sherman,* 418.

47. W. T. Sherman to Vinnie Ream, March 22, 1873, cited in Fellman, *Citizen Sherman,* 356.

48. W. T. Sherman to Vinnie Ream, April 19, 1873, cited in Marszalek, *Sherman,* 419.

49. W. T. Sherman to Vinnie Ream, July 1, 1874, cited in ibid., 419.

50. W. T. Sherman to Minnie Sherman, October 4, 1862, in Simpson and Berlin, *Sherman's Civil War,* 315.

51. Fellman, *Citizen Sherman,* 372.

52. W. T. Sherman to Tommy Sherman, October 10, 1863, in Simpson and Berlin, *Sherman's Civil War,* 557.

53. W. T. Sherman to Ellen Sherman, January 15, 1865, in ibid., 797.

54. W. T. Sherman to Tommy Sherman, January 21, 1865, in ibid., 804–05.

55. Fellman, *Citizen Sherman*, 375.

56. Ibid., 376.

57. Marszalek, *Sherman*, 402.

58. Fellman, *Citizen Sherman*, 378.

59. Ibid., 410.

60. Tom Sherman to W. T. Sherman, May 20, 1878, in Sherman Family Papers, Notre Dame.

61. Marszalek, *Sherman*, 410; Ellen Sherman to Minnie Sherman, May 24, 1878, in Sherman Family Papers, Notre Dame.

62. Ellen Sherman to W. T. Sherman, May 25, 1878, in Sherman Family Papers, Notre Dame.

63. W. T. Sherman to Samuel Beyer, cited in Hirshson, *White Tecumseh*, 366.

64. W. T. Sherman to Charley Ewing, cited in ibid.

65. Cited in Royster, *The Destructive War*, 402.

66. Cited in Marszalek, *Sherman*, 413.

67. W. T. Sherman to Henry Turner, July 24, 1878, in Sherman Family Papers, Notre Dame.

68. Marszalek, *Sherman*, 413; Fellman, *Citizen Sherman*, 386.

69. Cited in Marszalek, *Sherman*, 414.

70. W. T. Sherman to Minnie Sherman, August 25, 1880, in ibid.

71. Fellman, *Citizen Sherman*, 392.

72. Military Order of the Loyal Legion of the United States, "In Memoriam Joseph C. Audenried, June 3, 1880," in W. T. Sherman Papers, Library of Congress.

73. Fellman, *Citizen Sherman*, 361.

74. Marszalek, *Sherman*, 419.

75. W. T. Sherman to Mary Audenried, December 18, 1883, cited in Fellman, *Citizen Sherman*, 362.

76. W. T. Sherman to Mary Audenried, February 14, 1884, cited in ibid., 363.

77. W. T. Sherman to Mary Audenried, April 21, 1885, cited in ibid., 364.

78. Marszalek, *Sherman*, 403.

79. Hirshson, *White Tecumseh*, 377.

80. Marszalek, *Sherman*, 486.

81. Cited in Royster, *The Destructive War*, 379.

82. Kime, *Sherman Tour Journals*, 164.

83. W. T. Sherman to Charlotte Hall, November 18, 1879, in "General Sherman's Opinion of Centeral Grant," *Century* 31 (March 1879): 821.

84. Fellman, *Citizen Sherman*, 396.

85. W. T. Sherman to Ellen Sherman, December 27, 1884, in Howe, *Home Letters*, 392.

86. Korda, *Ulysses S. Grant: The Unlikely Hero*, 146.

87. W. T. Sherman to Ellen Sherman, July 27, 1885, in Sherman Family Papers, Notre Dame.

88. Cited in Lewis, *Sherman: Fighting Prophet*, 645.

89. W. T. Sherman to Ellen Sherman, December 15, 1887, in Howe, *Home Letters*, 400.

90. Ellen Sherman to Phil Ewing, May 16, 1888, in Sherman Family Papers, Notre Dame.

91. Thomas Ewing III to Basil Liddell-Hart, March 5, 1930, Thomas Ewing Papers, Library of Congress, cited in Marszalek, *Sherman*, 488.

92. Marzalek, *Sherman*, 488.

93. Ibid.

94. Lewis, *Sherman: Fighting Prophet*, 646.

95. Marszalek, *Sherman*, 481.

96. Fellman, *Citizen Sherman*, 354.

97. Ibid., 400.

98. W. T. Sherman to Vinnie Ream, April 23, 1887, in Marszalek, *Sherman*, 419; Fellman, *Citizen Sherman*, 358.

99. Marszalek, *Sherman*, 490.

100. W. T. Sherman to John Sherman, February 3, 1891, in Fellman, *Citizen Sherman*, 413.

101. W. T. Sherman to Alexander McCook, January 11, 1891, in McCook Family Papers, Library of Congress; Marszalek, *Sherman*, 490.

102. Moody, *Demon of the Lost Cause.*

103. W. T. Sherman to Mary Draper, January 3, 1891, in Henry Draper Papers, New York Public Library; Marszalek, *Sherman*, 490.

104. Cited in W. Fletcher Johnson, *Life of Wm. Tecumseh Sherman* (Chicago: M. A. Donahue, 1891), 479–80.

105. Cited in Hirshson, *White Tecumseh*, 386.

106. Ibid.

107. Howard, *Autobiography of Oliver Otis Howard*, vol. 2, 553–54.

108. Lewis, *Sherman: Fighting Prophet*, 653.

Index

Page numbers in *italic* type indicate illustrations or maps.

ROBERT L. O'CONNELL holds a Ph.D. in history from the University of Virginia and was a member of the United States intelligence community for thirty years. He is currently a visiting professor at the Naval Postgraduate School and lives with his wife in Charlottesville, Virginia.

About the Type

The text of this book was set in Janson, a typeface designed about 1690 by Nicholas Kis (1650–1702), a Hungarian living in Amsterdam, and for many years mistakenly attributed to the Dutch printer Anton Janson. In 1919, the matrices became the property of the Stempel Foundry in Frankfurt. It is an old-style book face of excellent clarity and sharpness. Janson serifs are concave and splayed; the contrast between thick and thin strokes is marked.